The Art of

HUNTING

BIG GAME

In North America

The Art of
HUNTING
BIG GAME
IN NORTH AMERICA

By Jack O'Connor

Drawings by Douglas Allen

OUTDOOR LIFE · NEW YORK

For H.I.H. Prince Abdorreza Pahlavi of Iran,
the most skillful and experienced sheep hunter
who ever lived and a great guy!

Contents

Contents

The Art of

HUNTING

BIG GAME

In North America

1 | The Country and the Animals

Big-game animals are to a great extent the product of the country in which they live, and every type of climate and terrain on this planet has some sort of game animal that has adapted himself to it. A wonderful example of this is the polar bear. He lives on the ice floes that swing slowly around the North Pole. He is the most carnivorous of bears since he lives almost exclusively on seals, and is one of the largest predatory animals on earth. He is far larger than a lion or a tiger and his only rival for size is the giant Alaska brown bear. The polar bear is a land animal that has learned to live out his life on the icy sea. The females come ashore to bear their young and occasionally, I understand, a restless old male is found wandering far inland from the salt water. But for the most part, Nanook, the great white bear, lives with the ice. He swims many miles through the open sea, he prowls along the ice ridges, preys on the seals, sleeps warm in the icy embrace of the bergs.

Another case of extreme adaptation of a large game animal is the addax, an antelope about the size of an American whitetail deer, which lives in the searing sands of the Sahara. The addax has learned to live completely without open water, and he has developed large cupped hoofs so he can travel rapidly in soft sand. He obtains his moisture from a gourd which sends its roots deep into the earth to tap underground moisture and from a tough, sparse grass which is also deep-rooted and which contains a tiny drop of water in each joint.

1

The polar bear and the addax are extreme examples of adaptation among large mammals. The polar bear might have a pretty tough time adapting himself to conditions on land. His warm white coat would make him very uncomfortable away from the cold sea during the arctic summer, and he would be pretty conspicuous as a hunter of caribou. Some polar bears might have trouble learning to live entirely on grass and roots after years of an all-meat diet. On firmer ground the big cupped feet of the addax would be a handicap rather than a help, and he might not be able to escape the swift rush of the leopard and the lion, animals kept out of most of his range by the extreme dryness. Take the ice pack from the polar bear and the Sahara sands from the addax and both of these animals would probably perish.

Indeed since mammalian life began, new species of animals have been evolving as an answer to some challenge of environment, and others have disappeared because of challenges they could not meet.

Our North American mammals are those which were adaptable enough to survive the rigorous climatic changes of the Pleistocene era, the age of the glaciers. This lasted around 600,000 years, during which great sheets of ice advanced and retreated, gouging out lakes, cutting off hilltops, dumping billions of tons of gravel, changing the courses of rivers. As late as the mid-Pleistocene, North America swarmed with camels, horses, elephants, mastodons, giant bison twice as large as those that survived, great saber-toothed short-tailed cats generally called "tigers," ground sloths, glyptodonts, giant elk-moose, species of wolves that are now extinct.

These are all extinct, but on this continent the Pleistocene ended only between 12,000 to 15,000 years ago, and some of these creatures survived until after the ancestors of the American Indians had wandered across the land bridge at the Bering Strait from Asia, just as most of the animals themselves had done. Primitive men hunted the giant bison, and the bones of this great herbivore have been found in association with his arrowheads. Dung left by giant ground sloths has been found in caves in the Grand Canyon of the Colorado above the remains of fires built by Indians, and in Utah bones and dried hide of extinct forms of camels have been discovered.

Africa south of the Sahara did not go through the rigorous changes of the Pleistocene, and consequently all of the land until recently swarmed with an amazing variety and numbers of the same game animals that lived there during the Pleistocene—the lion, the leopard, the cheetah, the elephant, the rhino, the buffalo, antelope no larger than hares and antelope as large as oxen. In areas of Africa where the country has not been overgrazed, turned into farms, or the game shot off, the animals still exist in great numbers and variety. To an American who sometimes has to hunt hard for a couple of days to see two or three deer, the numbers of African game animals seem incredible. I have seen places where the hunter was continually in sight of game—wart hogs, wildebeest, impala, sable, dik-dik.

During the glacial periods of the Pleistocene, so much of the waters in the world's seas were locked up in ice that the sea level was lower than it is now and a land bridge existed across the Bering Strait. It finally went under the sea for the last time only from 12,000 to 15,000 years ago. Over this bridge game mammals migrated from Asia to North America. Those that have been on this continent for a long time are quite different in appearance from their Old World relatives. The New World, for example, has only two of the great cats, the cougar and the jaguar. The cougar has been in the Western Hemisphere so long that it is found clear to the tip of South America. The jaguar, though marked much like the leopard, is descended from ancestors that crossed into the New World long, long ago. The pronghorn antelope is one of the most ancient of North American game animals, the last survivor of a numerous family. The pronghorn is a unique creature which shares characteristics with other species but is closely related to none. Like the giraffe, he has no dewclaws; like the goats and sheep, he has a gall bladder. His horns are branched like the antlers of the deer, but they are horns, not antlers, and they are shed annually. The North American mule and whitetail deer are ancient Americans and not closely related to Old World species, and the white Rocky Mountain goat is quite different from his Asiatic relatives, the short-horned goats, or goat-antelopes—the takin, the serow, the goral of Asia, and the chamois of Europe.

On the other hand, the more recent arrivals are just about indistinguishable from their Old World relatives. An Alaskan caribou is so nearly the same animal as the wild Norwegian and Siberian reindeer that the sportsman would not be able to tell the difference, and an Alberta or Wyoming elk is for all practical purposes identical to the Tien Shan wapiti of Mongolia. The moose of North America is called an "elk" in Scandinavia and the species is found throughout the evergreen forests that cross the top of the world.

The sheep of North America and those of northeastern Asia are so closely related that the British lump them all in one species, and even an old sheep hunter would be hard put to tell the skull and horns of a Kamchatka bighorn from those of an Alaskan Dall sheep.

This migration undoubtedly went both ways, west as well as east. Over the ages American sheep must have drifted back to Asia, and American brown bears surely established colonies on the Siberian side, where conditions are identical. Moose and caribou must have wandered back and forth.

Our North American game is descended from the more adaptable animals that survived the climatic changes of the Pleistocene. When the ice receded for the last time, many species had disappeared, but those that remained multiplied vastly. The first white pioneers on the Western prairies did not find the great number of species present in the southern half of Africa, but they were always in sight of game of some sort. There were millions of buffalo, millions of antelope, whitetail deer in the belts of brush and trees along the creeks and rivers, hundreds of thousands of elk out on those plains, mule deer in any rough and broken country almost to the Mississippi, bighorn sheep in the breaks of the Missouri River and on little hills and buttes clear out into the Great Plains, great truculent grizzlies roaming the plains and living off of buffalo and elk.

Two hundred years before, in the early seventeenth century instead of the early nineteenth century when the Great Plains were being explored by white men, Europeans found some of this game much farther east. The bighorn, the grizzly, the mule deer, and the white goat were never found east of the Mississippi, but the elk and the buffalo were found almost to the Atlantic seaboard. Some of my own ancestors hunted both species in Kentucky.

Some animals are more adaptable than others and are found in different types of climate and different terrain. The whitetail deer, for example, is found in the cold conifer forests of Maine, in the swamps of South Carolina, the brush country of Texas, and the low, hot granite hills of the Sonora desert. On the other hand, the much less adaptable Rocky Mountain goat is found only in high, rough mountains in the Coast Range and the Rockies from Alaska to the Salmon River country of Idaho. Today the grizzly bear is found in the United States only in high wilderness mountains and in the cold subarctic forests of the north. But, as we have seen, the grizzly was once found in numbers out in the Great Plains, and less than 100 years ago there were grizzlies in the isolated mountain ranges that rise from the southwestern deserts and also in the mesquite forests along the rivers down into Sonora.

In working its way south from Alaska, the mountain sheep differentiated into two species and four subspecies—Dall, Stone, bighorn, and desert—and made adaptions to all kinds of climate from the 50-below-zero winters of Alaska's Brooks Range to the searing 120-degree heat of the Southwestern desert hills. In fact, the mountain sheep did not invade the deserts of the Southwest until the country began drying up at the end of the Pleistocene era perhaps 12,000 years ago. There were human beings in the Southwest long before there were mountain sheep. Excavations in southern Arizona caves show that Indian hunters had camped in them and had hunted and eaten mule and whitetail deer and pronghorn antelope for many years before the mountain sheep began to drift in. In

This is desert sheep country in the lower Sonoran zone, a harsh inhospitable region where rainfall runs from two to eight inches a year. Most of this country is too rough for horses.

the heat and the dryness of the Southwestern and Mexican deserts, the bighorn evolved into a smaller, more thinly haired, tougher animal, able to live mostly by browsing instead of grazing, able to get by without open water in areas where he could get his moisture from water-storing cacti. In these same deserts the mule deer, whitetail deer, and antelope have also learned to survive with only the moisture they can obtain from dew on their browse and from the moisture in cacti.

The sheep, the deer, the antelope, the black and grizzly bears have made their adaptions to very different climatic zones. The sheep is highly migratory and as long as he can see a mountain in the distance he is willing to cover many miles of level country to get to it. Even that plains dweller, the pronghorn antelope, will work up into high mountains and is sometimes even found in the timber. I have seen antelope above timberline in Wyoming. The caribou is for the most part an arctic and subarctic animal and an animal of the open tundra. Nevertheless he is found in timberline country well down into Alberta and British Columbia, and there are even a few in the heavy forests of the north Idaho Bitterroot mountains.

The climatic zones of North America, starting in the south, begin with the Lower Sonoran. This is the warm, arid climate typical of the lower altitudes in the Mexican state of Sonora. This zone is characterized by mesquite, greasewood, cactus. The Upper Sonoran zone ranges from the high plains and foothills of the Southern states to the lower plains

5

The upper Sonoran zone of northern Arizona in the famous Kaibab Forest north of the Grand Canyon. The trees in the background are piñons and there is sagebrush in the foreground.

and valleys of the north. As I write these lines I am in Lewiston, Idaho, in the valley of the Snake River at an altitude of a bit less than 800 feet above sea level. This is in the Upper Sonoran zone. Here latitude takes the place of altitude. In Arizona the Upper Sonoran zone is found at from 4,500 to 6,500 feet and typical trees are the one-seeded juniper and the piñon. The Transition zone is cooler, moister but by no means humid. In Arizona and New Mexico it begins at from 6,500 to 7,000 feet. The typical tree is the yellow pine, but there are great plains of grass or sage, some aspens, some Douglas fir, cottonwoods along the streams. In the Southwest this is the climate that wild turkeys like. It is favored by mule deer, bear, and elk.

The Canadian zone is higher and the climate is like that of southern Canada. It produces forests interspersed with open grasslands called "parks" in the mountains of the West. This is elk summer range and in places summer range for deer. The still higher and colder Hudsonian zone is just below timberline. The climate is like that just south of the limit of trees in the Canadian north. This zone in the mountains of the West is characterized by moss and lichens, close-growing clumps of alpine fir called "shintangle" in Alberta. In the mountains this is one of the loveliest regions on earth, a land of rock slices, of melting snow banks, little ice-cold rills, small grassy meadows, tiny, perfect alpine flowers. This is the favorite summering ground of the Stone and Dall sheep and the northern bighorns. Because it is cool, caribou are often found right

6

up among the sheep and in the Wyoming Rockies the elk like to summer this high. Two of the finest bull elk I have ever shot were taken in lofty basins in the Hudsonian zone just under timberline, one out of Moran, Wyoming, near the Continental Divide in 1944, the other ten years later in a lovely basin off the South Fork of the Shoshone out from Cody.

In the Alberta and southern British Columbia Rockies, the arctic firs end at timberline as suddenly and as definitely as a clipped hedge, but farther north in the Yukon, where timberline is lower, the common timberline tree is the black spruce and the characteristic plants are the arctic willow and the dwarf birch, which the natives call "bug" brush or "buck" brush. With the first hard frosts the dwarf birch all turns red and inflames the hillsides. The willows turn yellow and the aspens bright gold. This is the loveliest time in the north country.

The upper portion of the Hudsonian zone occurs at 13,500 feet on the San Francisco peaks in northern Arizona, near which I used to live. In

A lone horseman crosses the Middle Fork of the Salmon River in Idaho. This is largely open grassland, a phase of the Transition zone, where sheep and deer spend the winter. However, even in summer some sheep are seen in the cliffs close to the water.

This hunter is above timberline where there is still some early fall snow. He has shot an excellent Stone ram on the high bench above the Prophet River in northern British Columbia.

Colorado this timberline is at about 12,000 feet, between 10,500 and 11,000 feet in Wyoming and 10,000 in Montana. As one goes north in the Canadian Rockies timberline drops rapidly. It is at about 6,000 to 6,500 feet around Jasper Park and about 5,000 to 5,500 in northern British Columbia around the head of the Muskwa and Prophet Rivers. In the southern Yukon it is 4,000 to 4,500.

Above the last timber is the Alpine or Arctic zone—dwarf willows, mosses and lichens, lovely little flowers, dainty grass, tiny trickling streams. There are always banks of old snow. Old rams with heavy blunted horns bed up here in the shale, drink in the rills, nibble on the tender grass and delicate plants. Often old bull moose spend whole summers in basins above timberline, fattening on the succulent willows, growing their great spreading antlers. Goats feed in the steep pastures, and grizzlies dig for hoary marmots. Caribou come to lie on the snow-banks and golden eagles patrol the polished skies. The game bird above timberline is the ptarmigan, just as the game birds of the Hudsonian zone are the blue and Franklin grouse. As the Pleistocene died and the ice retreated, little patches of arctic flora and fauna have been left far to the south. In Arizona some of the same arctic plants grow above timber-line on the San Francisco peaks that grow on the Canadian shores of the Arctic Ocean. Ptarmigan are found as far south as the Sangre de Cristo mountains in Colorado.

8

Country above timberline in Alberta. This is summer range for sheep, goats, and sometimes even moose.

Game country can be mountainous. It can be open or wooded, rolling or flat as a table, but the character of the country determines what game is to be found in an area, how the animal guards himself, and how it must be hunted. Let us look at some definitions:

The Plains

"Plains" means country that is flat or rolling, generally covered with grass but also with low brush such as the sagebrush on the plains of Wyoming, Montana, and south Idaho or the combination of mosses, lichens, and stunted willow that clothes the arctic prairie. Sometimes the plains are so arid that they are almost without vegetation. In some areas they are spotted with clumps of trees. Plains are always cut by water courses, often dry, and these are useful to the stalker. Before they were settled, the plains east of the Rockies were clothed with buffalo grass. Belts of timber grew along the creeks and rivers, and in these typical forests game like wild turkeys, whitetail deer, and black bear were found. Where plains are broken by sharp rough canyons, cliffs, rough escarpments, and rocky hills, mountain animals are often found.

On the plains of northern Arizona north of the Santa Fe railway, bighorn sheep were found not only within the Grand Canyon itself but in the canyon of the Little Colorado and on the rough little hills and buttes. Likewise bighorns also lived in the breaks of the Missouri and its

9

tributaries out in the Great Plains. They were found in the Badlands of South Dakota and on rough little hills far out in the plains from the main Rockies. On the plains of Kenya and Tanganyika (Tanzania) there are piles of granite boulders called *kopjes* (pronounced copies). Geologically this terrain is very ancient and the kopjes are all that is left of much higher hills that have eroded away. Every kopje has its quota of klipspringers, those gay little mountain antelope. On the plains of the Sahara clear down into the center of Africa there are hills and mountain ranges of various formations, and on these are aoudads or Barbary sheep.

The Great Plains of North America had millions of animals but few true plains species—only the buffalo and the pronghorn. The elk ranged out into the plains, but I am skeptical if elk (although they adapted themselves to the plains) were ever really a true plains species in the sense that the American pronghorn and many Old World antelopes are. In Asia and in Europe the wapiti and the red deer, relatives of the elk, are never found on the plains and have adapted themselves to open country only in the "deer forests" of the Scotch Highlands. But these heather-covered hills were once heavily timbered. The trees were cut down to run blast furnaces for the smelting of iron. In North America, the elk probably moved into the plains during the late Pleistocene when many plains species died off simply because the vanished species had left an ecological vacuum behind them and the elk's natural habitat, the foothills and the mountains, may have become overpopulated. Likewise the grizzly may have moved into the Great Plains to take the place of the enormous dire wolf, the lion, and the saber-toothed tiger, none of which survived into the modern era.

Grazing animals that are by nature plains dwellers depend on their eyes to discover their enemies and on their legs to get away from them. They have no instinct for concealment as brush and forest dwellers do. These creatures of the plains include the swiftest animals in the world— the American pronghorn, the Indian blackbuck, the Persian gazelle, and the cheetah which preyed on these and other Old World antelope. These animals when thoroughly frightened and on good ground can run in excess of fifty miles an hour. They can outrun their natural enemies— even the cheetah if given a little start—but they cannot outrun automobiles; and in areas where they can be chased by automobiles, as on the plains of India and Iran, these plains dwellers have become almost extinct. The chasing of plains animals by automobiles is wasteful of game and is unsportsmanlike. The practice should be prohibited everywhere. In India and Iran, meat hunters spray fleeing herds with buckshot from automobiles and probably wound and lose at least five animals for every one they kill quickly. In Mexico within the past twenty years it has become fashionable for rich Mexicans to hunt. In Mexico the rich are very rich indeed, and the Latin and Anglo-Saxon notion of sportsmanship is quite different. Mexicans in light planes enjoyed mowing down the antelope on the plains of Chihuahua with submachine guns. Peasants in trucks would follow and gather up the slain. A Mexican acquaintance of mine who is a multimillionaire tells me he used to do the same thing to the desert bighorn sheep in the low barren mountains of Sonora.

There is only one decent and sporting way to hunt plains game—and that is by stalking. Even in country that appears as flat as a billiard table, the hunter can sneak up a water course and get within easy range. He can get a small tree or a bush between himself and his quarry. In Africa the termite hills that dot the plains are the hunter's friends.

Almost as dangerous to plains animals as chasing them with automobiles and often combined with it is the cruel and unsportsmanlike habit of shooting at plains animals running and too far away. This is a cruel, calloused, and wasteful habit as at least 50 percent of the animals hit are not recovered.

Open Bush

Where open plains give way to scattered brush and trees, often with open grass between, the country is sometimes called "orchard bush," "open bush," or "scrub jungle." The first and second are used in Africa, the last in India. Although this type of country is common in the Western United States, I have never heard a specific term for it. Country like this is found in the semi-arid West in the Upper Sonoran zone, often where overgrazing by cattle has killed off the grass and has enabled the one-seeded junipers (usually called "cedars" by the natives of Arizona) to invade the range. This is country where some mule deer are found throughout the year, but if it is adjacent to higher and cooler country it is used by mule deer and elk and sometimes by antelope as winter range. This open bush country is always arid or semi-arid and is found all over the world. The arboreal deserts of southern Arizona and Sonora are country of this type, so are the drier jungles of India. Brush is generally heavy along the beds of dry or intermittent streams (*nullahs* in India, *dongas* in Africa, *arroyos* in northern Mexico or in the American Southwest), but otherwise the country is open enough so the game can be seen at from 30 to 150 or even 200 yards. In the rainy season in some country of this type, grass and vines spring up swiftly until the country is very thick.

In the very dry parts of eastern Africa, particularly the desert portions of Kenya and Somalia, this is the country of the lesser kudu, the gerenuk, the Beisa oryx. Farther south it is sable country and sometimes kudu country. In India it is the land primarily of the blue bull, and the little chinkara are also there as well as some spotted axis deer (chital). This type of country is typical of the central Indian Highlands, possibly the best tiger country in India. In some places this open bush country extends well up into the foothills. There is country of this type all over the Western states and since it is generally neither very rough nor very thick it is ideal in which to hunt mule deer on horseback.

Forest and Jungle

In common American usage the word "jungle" has a rather ominous sound. If you say that a patch of woods is a regular jungle you probably mean that it is very thick and is full of bugs and snakes and probably inhabited by some pretty formidable creatures. Actually, the word comes from Hindi and simply means uninhabited land. I have done some tiger hunting in India, have shot a couple and have been in on the kill of five. The only really thick country I have bumped into between monsoons has been the belts of high grass along streams in the Terai of northern India and in west Bengal–in each case near the Himalayas. Actually the "jungles" of the Indian foothills near the Nepal border (country made famous by the late Jim Corbett's tales of man-eating tigers and leopards) are, during the dry season anyway, not very thick at all. This is one of the most beautiful portions of the globe—great soaring trees, open parks, which the Indians call *maidans,* full of sweet-smelling grass.

Very thick country is difficult to hunt in because it is hard to move without making noise. About the thickest country in North America is the rain-forest country along the northwest coast from Oregon through the coast and islands of southeast Alaska. This is the home of the Pacific Coast blacktail deer, the Olympic elk, black bear, and in the north grizzly and Alaska brown bears.

Other forests that are hard to hunt because they are thick and noisy are the deciduous forests of the Eastern United States from Maine to the Carolinas and some of the woods of Wisconsin, Michigan, and Minnesota —all whitetail and black bear country.

Where tall, thick brush or heavy forests are combined with steep mountains the hunting is really tough. This is why that forest-haunting antelope of Kenya, the bongo, is considered a trophy of such high rank. He is found in heavy bamboo forest at high altitude where it is cold and wet. Even if the hunter gets within a few feet of a bongo he usually gets no more than a fleeting snap shot. In Idaho much of the elk country is composed of very high and very steep mountains thickly clothed in coniferous trees if it has not been burned over, high brush if it has. Since the elk season opens in wilderness areas on September 15 and in other areas on October 1, it is often quite warm and the elk stay in the heavy green timber during the day, coming out to feed in the openings only very late in the afternoon. By the time most hunters are up on the ridges, the elk are back in the timber again. When country is very thick and very noisy, still-hunting is impossible. Then the hunters either have to move the game by driving or they have to sit somewhere and watch the more open spots in case an animal wanders through.

Nature is never static. The face of the earth (the plains, the mountains, the forests) is always changing. Every time rain falls some earth is washed into the sea. Every time a herd of animals passed through a piece of country it changed it by tracking it up, by eating off grass. On the Great Plains there were millions of buffalo and also millions of antelope. When the buffalo runners shot the buffalo, the grass grew so tall and thick that it killed the weeds and forbs that antelope eat and the antelope almost died out. Overgrazing later by cattle took down the grass cover in Wyoming. The weeds and forbs came back and the antelope increased.

When Lewis and Clark came over the Bitterroot Mountains into Idaho, they were heavily timbered with fir, spruce, cedar, and pine. Such forests support little game because they grow little game food. Around 1910 a series of great fires swept the area. Brush grew up to take the place of the burned trees. The elk increased. By the middle 1960's, however, the brush was growing out of reach of the elk and the elk herds were decreasing.

There are now more whitetail deer in the Eastern United States than there were when Columbus discovered America. The second and third growth of cut-over forests support more game than do virgin forests. The lofty mountains of Iran were once covered with heavy forests, but these were cut over for building material and charcoal. Then the mountains were so heavily grazed by sheep and goats that new trees could not start. The big red deer and the little roe deer (both forest animals) died out and the tigers, which are also forest animals, disappeared. However, red sheep and ibex, which thrive in open country, moved in.

For thousands of years the natives of most of Africa have burned off the high, dry grass after the rains have stopped so that as they wander around they won't bump into lions, leopards, and other animals and also so that tender green grass that is more palatable to their cattle will come up. The small antelope flock to these burned-over areas because of the fresh, new grass and also because they can see their enemies and run swiftly over good ground to get away from them. In the Albert Park in the Congo the burning of grass was prohibited because the annual burnings destroy the topsoil and the fertility goes up in smoke. The result was that the park lost all of its small antelope. They could not see their enemies and so perished.

2 | *The Senses of Game Animals*

Like human beings, game animals see, hear, feel, smell. Some species of animals hear better than others, some see better, some have better noses.

Animals which dwell in open country generally have keener vision than those who live (or at least have evolved) in heavy forest. Woods dwellers may see less well than open-country animals, but they hear better (or pay more attention to what they hear), and they generally have keener noses.

Animals are well equipped with instincts, but some of their acts are not quite as instinctive as many used to think. The lioness which Joy Adamson tells of raising as a cub in *Born Free* hadn't the faintest idea how to hunt and had to be taught before she was liberated. My wife has a charming Siamese cat called Viggo. He bears the name of a Norwegian we know who like the cat also has large, round, very pale blue eyes. He (the cat) is instinctively interested in the birds and small mammals on which his ancestors preyed, and he is always stalking robins, sparrows, and starlings. Once he actually caught a starling, but he did the bird little harm as he did not have the remotest idea what to do with it. Some other starlings attacked him and scared him half out of his wits. He dropped his victim and fled.

Animals have just about the same emotions as human beings. They can love, cherish friends, be lonesome, jealous, frightened. They know rage and fear and after a fashion they think. They have long memories. Once a year a friend with a Brittany bitch used to come to my place to pick up my dog Mike in order to promote a romance between his Brittany and mine. Mike never saw him between visits, but he did not forget him from one year to the next and always greeted him with delighted barks.

Horses are among the most gifted of all mammals. Most of them have prodigious memories, and those who have worked much with horses on ranches and on wilderness pack trips say that when most horses are over a trail once they will remember it as long as they live and can follow it on the darkest night. In addition the horse has keen vision in daylight or darkness, excellent hearing, and a good sense of smell. I would guess, however, that in the scale of intelligence horses come well below dogs, cats, and bears.

The appearance of an animal gives some clue as to the keenness of its senses. Those dwellers in the forest, the moose, the elk, and the mule and whitetail deer, all have extraordinarily keen hearing—and large ears which are flexible and which they can cock in the direction a sound is coming from. The African greater kudu, another forest and brush dweller, is famous for his sensitive hearing and like the moose and the deer has large ears. On the other hand, the mountain sheep, the goats, and the pronghorn antelope, all mountain and plains dwellers that depend more on what they see than what they hear, have relatively small ears.

Vision of Animals

The best eyes in nature are those of birds, particularly those of vultures and birds of prey. It is common in Africa or India to make a kill with, as far as the human eye can detect, the sky completely empty of birds. In a few minutes the vultures start gathering and dropping down to perch in trees and wait for whatever is left of the kill. The birds have been floating so high in the sky that they have been out of sight. When I was on a tiger hunt in India, a kite dropped out of nowhere and grabbed one of a pair of tiger lucky bones (vestigial shoulder bones) out of the hand of a shikari who was taking them to my wife. The kite had been around 400 feet in the air when it started down. A lucky bone is about a quarter-inch wide and about three inches long. It has been estimated by scientists who have experimented by attracting hawks with carcasses of mice that a hawk (if he could read) would be able to read ordinary one-column newspaper headlines a quarter of a mile in the air.

Compared to those birds of prey, the eyes of human beings are nothing to get excited about, but the eyes of all primates, including human beings, are among the best possessed by mammals. Primates have binocular vision (seeing with both eyes at the same time) which gives stereoscopic effect and enables the creatures who possess it to judge distances better. They see better than most other mammals in front, but their vision does not have as wide a field as does the vision of herbivorous animals like deer and antelope, whose eyes are more nearly on the sides of their heads.

With the exception of those of the primates, the eyes of mammals do not distinguish color. Instead they see everything in shades of gray. For that reason it does not make much difference what color the hunter wears just so it does not contrast with the surroundings. The hunter can wear a red shirt and green pants with an orange hat and he is no more conspicuous than he would be in all gray, all green, or all khaki if these colors have about the same tone and degree of contrast. The fact that the human being can distinguish colors and has binocular vision means that in many ways he can see better than most of the animals he hunts.

All eyes detect movement quicker than anything else, and the quicker and the more extensive the movement the quicker it is detected. The flicker of the wings of a tiny bird will be seen instantly, whereas a moose standing still but in plain sight at the edge of the timber might not be noticed at all.

The ability to distinguish stationary objects depends on binocular vision, on the ability to see color, and also on the human brain, which interprets what the eyes see. Stationary objects do not mean much to most mammals. In 1950 in the Yukon my guide and I made a long stalk on a bunch of Dall rams, one of which was the finest I have ever shot. They were lying at the head of a big basin about three-fourths of a mile wide under a bluff about thirty feet high. Three of the rams were lying with their broad rumps toward me and the other was lying sidewise. All were looking off into the basin and had probably seen our horse wrangler ride out to drag in a dead spruce so he could saw it up for firewood.

The middle ram of the three facing away from me had a tremendous head, but I did not want to shoot him in the rump or through the backstraps and destroy meat or in the neck and ruin the cape. I knew that there was no way he could get away, so I simply sat there above the cliff with my scope-sighted .30/06 across my knees. Presently the ram that was lying sidewise got tired of looking down into the basin, so he turned his head and neck in line with his body. That meant that he was "seeing" me with the vision of his right eye. For three or four minutes nothing happened. Then the fact that I was rather oddly shaped seemed to register. The ram turned his head and stared right at me with both eyes.

I knew then that the jig was up. He had no idea what I was, but he was suspicious as he could not remember seeing that odd shape before. I moved my right thumb to switch off the safety of my rifle. Instantly the ram was on his feet and off. The other rams didn't even look back but ran like the devil. I had to shoot the big fellow in the fanny after all.

Mountain sheep have eyes that are famous throughout the hunting world. I have seen them watching human beings, bears, and coyotes at distances so great that I could only pick up what they were looking at with binoculars. Yet if an object is not moving, the sight of it doesn't mean much even at thirty feet.

I have had experiences like the one with that band of Dall rams with many other animals. Once many years ago in Sonora I sneaked up on a young desert bighorn ram, got on top of a boulder above him. He paid no attention until his browsing brought me in line with his vision. He stared at me fixedly until I spoke to him and waved a hand. I have had deer almost walk over me when I was motionless and they seldom pay any attention to me unless they catch my wind.

I may be wrong about this, but it seems to me that the pronghorn antelope has keener eyes even than the mountain sheep. Many times I have put my head over a ridge to look at antelope, and even when the outline of my head was broken by thin brush, antelope would quickly detect it—quicker, I think, than sheep. They wouldn't know what my head was but they knew that whatever it was it did not belong there.

Deer and elk pick up movement well. I remember on one occasion I was packing in to some sheep country above timberline at about 11,500 feet in Wyoming. My guide and I were riding and leading a couple of pack horses. We stopped to look things over from a ridge. Below us was an enormous rolling plateau covered with yellow grass. In a few minutes we had discovered a herd of about a dozen big six-point bull elk lying on a rise about a mile away. Every one of those elk was staring right at us. They had seen us before we had seen them—undoubtedly when we were moving.

Most members of the deer family have pretty good eyes for moving objects, and when they are spooky the movement of any strange object is apt to send them flying. I have seen both mule and whitetail deer that had been chased around a great deal by hunters get up and run wildly when I was 400 yards or so away. That is why it is important for the hunter in open and semi-open country to avoid making himself conspicuous. He should never hunt along the top of a ridge, as every deer or sheep in the country can see him. Instead he should work along just below the ridge, as he is then far less conspicuous than he is against the skyline. He should wear clothes that do not contrast violently with the surroundings. A white shirt is very bad, as is any light color—even faded khaki. Clothing of camouflage material helps in that it breaks up the outline. He should remember that the quicker his movements are the easier he is to see. If he wants to look over a ridge into a basin where sheep may be, he should raise his head very slowly. In Kenya cloth hats are made and sold with little pockets around the cloth band to hold twigs. The stalker who wants to remain inconspicuous can put grass or twigs with leaves on them in the hatband and when he pokes his head over the hill he is less easily seen. Since there is nothing like a ten-gallon cowboy hat in nature, if I am wearing one I always take it off, put it down, and lay a stone on it to keep it from blowing away before I take a peek.

The hunter should avoid conspicuous equipment—anything that will shine or glitter. Once when I was hunting sheep I saw a bunch of ewes and lambs on their feet staring at something below them. I looked in that direction and in a moment I saw a bright flash. Then a few seconds later I saw it again. I looked in that direction with binoculars. There was my companion and his guide. The flash I had seen was the polished bolt of his rifle.

Moose have extraordinarily keen hearing and good noses, but I have never been impressed with their vision. I have seen big bulls browsing on willows a half mile away who paid no attention to a whole packtrain unless they got the wind or heard a strange noise. A grazing deer or sheep would have seen it quickly. The caribou has very poor eyes and doesn't even trust what little he sees with them. If he does make out something that looks suspicious, he always circles to catch the wind. Then the instant he gets the rancid scent of man his little white tail pops up and away he goes. I have stalked caribou by getting the wind on them and walking slowly toward them, taking no precautions except to stop and stand motionless if any of them happened to look in my direction. Generally I have been in easy range before I have been noticed.

The hunter should remember that even if an animal sees him, jumps to his feet, and runs wildly off, it is no sign that the animal has identified him as a hunter. The animal only knows that something is moving and that its shape is odd. Sad experience has taught the animal that the sight of such odd shapes is followed by the loud crashes of rifle fire, cause bullets to snap and crack over his head, gravel to fly around. The creatures that are hunted associate the upright shape of man with trouble. That is why bending over or crawling is a good idea for the stalker.

Bears (or at least grizzlies, blacks, and browns) have very poor eyes. I have never hunted polar bears and for all I know from personal experience they may be able to see like eagles. On several occasions I have stalked bears feeding in the open with no other precaution than to stand still if they looked in my direction. I have had grizzlies look at me when I was standing within a hundred yards, decide I was a rock or a tree, and go on feeding. In Alaska I once lay in plain sight on a beach while an enormous brown bear walked toward me. Rain was pouring down. At about sixty yards I let him have it.

Bears, pandas, raccoons, and members of the dog family are all vaguely related, and all have excellent noses, good enough hearing, but indifferent eyes. The coursing dogs have been bred for speed and to chase what they can see. Their eyes are probably much better than those of dogs bred for keen noses.

However, I believe that dogs and all their relatives in the wolf family depend much more on their noses than they do on their eyes. When my Brittany spaniel, Mike, made a wide swing in a stubble field, he used to stop and look for me. I could be standing in plain sight 200 or 300 yards away, and he would not be sure it was me until I made a circle above my head with my right hand. Then he'd come in. Until I did that I am sure that to his eyes I was simply an indefinite upright shape that *might* be me.

I remember one time when I was hunting pheasants in a stubble field on a hillside. Mike had made a circle and had started to come back when a hunter about 300 yards from me blew a whistle for his own dog, a German shorthair. Mike trotted over to the hunter and fell in beside him about twenty feet away but upwind. The hunter was looking for his own dog and did not see Mike. I watched to see what would happen. Mike went along for about thirty yards. Then he took a good look at the hunter and decided there was something odd about his appearance. He trotted over to him, sniffed his leg, and jumped backward ten feet in astonishment. Immediately he started looking around to see where I was. I waved my hand above my head and he came in.

Scenting Ability

As anyone knows who has done much hunting with hounds or pointing dogs, scent is a mysterious thing. I have seen my old dog Mike go right to a cock pheasant over 200 yards away, but I have seen him fail to pick up the scent of a wounded bird I had knocked down on hot, dry ground. Scent lies best and lasts longest on cool, still, damp days. It dissipates most quickly on hot, dry, windy days. Probably dogs which have been specially bred for keen noses can smell better than most wild animals. Some of the scenting feats performed by bloodhounds are incredible.

I think that under favorable conditions, on a damp, cool day with a gentle, drifting wind that does not dissipate the scent a deer or a bear can smell a man a half-mile away, possibly farther. I have seen deer spooked by hunters they could not possibly have heard or seen at that distance. I have seen disturbed elk move out of a basin and then long afterwards have seen a hunter they had smelled show up.

In damp, cool places out of the wind man-scent must lie for a long time. I have seen deer and bears cross my trail, made an hour or two before, and show all signs of alarm. I remember one old grizzly sow with two cubs who wandered into my trail in a Yukon basin. She jumped as if someone had stuck a pin into her, batted one of her cubs, and then took off at a dead run with the cubs right behind her. One of the reasons that a big party hunting a valley will run all the game out is that they stink it up.

Many times I have read that a hunter should not smoke because tobacco smells bad to an animal. I think a human being smells so bad to an animal as it is that tobacco could not possibly make him smell worse. Actually, a pipe or a cigarette is often very useful for determining the direction of a fitful and gentle wind. I have hunted with guides who were so filthy, even with my poor human nose I could smell them at considerable distance. It would seem logical to me that a hunter wearing clean clothes would be somewhat more difficult for an animal to smell than a man in dirty, sweaty clothes. Bottled scent which is supposed to kill the human odor is sold, but I have never used it. Once when I was hunting in Africa I had shot an antelope for meat and a native hunter with a bow and arrows and wearing nothing but a breechclout came out of the bush and rubbed the contents of the animal's stomach all over his body. The idea, of course, was to kill his scent.

Human beings have generally rather poor noses, but some are much more aware of odors than others. In spite of the fact that I smoked for many years I have always had a pretty good nose. On many occasions I have smelled elk and deer before I have seen them. Once when I was hunting Dall sheep I stopped right in the middle of a little basin and told my Indian guide I smelled a ram. A moment later a big ram jumped off a point upwind where he had been lying quite well concealed and I nailed him.

Different human races have different odors, just as different species of birds and animals do. I see nothing disgraceful about this. African gun bearers who work for good Kenya safari companies are scrupulously clean. They bathe and put on fresh clothes daily, but they have their distinctive odor just as members of other races do. A strange Indian can walk into an Indian village and the dogs pay no attention to him, but if a white man does his exotic odor drives them mad. I have been told by Japanese and Chinese friends that Europeans have a peculiar odor that they find rather offensive.

With the exception of man the sexes of mammalian species are attracted to each other by odor. Men are largely like birds in that they are first attracted to prospective mates by what they see. We have let our noses degenerate and do not use them as much as do other mammals. But we should not write them off as we still use them more than we are aware of. If we didn't the gals wouldn't spend millions of dollars annually on perfume.

In order for an animal to smell the hunter, the scent must be wafted to it by moving air. That is why the hunter always tries to hunt upwind or crosswind. Sometimes the air is moving so slowly (as the hunter can tell by tossing up a handful of grass or dust or by watching the smoke of a pipe or cigarette) that he can walk briskly and travel faster than the scent. As air is warmed on the surface of the earth it rises. As it cools off it flows down. When the earth is warming up from the sun, the current of air runs up a canyon. In late afternoon the higher air cools off and flows down.

In the mountains the air currents are fickle. Sometimes air rises rapidly or swirls around a peak and an animal that looks as if he is getting scent is not getting it at all. That is why, I believe, some hunters think mountain sheep do not have keen noses. Sheep have good noses but the erratic air currents of the mountains do not always give them a chance to use them.

The big cats are not supposed to smell well. Cougars, jaguars, cheetahs, leopards, lions, and tigers are supposed to hunt by sight and probably do so largely. In India native shikaris claim that tigers have noses no better than human beings. However, I have found that I have more luck in getting a tiger to come back to the bait when I keep the natives from hawking, spitting, and urinating around it.

There are many cases where tigers go near young water buffaloes tied out as bait and do not touch them. Presumably this is because they hunt by sight alone and do not smell. In the chapter on types of hunting, we will see that in Africa the baits are dragged so lions are led to the bait tree and that leopards are attracted to the bait by the smell when it gets high. Why the tiger should have a nose less keen than those of lions and leopards, I cannot say. But there is no doubt but that cats see better than dogs, bears, and most herbivorous animals. Anyone who has hunted tigers knows that they have excellent eyes.

Hearing of Animals

How the hearing of human beings ranks with that of game animals I cannot say. Undoubtedly, deer, moose, and elk hear better than human beings. Game found in mountains and plains game doesn't pay much attention to what it hears. Sheep and goats live in a region of unstable rocks and slides where all the stones are looking for an excuse to roll. I have seen large stones roll within a few yards of bedded goats and rams without their paying any attention.

Familiar sounds do not bother animals, and in some cases neither do sounds they cannot interpret. Deer and elk are not bothered by the rustle of the wind in the trees, the patter of the raindrops, the rumble of thunder; but a breaking twig, a stealthy footstep, the unnatural clank of metal on stone sends them off. I doubt if a shot means much to most animals unless it is close by. As Ralph Young demonstrated to me in Alaska in 1963, a brown bear is not bothered by the human voice. Two people can carry on an animated conversation within thirty or forty yards of bears and it doesn't bother them as they don't know what the noise is and it does not sound menacing. But pick up a twig and break it and the bears are off like shots! I would not believe this if I had not seen it demonstrated.

As I have found out to my sorrow, tigers have ears like bats. They will take off at the sound of a camera shutter, at the snick of a safety, at the nervous distant clearing of a throat. Why Ralph Young's brown bears are not bothered by the human voice and tigers are frightened by any tiny and harmless sound, I do not know.

Game animals tend to have one-track minds, and most animals will almost run over another hunter when they are sneaking away from one behind them. This is why the drive is a good hunting tactic: the animal's attention is fixed on the driver, not the stander.

Instinct and Intelligence

Game animals exist in a fierce and uncompromising world. Few live into advanced old age. When the mountain ram gets old his teeth go bad. He becomes thin and weak and the wolves pull him down and devour him. When deer get too plentiful they eat down their forage and perish miserably of cold and malnutrition. The bull elk tries to make it across the river to a spot where the browse may be better, but he breaks through the ice, scrambles to get out, grows weak, gives up and is swept away by the current. The old lion with bad teeth, weak and dim of vision, can no longer find game he can catch. For a time he lives on small creatures but he grows weaker and the hyenas close in and kill him. When an Eskimo grows old and cannot move, the rest of the clan leave him with a little food to die when they move off. In Africa it is common for natives to carry grandma out into the bush so the hyenas can finish her off and eat her when the old girl is plainly in extremis.

Animals are afraid of any unfamiliar thing. A great fierce tiger will turn away from a piece of white cloth or paper fluttering on a bush or from a "stop" tapping lightly with a stick against a tree trunk. A 1,200-pound horse can be thrown into a wild, unreasoning panic by a cotton-tail rabbit that hops across the trail or by a grouse that flushes under his feet, or a gum wrapper in the trail.

It is instinctive for every animal, even large, fierce predators, to run from anything that chases it. The assumption is, I suppose, that the animal flees because he feels that the animal coming at him is certain that he can devour him. When my wife and I were hunting in Tanganyika in 1959 with the famous white hunter Syd Downey, we found a large hungry lion sitting under our bait tree sniffing hungrily at the quarter of rotting zebra. On the highest limb that would bear his weight was an unhappy leopard who was not about to come down as long as that damned lion was hanging around. Syd wanted to get rid of the lion and he did not consider it sporting for me to knock off the leopard, which I could easily have done, as long as it was kept up the tree by the lion.

He drove the hunting car up to within fifty or sixty feet of the lion, told him to go away. For whatever the reason, a lion apparently cannot identify the things in an automobile as human beings. The lion batted insolent yellow eyes at Syd and did not move. Syd leaped out of the car, rushed at the lion, waving his arms and yelling. The king of beasts fled as if it had been turpentined.

My friend Robert Chatfield-Taylor tells this one. He was hunting elephants in the northern frontier of Kenya when the hunting car got stuck and his white hunter and the gun bearer were trying to dig it out. Suddenly there was a pounding of heavy feet and a crashing of brush and a big rhino came trotting to investigate. Bob made a dive for his double .470 to defend himself but the white hunter rushed at the rhino, threw a handful of sand in its eyes and shouted: "Bugger off, you bawstard!" The rhino buggered off.

A predatory animal will chase anything that runs from it. The reason that dogs chase cats is that cats generally run. If the cats ran toward the dogs the dogs would run. In my town there is a truculent Siamese cat that has a very low tolerance as far as dogs are concerned. Whenever a dog comes into what the cat considers his territory he is after it like a flash. The dogs always flee, generally yelping in terror.

If a wounded lion charges a group of men he will always ignore the ones who stand their ground and chase the ones who run. Some years ago I used to walk my dog on a leash on the grounds of a local normal school. A large, noisy neighborhood dog used to leave his yard, cross the street and bark and growl at me. Finally I grew tired of this and one day I rushed at the dog, barking at *him*. He fled howling and from that day on he would never get closer than 100 yards to me. If I even looked in his direction he would flee as if the devil were after him.

All animals interpret signs of weakness as fear and think they have the upper hand. Stand your ground with a mean range bull and you'll get into no trouble. Run and he'll chase you. The first time you ride a horse, belt the hell out of him the first time he decides to poke along at his own gait. Otherwise he'll think you're afraid of him and will make your life miserable.

Game animals cannot talk but they are by no means dumb brutes. I have often seen them do very intelligent things. The whitetail buck that circles to watch his backtrack is no boob, and neither is the mule deer that beds on the end of a point, goes off to his left and then sneaks around the point to get behind the confused hunter.

I was once hunting sheep in Sonora when I had to sling my rifle across my back and use both hands to climb out of a canyon to a narrow point that projected out from the main ridge. When my head cleared the top I found myself looking right into the startled eyes of a fine old ram with pelage so dark as to be almost black. He dived off the point and I scrambled up. I looked across the side canyon expecting to see him. I did not. The sneak had run around the point to get behind me and I realized this just in time to see him going over the crest. It would seem to me that the natural and instinctive thing for that ram to have done would have been to run directly away from me across the side canyon and up or around the other point. His maneuver really fooled me and I think it was a sign of genuine intelligence.

A hunter I was on safari with in Africa had a tough time getting a greater kudu, but one day a villager came in and told his white hunter that a bull kudu was feeding in a brushy ravine about a half-mile away. When the sportsman and the white hunter got there they could see the kudu in the brush. The sportsman blazed away. Nothing happened. The kudu simply disappeared. A moment later the white hunter happened to look directly below him. There was the big kudu bull, his horns laid along his back, sneaking along. The white hunter punched his client and the client shot the kudu at a distance of a few feet. They found that the first shot had hit the kudu low in the neck. The kudu did not know where the shot came from. In spite of the wound it gambled on sneaking out. The fact that he lost the gamble does not detract from its being a cool and intelligent decision.

It is, I believe, generally agreed among hunters that the smartest North American game animal is the whitetail deer. I have done a lot of hunting for the small Southwestern variety of whitetail and I'll string along. I think that elk are very intelligent and mule deer are by no means dumb. All of these animals are born wary and suspicious. Caribou are, I think, not only rather dumb but also eccentric. Mountain goats have never struck me as being very smart but perhaps that is because the lofty country they inhabit gives them a sense of security.

Mountain sheep are not born suspicious like deer, but they learn and the more they are hunted the smarter they get. I have never hunted smarter animals than old desert bighorn rams that have been shot at a few times.

Game animals have good senses, are wary and intelligent, but man isn't too badly off. With good binoculars he can see better than any other animal. With care, patience, and proper footgear he can move as quietly as a soft-footed cat. He can climb anywhere the goat or sheep can go. His nose may not be very keen, but his hearing if unimpaired is quite good. With a modern rifle he is far more deadly than any grizzly, lion, or tiger that ever walked. But most important of all, he is smarter than the game he hunts!

3 | *Evaluating Game Country*

In the early 1930's I lived in Flagstaff, Arizona. It was then a charming little city of about 5,000 sitting at the foot of the 14,000-foot-high San Francisco peaks and in the midst of the great forest of yellow pine that grows on the 7,000-foot-high Mogollon Plateau. This was a great country to be alive in in those days. There were plenty of wild turkeys, fine hunting for mule deer, quail shooting about forty miles away in the Verde Valley. Although the season was not yet open on them there were plenty of elk and antelope.

For a month before the hunting season opened (about October 15, if I remember correctly) my favorite pastime was scouting for good deer and turkey areas. I would pick a forest service road, drive out on it and inspect the ponds or the "tanks," where earth dams had collected water. Wild turkeys water every day and when they do so they leave tracks and droppings. I would always try to have several spots located where the turkeys were coming to water regularly. I would look for tracks, feathers, droppings, scratchings in the pine needles where the birds had been hunting the seeds of the yellow pines. Partly to see if the birds were watering in a certain place every day and partly to confuse other low fellows who liked to sneak out and get bunches of turkeys located, I used to use a pine branch to whisk turkey tracks out of the dust around a nice water hole. Once I happened to notice a great many tracks around a

26

water hole where I had until then seen no signs whatsoever of turkey use. This was pretty suspicious and it was even more suspicious to note that all the tracks were exactly the same size. Later I found out that a rival turkey hunter owned a dried turkey foot. He had used it to track that dead water hole up hoping he could lure me away from a spot where three bunches were watering.

Tracks would tell me what direction the turkeys came from when they came to water. I also liked to find out where they were roosting. Then if there was no natural blind such as a dead tree or a little thicket, I would build myself a blind from the basaltic boulders strewn thickly over the Mogollon Plateau from the eruption of the gigantic volcano that became the San Francisco peaks. I'd try to build the blind a couple of weeks before the season opened so the turkeys would get used to it. I imagine my old blinds are still there—and probably still in use by turkey hunters.

I also used to scout for deer areas. I would look for tracks, for droppings, for beds, for signs of browsing. I would try to make an estimate of the age of tracks and droppings, the numbers and the sex of the animals that made them.

In some areas I would find no tracks but plentiful old droppings. These were places where the deer wintered. Since the bucks were not with the does in early October I tried to find areas where big tracks told me bucks were hanging around. I looked for places where the bucks had been "horning" trees to get the velvet off. Now and then I'd find places where a couple of bucks had been sparring.

Almost all animals have their home territories. In many areas, particularly in the West, deer, elk, and sheep have summer homes and winter homes. In the summer they migrate to high, cool country of pure water and fresh, tender grass and browse. As the snow gets deep in the high basins, the game moves to lower, less frigid country where the snow is less deep.

But in general all animals have their home range. A cottontail rabbit may live and die within a radius of a hundred yards, a deer within a radius of a few miles. Desert bighorn sheep migrate from dry ranges to those where they see rain falling, as in their arid habitat they have had to learn to do this in order to exist.

But almost all mammals love the little space of the earth they think of as home. I have been fortunate enough to have traveled and hunted over much of the world. I have shot wild sheep and ibex in the mountains of Iran, tigers in the teak jungles and grassy Terai of India, Barbary sheep and addax in the Sahara, lions, leopards, and kudu in Angola and Tanganyika, brown bear in the rain and mist of Admiralty Island. But I grew up in the southern Arizona desert, and I have never felt completely at home anywhere except in desert country. I like to be able to see great distances. Heavy forest makes me feel hemmed in. I do not sleep well in damp climates. When the population explosion drove me out of Arizona into less crowded Idaho, I instinctively did my first hunting across the Snake River on the Washington side because it was drier and more open.

I imagine that exactly the same sort of mechanism works with other mammals. A deer will starve to death on his overpopulated, overbrowsed mountain because it is "home" when across a valley fifteen miles away there is another mountain with few deer and much deer food. We think the deer is stupid, yet thousands of American mountaineers who are out of work because the mines on which they have depended for their livelihood have closed will eke out a miserable existence on relief rather than leave their native hills and hollows for industrial areas where there are plenty of jobs.

Apparently the love of the old and familiar and the fear of anything strange, new, and different is common to all mammals including man. With vast empty spaces in Canada, Australia, and New Zealand crying for settlers, the English have preferred to exist miserably in their crowded, smoky cities rather than to emigrate. To send great numbers of people into a new environment, it is generally necessary for them to be forced out by some genuine catastrophe—the confiscation of the lands of the clans in the Scotch Highlands by the English, the Irish potato famine, the pogroms against the Jews in Russia and Poland. Then almost always the immigrants have settled with their kind in Little Italys, Little Hungarys.

Some species of animals are much more adaptable than others, just as some human beings are. The mountain sheep is found in North America from the artic to the searing summer heat of the southern Arizona and Sonora desert, from 12,000 feet above sea level in parts of his summer range in Colorado and Wyoming to the rocky hills on the shores of the Gulf of California in Sonora. The restless sheep will cross great stretches of level country if ahead of him he can only see another mountain. The less adaptable Rocky Mountain goat, however, is never found far away from his alpine environment in his rugged mountains.

The hunter scouting for game before the season opens is primarily looking for the home grounds of the game he is after. For whatever the reason a certain piece of country will appeal to certain species of animals more than another stretch of country that may look to the human eye just about like it and equally desirable. Generations of wild sheep will prefer one part of a mountain range to all others. Generations of elk will like a particular basin, and when they are forced out of it they will always go by a limited number of routes.

Once when I was camped by the road with my outfit in the Yukon, we fell in with a very ancient Indian. He told us of a big basin in a little isolated range of mountains only about a half-day's pack from the road—perhaps twelve miles. For years he had trapped there, he said, and in or immediately around the basin there were always from four to six rams and of these, he went on, one or two were always very large. He was sure we would find rams there, he said, in spite of the fact that he had not seen the basin for ten years. He was sure no one else had been there either. Since we were not far from the mountains, had plenty of time, and the old Indian's tale sounded straight, we decided to investigate. I believe ours was the first horse outfit in there. We found trails, but they were old trails made by pack dogs, not by horses. At the campsite the old Indian had suggested most of the trees that had been cut had been chopped down with stone axes. The next morning we went out and I nailed a magnificent Dall ram. There were four rams in the basin and one was a big one.

"Home," then, affords the game animal a combination he likes of food, water, shelter, protection from his enemies. His home range may be very small or quite large, depending on the size and habits of an animal. He may have two homes, one for summer and one for winter. An old buck mule deer I knew used to appear along with the first tourists in early summer at the camp grounds of the national park on the North Rim of the Grand Canyon in Arizona. He stayed there all summer posing for his picture, bumming cigarettes and hamburgers, eating celery stalks and lettuce leaves out of the garbage. This was his summer home.

But when the frosts came, the park closed, and the hunters invaded the surrounding forest, Old Bill disappeared. He probably wintered far down in some little rocky canyon, and when he grew old he probably died there. He was well known and throughout the last years of his life he carried a magnificent, many-pointed head. It would have been recognized if it had come through a checking station.

In India hunting is done in "blocks." These are portions of the national forests which are reserved for hunting parties for fixed fees. Before the block is reserved the conscientious gentleman *shikari* (head guide or white hunter) always spends a week or two scouting it, finding out how many tigers call it their home, where they water, what their hunting routes are. A big tiger will stay in his home area for many years—as long as he has sufficient game or cattle for food, water, and cool thickets or canyons to lie up in. In the spring of 1965 my wife shot a mean old tiger that had made his home in a certain block in Central India for at least five years. This must have been a very desirable block because within a week after my wife shot the old boy, another tiger had moved in and had taken over, just as a new sales manager always shows at the same desk when the old one is fired!

The old whitetail almost always bedded down at X or Y. If he saw hunters coming up either trail A or trail B he would slip out, drop below the rimrock and come up to his other favorite spot. O'Connor ambushed him by having his wife go up trail B while he went below the rimrock. The buck was at D when O'Connor shot him from F.

I remember an old whitetail buck who lived for many years on the southern end of a little chain of hills in southern Arizona. His "home" consisted of an area of canyon, rimrock, rocky hillsides covered with grass, and patches of live oaks. I caught many glimpses of him, but never did I see him out of an area measuring about one and a half by two miles, and most of the time he was within a stretch about one mile long and a half-mile wide. He was a very wary buck. He always bedded down so he could get up and slip away without being seen or at most giving only a brief glimpse. This old buck was not difficult to see since his area was not large and relatively open. But he was almost impossible to get a good shot at.

I was finally responsible for his downfall. By following his tracks I found that he always did about the same things when he was jumped from certain places. So one brisk November morning, I sent my wife and a woman friend up a canyon while I went around under the rimrock at the south end of the chain of hills. I had discovered that if he were lying at the head of the canyon he'd sneak out, drop down, and skirt the rimrock where he was partially concealed by live oaks, cliff rose, and mountain mahogany. If he were under the rimrock, he would sneak out through a notch and drop into the head of the canyon the gals were in or into the one just north of it.

That morning the old buck went out of the head of the canyon without the gals seeing him. I was riding slowly along a trail at the foot of the slope and keeping my eye on the rimrock. Most game animals have one-track minds. This old buck was thinking of the two people he was slipping away from and although I was in plain sight he did not notice me.

I slipped off my horse, dropped the reins, and yanked a .270 out of the saddle scabbard. The sun was just over the horizon then and every point of the buck's antlers glistened like the lights of a Christmas tree. I guessed the buck to be about 250 yards so I got a good rest on a boulder, held the horizontal crosswire about one-third of the way up the body and moved the vertical crosswire about two feet ahead of the buck's chest and squeezed the trigger. The buck disappeared. I watched for ten minutes or so with binoculars but I saw no movement. I then tied my horse and climbed painfully up the steep rocky slope toward the spot where he had fallen. If I had not been convinced he was dead I would have gone around so I could come on him from above. I heard him go out ahead of me, went a few yards and found a tremendous pool of blood. A couple of minutes later I heard a shot from above. My wife had come on the poor old buck standing head down under an oak. My .270 bullet had almost taken his left front leg off close to the body. I guessed this old buck to be thirteen or fourteen years old. His antlers had eighteen points, his muzzle was gray, and there was not an ounce of fat on him.

The game in an area leaves a lot of sign and it is up to the hunter to interpret it. In the course of a day one deer or one sheep makes many tracks and leaves behind him many piles of droppings. The inexperienced man thinks of one track meaning one deer, a pile of droppings meaning another. The experienced hunter tries to guess how many deer there are in a certain area by comparing the size of the tracks and the size of the pellets. Big deer make larger tracks (obviously) than small deer and drop larger pellets. Also obviously, the beds of large deer are large.

The appearance of a track depends not only on its freshness but also on the kind of soil it was made in, how the weather has been. Very fresh droppings are not only soft to the touch but warm. Droppings made within the night are soft but cold. Droppings made within the past few days are dry, black, with a hard glaze. Old droppings have the glaze dissolved by rain and they are bleached by sun. Gradually they disintegrate, but they last a very long time if they are sheltered. I have seen droppings made by desert bighorn sheep in Arizona caves where no sheep have been for fifty years, and the dung made by giant ground sloths thousands of years ago has also been found in Arizona caves.

In scouting a piece of country the hunter should get to know roughly about how many deer call it home, and he should have a fair notion as to how many of them are bucks. He should also have an idea about where they bed down and where they water and feed.

A friend once told me he knew of a place that was all tracked up by deer, but that he could never see one. I went out with him. It was a stretch of abandoned orchard and alfalfa field between some cliffs and a river. The cliffs were about 500 feet high, but between the cliffs and the orchard was a rocky talus slope that came down at an angle of about 45 degrees. It was covered with brush. My friend was the only one who had been hunting in the area. He had not disturbed the deer and it was obvious to me that the deer must be bedded in the brush on the talus slope just under the rimrock. The orchard was on a sandy alluvial bench and between the bench and the river was heavy brush full of quail. The narrow sandy beach was all tracked up by deer. This was really home-sweet-home to a nice little deer herd. They fed at dusk, at night, and very early in the morning. They would eat stunted but sweet little apples, alfalfa, various browse. They watered at the river and then went back up to lie down in the brush. No doubt they had been watching with much interest as my pal plodded around through the orchard.

The next time we came back I put my friend in the alfalfa field where he could watch a stretch of talus slope that was almost bare of brush. I then went downwind along the river bank, climbed up the talus slope and started working through the brush. I saw all sorts of droppings and beds, and the deer had a regular trail right at the foot of the cliff. I had gone not over 100 yards when I heard stones roll and knew a deer was moving ahead of me. When I had gone perhaps another 100 yards, I caught a glimpse of a gray form below and ahead. It was a big four-point buck trying to slip out through the orchard. I shot him offhand at somewhere around a hundred yards. A moment later I heard my pal open up.

I field dressed my buck and went over toward my amigo. He also had a buck and he told me he had seen two deer slip out through the orchard well ahead of me and his buck and several does and fawns had come out of the brush and had crossed the open space.

These deer had been given a rude shock. Their inviolate sanctuary had been invaded by bad-smelling people on two legs. They had heard loud noises and later had found piles of offal that smelled both bloody and deery. Probably they avoided the orchard that night, but I'd be willing to bet that in a couple of days they were again bedding down at the foot of the cliff and feeding in the orchard and field.

As long as they have food, water, and shelter, and are not badly spooked, game animals will stay in one small "home." Often they will lie in the same bed for many days. Many times fat, lazy old rams will spend an entire summer in one basin, feeding around through it but going back to the same beds.

Once in Sonora years ago I was camped with one Mexican by a little well. A big ram had been seen in a little chain of hills and for three days I had ridden about three miles over from camp. Then I tied my horse and hunted on foot. Every morning a handsome whitetail buck got up from beneath one particular tree and trotted off in exactly the same direction. When I discovered the ram had left the hills and had headed over toward some higher and more rugged mountains, I decided to see if I couldn't bushwhack that buck. I asked the vaquero to saddle up and go with me. When we got about a quarter of a mile from the spot where I had always seen the buck, I told the cowboy to wait for about fifteen minutes and then to follow my horse tracks toward the tree. I rode around to a spot where I could see the country toward which the buck had always headed. I got off my horse, tied him, and sat down with my rifle across my knees. In a few minutes I heard the buck trotting along and presently here he came right at me.

When the hunter discovers tracks of the game he is after, he should try to figure out what the game was doing. Was it feeding, watering, or just passing through? In the Sonora desert back in the 1930's, the big-horns used to come down into the valleys to feed early in the morning and very late in the afternoon. It was easy to find fresh tracks and droppings there, but the sheep went back into the rough hills to lie up during the day. The sign low down simply told the sheep hunter he was in an inhabited range.

In 1944 I hunted for the first time in Wyoming, and my outfitter, the late Ernie Miller, my guide, and I headed for a narrow plateau something over 11,000 feet above sea level where for many generations bighorn rams had come to spend the summer. The top of the plateau was above timberline but stunted whitebark pine and alpine fir grew in the heads of the canyons and on the little benches that broke off the top. We had three saddle horses and a couple of pack mules, and we made camp on a little bench overlooking a tremendous canyon.

Miller told me that just above our camp on top of the plateau was a little pond and asked me to get a bucket of water. The edge of the pond was all tracked up by watering rams. There were droppings lying around in various stages of freshness. Rams had been watering there for at least two weeks. Since this was the first day of sheep season, the guide and I ate a hasty sandwich and went off to glass the heads of the canyons. I shot a fine ram in the second canyon.

On another Wyoming hunt my wife and I were camped with a cook and a guide in a beautiful valley just under timberline. The first day we hunted we saw a spike bull and a couple of cow elk. We also saw a few fairly fresh beds. We hunted up and down the valley and above timberline on the ridges on both sides. We found tracks, many quite fresh, but comparatively few droppings and no beds.

We finally decided that for whatever the reason the elk were not staying in that valley but were simply traveling through. Possibly noise of the horse bells or the smoke of our fires kept them from tarrying. We climbed a steep trail so we could look into the next drainage and from the top we could see three bunches of elk above timberline on a mountain across the valley. We dropped down into the bottom and as soon as we hit the belt of timber that grew along the creek we ran into beds, fresh soft droppings, fresh tracks, muddy elk wallows, trees all battered by bulls polishing their antlers. You simply do not see sign that fresh without being close to elk. It wasn't long before we heard a bull bugle.

No hunter is going to have any luck if he hunts where there is no game. And if there is game in an area it leaves the signs of its presence, just as civilized man strews the countryside with tin cans, cigarette butts, chewing gum wrappers, worn-out tires, and rusty automobile bodies. If there is no fresh sign there is no game.

In 1949 a friend and I made a trip into the Pelly Mountains of the Yukon. We got into what was to be our first hunting camp along about noon and while the hands were making camp I took a rifle and a pair of binoculars and climbed the highest nearby mountain. I didn't like what I saw. There were plenty of sheep trails but they were grown up in grass, and what few droppings I found were in protected areas and they looked to be a couple of years old as they were leached out almost white. I found on that mountain not a single sheep track. I found a few caribou tracks I judged to be a week or more old and some signs of grizzlies digging for gophers the spring before.

In the saddles and out on the points there were still signs that sheep had once bedded there as there were depressions where sheep had pawed out beds in shale and gravel. I also found a weathered ram horn and part of a weathered sheep jawbone. The few wolf scats I ran across contained sheep hair but they were at least a year old and had been weathered white.

I found a good spot and sat down to glass the surrounding mountains with my binoculars. I saw sheep trails across shale slides but they looked old. The sun started dropping in the west and if there was anything in the country it should have been coming out to feed. I saw nothing. Ten years before a friend of mine had hunted in this area and had found it full of sheep, grizzlies, caribou, and wolves. Now there seemed to be almost nothing.

I got back to camp about dark and told my companion that I did not like the looks of things, that I was afraid that we'd have a tough time finding game. The next day he and I left in opposite directions to scout out the country. Each of us had a couple of pack horses and an Indian guide. My one look had made me pretty gloomy about the prospects, but we had made our move, had spent our money, were way out in the wilderness, and had to make the best of it.

On that whole trip I saw seven sheep, all ewes, lambs, or small rams, one grizzly and one young bull caribou, which I killed for meat. My pal saw a caribou cow and a calf and a bull moose about three miles away. We hunted hard and long.

What happened to the game? I do not know. It had not been shot out because no one had been in the country for ten years. Had it been decimated and driven out by wolves? Had everything died off from disease? Wherever records have been kept of sheep herds these die-offs occur periodically. Lung worm is endemic in most varieties of North American sheep. They get the infestation from each other's droppings. Then when range conditions become poor, the sheep lack the strength to combat their affliction, get pneumonia, and die. On various occasions lung worm has just about wiped out Colorado's Terryall herd. An epidemic of some disease would explain the absence of sheep, but what about the caribou and the grizzlies?

At any rate this experience shows that unless there is fresh sign in an area there is not much use hunting.

4 | *The Different Methods of Hunting*

Since animals come in a variety of sizes and shapes, are found in all kinds of country, and possess a great diversity of dispositions, human beings have devised many methods of killing and capturing them. A whole book could be written about hunting methods alone. Hungry and intelligent human beings have driven animals over cliffs, into corrals, past hunters armed with arrows and spears. They have dug holes into which game animals have fallen, have killed them with deadfalls, with weighted spears that drop upon them from trees as they pass in a trail. They have captured them with steel traps, snared them, shot them with poisoned arrows, chased them with dogs, captured them in nets, speared them.

In some parts of Europe it is still considered sporting, I understand, for the hunter to corner wild boars with dogs, then to slip up and transfix a boar with a spear. This is a very ancient sport which was practiced by the Celtic and Teutonic tribesmen of Europe and throughout the Middle Ages. In the days of British India it was considered very sporting to ride down wild boars with fast ponies and spear them. A friend of mine, a European nobleman who now resides in Portuguese Africa, amuses himself by hunting the big truculent Cape buffalo with dogs. These cut a buffalo out of a herd, corner it, distract its attention. Then my adventurous European friend slips in and drives a heavy, wide-bladed spear into its lungs.

Hunting game animals with missile weapons is simply common sense applied to the problems of the animal and his habits, the cover and the terrain in which he is found, the size and disposition of the animal, and the efficiency of the missile weapon employed. Naturally, the crack shot with a scope-sighted, high-velocity rifle does not need to approach as close to his game as does a hunter using a bow and an arrow. Naturally, also, the fierce grizzly or the savage tiger must be dealt with differently from the timid and harmless deer.

Obviously the hunter must get close enough to the game for a certain shot no matter whether he is using a spear, a bow and arrow, or a scope-sighted rifle. To get close, he must generally keep the animal unaware of his presence. That means that the hunter must prevent the animal from smelling him, from hearing him before he is in range, and if not from seeing him at least to keep him from knowing that he is being hunted.

This means that the hunter should do his best to make certain that the moving air does not carry his scent to the game. He hunts against the wind, across the wind. Sometimes he can go to the side, let his scent blow past the animal as he approaches, then when the hunter himself is beyond the animal he can turn and approach upwind. Sometimes when the air is barely moving he can walk faster than his scent is moving. The hunter also learned long ago that in addition to seeing that the animal does not smell him he should also do his best to make sure that the animal does not hear him.

Still-Hunting

The hunter who moves quietly through brush and timber, taking great pains to make as little noise as possible and to hunt into and across the wind, hoping by this means to see a game animal before it is aware of him, is said to be *still-hunting*. This is a favorite, a sporting, and an effective way to hunt all forest game.

The still-hunter has one very great advantage. He is looking for the deer, the moose, the elk or whatever he is after, whereas the game animal is not necessarily looking for him. If he is out early enough or late enough when the animals are feeding, he also has the advantage of having hunting on his mind whereas the animal's principal concern at the time is food. During the rut, male animals are much less cautious than they are at other times and are much easier to hunt, as they think far more of perpetuating the race than they do of preserving their own hides. I have had rutting buck deer almost run over me and apparently never see me, and I once had a bull elk come up and offer battle when I was sitting with a rifle over my legs and tootling on a tin whistle which he thought was the bugling of another bull.

Stalking

The still-hunter knows where his game may be feeding or may be bedded, but he seldom sees the animal until it runs or otherwise makes a move. The *stalker,* on the other hand, locates the animal from afar and then tries to approach to within sure shooting distance by keeping the wind right and staying out of sight behind ridges or bushes or in gullies. Sometimes he makes himself so inconspicuous by crouching low and by moving only when the animal is busy feeding or looking away that the animal is not aware of his presence. Sometimes by his gait or posture he pretends to be another animal or by approaching behind a familiar vehicle he keeps the game unaware of his presence. Primitive hunters have long pretended to be various animals in order to get close to game. Indians have worn the hides and antlers of deer to deceive other deer. Eskimos flop around and make seal-like motions in order to fool polar bears. In India a common way of hunting black buck on the plains is to approach behind a native bullock cart. I have seen deer feeding across an open mountain meadow and have approached them by walking behind a saddle horse, and in order to cross an open space when I was stalking elk I have got down on my hands and knees and walked along on all fours, pretending to be a grazing cow.

Calling

Ingenious human hunters have learned to call and lure animals to them. An Indian guide grunting through a birch bark horn sounds to a love-sick bull moose just like an amorous lady moose. The whistle of the elk hunter sounds to an old rutting bull like the noise made by a pushy young bull trying to horn in on the old fellow's harem. In India hunters have invented devices that enable them to sound like a roaring tiger and other tigers will approach. Down in the Texas brush country one method of hunting whitetail deer is to rattle two pairs of antlers together. During the mating season a buck who hears the racket will approach. He thinks two bucks are fighting and reasons there must be does nearby. He investigates. Since the war the sport of varmint calling has become enormously popular throughout the West. With his call the hunter makes a noise like a trapped and suffering rabbit. The coyote, the fox, or the bobcat comes at a rapid incautious run to be the first diner at an easy meal. I once read somewhere that an American in Malaya tried an American varmint call in the jungle and up came a tiger. Deer can be brought up with a call that sounds like a fawn in distress.

Game should be protected from the wonders of modern electronics. Records of the sounds made by feeding and contented ducks have been used to bring flocks into the decoys and to the guns. I have heard that there were recordings which when broadcast with a loudspeaker would bring in African lions on the gallop. The turkey hunter with his cedar box call makes noises like those of a hen wanting to assemble her scattered brood and the young turkeys come running.

Mammals and birds, like most human beings, have one-track minds. We have all seen fatuous husbands who had made up their minds that their wives were dream girls who could do no wrong. We have seen these husbands remain blissfully unaware that their wives were cheating on them right under their noses long after the duplicity of the gals was apparent to everyone else. Animals that are called up act with the same stupidity. The coyote who comes galloping up to the caller picturing a juicy rabbit caught in the brush by some mischance simply cannot believe it when the rabbit turns out to be a man with a rifle. The bull elk is flabbergasted when it dawns on him that the man with the elk call simply is not a spike bull. The young turkey, worried and alone, anxious to see his mother and his brothers and sisters, will trot right up to the caller.

Driving

Another ancient method of hunting and one widely used on elusive forest game is driving. This was probably one of the first methods of hunting worked out by primitive hunting tribes. It is even used by animals. Male lions in Africa show themselves, give their scent, and roar so frightened antelope will rush blindly away to where the swift and agile lioness lurks in the grass. Wolves drive deer, caribou, and moose toward a spot where another wolf lies in wait.

Primitive hunters everywhere drive game—into traps, into pits and snares. Driving is also a favorite method of hunting in aristocratic societies where the rich are few and very rich and the poor numerous and very poor. Partridges are driven in Spain, pheasants in England, grouse in Scotland. But in Britain the peasants are getting uppity and their services hard to secure. In Iran whole villages turn out to drive wild boars through a river valley past the "guns," and villagers also drive ibex down the length of a mountain toward those who will do the shooting.

Driving in combination with baiting is the preferred method of taking tigers in India. The tiger is located by tying out a young water buffalo. It is the nature of a tiger to eat a tremendous amount of meat, drink heavily, and then go to the nearest cool, secluded thicket and go to sleep. When the shikaris find that the tiger has killed they track him to his thicket, go all around it to make certain he has not left it. If he is still in residence a drive is set up. Men called "stops" are put in trees in the form of a V to tap on limbs and to turn the tiger if he tries to break out of the beat. A line of beaters whooping and yelling then advances to

O'CONNOR'S ROUTE

HILL

BUCKS SHOT HERE

SADDLE

MRS. O'CONNOR

HILL

On a deer hunt in Sonora, O'Connor placed his wife on one of two adjacent hills from where she could observe the saddle below. He moved counterclockwise around the other hill about one-third of the way up. When O'Connor reached the saddle, he found that Mrs. O'Connor had shot two bucks which he had moved off the hill.

drive the tiger toward a "gun" or "guns" at the apex of the V. This sounds easy but it often does not work out according to the script. Tigers often break through the line of beaters or refuse to turn back when the "stops" tap. Often when the tigers do go by the guns, they are running like greyhounds and roaring like fiends from hell. Not a few tigers have been missed by excited "guns" who simply closed their eyes and yanked the trigger.

In democratic societies like that of the United States everyone is a "gun" in that all those who take part in a beat are armed and the hunters are divided into drivers and standers. A line of beaters advances slowly toward a line of standers placed strategically where deer are apt to sneak out ahead of the beaters—along trails, in saddles. Often bucks, particularly wise ones that have been driven before, break back through the beaters, or hole up in the brush and let the beaters pass them by, go off at right angles to escape the drive. If there are many deer, both beaters and standers get shooting.

Driving for deer is almost never used in the West, but I have seen a couple of drives in Pennsylvania and a few in South Carolina. In Pennsylvania the beaters walked quietly along, depending on their scent and their presence to move the deer. In the South a line of hounds and men raised all kinds of racket, baying (the hounds) and yelling (the men).

In the West what driving that is done is a much more modest production. One or two hunters place themselves where they can see fairly well the routes that deer or elk would take if they got nervous and moved out ahead of the drivers. If animals are merely nervous and not hard pressed they tend to move by well-established routes. Their instinct, particularly when nervous, is to move in the open as little as possible, and like anything else they prefer to go the easiest way. That means that they will travel a trail if there is one and will go through a saddle instead of climbing the peaks on each side. Anyone who has hunted an area much knows just about where game will travel when it has decided to leave a hillside or a basin. Likewise any experienced hunter with an eye for topography will have a fairly good idea where the trails will run.

I remember one trip into Sonora for whitetails many years ago. My wife and I arrived at a little cluster of huts called Purgatorio. We unloaded our car, set up our cots. By that time we still had three or four hours of light left. About a mile away I could see two little round hills. The top of each was about 150 feet higher than the surrounding country and perhaps 50 feet higher than the saddle between them. We saw a great many droppings and lots of fresh tracks as we headed toward the hills. About halfway to the hills a young doe jumped out on the slope above us, flirted a big white tail, and took off.

I placed my wife about halfway up the hillside to our left in a spot

WIND

SADDLE

CREEK

DIRECTION OF FLOW

GAME TRAIL

ELK BEDDED HERE

JACK O'CONNOR

ELK SHOT HERE

MRS. O'CONNOR

ROUTE OF GUIDE

In this elk drive O'Connor and his wife posted themselves about 400 yards apart on hills overlooking a basin where a well-used elk trail followed a creek. The guide went around to the right, dropped into the basin and moved up the trail, driving an elk from his bed in the brush. O'Connor shot the elk as it emerged and headed for the saddle.

from which she could see anything that moved through the saddle. Then I started to move counterclockwise around the right-hand hill about one-third of the way up. The brush was thick and thorny but I had not gone far when I saw a doe and fawn staring at me. Then they ran. A little farther on I heard what sounded like several deer moving ahead of me. Then I heard a deer run. A minute or so later I heard two evenly spaced shots, and when I got to the saddle Eleanor was perched on a rock smoking a cigarette and contemplating a couple of handsome four-point bucks (ten points Eastern count). Our little maneuver had worked perfectly.

As I write this the last elk I shot came as the result of a modest little drive. My wife sat on a point overlooking a big basin where a little brook had its source. I sat on a hillside about 400 yards away. Between us was a saddle with a well-used elk trail. To my wife's left perhaps a half-mile away was another saddle. Beyond it was a second basin. Our guide, Dave Christensen, said that a trail ran along the bottom of the basin along the creek and went over the saddle to my wife's left into the next basin. He proposed to go around to the right, drop into the creek bottom about a mile away and then work slowly up the trail.

For about an hour nothing happened. I ate my lunch and with binoculars I saw my wife eating hers. Then as I watched Dave came out of the brush above my wife and sat down on the point beside her. Presently I became aware that they were both trying to attract my attention. Dave was looking at me with binoculars and when he saw that I had mine trained on the point they both made motions for me to look down.

I stood up and below me I could see the tips of a fine pair of elk antlers moving through the high snow brush. The bull had apparently heard or smelled Dave some time before. He was nervous and was on the move and headed for the saddle. Slowly the antlers moved through the snow brush and I hoped that the bull would come out on the fairly open hillside. But when those antlers moved to the edge of the tall brush they stopped. Apparently the bull had seen Dave and Eleanor over on the point.

The antlers turned back then and slowly moved to my right once more. It looked as if the bull had turned back to go around below. I knew I was going to have to shoot. The bull was about 125 yards away. I waited until he went past a spot where the brush was thin enough so that I could dimly see his head and the front part of his body. With the crosswires to the left of his spine just behind his shoulder, I squeezed the trigger of my 7mm. Remington Magnum. I had barely been able to make out the elk through the brush and when I shot absolutely nothing happened. I could no longer see the elk. Nothing moved. I suspected that I had dropped the bull in his tracks—and so he had. He was a fine big bull with an excellent head, the best elk trophy I have ever taken in Idaho. He had six ivory-tipped points on one side, seven on the other.

Baiting

As we have seen in this chapter in the section on beating and driving, tigers in India are generally located by tying out a young water buffalo in a spot where a hunting tiger is apt to pass. Then if things go well the tiger kills the buffalo, gorges himself, drinks heavily, and goes to sleep in some cool and shady hide-out not far away. Then a beat is organized so the tiger can be driven past the machan where a hunter sits with a rifle. If the tiger has not bedded down nearby and cannot be located the man with the rifle sits in a machan over what is left of the kill and hopes that the tiger will come back for another feed. If he does so his shikari, who is sitting with him, turns on a powerful flashlight and if all goes well the hunter rolls the tiger over.

Baiting is also used for African lions and leopards and American black and grizzly bears. To bait for lion the hunter shoots a zebra or a large antelope, opens the belly cavity so stomach and intestines hang out. Then he drags it behind a four-wheel hunting car to a tree about a mile away. He then puts it in the car, takes it about a mile in the opposite direction, drags it toward the tree. He then ties it to the tree with ropes strong enough so that the lions cannot pull the carcass down and drag it away, low enough so they can reach it, and high enough so that a whole pride of lions cannot gobble it up in short order.

Any hungry lion crossing the scent trail will follow that delicious smell in the direction in which the scent gets stronger–toward the tree. In good lion country baiting will almost always bring lions. The hunter stalks the bait and if there is a good trophy male on it, he lets him have it.

In Africa baiting for leopards is an art. A tree is selected near the sort of a rocky kopje (small hill) that leopards like to den up in and also preferably not far from water. Leopards like to feed on trees with strong, horizontal branches and some concealment from leaves. In addition, for the sake of the hunter, there should be a good spot to shoot from in a direction where the prevailing wind is favorable and from which the leopard is not apt to approach.

Then one of the smaller antelopes like an impala or a Grant's gazelle is shot and hung from the limb. It is important to keep the hide on, for if the animal is skinned the vultures can get at the flesh and will devour it in short order. The bait quickly ripens and attracts a leopard. Leopards like their meat high, just as some gourmets like very fruity cheese. When it can be seen that a leopard is feeding on the bait, the hunter stalks it early in the mornings, sits in his blind, in the brush, or behind a rock in late afternoon waiting for the leopard to show up about sundown.

Baiting for bears in the United States and Canada is much the same. Generally the guide or outfitter buys a broken-down old horse that is about to go to the dog-food factory. He drives him out to a spot where bears are apt to pass, shoots him. Then the guide and the hunter select a spot to watch and shoot from. With luck a bear will show up. When the French were firmly in control of Viet Nam, Laos, and Cambodia (all of which they called French Indo-China) the method of taking tigers was much the same as baiting for bears in the United States. Apparently the beat system as used in India was either unknown there or not practical. They built a blind, shot an animal in front of it, and then the hunter sat in the blind with his rifle until vultures and insects had eaten it up or a tiger had found it.

Most states in the United States require that game carcasses be brought in and utilized, but in Canada it is common practice to leave much of moose, caribou, and grizzly carcasses out in the bush. Then if the hunter is in the vicinity for some time he keeps an eye on the carcass in hopes of finding a bear on it.

Hunting with Dogs

Cougars (mountain lions), unlike most of the great cats, prefer to kill their own meat, and the most successful way of getting them is hunting with packs of well-trained and keen-nosed hounds—usually foxhounds, mixtures of foxhound and bloodhound, or occasionally straight blood-hounds. The hunters follow the baying hounds on foot or on horseback and shoot the cougar out of a tree or off the top of a rock after the dogs have brought it to bay. In Mexico and Central and South America, jaguars are hunted in the same way, but these spotted cats are more courageous, have shorter tempers, and less patience than do cougars.

Another method of using dogs in the hunting of big game is one that I have never seen—the hunting of deer with jump dogs. The hunter takes with him a small dog like a fox terrier. It is trained to stay with the hunter and to keep quiet. When the hunter is near a deer, the dog indicates his presence and the hunter sends him in to "jump" him—to put him out, in other words. This sport is legal in California and is confined to that state, I believe.

The good hunter is the man who can combine patience, common sense, and observation. He does not have to be a crack shot but he should be a cool shot. Most shots at big game are missed not because they are difficult but because the hunter got excited and blew up.

5 | *The Woods*
Hunter

In the chapter on the types of hunting we did some defining. We learned that game has been hunted by calling it, by driving it, by stalking, by chasing it with dogs, by having it fall into a cleverly concealed pit, by snaring it, by trapping. Some of these methods are sporting; some are not. There is nothing sporting, for example, in digging a hole in a deer trail and concealing it so a deer will fall into it, and as far as sport goes I'd certainly rank the shooting of driven game pretty far down the list.

The two methods of hunting generally considered the most sporting and requiring the most skill are *stalking* and *still-hunting.* The stalker generally operates in more open country than the still-hunter. He locates the game, often with binoculars, spotting scopes, or telescopes. Then he tries to approach close enough for a sure shot without disturbing it.

The *still-hunter,* on the other hand, moves quietly through game country trying not to disturb the game by making noise or by letting it get his scent. The still-hunter operates in brush and forest country where visibility is limited to relatively short distances. He plans to see the game before it sees him, if this is possible. If it isn't he hopes to be so close to the game and in such an advantageous position that he can shoot it before it gets out of sight.

To illustrate the difference between stalking and still-hunting, and to serve as an introduction to forest hunting, let me tell a story. In 1943 when I made my first hunt in Alberta, I had never shot a moose and was very anxious to get one. When my companion and I were camped with our outfit at the head of Copton Creek right on the Alberta-British Columbia boundary, we were in a country that abounded in moose sign. For three straight mornings I went out either with Roy Hargreaves, who owned the outfit, or with Isaac Plante, a Cree Indian guide. We were camped just under timberline, but along the creek and for about 500 feet up the side of the mountains the timber was very thick.

By climbing up above timberline we could look down with binoculars into the timber along the creek. All the moose in this high country were bulls. They had cleaned the velvet off their antlers but as yet they had not started hunting for cows and they were still feeding. When the rut is in full swing bull moose do not feed at all. By getting out and up on the mountainsides early we could look down into the little muskeg meadows within the heavy timber. Every morning we would find from one to three bull moose feeding. The job was made easier because their freshly cleaned antlers were still snow white and unstained from contact with brush and trees. These wide, snowy antlers moving as the bulls fed enabled us to pick them up quickly, often with the unaided eye.

But seeing moose and getting a shot were different things. We were generally around a mile from the bulls. We would have to find something by which to mark their location—a conspicuous tree, an outcropping of rock, a bend in the creek. Then we had to go down the mountainside through the timber, wade the creek, and try to sneak up on the feeding moose.

Since we had located the moose from afar we were *stalking* them. But, alas, we had little luck. It was a time of moonlight nights, and the moose were filling up early, going back into heavy timber, and lying down. By the time we arrived at the little meadows with their tall grass and dwarf willows, the bulls were gone. One time the tracks showed the bulls had left in a hurry. They had probably heard us.

One reason we were having no luck, I decided, was that we were starting our stalks just about the time the bulls were ready to go off and lie down. Another reason was that about the time we were sneaking up on the meadows where we hoped to find moose, the wind became unpredictable. All night and early morning the heavy, cold air had been drifting gently from the high country down the creek bottoms. Now with the sun up and warm in the high altitude the ground was warming up and the flow of air was beginning to reverse.

In the course of our stalking we had seen several moose beds, and it appeared that when the bulls had finished feeding they moved uphill a bit and lay down in thick timber. The fourth day, I told Isaac Plante that I'd like to try hunting alone since two men made more noise than one.

I planned to still-hunt to see if I could not come across a bedded bull. I waited until the ground had warmed up enough so that the air was moving gently upstream toward the camp. I planned to work slowly downstream across the creek from camp, hunting into the wind. I planned to go three or four miles. Then if I had not got a moose I'd eat my sandwich, take a snooze in the warm sunshine, and then as the sun went lower and the cold air from the high country once more started rolling downhill again I'd hunt upwind toward camp.

I put on a pair of rubber-bottom shoe pacs, wore wool trousers and shirt instead of stiffer and noisier cotton. I worked slowly through the forest along the foot of the hill perhaps 100 to 150 feet above the creek and above the muskeg meadows where the moose had been feeding. It was along about this elevation that I had been seeing the moose beds.

I walked slowly. The moss was soft underfoot. There was a great deal of moose sign—the big, sharp-pointed, deer-like tracks, droppings, some old and weathered, some still soft. Every fifty yards or so I'd stop, listen, look carefully to see if I could make out the white of moose antlers, the brown-black body of a bedded bull. Now and then I'd squat down to see if I could make out anything under the trees.

It was an enjoyable hunt. The wind was steady in my face. The going was easy and quiet. With all that fresh sign and with all the moose we had been seeing, I did not see how I could miss. I thought I'd have to be very unlucky if I did.

I had been gone over an hour, perhaps an hour and a half, and covered over a mile when a bull moose rose out of his bed on the other side of a tree not over twenty or thirty yards away or maybe not over that many feet. I could see white horns and an enormously tall body about half concealed by the tree. I had been carrying my rifle across my body as if I had been walking up quail. I threw a 130-grain .270 bullet at him through the tree, saw twigs and small limbs rain down, shot again as fast as I could work the bolt. This time I had a pretty clear shot and I called a hit angling up from behind the last rib on the left side toward the right shoulder. Those shots sounded frightfully loud down there in the timber. The bull disappeared and all was quiet.

I found myself shaking a little from excitement. I listened, but the only sound I could hear was the distant tinkle of a horse bell toward camp. I found the bull's track. He had run out of the timber into a little muskeg meadow where he had probably fed that morning. Twenty or thirty feet into the meadow I found where he had gone to his knees in the mucky ground. I knew he was hit. I had walked perhaps thirty yards through the waist-high willows when the bull rose out of them like a spook and started off. I shot him this time right behind the shoulder. He continued on across the meadow, but I did not shoot again as I knew that last bullet was perfectly placed and he could not go far. He went down at the far side of the meadow just at the edge of the timber.

This is a case when still-hunting worked when stalking had failed.

Most game animals are pretty adaptable. I have seen forest animals like moose and deer in open country above timberline, and open-country animals like caribou, pronghorn antelope, and even bighorn sheep in timber. I have shot about a dozen grizzly bears, mostly above timberline, but the biggest one I have ever knocked off was down in heavy timber tearing open logs to hunt for grubs. The forest and brush-loving white-tail deer of the Eastern United States often comes out of the woods to feed in open pastures. One of the handsomest whitetail bucks I ever shot was lying on a grassy hillside under a lone oak tree. The principles of still-hunting are the same if you are after whitetail deer in Pennsylvania, moose in Quebec, greater kudu in the rocky, brush hills of Tanzania, elk in Idaho, or bongo in the bamboo forests of the Abadare Mountains of Kenya.

Boiled down to their essentials the principles of still-hunting would be about like this: Go very slowly and very quietly. Stop often and look carefully. It isn't how much country you cover but how well you cover the right country. When the hunter stops he can hear a bit better and see a bit better himself, and in turn he is more difficult to hear and to see. Furthermore, when a hunter stops he often moves an animal because the animal may be close by, watching him or listening. When the hunter stops, the animal may think that he has been detected and the jig is up. He'll then take off. The hunter must hunt in a direction where the wind will not carry his scent to the game and he must hunt where the animals are.

This last bit of instruction is obvious but it is very important. There is always a temptation to hunt where a great deal of sign is found. But the hunter must decide what the animal was doing when he made the sign. Was he feeding, traveling, or resting?

Habits of Woods Animals

Herbivorous animals all have pretty much the same daily schedule. They are out feeding at the earliest light. On moonlight nights they move and feed more than they do on dark nights, and they bed down earlier. This is the reason hunting is generally poorer when the moon is full. The game simply fills up and beds down before the hunter is afield. Deer will do some feeding even on very dark nights, but open-country animals like antelope and sheep stay in their beds. Members of the deer family, like horses, have much better night vision than human beings, but I am doubtful if open-country animals do. Once in northern Arizona I stayed too long on a high mountain hunting mule deer. By the time I got down it was very dark. I couldn't find my car. As I was stumbling around a plain covered with volcanic boulders, I found myself right in the midst of a herd of bedded antelope. I don't think they could see any better than I could. I am quite sure that desert bighorn sheep do some feeding on bright moonlit nights and once I saw a big lone ram crossing a paved road in Arizona on such a night.

The reason the hunter is told to get out in the woods early is that any animal is easier to see when it is moving, just as it is easier for the deer to see the hunter when *he* is moving. The hunter who is out at dawn will see feeding game and a bit later game moving back to its bedding ground. Still-hunting for bighorn sheep may sound silly, but it has been done. In Sonora back in the 1930's the best sheep country had no cattle and very few deer, as sheep can get along with less water than deer can. The sheep would come down from their rocky hills into the valleys to feed on cholla fruit and various plants. If the hunter were out early enough he could find the sheep feeding or catch them moving up a mountainside to their bedding ground.

When I first started hunting mountain sheep in Sonora, it came as a great surprise to me that the animals were often found low—feeding in the valleys, bedded down on points not very far up. The first desert ram I ever saw had been feeding in a valley and was headed back to a mountain to bed down. I know of one hunter who was wandering around looking for mule deer when a feeding bighorn ram heard him, jumped up on a big granite boulder to see what he was. The hunter popped the ram off the rock and got his desert bighorn trophy without setting a foot on the mountain.

If the hunter is out at the crack of dawn when the game is feeding, that is well. If he is not out when the game is feeding, he can hunt in the feeding area until he wears his legs off at the knees without seeing much. There are always exceptions that prove the rule. Now and then an animal will lie down in an exceedingly unlikely place. I once knew a hunter who killed a bedded desert ram under a palo verde tree out in a flat. I have mentioned a beautiful whitetail buck that had bedded down under a lone oak on a grassy, open hillside.

Once the animal has eaten his fill he wanders back to the place where he wants to rest, doze, and chew his cud during the day. Generally he takes a bite now and then if anything looks good. Then he gets to his chosen spot and lies down.

Game animals, like human beings, like to be comfortable. They don't like to be cold, to be too hot, to be chewed on by insects, to lie on sharp rocks, to be buffeted by strong wind. Just as the family cat chooses a comfortable bed where it is warm when the house is cold and drafty and a cool spot when the house is hot, so does the deer or the elk. In Sonora mountain sheep often seek out caves to lie down in when it is rainy or very hot, and sheep likewise use caves all over their range. Goats do the same thing. I once saw several desert rams lying on rocks where they were cooled by the salt spray from the Gulf of California.

On rainy days, particularly if the rain is cold with wind, deer and elk stay in heavy timber and feed but little. Then when the storm is over they are out feeding early and since they are hungry they feed late. A soft, warm, gentle rain does not seem to bother deer and they will move about and feed in it.

On hot days deer and elk seek out dense, cool timber if it is available, and they bed down early. When it is warm they do not come out to feed until almost dark. The fall of 1965 was very warm throughout the West and the hunter success ratio, particularly on elk, was down. Part of the explanation lay in the fact that elk remained in high, rough country that was difficult to get to, but probably more important was the fact that the elk fed at night, very early in the morning, and did not come out of the heavy timber until almost dark. My wife and I hunted in the fall of 1965 for a week in country where in other years we had never failed to get a couple of bull elk in two or three days. In that time we saw only two bulls. These, both magnificent six-pointers, had come out of the timber almost at dark. They were a mile away and it was too late to go after them.

When you are hunting, ask yourself where *you* would be if you were a deer. If the night had been bitterly cold and you did not have access to fire, you (and also the deer) would probably bed down on the sunny side of a hill in brush or timber thin enough so the sun could get the frost out of your bones.

If there are no hills deer like to bed down in a thicket, most often, I believe, close to the edge where they can look out. If there are hills the deer like to go up into a patch of brush or timber just under the crest of a hill. I think they do this because the warm air rises and they can get the scent of anything approaching from below better than on top of a ridge, where the wind is less steady. In the West both mule and whitetail deer like to bed in brush at the head of a draw or canyon. Then if they smell something from below they can slip out and go over the top. Likewise in the West, a favorite bedding spot for both species is in the brush at the top of the talus slope of broken rock and gravel right under a rimrock. If there is brush and timber at the end of a point, both species like it. If there is a cold, raw wind the game will try to get out of it.

But we must not make up our minds in advance where deer are going to be. Those whose notions are completely fixed are often in for some surprises, as deer, like gold, are where you find them and you can find them in some pretty unexpected places. I remember one morning in southern Arizona when I stopped to rest and smoke on an open hillside. Below were draws filled with oaks and brush where the deer ought to be.

Up high there the gramma grass was not heavily grazed. It was around a foot high, frost cured and yellow, and out of it were sticking some brown, dead, frost-killed stalks. It runs in my mind that they were something like sunflowers. While I rested I used my binoculars on the opposite hillside about 600 yards away, hoping to see a bedded deer. I didn't pay much attention to the ground immediately in front of me. Presently I noticed idly that one of the dead plants fifty or sixty yards away looked strangely like the antlers of a whitetail buck. Then I decided they looked too much like antlers to be anything but antlers. I focused my binoculars on them. They were antlers. That darned buck tried to brazen it out until I was within twenty feet of him. Then he jumped up and took off. I nailed him.

When deer are bedded we must hunt where they are likely to be lying, and when we hit the bedding area we'll see beds. The size, the tracks, the droppings (in case there is more than one species in the area) tell us what the animals are and often the sex. If the ground is not too noisy, the hunter can stroll quietly along, watching, listening, stopping often. If it is noisy from dry leaves or from loose stones, still-hunting is simply impossible and some other means of hunting must be employed.

The whitetail deer is a very foxy animal. He has a keen sense of smell, ears like a bat, and pretty good eyes for moving objects. Anyone who hunts whitetails and who pays any intelligent attention to tracks quickly learns that he moves a lot of deer he does not see or hear. Once in Sonora I was on a hill overlooking a brushy valley with a dry arroyo running through it. I had been hunting alone and I had tied my horse on the other end of the little chain of hills about a mile away.

Presently I saw my hunting companion and a vaquero named Miguel riding toward the valley from out in the flat country. I waited to see what would develop. They entered the valley and headed toward me. I watched ahead of them with binoculars. In a minute or two I saw a whitetail doe and a fawn looking in the direction of the riders with their ears cocked toward them. When they saw that the riders were not going to come right toward them they faded back into the brush.

Then right ahead of the riders, not over seventy-five yards from them, I saw a larger deer sneaking along. When he went through an open space I could tell he was a large buck with good antlers. Presently he turned to his right, sneaked around back of them, and kept on with his head low until he got to the mouth of the valley. He then came out on the flat brushy desert, threw up his big white tail, and ran as if the devil were after him. I could see him while he ran at least a half mile. Presently my pal and the vaquero came jingling up. They were surprised to find me sitting there and also to be told that they had moved that fine buck.

On another occasion, my friend Carroll Lemon was hunting over the top of a brushy hill, Frank Siebold on one side, and I on the other. I was perhaps 150 yards from Lemon and about 100 feet below. I could catch a glimpse of him now and then. The ground was rocky and in spite of the fact that both of us were trying to go quietly I'd hear him now and then and I am sure he heard me. I thought he might move something. So I looked toward him now and then. Presently I caught a movement in front of him. I knew it was a deer, suspected it was a buck. I sat down, threw the safety off and watched. The buck was sneaking along about fifty feet ahead of Lemon, his tail between his legs, his head down. When he began sneaking through a little opening I let him have it. The snapper on this tale is that there were two bucks, one of which I had not seen. The shot that killed his pal startled the other and he ran. Carroll nailed him as he went up the other side of a little draw.

Whenever he is found the whitetail is an exceedingly intelligent animal. He makes up his mind whether he is going to sneak off or sit tight. If he does decide to lie low, he lies very low indeed. If he decides the jig is up and he must leave in a hurry, he never pauses for a last look as the mule deer often does. Most of us undoubtedly pass up far more deer than we realize. I remember one occasion when around noon my wife and I tied our horses to an oak just above a small, brushy ravine. While my wife got the sandwiches out, I tossed stones into the brush hoping to move something. Nothing came out. We ate our lunch, dozed for a half hour in the sun. When we were ready to go I pushed a big stone with my foot into the heavy brush right under me. Out came a fine whitetail buck. He had been within yards of us all the time.

The hunter of wooded and brushy hills should always keep his eyes open around the middle of the day. Most herbivorous animals will get up, stretch their legs, and feed for a few minutes around noon. Many times I have been sitting on a hillside at lunch time glassing the opposite slopes. Then I'd suddenly see the tan body of a bull elk where nothing had been before. Sheep almost always get up and feed a little around noon, and since they are generally in open country they are easily seen. I have sat on points overlooking sagebrush flats with nothing in sight, then suddenly I've seen an antelope that had been lying down pop up for a few bites.

Many years ago I used to do some hunting with a man who was the most energetic and least successful deer hunter I have ever seen. He was then in his early forties, tough, muscular, and enduring. He seemed to feel that if he just worked hard enough, covered enough territory, crashed through enough brush he would be rewarded with a buck, just as the medieval sinner who wore a hair shirt and walked far enough bare-foot over sharp stones would be rewarded with a trip to heaven. I quickly decided that it was futile to hunt with this guy but that his boundless energy and iron determination might as well be put to good use.

The country where we hunted was composed of rolling limestone hills in the Big Bend of Texas. Because it was rocky it was a difficult country to go quietly in, and since much of it was fairly thickly wooded with piñon, juniper, cliff rose, and mountain mahogany it was not easy to see deer, particularly if the hunter moved them himself. In Arizona, hills like this would have been whitetail country exclusively, but there in Texas there were a few whitetails but it was mostly occupied by a rather small variety of mule deer. In the three years I hunted off and on with this human bulldozer I shot two buck mule deer that he had moved and a whitetail that I got by sneaking around through the heads of three canyons, taking a half day to cover a mile. I was wearing shoes with crepe-rubber soles and I wasn't making much noise. I shot the whitetail as it lay in its bed not knowing that I was in ten miles of him. The buck was watching my friend who was plowing purposefully along about a half-mile away. I was proud of the buck since of all American game I think the whitetail is the most difficult to bushwhack in his bed. My pal heard the shot, came over and helped me carry the whitetail back to the car. He had covered far more territory than I had and simply could not under-stand my luck. Again, it isn't how much territory the still-hunter covers but how well he covers it.

The Problem of Wind

The still-hunter must always consider the wind and approach likely spots in such a manner that deer will not catch his scent. This does not mean that the still-hunter should always move directly into the wind. He can hunt across the wind and sometimes he can even step out fast enough to beat a gentle drift of air and actually hunt downwind. The biggest grizzly I have ever shot, a real monster for an interior bear, was down-wind. Since the wind was strong and steady, it was possible to go to one side, let the wind blow past the bear, and then come back upwind and nail him.

The worst type of wind for either still-hunter or stalker is the un-steady, shifting, eddying wind. The hunter out in such a wind should keep constant track of it—by dropping a bit of dust or leaves, by watch-ing the smoke of pipe or cigarette, by wetting a fingertip and feeling for the direction. I have known hunters who carried a little Bull Durham tobacco sack full of powdered chalk. When in doubt they'd shake the sack and see which way the chalk dust drifted.

In one of my favorite hunting areas years ago down on the Sonora desert the ground was generally level, with low trees, cholla, cactus, and brush. The mule deer were in this flat country. But here and there were little rocky hills, some not over 100 yards in diameter and over 100 feet high. Many whitetails made these little hills their headquarters. They would feed out around them and then when they had filled up they'd go back and lie down about two-thirds of the way to the top. I have moved many of them by hunting around the little hills in such a way as to give them my wind. When a buck would try to sneak out, I would try to cut him down before he could get over the top.

Shifting, unsteady winds are bad and so are hard, gusty winds that rattle the branches and blow everything around. I do not like to still-hunt on such days. The deer are jittery. They tend either to move out wild or refuse to move at all. If you have plenty of time, such days are good ones to spend in camp.

Sitting and Waiting

The still-hunter should remember that he is *hunting*, not traveling—that his object is to get himself a decent shot at a deer and not simply to cover territory. He should go slowly and he should spend from one-half to one-third of his time standing still. He should pause and look carefully and listen wherever he thinks a deer might be. If he is not moving he is less easily seen and heard, and when a hunter stops near a bedded deer that is conscious of his presence the animal often gets nervous and makes a break for it. It doesn't hurt for the still-hunter to find a good spot and sit still and watch for a half hour at a time.

Ideally still-hunting should be done when the woods are not full of hunters. If hunters are crashing through the brush in every direction all bets are off. That is the time when it is just as productive to sit and wait and let the deer come to the hunter. I have done a little of this but not much, as I am congenitally a nervous type. I am easily bored and when I am bored I itch.

However, the man who doesn't mind inactivity and who doesn't bore easily can get a lot of deer simply by finding a good spot and *sitting still*. A good bet for the sitter and waiter is to find a tree or a rock to rest the back against and to make him less conspicuous. Then he should sit as still as possible. He should locate himself so that wind will not blow his scent in the direction he expects the deer to come from. He should not smoke, not because the animals will smell him (as they will not if the wind is right) but because the smoke moves and the smoker moves his hand to his cigarette. A nervous deer, unless he is fleeing in terror, will nearly always stop, look, and sniff before he crosses any sort of opening.

The man who sits and waits should dress much more warmly than he would if he were still-hunting. The surest way to keep a deer from coming toward you is to get up and walk around, to stamp the feet and swing the arms to get warm, to build a fire.

Deer have runways. Often they are used so much that regular trails are established. Incidentally, it is easy to tell what sort of animals made a trail even if no tracks are seen. The larger the animal is the wider the trail. Horses, cows, and moose make similar trails, but a pack trail can always be told from a game trail because it is more cleanly cut, more nearly straight (though never straight as a highway is straight), and it heads for the passes. A moose trail wanders more, is less clean-cut and definite, and does not show uniform use like a pack trail. Trails made by elk and caribou are somewhat narrower than moose trails. A deer trail is much narrower and it will go under branches a moose or horse trail would go around. Trails made by mountain sheep are found more in the open, whereas the deer like to move concealed as much as possible, and they are more clean-cut because sheep like to travel in a line, nose to tail, like a pack string. The brown bear trails of Alaska are actually two tracks like an automobile road with a high center between them, since the great bears have a wide wheel base. In rough country both deer and sheep like to travel around under the base of a rimrock and game trails are nearly always found there. When deer are not pushed they like to follow the path of least resistance and take an easy grade, even as you and I. Their trails run through saddles and up ravines and around easy contours. Both deer and elk will follow pack trails because the going is easier and the footing is better and also because the original pack trail probably followed a game trail anyway. A deer or an elk doesn't like to climb up over a peak or scramble straight up a hill any more than the hunter does.

In addition to definite trails there are always routes used by animals when they are going from one place to another. Generations of deer when pushed from a certain direction will try to sneak out of a particular area by more or less the same route, just as generations of Indian tigers always go about the same way when they are driven. In the South, where deer have been driven by hunters for hundreds of years, the good stands on productive routes are well known.

The man who sits and waits must keep alert, something that is easier said than done, as it is very easy to daydream or even to doze. To beat boredom some have tried sitting on a runway with a pocket book, but alas many get so interested they let deer go by without seeing them.

A variation of the sitting and waiting caper that is popular in the brush country of Texas is to do the sitting and waiting in a platform in a tree. Since scent generally rises, the deer seldom smells the hunter; and since a deer almost never looks up, it does not see him. The same method is employed by natives for waterhole hunting in Africa and India.

Another Texas method of getting whitetails is that of rattling two pairs of antlers together during the rutting season. A love-starved buck hears the racket, thinks two bucks are fighting and if they are that a doe must be near. So he comes up to see if he can't horn in and when he does the hunter knocks him off. Still another method of attracting deer is the use of a call which sounds like the bleat of a fawn in distress. I understand that it works, but I have never used it.

6 | The Art of Stalking

A pal and I had been seeing fresh sheep sign that February morning down there in the San Francisco Mountains in northern Sonora. There had been a lot of rain in the "Friscos," and a good many sheep had moved in. Grass and weeds were springing up green and succulent. The ocotillos were feathery with shining new leaves, and the leaves of the prickly pears were plump and distended with moisture.

It had rained within a week, but the sands of the arroyos were dappled with fresh sheep tracks and there were fresh droppings and tracks in the valleys between the rugged hills. The sheep had been feeding down in the valleys late in the afternoon and early in the morning, and I found where some had even bedded down there under the palo verdes during the day.

Yet for all the sign it was not until about 10 o'clock that I saw the first sheep—three rams. They were lying under the ridge across a canyon about a quarter of a mile away. I discovered them with binoculars, but if their outlines hadn't been broken up by a little thin brush they could have been seen with the naked eye.

I handed my amigo the glass, told him where to look. Presently he said excitedly he could see them and handed the glass back to me. I was lying there peeking over the ridge with only my head exposed, trying to figure out which ram had the best horns when my companion's .30/06 bellowed in my ear. I saw the rams jump to their feet. The rifle went off again. The rams took off. The last I saw of them, they were going over the skyline and my amigo was speeding them on their way with his last bullet. We never saw those rams again.

The rams had been in a spot where stalking them would have been easy. Staying behind the ridge we were on we could have gone around the head of the canyon and could have sneaked to a spot above and behind the sheep. The shooting would have been at about sixty yards. As it was, my eager friend blazed away with only a vague idea of the range and ruined what would have been an interesting and exciting stalk.

By prematurely bombarding game thousands of American hunters spoil their chances. Not only do they miss and wound game but they likewise deprive themselves of the opportunity to enjoy one of the world's most thrilling types of hunting.

Take antelope hunting, for example. Probably more ammunition per kill is expended on the pronghorn antelope than on any other North American game animal, and likewise probably a higher percentage of wounded antelope escape to die miserably than any other animal. The antelope is found in country made to order for stalking, but the average hunter cruises around the plains in an automobile until he sees antelope. Then he jumps out and starts smoking them up. I have seen hunters shooting at running antelope at a half mile or more. Unless an antelope turns a double somersault and lies kicking the hunters drive on and look for another herd to bombard.

Twenty and thirty years ago, sheep hunting was not fashionable and there was only a handful of sheep hunters in the United States. Most of these I knew. Now and then when things went wrong and a stalk was impossible one of these veteran sheep hunters took a 300-yard shot at a ram—or even a slightly longer one. But most rams were taken at short range after a careful and skillful stalk. Nowadays, judging from the stories I read, banging away at rams 300, 400, and even 500 yards away is routine.

It is a lot easier to kill a ram at a quarter of a mile away with a typewriter than it is with a rifle, and actually because of the terrain in which sheep are found it is almost always possible to stalk within easy shooting distance. When I first started hunting sheep I scared some out of the country by blasting off at long and uncertain ranges. Then I decided it was a sucker's game. I have shot a good many rams of various American and foreign varieties. Most of them have been shot at fairly short range and have been killed with one shot.

Of the various methods of hunting, stalking sustains the interest and excitement the longest. The hunter first locates the game and then tries to creep up to within easy range for a certain hit and a quick, humane kill. In these days of flat-shooting, scope-sighted rifles, the temptation is to blast off prematurely and hope for the best. Shooting equipment has improved greatly in the last fifty years but no matter how skilled the rifleman and how good his rifle and his scope, he is more certain of an exactly placed shot at 200 yards than at 400, and at 100 than at 200. From a benchrest old Betsy may put five shots into a 2½-inch group at 300 yards, but game generally isn't marked off with conspicuous black bulls-eyes for aiming. It is likewise inconvenient to carry a bench rest around to shoot from, and game doesn't always give the hunter time to get his heart and respiration back to normal. As an English sportsman wrote more than a half century ago, the cream of all hunting lies in the last 50 yards of the stalk.

In some ways stalking mountain game like the various wild sheep and goats is the easiest of all. The stalk may be long, the climbing difficult and laborious, but generally it is possible to approach the game out of sight and from behind a ridge. There is generally definite wind in high places and keeping the wind right is usually not a problem. Neither is noise, since in high, steep mountains rocks are always rolling and the game pays little attention to them. The hazards of high mountain hunting are that the game may move before a long stalk is completed, that the hunter may blunder into unexpected animals which in turn spook the game, or that another hunter may spook it.

A friend of mine had just completed a stalk on a fine bull elk and was about to take a shot at it when his hunting companion, who had also seen it, shot it from a distance of about 300 yards. The stalker, who was within 100 yards of the bull and about to touch off his shot, told me he could see the bull's hide fly out as if someone had jabbed the animal with a stick and pushed the hide out from within. Afterwards when they skinned the elk they found the bullet under the hide at the point where he had seen the hide expand. Apparently the bullet had had enough power left to stretch the hide but not to break through.

One of the most interesting stalks I have ever made was for a very fine greater kudu bull in Tanganyika in 1959. A gun bearer had spotted the bull as he got up to stretch about midday. He was somewhere in the neighborhood of a half-mile away in a hot, dry basin full of brush. We marked him just to the right of a big baobab tree. The wind was favorable, and from the pile of rocks where we had been glassing it looked as though we could keep to the left of a ridge and out of sight of the kudu.

Expecting I would have to make a stalk that day, I had worn a pair of light boots with soft, crepe-rubber soles, and my white hunter, John Kingsley-Heath, Kiebe, the gun bearer, and I sneaked along as quiet as a drifting fog. A kudu has ears as keen as those of a moose, so we took great pains to avoid loose stones and dry leaves.

Before we had gone far we discovered that the ridge we had counted on stalking behind was too low to conceal us. We had to gamble on keeping our eyes open and making like little mice.

We were just short of the tree when Kiebe jabbed me with a finger and pointed into the brush. In turn I jabbed John. Kiebe could see the kudu, and presently John whispered that he could make out a patch of gray hide striped with white. The bull was lying down within thirty-five yards in very heavy brush.

I decided to walk in and take the kudu when he jumped. Before I had gone ten feet the big bull shot out of there like a rocket and I put a bullet in him in the middle of a jump. We found him within 300 yards or so—the biggest kudu I've ever shot or probably ever will shoot—sixty inches around the spiral. I still think this was a very lucky stalk, as a bull kudu in the dry and noisy brush and rocks of the Tanganyika hills is one of the world's most difficult animals to sneak up on. I have laid too many eggs in stalking too many kudu to think otherwise. This old boy must have had his mind on something else that day.

One of the most exciting aspects of African hunting is the stalking of lion and leopard baits in the gray of dawn. The secret of success is to go upwind or crosswind very slowly, very quietly, being constantly on the alert to see if there is anything on the bait and to avoid spooking anything else that may be lying up nearby. Grizzly and black bears are stalked on baits in exactly the same manner in North America.

The stalker will do his best to get the wind right, but often the animal being stalked will fill up, then move off and lie down in an unlikely spot to keep his eye on the meat. In Tanganyika in 1959 Syd Downey and I had a big leopard coming to a bait in a tree. We had it figured out just where the leopard would lie up to watch the meat in case he was not eating when we arrived. We made our stalk accordingly. But the leopard did not follow the script. We caught a glimpse of him as he dived off a rock where no orthodox leopard would think of being.

Stalking in open country is the most difficult of all because it is often hard to find cover to approach behind. However, a careful survey of the terrain will usually show shallow water courses that can be utilized. Most of the Wyoming antelope country is rolling and cut with shallow, dry ravines called "coulees" there and known in Arizona and Sonora as "arroyos." These can be made to serve as cover for an approach if the hunter is willing to stoop over or even to crawl. To me it is far more exciting to creep up to within 150–200 yards of an antelope and kill it cleanly than it is to cut loose at 400.

A pile of stones, an isolated bush, or, in Africa, an ant hill can be used for concealment during the last stages of the stalk. I sneaked up behind an ant hill to within seventy-five yards of so of my first lion. He was gazing off in the direction of a nice ripe kongoni bait he had left when he had heard the hunting car in the distance. His sign at the bait was so fresh that Don Ker, my white hunter, felt he was close by. We sneaked around through open bush on ground covered with tall grass hoping to see him before he saw us. Luckily we did. The old boy's benign countenance stares down at me from the wall of my study as I write these lines.

A switcheroo I have used to close the range on pronghorn antelope and African plains game goes like this. Let us suppose that the animal has seen the hunter, is suspicious but not spooked. Let us also assume that within range of the animal is a patch of trees or brush that will conceal the hunter. If the stalker, once he has been detected, tries to approach behind the bush slowly, the animals move off.

The thing to do is to walk slowly at right angles until you are hidden by the bush and then to run toward it. You should pause for an instant to get your wind and collect your wits—and then step out and shoot. If this maneuver is performed quickly it generally works. The animal has been expecting you to continue your line of march and has been waiting for you to come out on the other side of the bush. I learned this stunt hunting pronghorns in northern Arizona and in Sonora and I found that it worked as well in Africa.

But sometimes the game must be approached when there is absolutely nothing to hide behind. Then all the stalker can do is to make himself as inconspicuous as possible, to keep the wind right, and to advance when the animal being stalked is looking the other way and to stop when it glances in his direction. In 1956 when Bill Rae, the editor of *Outdoor Life,* and I were hunting white sheep in the Yukon, we glassed at about a mile the big ram he later killed. The first part of our approach was out of sight up a canyon. The ram was feeding on the slope of a big, rounded mountain. To get within 250–300 yards we had to crawl about 300 yards on our bellies with no cover but some scrub willows about ten inches high. I was really weary of crawling when Bill got close enough to risk a shot!

Once in Wyoming the late Ernie Miller and I glassed a fine bull elk about a mile away across an enormous canyon. He had just taken a bath in a wallow and as we watched him he viciously horned some timberline trees; then he threw back his head and bugled.

Over much of the distance we could stay out of sight, but we had to cross one open space about 200 yards wide. To do so we got down on hands and knees, wandered erratically about, pretending to be grazing. We could see the elk watching us (and elk, incidentally, have about the best eyes in the deer family) but the bull apparently decided we were cows or bears. He bugled again and then went back to horning the trees.

We worked around the head of the canyon and up the side on which the elk was on. Presently we were lying in a little draw not far from where we had last seen the bull. The wind was blowing from the bull to us and we could smell the sweet, musty odor of a rutting bull elk. I crawled up the slope. No elk. I crawled further. No elk. Presently I could see the ivory tips of his antlers above the tops of some low, stunted alpine firs. He was lying down and as far as I could tell from the antlers he was facing my way.

I continued to crawl, pushing my .270 ahead of me. Elk have good ears as well as good eyes and good noses. The elk must have heard me. Possibly he saw me. Anyway, he stood up in the midst of that little patch of trees and stared right at me. I put a 160-grain Barnes bullet into his chest. He lurched, ran in a little semicircle, and fell.

This business of pretending to be a horse or a cow is an ancient ruse used by stalkers for hundreds of years. In areas where antelope, elk, and deer are used to range horses, hunters often approach by keeping a saddle horse between hunter and hunted. In India one of the successful ways to hunt black buck on the open plains is to approach the herd by walking behind a native bullock cart. Incidentally, game quickly discovers the difference between a horse with a rider and a horse without one, and animals that pay no attention to a riderless horse will bolt at the sight of a mounted one.

Since all mammals except man and the other primates are color blind, it makes no great difference if the stalker's clothes are the same color as the surrounding rocks and shrubs. What is important is that they be of the same value. Anything that stands out sharply from the surroundings should be avoided—white, vivid red or orange, black. A neutral shade of gray, tan, or green does all right and all of them, I imagine, look about the same to an elk, an antelope, or a sheep.

No stationary object means much to an animal. A sheep is traditionally sharp-eyed, yet on several occasions I have had sheep come close and stare at me. If an animal looks in the direction of the stalker he should stop immediately and remain still.

Locating bull elk by their bugling and then stalking them is one of the most exciting ways to hunt I know of. It is difficult to pinpoint a bugling elk exactly, even if he doesn't move. It is not easy to stalk an elk at any time and it is doubly and triply difficult to make a stalk during the rut. At that time the big six-point bulls have collected harems of sharp-eyed cows, and in addition smaller bulls are generally hanging around to see if they can't steal some cows. The same thing is true of mountain sheep—except that sheep are usually not hunted during the rut.

Often bull elk will come right to the caller, and if the elk seems to be moving toward the call the thing to do is to sit tight and wait.

But often a bull will bugle his answer but not move. Often such a bull is surrounded by his harem and can't very well move. At other times it is an old lone bull that is either lazy or cautious. In my limited experience in calling elk, it seems to me that big mature bulls who have not yet collected harems will nearly always come to a call if the call sounds natural and if the caller doesn't arouse his suspicions by whistling too often.

For whatever the reason, those coy old bulls that stay put are almost always in the bottoms of the steepest canyons, in the thickest timber, on the steepest, rockiest slopes. Getting to them without making too much noise is a tough proposition. A wise old bull elk is as tough to stalk as a bull kudu or a bull moose.

The last bull moose I shot came as a result of a long and interesting stalk. My guide and I saw the bull across a creek right at timberline feeding in what to the naked eye looked like a green and level lawn in the midst of a great willow patch. He was a big bull with what later turned out to be a 62½-inch spread and he loomed up like a silo on a Kansas prairie. Binoculars showed us that what looked like grass were willows about four feet high, and that the surrounding willows were probably around ten feet high.

We decided that since I would be stalking on a tilted hillside in willows for the most part higher than my head, the thing for the guide to do was to stay put so that he could direct me to the moose by hand signals when I came to open spaces.

The willows were worse than they had looked, so tall and so thick that the only way I could move through them was by trails made by the browsing moose. I might as well have been inside a sack. I could go along the trails without much noise, but I knew that if I tried to force my way through the willows I would frighten the moose.

Now and then I'd come to one of the open spaces and I'd look back across the creek toward my guide. Seeing me looking at him, he'd signal where the moose was located. There was no rhyme or reason to those damned wandering moose trails. Once I was within a few yards of the moose. I could hear him feeding, but I knew that if I tried to force my way through the willows he'd hear me and take off.

Finally I found a moose trail that took me out of the tall jungle to the edge of the open space. The moose was around 150 yards away, and as I was standing in willows almost waist high I had to shoot offhand. I laid a 130-grain .270 bullet in his ribs. I heard the bullet strike and saw him flinch, but if I remember correctly he didn't go down until I had shot the third time. All the bullets were in about an eight-inch group squarely through the lungs.

The wind is a big factor in stalking, as many animals depend more on

When the weather gets warm the wind generally blows *up*. To keep upwind of the game, the hunter should keep above it. Hunting high, as it is often called, is one way of preventing the animal from getting your scent.

65

their noses for protection than they do on their eyes. Many a well planned and executed stalk has gone sour because of a sudden shift in the wind. The stalker should remember that it is just as good to stalk crosswind as upwind. If a wind is strong enough and steady enough it is possible to go to one side, stalk downwind, and let the scent blow past the game.

I have made two successful stalks on grizzly bears that way. In one case my guide and I came down a hill with a strong wind at our backs blowing our scent about 200 yards to one side of the grizzly. We went beyond the spot where we had marked the bear, then turned, stalked him upwind, and knocked him over.

On another occasion I had shot a couple of fine bull caribou in a big basin above timberline. The guide and I were carrying the heads and scalps up to our tethered horses when I noticed a moving dark spot about a mile away. It was a grizzly. The wind was blowing strong and steady from the carcasses of the caribou to the bear, and I am sure he was investigating the delicious smell.

My guide and I figured that the wind was strong enough to blow our scent past the bear if we stayed to one side. Taking advantage of the fact that bears have poor eyes, we hurried toward the bear, keeping above him and to the side. Whenever he looked our way we stopped. Presently the bear apparently wondered what he was doing out on a lousy day like that. He found himself a little hollow out of the wind and lay down. We completed the stalk and gathered him in.

As a rule those animals that live in the open plains and mountains see well, but those who dwell in the brush do not. The eyesight of wild sheep and goats is legendary. The eyes of elk are good, as are those of the big cats. The eyes of deer have never seemed to me to be as good as those of elk, but they are by no means poor. The eyes of the plains-dwelling African antelope are good, but those of the tundra-dwelling caribou are not. The eyes of bears are very poor, as are those of rhinos and elephants. Wolves and coyotes have good eyes, keen ears, and sensitive noses. A coyote is one of the world's most difficult animals to stalk.

In my years of sneaking up on animals, I have continually been impressed by what an enormous advantage it is to see an animal before it sees the hunter. The hunter can focus his attention on approaching the animal, on standing still when the animal looks his way, on watching the wind, on moving quietly. The animal, on the other hand, generally has his mind on something else—on eating, on making love, on keeping flies off. He is expecting danger only in a general way.

The long and lanky gerenuk or giraffe-necked antelope is a keen-eyed desert dweller, but once, as a stunt, I got the wind on a gerenuk and with only a little cover to help me I sneaked up within twenty-five feet and

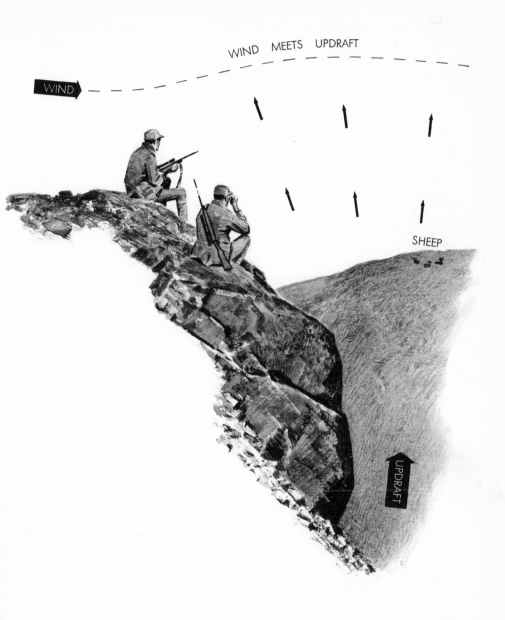

When hunting mountain sheep in high country, it is not always true that the game will pick up your scent if you are downwind. Often an updraft in a saddle between you and the game blows your scent over the animals.

shot him. There is no warier or keener-eyed animal in Africa than the eland, but I have approached lone bull eland within forty yards. On many occasions I have stalked to within a few yards of mountain sheep.

One thing the stalker should remember is that if he has to move when he is in sight of the animal he should move very slowly. Watch a cat stalking a bird sometime, and you'll see what I mean. The more rapid the movement, the quicker it attracts attention. He should also remember that a little brush breaks up his outline and makes him harder to see. He should try to shield his head with a little brush when he looks over a ridge. Putting twigs and leaves in the brim of a hat helps break up the outline.

If, during the stalk, he has to cross a ridge against the skyline, he should do so as slowly as possible and make himself inconspicuous. If he is bent double or crawling, he does not have the upright human outline that animals fear. Even if they see him they may mistake him for another animal.

Seeing game is not so much a matter of eyesight as knowing what to look for. The eyes of Indians and trappers are traditionally good, but this is because they are able to interpret what they see, whereas the city man is not. The man who lives in the hills can tell at a glance that one brown spot is a stone and another is a sheep. He can tell from the way a distant animal stands or walks what it is.

The subject of eyes brings up another tale about my pal who smoked up the rams instead of stalking them. A couple of days later we were skirting one of the big, rough hills of the San Francisco range when I saw above me about 200 yards away a nice shootable ram walk out from behind a rock and stand quartering away from us.

"Look up there," I said. "See that big triangular rock just to the left of the tallest organ cactus? Well, see the ram standing by it with his rump toward us? Can you hit him?"

"Boy, I'll say I can hit him!" he whispered.

I saw him sit down and prepare to shoot.

As I watched the ram, he shot three times. The ram was not hit. I couldn't see the bullets strike. The ram finally ran around a big rock, got into a draw and came out about 500 yards away toward the top of the rugged hill.

My pal had been shooting at a rock about a half-mile away and as large as a small house. He had good eyes, he was a gun nut of the first water, and a fine target shot. If the ram had been moving when I tried to show it to him he would have seen it, but although he could see things he couldn't interpret them.

Afterward he told me that the rock looked more like a sheep than any sheep he had ever seen. I guess maybe he was right!

7 | *Tactics for the Hills*

In the western part of the United States most big game is found in hilly and mountainous country. Sometimes the hills and mountains are covered with brush and trees. Sometimes there is brush only in the draws. Often the south sides of the hills are quite open, but the north sides, where it is cooler and the moisture stays longer, are wooded.

Sometimes the hillsides are gentle enough and the ground is soft and quiet enough so that the most productive method of securing a deer in the woods and brush is still-hunting. Then the hunter employs the orthodox tactics of going quietly upwind or crosswind, stopping often to look and listen. But often this type of hunting is just about impossible. The hills may be too steep, the ground too noisy, the brush in the draws or on the north sides too thick and too brittle. Sometimes the hills and mountainsides offer good footing for horses anywhere, but sometimes they are so steep and so rocky that horses must stay on the trails.

Resting Places of Game Animals

All members of the deer family prefer quiet shady spots to lie down in—cool timbered basins, the brush and trees at the heads of draws and canyons, the brush of north slopes. They like to rest where they are comfortable, where they can see but not be seen, and where they can get the wind of a possible enemy. In my native Arizona the small South-

69

western whitetail deer are often found in quite open country, but as a rule whitetails prefer more cover than mule deer. Both whitetail and mule deer, if given protection, are found close to farm houses, ranch houses, and towns. The more deer are bothered, the more often they are found where people seldom come—in heavy brush, steep hillsides, deep, rough canyons.

Elk are much less tolerant of human presence than are deer and are generally found farther from roads and in wilder, rougher country, and mountain sheep are still less tolerant. However, in both Wyoming and Idaho I have seen sheep and elk in the same country. Once in Wyoming I shot a big bull elk in a basin just above timberline and frightened the wits out of three big rams that I had not seen. They had been lying down in a shale slide around a point from the bull elk. I have also seen mule deer and sheep not far apart in Idaho, and sheep and caribou using the same range in British Columbia and the Yukon. In some ranges in Sonora I have seen whitetail deer not far from desert sheep.

Sheep generally prefer to bed on a point, in a saddle, or at the head of a basin, but particularly early in the season when the weather is warm, they sometimes lie down in the thick patches of stunted alpine fir called "shintangle" in the southern Canadian Rockies. In Idaho, where timberline is much higher than it is in Canada, bighorns during the warm, early September season often lie down in timber, particularly on the cool, shady north slopes. Alberta guides tell me that the habit of bighorn rams bedding down out of sight in shintangle has become more common as hunting pressure has increased. However, whereas deer and elk almost always bed down in brush or timber where they are difficult to see, open country animals like sheep, goats, and caribou give little thought to concealing themselves and generally bed down in plain sight.

When animals are bedded in the open, they can be located at a distance and stalked. Feeding animals are often difficult to stalk from a great distance because they may move away from where they were located and bed a considerable distance away. Then the hunter does not know where they have gone. Unless the hunter in the hills can get to a shooting position within fifteen or twenty minutes, it is generally better to watch an animal, see where it goes, and then make the stalk.

The tactics adopted by the hill hunter depend on many things—what time of day it is, how the weather has been, what game he is hunting, how plentiful it is, how steep and rough the country is, whether he is afoot or on horseback.

For any kind of hunting it is always best to be out in the game country as early as possible because the game animals can then be seen moving, either feeding or traveling from feed or water to where they plan to bed. But sometimes this is difficult, as a suitable spot for camping, where wood, water, and horse feed are available, may be some distance from the hunting ground. I have probably shot more deer after 10 o'clock in the morning than before, because in so many instances I have had to camp so far from where I wanted to hunt that I have not been able to get into the area where the big bucks were until between 9 and 10 o'clock in the morning.

Let us take a look at the time of day when I have shot some outstanding bucks. The best desert mule deer I have ever taken was shot probably about 4 o'clock in the afternoon. It was about the end of December and this big buck had just started the rut. (Desert mule deer rut in January, about two months later than the Rocky Mountain mule deer.) He had collected a bunch of does and the whole lot were on foot and on the move. Two of the best heads I ever took in northern Arizona were both shot fairly late—one at about 10:30 and the other at about 1:30. The last mule deer I shot in Idaho was knocked off at around 1:30.

Most of the whitetails I have taken in the hills were also shot at between 10 in the morning and 4:30 in the afternoon, because they were in high steep hills and it often would take two and a half or three hours to get to where they were. Then if I got to camp in time to cut some wood and make a start on supper before dark I had to head down the mountain at around 4:30.

Getting Game to Move

Since most of the western deer mountains are not very heavily timbered and since the animals being hunted are bedded, the hunter has to get them to move—and to move in such a direction so that he can get a shot. Where the country is fairly open and where game is plentiful, it is feasible simply to ride along the trails. Enough deer will get nervous and move out so that the hunter will get shooting—and generally a deer. If the footing is good enough so that the horses do not have to stick to the trails, the hunter can ride through likely spots and can travel so that he can see anything that moves on the opposite hillside. The man on foot follows the same tactics. He has the advantages of being able to get into action quicker if a deer jumps, and he can also go through likely spots where taking a horse would be difficult if not impossible. However, the horseback hunter can cover more territory, has a more pleasant and less taxing hunt, and has his mount to carry his deer in on if he is lucky and connects. In most brushy or partially wooded hill country, far more opportunities present themselves on the far side of a draw or canyon. If the game is on the same side as the hunter, it is too quickly out of sight if he sees it at all. This is particularly true if the hunter is on horseback, as he makes more noise and cannot get into action quite so fast.

This horseback hunter is riding along the edge of a ravine, hoping the sound of his horse on the stones may move a deer on the opposite hillside.

he crack shot there is no more pleasant hunt than the leisurely
er rolling Southwestern hills on pleasant October and November
ith an occasional big buck dashing out of a draw to try to make it
ty by running up an almost open hillside.

great place to do horseback hunting like this used to be the winter
in Arizona's Kaibab Forest north of the Grand Canyon. There a
could go almost anywhere. The draws were wide, the piñon and
per trees not thick, and many of the old bucks had spectacular heads.
ot one of the best mule deer I have ever taken there in 1932. He was
ded in the brush in the bottom of a wide, shallow draw. I was on
seback. I happened to see him as he got to his feet and headed uphill
f he would go through scattered trees and over an open ridge. I got off
horse, yanked my .30/06 Springfield out of the scabbard, and waited
r him to appear.

I expected him to show up through the openings between the trees
bout 250 yards away, so I sat down to wait. Apparently when he got to
the edge of the open stuff he had decided it would be pretty risky, as he
had cut over to his left to stay in the heavy stuff. When he had traveled
about 300 yards he cut back to my side of the draw to get behind me.
That old boy had undoubtedly been shot at a few times before!

When he failed to show up among the scattered trees or on the open
ridge I knew he planned something foxy. He was, I knew, either skulking
in some heavy brush or he had planned some maneuver. If he had holed
up in some brush to wait it out I wouldn't have had a chance, as he
would have been able to hear me and he could have sneaked off without
my seeing him. As it was, my luck was in that day and his was out. He
had been on the north slope of a hill and I on the more open south slope.
I happened to see him as he sneaked through an opening about thirty
yards wide and not far from the foot of the draw. I swung ahead of him,
shot, and he went down at the forequarters but did not fall. I shot again
as he recovered and went behind a tree. I got on my horse and rode over
to the opening. At once I picked up a good blood trail. Most of the blood
was bright scarlet and frothy and I knew he had been hit in the lungs. I
could follow on a trot. He had traveled about 300 yards. The second shot
had broken a leg high. This buck had high close-pinched antlers with
beams 28½ inches long.

Another spot I used to enjoy hunting was a big conical mountain
called Cerro Azul (the blue hill) in Sonora. The only water was low in a
creek so the cattle did not graze clear to the top of the mountain. There
the tall, rich gramma grass was ungrazed and full of Mearns quail. There
were deer in every draw and canyon, and the vaqueros told me there
were some black bear but I never saw one. I used to ride out from a ranch
house with a vaquero named Palacio, and when the bucks came booming

This country here is almost slide rock and so rough it would be difficult to get horses over. The tactics used here were to hunt right along the edge of a hill to shoot at anything that was bedded above and tried to move.

out of the heads of the draws I'd do my best to cut them down. Back in the 1930's the Mexican limit on whitetails was three, and two bucks a day was about par for Cerro Azul. Palacio used to take a pack mule with him to bring in the game.

About all Palacio and I ever did was to ride along about halfway up one side of the draws 150 yards or so above the oak trees and manzanita and cliff rose where the deer bedded. They were spooky but unsophisticated.

Deer learn quickly, and when they are shot at a few times the bucks learn that if they get nervous and take off in the open, all hell breaks loose. Bullets snap through the air around them. Fragments of rock sting them. Companion bucks fall and bleed. Deer are natural skulkers, so they learn to sit it out if the hunter is on the opposite hillside. The foolish bucks that run into the open when they hear or see a hunter get killed. The smart ones play it cool, often letting a hunter pass within a few feet.

When deer are reluctant to move, one mountain hunter will go along on one side of a draw or canyon, one on the other. Then if there is much brush or many trees the hunters will almost never see the deer they move but they see and shoot the deer their companions on the other side move. I remember one time when a companion was on one side of a draw, I on the other. I had seen a good deal of sign and there were occasional pools of water in the draw. This looked like an ideal spot for a smart buck to brush up. My companion was on his horse, but I was off walking and leading mine, my scope-sighted .270 in my hand. I was watching the opposite hillside when I saw a movement that materialized into a big whitetail buck that got to his feet about fifty yards in front of my companion and left in a dead run. I swung ahead and shot when he was about ten feet from an oak. He gave no sign that he had been hit, and in this case I did not hear the bullet strike. But he did not come out from behind the oak, and a few seconds after he had disappeared I heard him bleat. My companion found him on the far side of the oak, stone dead and shot through the lungs.

It is generally wise for two hunters to split up when hunting a canyon or when hunting rolling semi-open country. Deer will often move off to one side and give one of the hunters a good shot. I have got many deer and coyotes by this simple maneuver. As I have mentioned elsewhere, most animals have single-track minds and if they are moving away from one hunter they will almost run over another without noticing him. I was hunting with a companion one time, he on one side of a canyon, I on the other, when I heard a stone roll toward the bottom of the canyon. A moment later I heard another noise somewhat closer. I stopped, switched off the safety of my rifle. Presently a buck walked within sight about

O'Connor with a good Arizona whitetail buck shot across the ravine behind him. He was just to the left of the two conspicuous trees just under the ridge when the deer jumped.

twenty yards away and stood there wa... not move and since I had the wind on hi...

On another occasion a friend, Frank ... the north side of a long hill that was par... north of the Mexican border near Patagoni... deer on the hill they would be on the north... there and there were plenty of trees and brush ... ridge, however, was quite open and a trail used ... along the top. I carried a .270 in my hand as I wa... horse. Frank was to ride along the bottom. If the ... should get a shot. If they moved up, there was a chan... me. As I strolled along the easy trail, I could hear the ... of Frank's horse below me now and then. Presently five ... sneaking uphill out of a brushy little draw. I dropped ... position and put a 130-grain .270 bullet right through t... horse and I were in plain sight, but those bucks were so i... Frank that they did not see me.

Generally, hunting the hills requires a combination of tacti... times putting a man at the head of a canyon while two others go ... side is productive. One hunter can stay in a saddle while anothe... around a hill or through a basin.

Deer like to bed down in brushy draws near the top. It is a good stu... for one hunter to go along just under the top of a ridge and anothe... about one-fourth of the way down. When deer move out of the ... brushy bottoms across the more open ridges, the hunter near the top will get shooting and sometimes both will shoot.

A horse is a great help, particularly to the middle-aged or elderly hunter, but many a fine buck has got away because the hunter was on his horse when he should have been off ready to shoot. Whenever the mountain hunter comes to a particularly likely area he should dismount and have his rifle in hand so he can get into action quickly. He should not be afraid to get off, tie his horse, and still-hunt through a basin.

Often deer simply will not move if they think they have not been seen. Then the hunter can roll rocks into the head of a canyon or drop them down into the brush just under a rimrock. The deer can't stand the racket and try to sneak out.

What I have written about hunting deer in the hills applies also to elk. However, elk move around much more than deer. A deer may spend his life in three or four basins and never travel more than two or three miles from where he was born. An elk, however, has a larger area of home territory, tends to range higher in the summer, lower in the winter. He moves farther when he is shot at. However, the elk is just about as adept as the deer in sitting tight if he thinks he has not been seen.

Typical Southwestern hill country. In this area the game animals are whitetail deer. The bare hillside in the background is the southern exposure. Notice that there are more brush and trees on the northern side. Deer would be in brush and trees.

Like human beings, game animals tend to repeat maneuvers that are successful, discontinue those that get them into trouble. If a buck finds he can slip out of a favorite bedding spot without getting shot at, he will try exactly the same tactics again. I have told elsewhere about an ancient whitetail buck who for years slipped out of the head of a canyon and around under a rimrock if a hunter approached from the bottom of the canyon. If he had bedded down in an oak grove at the top of a hill, he sneaked out of it into the head of the canyon. I learned his two escape routes and bushwhacked him.

A big buck mule deer lived for years around a spring near the head of a canyon. It was possible to get to the mouth of the canyon by automobile, but from then on a hunter had to hike about four miles uphill to get to the head of the canyon. Many hunters reported seeing the big buck and he was shot at and missed at long range dozens of times over a period of four or five years. He always crossed over a saddle and disappeared over a ridge into the head of another canyon. This point was eight or ten miles from another road.

I didn't shoot at this big buck but I got binoculars on him three or four times when he was trotting over the ridge 500 or 600 yards away. I knew a rancher who lived by the road so I arranged to spend a Saturday night at his place and leave before daylight for the saddle the old buck crossed. I knew some Sunday hunters were certain to be out that morning and I was pretty sure they would push the old buck across the saddle into the chaparral on the other side.

When I got to the saddle, the sun was up, but it had been very cold the night before and there was a heavy frost. I tied my horse out of sight, found an inconspicuous spot in the sun, sat down on a boulder and waited. I had my rifle across my knees, and now and then I took a look down the canyon through my binocular. About 8:30 I saw my first hunter, a chap with a plaid cap and a red jacket. He was toiling slowly up the trail. A little later I saw another hunter moving slowly along on the hillside opposite the man on the trail.

About 9 o'clock I heard a shot. Through my binocular I could see that the man on the hillside was kneeling and shooting at something below me. Then the hunter on the trail opened up. I could hear the crack of the bullets before I could hear the report of the rifles.

A little later I caught a glimpse of something gray moving in the brush below me and about 150 yards away. It was the old buck. As he went through the brush his chin was up and his head was back so his wide-spreading, many-pointed antlers would not get hung up. He trotted out into the open about sixty-five yards away and came almost directly toward me. The temperature was still well below freezing, and I'll never forget how magnificent he looked with the steam coming out of his nostrils and the sun glistening on the polished points of his antlers and on his gray hide. He did not see me until I raised my .30/06.

I have always wished I could have weighed that buck, since I am sure he was one of the heaviest mule deer I have ever shot. I couldn't get him on the horse whole, so I skinned him, quartered him, and packed my saddle with head, scalp, and quarters. When I finished the skinning I washed my hands in what was left of some early snow back in the timber and took off down the trail, leading my horse and eating a sandwich I had brought with me.

Anyone hunting deer and elk in semi-open hill and canyon country should remember to choose his route so that if he moves game he can see it and get shooting. It does no good for a hunter to move game if he is tangled up in brush or is behind trees and can not see out. Neither does it help the hunter if he moves game and it is so far away that he cannot be certain of a solid hit. If it is necessary for one hunter to go through heavy brush, another should always be stationed where he will see anything that moves.

The hunter should also be ready to shoot, quickly and accurately. That means that if he is hunting on a horse he should get off and have his rifle in his hands when he comes to an area where he is liable to get a shot—for example, if a companion is about to go through the head of a brushy draw where something may be bedded down; if sign tells him a deer or elk has just gone into a draw or the head of a small basin; or if he hears shooting down in a canyon or on the other side of a hill and thinks something may come by him.

Too many would-be big-game hunters are lazy—and I have had attacks of indolence myself. I have seen hunters remain on their horses like sacks of flour when a companion was just about to come through an area where there were chances that game might move. Then when something does show, such hunters generally frighten their horses by scrambling off and grabbing wildly for their rifles. In very open country the hunter may have a good many seconds to get into action, but in much mountain hunting he has only from three to ten seconds while his buck goes across an open spot or before he gets over a ridge.

A horse is a great aid for mountain hunting, but hunters who seldom get out of the saddle are severely handicapped. One day in November I was hunting some whitetail hills in an Arizona national forest. I had shot a buck just before noon. A friend and I had horses. We had put the buck across one saddle and we were taking turns riding the other horse. A storm was coming on. A bitter wind was howling, and we were about to freeze as we came down a long open ridge. We had stopped because the buck was slipping over to one side. We were tightening the cinch and trying to balance the buck when I noticed two riders coming down a

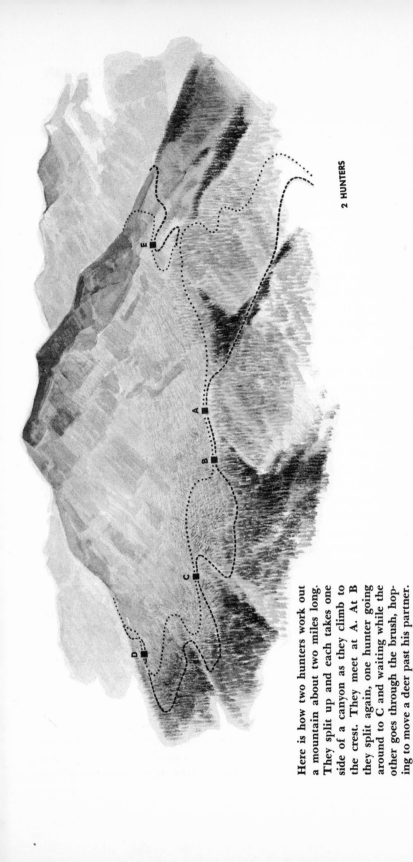

2 HUNTERS

Here is how two hunters work out a mountain about two miles long. They split up and each takes one side of a canyon as they climb to the crest. They meet at A. At B they split again, one hunter going around to C and waiting while the other goes through the brush, hopping to move a deer past his partner. They hunt all heads of draws and canyons, split again at D and work opposite sides of the brush and meet at E.

similar ridge about three-fourths of a mile away. They had rifles with them in saddle scabbards, and my companion, who had looked at them with binoculars, told me that the two were a wealthy Easterner and his wife. They had bought an adjoining ranch a few months before and had a permit to run some cattle on this portion of the forest.

Just below the crest of the ridge and on our side was a bluff of hard red rock. Bushes and oak trees grew just below the rimrock and anything lying there would be sheltered from the wind. My companion and I had booted the buck we had got out of a similar spot. While we watched, the two covered about a half-mile, three different deer got up from under the rimrock and went off. One of them ran downhill toward us in plain sight but the pair didn't even turn their heads. Before the deer got out of sight in the wooded draw between the two ridges, we could see antlers. When we got down off of our ridge, we met the other hunters on the trail. They congratulated us on the buck, but said that they had seen nothing.

Pointing Out Game

A thing the man who hunts the hills (or for that matter anywhere) should do is to learn to point out game to someone else.

Typical conversation:

1st Hunter: I see a big buck.

2nd Hunter (excitedly) : Where?

1st Hunter: By that big rock.

2nd Hunter: For Heaven's sake. This country is made of rocks. I can see 500. Which rock?

1st Hunter: By the tree . . . the rock by the tree! I can see him as plain as day. He's standing there looking at us. If I had a rifle with a scope on it like you do I could hit it.

2nd Hunter (now frantic) : I can't see him. There are rocks and trees all over the damned hillside. Which rock, which tree?

1st Hunter: Oh hell, he's moving off now.

The second hunter sees the buck for the first time just as it disappears.

To show someone else an animal he does not see, pick out the most conspicuous object in the general direction of the game. Then tell the hunter exactly what direction the animal is from it and what reasonably conspicuous object it is near, how far it is both from the most conspicuous object and the object close to the animal.

Example:

I see a deer. I think it is a buck. I can see antlers now. It *is* a buck and a good one. See that big triangular rock about 300 yards away in the middle of the hillside, the big rock shaped like a pyramid and with green lichens growing on the left side? O.K. Now see the dead piñon tree about

100 yards to the right of the rock at 4 o'clock? Just to the left of the dead piñon and a little below you'll see sort of dirty white spot. That is the rump patch of the buck. He is browsing on a bush. You'll see his antlers when he lifts his head. See him? Good!

The last example no doubt seems very simple. It is—both simple and logical, but I have seen few hunters and not very many guides who could quickly and clearly pinpoint an animal for someone who had not yet seen it!

8 | *Tracks and Tracking*

Almost as many giddy tales are told of the fantastic skill of trackers as are told of the unbelievable feats of rifle and revolver shots. The exploits of the Western badman who could gallop past a six of spades nailed to a barn door and shoot all the spots out of it, and the white hunter who could always break the neck of a running Thomson's gazelle at 400 yards with an iron-sighted .470 Nitro Express, are akin to some of the tracking tales one hears.

I remember a dandy. An Arab guide was following the track of a hare across ground composed of coarse gravel and small stones. The tracking was so difficult, the narrator said, that he could see no tracks at all. Presently the Arab stopped. "Something is wrong here," he said. "I was following the track of a pregnant female. This is the track of a female that is not pregnant!" So they looked around and presently they found the new-born leveret. I have also read stories of trackers so good that they could follow the track of a sheep or an ibex over bare rock.

Tales like these arise in many ways. In the first place, there is the human tendency never to let a good tale suffer in the telling. In the second, many people are so unobservant that the most ordinary bit of tracking seems to them like black magic. In the third, a great many guides are showmen. When they discover a client is gullible they like to con him by making their tales juicier and juicier.

I used to hunt deer and quail in Arizona with a friend who grew up in a very large city. He was (and I suppose still is) about the most unobservant human being I have ever met. To him all mountains looked exactly alike and he couldn't tell the track of a horse from that of a cow. He saw me do a little very ordinary bit of sign reading and tracking and from then on he told our mutual friends that I was a veritable Leather Stockings, a steely-eyed outdoorsman who could track a soft-footed animal over solid rock. Once we were quail hunting. He had an ancient, obese, and asthmatic cocker spaniel of which he was very fond but which was about as useful on a quail hunt as an alligator. We got separated and presently I heard him shouting for me. He told me he had lost the miserable old mutt and he was afraid the poor creature would perish in that dreadful desert. I asked him if he could show me about where he had seen the dog last. I cast around and found dog tracks crossing a sandy arroyo and heading up a rocky little ridge. I assumed that the dog would travel across the ridge in a fairly straight line so I crossed the ridge, picked up the tracks again in the next arroyo and presently I found the dog snoozing in the shade under a bush. You can't tell my friend that I cannot track a dog across solid rock.

Another time he broke high the left front leg of a whitetail buck. I found a piece of bone. From the facts that the animal was leaving only tracks from three hoofs, that occasionally I could see a scrape mark made by the hoof on the broken leg, that the blood was on the left side of the tracks and that occasionally the left hind foot left a track over a spot of blood, I told him that the buck's left front leg was broken. Presently the tracks and the blood disappeared into a patch of brush. I circled it and found no tracks or blood going out. I told my pal that his buck was in there lying down. To any reasonably experienced hunter this was simple but to him it was a feat to stagger the imagination.

Learning to track is a combination of observation, experience, common sense, and patience. To observe well one must be interested. Anyone who is bored by animals, hunting, and the outdoors will never be a good observer and anyone who does not observe well will never be a tracker. Likewise anyone who is not patient will never become a good tracker.

I have seen some excellent trackers in action. I have hunted with the famous Dorobo trackers in Kenya and Tanganyika and with skillful Masai and Wakamba gun bearers there. I have seen them do some good tracking but never have I seen them do anything that was beyond explanation. I have hunted with the famous Geraan, wild Arabized Negro tribesmen who live in the Sahara desert and of whom many fantastic tales are told. I have hunted with Luhr and Turkoman shikaris in Iran, with Dravidian tribesmen in India, with Papagos in Sonora, and various Indian guides in Alberta, the Yukon, and British Columbia.

I have seen them do some excellent tracking, but none of them are magicians. None of them can track an animal across solid rock or perform any of the other feats that trackers are supposed to accomplish in the windy tales one reads.

In 1953 when I was hunting in Tanganyika, my white hunter Don Ker and I were out early one morning before the sun was up. We ran into two beautiful lions with heavy manes—one dark and one light. Since it is against the law to shoot within 200 yards of a motor vehicle, Don drove on until he could park the hunting car out of sight in a patch of brush about 400 yards from the spot where we had seen the lions. Then we sneaked back along a donga (dry stream bed) to the point where we had seen the lions. Our pious hope was to bushwhack one of them.

But those lions had apparently been shot at, as their tracks showed that the moment we were out of sight they had started to run. Don and I, with a Dorobo tracker, took after them. The tracks showed that after they had galloped about a half mile they had settled into a walk. We had started tracking about 7 or 7:30. The lions had gone across a plain spotted with thorn trees and threaded by occasional dry dongas. Where the ground was soft and dusty the tracks were easy to see and we traveled fast. Where the ground was hard we often had a tough time. In places they had walked through patches of grass already tracked up by eland, wildebeest, and zebra, we had the best luck by circling the patch and picking the tracks up on the other side. I don't think the Dorobo was a bit better at tracking than Don Ker and not too much better than I was. He certainly couldn't see any tracks that I couldn't see.

Much of the superior skill of people who live in the game country can simply be laid to patience. The average once-a-year hunter doesn't have much of that commodity. As soon as he finds tracking a bit difficult he says to hell with it. But not the chap who lives in the back country.

Many years ago a hunter I knew gut shot a fine desert ram in Sonora. He and his Mexican guide tracked it down a mountain, across a flat, and into a canyon of another sierra. By this time the American was tired, thirsty, and discouraged. He told the Mexican that if he found the ram he would give him $100. At that time the Mexican peso was 5 to 1—and for 500 pesos a poor Mexican would follow a wounded ram to hell and back barefoot across broken glass. The ram had stopped bleeding as some abdominal fat or an intestine had blocked the exit hole. Two days later, the Mexican came into camp carrying the ram head and scalp. He collected his $100.

Since the ram had traveled in very rocky country, he had to look for sign along trails, in saddles, and in soil between stones. He knew that a gut-shot ram would probably take an easy path up the canyon and follow a sheep trail when it could. He also knew that a ram so wounded would eventually head for water. It was in a time of winter rains and the Mexican knew the few natural tanks in the area that would have water in them. He eventually found the ram almost dead by a water hole, sneaked up on it and finished it with a knife. In this case what did the trick was the patience begotten by that 100 bucks.

Some people are observant and others are not. Most people observe well what they are interested in, poorly what they are not. Once I asked a friend and his wife to have dinner at an expensive restaurant with my wife and me and another couple who were from Europe. When my friend's wife got home, she told the society editor of the local paper about her experience. She got everything cockeyed except the clothes of the European woman, who was an internationally famous beauty widely known for her jewels and her clothes. These she described in minute detail down to the last stitch and the last emerald. Obviously she was interested in clothes, but she didn't know whether the woman's husband was famous for polo, badminton, large gifts to charity, or tiger shooting. My own wife is interested in hunting and in animals, but she is by no means a gun nut and can hardly tell one rifle from another.

Anyone brought up in the country has a head start in learning to track. I grew up in a small Arizona town with great expanses of desert within easy walking and easier bicycle-riding distance. During summers I spent much time on a relative's ranch. I cannot remember when I could not tell a roadrunner track from that of a quail, a desert mule deer track from that of a javelina, a mule deer track from that of a whitetail, or when the tracks were clear and well defined those of deer from those of desert bighorn sheep.

Later I learned to tell the cow-like track of an elk from that of a moose, which is shaped like that of a very large deer; the tracks of a Rocky Mountain goat from those of a bighorn sheep; those of an antelope from those of a deer; those of a caribou from anything.

The city man, the highly educated man, is probably at a disadvantage in learning to track as compared, let us say, to some simple Mexican vaquero, a trapper, an Eskimo, or a wandering Dorobo hunter in Africa or a Dravidian tribesman in India. The city man is used to finding his way about by street signs and numbers—not by the appearance of hills and trees. Because tens of thousands of human beings leave their "spoor" about constantly—empty cigarette packages, chewing gum wrappers, tread marks of automobile tires—he pays no attention to them. I have hunted with men who hadn't the faintest idea what the tread marks of the tires on their own automobiles looked like or what sort of tracks their own shoes left.

The man who lives in the backwoods has a mind free from worthless information such as stock market prices, big league batting averages, the date of the Norman invasion of England, the real names of movie stars, the blue book value of a 1965 sedan, and the cute things said by Princess Grace's young as recorded by their British nanny. If he is a cowboy he must constantly be on the lookout for tracks that tell him of the presence of predators—mountain lions, wolves, coyotes, for sign that tell him of the movement of his cattle, or the presence of a cattle thief. The trapper must be able to get a notion as to the kind of animals that inhabit a bit of country, their numbers, the routes they follow when they hunt or feed.

To the city man an elk track looks about like a moose track. He cannot tell the difference between the track of a mule deer, a whitetail, an antelope, or a mountain sheep. But the cowboy should even be able to recognize the tracks of some individual animals. A rancher I used to know remembered that he hadn't seen for several days a range bull that had cost him important money. He rode around until he picked up the bull's track, followed it until he found the beast bogged down in the mud of an almost dry waterhole and in desperate straits. He brought back a couple of cowhands. They got ropes on the bull and pulled him out to dry land.

It will shock horse lovers to be told that to non-horse lovers one horse looks about like another. Caucasians often say that all Chinese look alike to them, and I have no doubt but that Chinese say the same thing about Caucasians. A Hopi Indian I knew once told me that if I should ever run into him and he did not speak to me that I should not feel slighted as he found it extremely difficult to tell one white man from another.

The reason for this is a lack of interest and observation. When I was a lad I was keenly interested in automobiles. I not only could tell any make of automobile at a glance, but I could almost always identify the make by the sound of the motor. Now I feel about automobiles as a non-horse lover feels about horses. The only way I can tell one from another is to read the nameplates.

And it is the same with tracks. The man who cannot distinguish between the tracks of mule deer, whitetails, sheep, and antelope has never observed them very carefully. I have never been good enough to tell the track of one large buck from that of another large buck of the same species, but there are plenty of people who can. Many years ago the most remarkable tracker I have ever known lived in a little Sonora village called Piti Quito. He was a simple rancher who was barely literate and who was apparently psychic as well as being an astounding observer. He told me that he could tell at a glance the footprints of any person in Piti Quito and the tracks of any of the horses owned thereabouts. The first time I met him he asked me if I hadn't stopped at a certain store in Piti Quito a couple of weeks before. I said I had. He told me that he had seen my footprints there and he would know them anywhere. He added that I had at one time injured my right foot. This was true.

This Mexican rancher was a sort of a genius. I never did hunt with him but those who have tell me that in tracking a deer he depended as much on intuition and knowledge of the deer as he did on observation. He would follow a buck for a mile or so, perhaps; then he'd suddenly say, the buck is just on the other side of that hill, and he would be!

Anyone interested in learning to track should try to interpret all the tracks he sees. Here is the track of a deer. Do you think it is a buck or a doe? Is it traveling or feeding? If traveling, was it walking, trotting, or running? When were the tracks made? If it was running, why was it?

Determining Age of Tracks

Learning to determine the probable age of a track is a combination of observation and common sense. The would-be tracker should continually compare game tracks with other tracks of a known age—his own, the tread marks of an automobile, the tracks of a horse.

If it has been raining until 7 o'clock in the morning and the track was made since the rain, the track was obviously made sometime since 7 o'clock. If the track is sharp and clear, it is probably pretty fresh, but how long a track remains sharp and fresh looking depends on the character of the soil and on the weather. Sometimes damp clay will dry and keep a track looking sharp for weeks or even months. Tracks in gravel or dry sand are never much good as these materials do not hold the impression. It is then possible to mistake a sheep track for a deer track.

A track made since the frost has gathered is obviously fresher than one made before, and even after the frost has melted it is possible to tell if the track was made before or after the frost, or before or after dew fell. The trail of an animal that has passed across grass heavy with frost or dew is easy to follow even though the tracks themselves are hard to see. Animals can be trailed across the heavy grass because they disturb it as they pass over it. The heavier an animal is the easier he is to trail this way. A small deer or a little antelope does not displace much grass, but an elephant or a rhino is almost as easy to follow across some types of grass as a truck would be. Even a large soft-footed animal like a lion, a tiger, or a grizzly bear can be followed.

An animal going through fairly tall grass bends some of the stalks down, rearranges others, and it is the bent grass one follows. Why this is I am not sure, but closing the eyes and looking ahead at the grass through the eyelashes makes it easier to see this displaced grass. When the tracker sees grass that an animal has stepped on slowly rising, or a branch still swaying from the passage of an animal, he knows the trail is very hot.

I'll never forget one occasion when I stalked a bait in India. I crept through brush and tall grass as quietly as I could. When I got to the bait, grass was slowly rising in the bed where the tiger had been lying. I didn't need the tiger's growl a moment later to tell me that the tiger had heard me and had moved off a few seconds before I got there.

Sometimes when I am doubtful of the age of tracks along a trail or around a spring or waterhole, I take a branch and sweep the ground clean late in the evening. Then when I look for tracks the next morning I know those I see have been made during the night.

A track in a sheltered spot in a dry windless climate can look very fresh for a very long time. I remember one time when I had been hunting sheep in the coastal ranges of Sonora north and south of Puerto Libertad. That was in April. In December I took my wife back there and we camped in two of my old campsites. No one had been there since and much of the sign looked as if it had been made within a week. On another occasion I drove into a bit of isolated sheep country that I had been into ten years before with the late Charlie Ren. I could still see the automobile tracks we had made ten years before.

In tracking an animal, other signs can show about how old the tracks are, even if the tracks themselves do not tell the story. If the animal has defecated and the pellets are still wet, the animal has passed there recently. If the pellets are both wet and warm, you are on a very hot trail. If a wind is blowing, tracks in loose and sandy soil quickly fill up in exposed places and a track that looks fresh *is* fresh.

Learning to Detect Differences

Much that can be told from tracks is a matter of observation, common sense, and experience. A large, fat animal will make deeper tracks in the same sort of soil than a smaller, lighter animal of the same species. The tracks of a heavy animal with cloven hoofs show more splaying than those of a lighter animal, and a certain amount of splaying of the hoofs is a sign of old age in an animal, just as fallen transverse arches are a sign of age in the human race.

Often animals have certain peculiarities about their tracks—as witness the dozens of bear stories about Old Clubfoot, Old Two Toes, Old Splay Foot. If the peculiarity is marked enough even a half-baked tracker like me can identify a track as belonging to a certain animal.

As a rule the tracks of males are larger than those of females, and particularly with horned and antlered game the front feet are larger than the hind feet, but the lads who look at a track and say, "This is the track of a big bull," or "this is the track of a barren doe," are often wrong.

Once many years ago in Arizona I followed the track of a lone elk in fresh snow. It was a very large track and I was convinced it was that of a large bull. After a couple of hours it became apparent that I was very close to the elk. The tracks entered a thick patch of juniper and I sneaked silently in. Presently I could make out part of the tan body of an elk lying down not over twenty feet away. I took a couple of steps so I could be certain of a shot through the lungs. Inadvertently I stepped on a brittle twig beneath the snow. It cracked and the elk floundered to its feet. I had the gold bead front sight of my .35 Whelen against the ribs when it dawned on me that my "bull" hadn't the slightest sign of an antler. It was an enormous cow.

In Africa hunters after big ivory get out at dawn to try to pick up very large tracks of elephants who have come down to water during the night. The big tracks are always those of big bulls. They follow the tracks until about noon. Then the bull generally stops beneath a tree and dozes the hot hours away. The hunter can then overtake the elephant and look him over. Sad to say, big tracks go with big bodies but not necessarily with big tusks. Often the tusks will be only of moderate size and occasionally the animal will be a one-tusker.

Tracking and Terrain

Some types of country are easy to track in and some are just about impossible to track in. Soft, thinly grassed or bare soil that is sandy or loamy is easy. Rocky ground is just about impossible to track in. I lost the first elk I ever shot at because he did not bleed externally from a high .30-caliber lung shot and he ran off across a type of volcanic rock called "malapai" in the Southwest. I could not find any tracks at all, and the cowboy who was with me couldn't find a track. We ran across the bull a couple of days later after I had shot another elk. He had lain down in an oak thicket and had died not much over 300 yards from where I had shot at him. If we had been blessed with enough patience to comb the whole country we would have found that bull. We had seen the elk stumble, had seen hair fly, and had found a few hairs cut off by the bullet. But because we had found no tracks and had seen no blood we gave up.

Hunters like a fresh "tracking" snow. Then one can follow a deer, an elk, or a moose as fast as he can walk—or if he is on horseback just about as fast as he can ride.

A couple of days after I had wounded and lost the elk I tell about above, snow began to fall up there on the Mogollon Rim. My cowboy pal and I were out hoping to run into another bull when we found very fresh tracks of a herd of seven. We guessed the trail was not over fifteen minutes old. We caught up with the herd within an hour. They had stopped to rest and think things over about 150 yards from us on the

Sheep tracks along a creek bed in British Columbia.

Track of a front foot of a Yukon grizzly.

A caribou track. Notice the semicircle of the hoofs and the imprint of the pasterns behind.

Sheep tracks in the sandy desert between two mountain ranges in Sonora.

Wolf tracks in the sand.

other side of a draw. There was a spike bull and a five-pointer in the bunch. I knocked off the five-pointer.

When I lived in Tucson, Arizona, I used to do a great deal of hunting in the lowland deserts within thirty miles of the Gulf of California. This is very dry country and the soil is largely decomposed granite sand. The desert is clothed with many kinds of cactus including the wicked cholla, the barrel cactus (bisnaga), a form of giant cactus called sahueso, organ cactus, and low mesquite and palo verde trees about the size and shape of the trees in a peach orchard. These lowland deserts are to me one of the most interesting spots on the globe. I grew up on them, shot my first deer, my first quail, my first sheep, my first javelina on them. In Sonora rugged

93

and sometimes fairly high sheep mountains rise from these deserts, and the handsome little Coues' whitetail lives on the little hills that spot it. The mule deer stay out on the flats. They leave their long pointed tracks all over the flats when they travel from place to place and browse on cholla fruit, on tasty shrubs like jojobe, and on ironwood leaves. Now and then the smaller, more heart-shaped tracks of the whitetail show where one of the beautiful little bucks has crossed a flat from one hill to another or a doe and fawn have fed out around one of the little hills. There is no mistaking for deer tracks the little round dainty tracks of the javelina, which are always more deeply indented at the points—as if the animals walked on tiptoes. Now and then an observer will see where a small herd of desert bighorns or possibly a lone and restless ram has passed en route from one high rough sierra to another. The tracks are about the size of those of mule deer but the shape is slightly different. I generally need a clear impression to tell the difference, but the tracks left by a big ram's front hoofs are usually unmistakable.

Besides the game, other desert dwellers leave their tracks—the dainty little tracks of the nocturnal ringtail cat, those of gray desert foxes, coyotes, and bobcats, the tracks and scratchings of a covey of desert Gambel's quail, the big round pug marks of an occasional mountain lion or the slithering spoor of a rattlesnake.

Many times I have picked up and have followed the tracks of a feeding buck mule deer. Sometimes the tracks have not been as fresh as I thought. Sometimes, alas, I have been wrong and my buck has turned out to be a big barren doe. On other occasions the erratically wandering buck has got downwind from me and my reward would be only a snort, the sound of breaking brush and pounding hoofs and a fleeting glimpse of a flashing gray body.

The best time to trail up and knock off a buck down on the desert is early in the morning right after a long rain has stopped. Then the raindrops have washed the sandy floor of the desert clean and all the tracks to be seen are fresh. The deer and other game have been bushed up during the rain and now they are out and feeding.

I remember one time back in the 1930's when a friend and I drove down to a desert cattle ranch about 150 miles from the border and about thirty miles from the Gulf of California. It had started clouding up when we cleared the border at Nogales. We had no tent with us so when we got to the ranch we made camp in a dilapidated hut made of ocotillo stalks plastered with mud. One end of the hut had fallen in, but the area near the door was dry. We set up our camp cots, discovered that the smoke found its way out of a hole in the roof when we built a small cooking fire. We put on a pot of frijoles and made ourselves comfortable.

It rained steadily for two days and two nights. The morning of the third day we awoke to a damp and dripping world but the rain had stopped. We cooked bacon and eggs, dressed hurriedly, got into our car and drove off down the road toward Puerto Libertad. Four or five miles from the ranch we found a fairly high hill at the right of the road and parked the car near it. The country was flat and dotted with low brush, cholla, and trees from ten to fifteen feet high. In places it was possible to see for a hundred yards or so, but for the most part visibility was limited to from thirty to sixty yards. Parking the car by the hill would enable us to head straight for it, as it was high enough so that it could be seen from any of the other little hills that were higher than those desert trees.

My companion and I split up. He wanted to go to the right toward a chain of small hills about two miles away, and I liked the looks of a big cholla patch at my left. I had not gone more than 200 yards when I picked up the tracks of two mule deer. Tracks of one were large and I was certain that they had been made by a buck. Tracks of the other were somewhat smaller. I decided the tracks were made by the familiar combination among mule deer of an old buck and a younger one. The tracks wandered erratically out of the chollal. Sometimes the bucks would be right together and sometimes they would be fifty yards or so apart. They were feeding, nipping a few leaves off a bush occasionally, pausing now and then to browse on an ironwood tree.

The tracks were very fresh. When I picked them up, the droppings were cold. When I had been on the trail about forty-five minutes, the droppings were warm and the signs of their feeding were fresh. A gentle breeze was blowing in from the sea. Since the tracks were easy to follow I kept to the right of the trail on the downwind side as much as I could. I didn't want them to wind me if by chance they made a loop that brought them downwind. The floor of the desert was dotted with occasional little hills and now and then a little pile of eroded granite boulders, probably the only part of a hill that had not been weathered away over the centuries. Every time the trail of the deer led near one of these piles of boulders I'd climb up and look down into the brush and trees ahead.

The trail got fresher and fresher. It was easy to follow and I was walking as fast as I could cover the ground quietly. The tracks told me the deer were still feeding and were not disturbed. Presently the fresh tracks led just to the right of a little pile of those granite boulders about twenty feet high. As I looked at the track of the big buck I could see some sand slide down into it. I knew the deer were very close.

As quietly as I could I climbed up on the boulders and looked down. At first I saw nothing. Then about sixty yards away I noticed a movement in the branch of an ironwood tree. One of the bucks was browsing there. As I watched I could make out the shape of a big four-point (ten-point Eastern count) buck.

I was carrying one of the handsomest, fastest-handling rifles I have ever had—a 7 × 57 Mauser fitted with a ramp front sight with gold bead and a Lyman 1-A cocking piece rear sight. It wore a stock by one of the finest craftsmen ever to practice the trade of stock making—Adolph G. Minar of Fountain, Colorado. Presently the buck moved just enough so that I had a clear shot at his chest. I held the gold bead for a high lung shot and when the little 7 mm. cracked I could see the buck collapse. Then about twenty yards to the left I saw the other buck for the first time. He was getting out of there, and I had only a shot at his bounding rear end. The front bead found his dingy white rump patch. The 7 mm. cracked again—and the smaller buck went down. However, he needed another shot.

The big buck was a dandy. He had heavy antlers and a wide spread. I would imagine that he weighed between 180 and 190 pounds field dressed. The other buck was about a three-year-old and I guessed his weight as about 140–145. He had a small, spindly, four-point head. I dressed the two bucks, laid them over a boulder under an ironwood tree, and propped their belly cavities open with sticks.

From the top of the pile of boulders from which I had shot I could see the conical hill near which we had parked the car. It looked to be no more than a mile away. I took a careful bearing. I was on a straight line between the little conical hill and the highest peak in a chain of low hills to the southeast. As a further precaution, I climbed the tree under which the bucks were lying and tied a red bandana handkerchief to one of the top branches. My plan was to go to the ranch, pick up a cowboy and some horses and come back for the bucks. If no more rain fell it would be easy to backtrack myself, but a hard rain could obliterate the tracks.

I had thought I'd heard a distant shot while I was trailing the two bucks and when I got back to the car, my companion was waiting for me. He had shot a very fine whitetail buck, he told me. He had taken a picture of it. Later, he said, he'd get a horse and go back for it.

While we were headed back to the ranch the clouds thickened up again. It grew darker and rain began to fall. By the time we got back with horses the tracks were so badly washed out that we could not follow them, but because of my precautions we found my two bucks with no difficulty. My companion, however, never did find his whitetail. He hunted for it off and on for a couple of days. He even offered a reward of fifty pesos to any of the cowhands who might run across it.

He had not marked it as I had. He had not even located a line to it. He had counted on backtracking himself. The moral of this is, I suppose, that tracks are good to follow but at best they don't last forever.

9 | *Following Wounded Game*

A score of years ago, a companion and I were hunting that grand little deer called the Arizona whitetail. Our luck had been poor. We had seen some does and fawns but no large bucks. Along toward noon we decided to ride the trail back to camp, eat some lunch, and then hunt another area.

We were jogging along a cattle trail when I noticed ahead of me a well-marked blood trail. It went right across a solid limestone outcrop in our path and disappeared into the brush on one side. Whatever had made that blood trail was bleeding so heavily that it looked as if someone had been carrying a bucket of paint with a large hole in it.

I turned my horse, followed the blood thirty or forty yards into the brush and there I found a dead Arizona whitetail buck. It had been hit in the last ribs on the right side, apparently as it was quartering away. The bullet had gone through and had come out the brisket leaving a hole you could stick an arm in.

An hour or so before we had heard a furious fusilade and before that we had seen three hunters on the sidehill. Now they were nowhere in sight. Apparently they had smoked this buck up but because he hadn't turned a double flip-flop they hadn't bothered to cross the canyon to see if they had connected.

My amigo and I dressed the buck, hung him in an oak near the trail and marked the spot with a red handkerchief. Later we ran into the

97

hunters, told them where their buck was. They didn't return the hand-kerchief.

Thousands of head of game are wounded and left to spoil in this country every year simply because hunters won't go over to the spot where the animal was and look for blood, cut-off hair, or other signs of a hit. At least 50 percent of all wounded animals can be recovered simply and easily, as in a high proportion of the cases they do not run over 100 yards and leave a trail a child could follow.

How can the hunter tell he has made a hit?

The answer is that he cannot always tell and that is why it is so important to follow up every shot, even if the hunter is pretty sure he has missed. If the hunter is a reasonably good shot and has learned to "call his shots"—to remember what his sight picture looked like when his rifle went off—and he thinks he should have hit, he should always follow up his shot, even if there was no indication of a hit.

In Tanganyika in 1959 I got a quick shot at a bounding greater kudu bull in heavy bush. My white hunter, my gunbearers, and I charged after it, hoping I could get another shot. The kudu, as far as any of us could tell, didn't stumble and didn't flinch, and we were so close that the bullet could not be heard striking even if it did hit. My white hunter was convinced I had missed, but I retained the picture of the crosswires looking just right when my .30/06 went off. So on my insistence we went back to the spot where the kudu had jumped and immediately found blood. We followed it up and gathered in the biggest kudu I'll ever shoot—sixty inches around the spiral.

My last desert bighorn ram was going at full throttle and about to disappear behind a big rock when my rifle went off. He gave no sign of being hit, but the sight picture had been right. He hadn't gone twenty-five yards after he had disappeared.

Reactions of Wounded Game

In the majority of cases the experienced hunter cannot only tell that he has made a hit but he can make a pretty good guess as to where.

Often, but not always, the bullet can be heard to strike. A sodden, squashy thump means a hit in the water-filled abdomen. A harder hollow thump means a hit in the chest cavity. A sharp crack means that the bullet has struck bone. A gut-shot animal generally humps up and goes off with its head down. If an animal sags at the forequarters and then goes off this generally means a hit in the forward portion of the body, generally in the lungs. Why this is I cannot say, but if an animal jumps in the air and starts off on a wild, blind run, it generally means a heart shot.

A bear hit almost anywhere will generally fall down, get up, and if he is not hit hard, run off like a streak. I have seen big grizzlies fall flat from a shot in the foot. I have never heard a black bear make a noise when he is hit, but grizzlies almost always roar when a bullet hits them.

The smaller an animal is the more it reacts to the shot. A well-placed shot in the chest cavity from a fast-expanding bullet will generally knock an animal the size of a deer, sheep, or antelope flat. Sometimes the animal is flattened so fast that the hunter is not aware that the animal has fallen. The .270 with a quick-opening 130-grain bullet is particularly deadly in this respect. Once in Sonora I was sitting on the side of a hill when a companion started shooting in a canyon below me and on my left. In less than a minute five or six bucks came boiling out of the canyon and started running through the brush below me about 200 yards away. I swung ahead of one and fired but did not think I had connected.

A few minutes later my pal called that he had wounded a buck and was on the blood trail. Thinking that one of the bucks in the bunch I had shot at was his wounded buck I went down to where they had run to see if I could cut a blood trail. Almost immediately I stumbled over a dead buck. I called to my companion that I had found his buck, but a moment later he told me I was wrong since he had found the buck himself about 150 yards away. I had killed a buck instantly but didn't know it as I had lost sight of him for an instant when the rifle recoiled upward.

On the other hand, large and phlegmatic animals like elk and moose will often walk away with no sign of being hit. A Rocky Mountain white goat will also take a solid hit without flinching. I once took a careful shot from a rest over a log at a bull elk. Because of the wind I couldn't hear the bullet hit and the elk gave no sign of being hit. He simply walked a few steps into heavy timber and disappeared. The chap I was with was certain I had missed but I didn't see how that was possible from such a solid position. We crossed the canyon and found the bull dead within fifty yards.

If an animal that has been shot at does anything out of the ordinary it is generally a sign of a hit. If one animal in a bunch turns away from the others and runs downhill, let us say, he is generally hit. If you are shooting at a deer and he stops behind a bush this is almost always a sign of a hit. If an animal makes a leap at the shot it is almost always the sign of a serious hit, generally in the heart.

My wife's first kudu took a tremendous bound when she fired her first shot. The cows he was with ran off like scalded cats but he went slowly. She shot again and this time I heard the thump of the bullet striking ribs. He went twenty yards, stopped, and she shot again. He went down.

As we walked up I told her I thought she had shot the bull in the heart with the first shot—and indeed the autopsy showed that a bullet had gone through the lower part of the heart.

Locating Wounded Game

Let us suppose that the hunter has shot at a game animal and thinks he may have hit it. He should mark the spot well and go to it. When the hunter is on one side of a canyon or a ravine this is easier said than done, and often the hunter can miss the spot by fifty or seventy-five yards. Before he crosses he should stop, look the country over, pick out a definite landmark—a large rock, a dead tree, an open meadow—anything which will enable him to get definite bearings. If there is no landmark and he has a companion, he should have his pal stay where he was and keep his eye on the spot. Things often look different on one side of a draw than they did on the other.

One of my most frustrating hunting experiences came from neglecting this precaution. My wife and I were hunting whitetails in Sonora and were riding with a Mexican cowboy along a trail. Suddenly about 175 yards away a handsome whitetail buck jumped up out of high grass and stood there looking at us. We piled off our horses, shot at the same instant, and the buck went down as if poleaxed in the grass.

It did not occur to any of us that we could lose anything as large as a buck on what we thought of as an open hillside. But when we went over there we discovered the grass was as high as our middles and as thick as the hair on a grizzly bear. We hunted for an hour and never did find the buck. We could have been within two feet of him without seeing him. If we had left the cowboy on the trail to keep his eye on the spot, we would have found the buck in five minutes.

Once the spot where the game has stood has been located, the hunter should look around for signs of a hit. Blood is the obvious thing to look for but sometimes an animal may not bleed immediately. Small-bore high-velocity bullets often stay within the animal, and the tiny entrance hole in the hide may not match up with the hole in the body when the animal moves. The bleeding is then largely internal. The hunter should also look for hair cut off by the bullet, and sometimes he can tell about where the wound is by the character of the hair.

Bright, frothy, scarlet blood means a lung shot, and almost never does any animal shot squarely through the lungs go far. I can remember offhand only two such cases. Many years ago in Sonora when the .257 first came out I was hunting deer with a rifle of that caliber and bullets so strongly constructed that they opened up very poorly on light animals. It was almost dark when I got a shot at what I believe was the finest

Tracking a wounded buck, Eleanor O'Connor examines a spot of blood on a twig for freshness.

101

whitetail buck I have ever seen in the hills. He was only about 100 yards away. I shot from the sit and had him cold turkey. I found minute particles of frothy blood, but since the country was all tracked up by deer, following was slow. Darkness came on and that night it rained. I never did find the buck.

On another occasion in central Africa I took a shot at a big bull roan antelope, a creature as large as a bull elk. I forgot that my .375 was loaded with solid bullets. It was a lung hit all right and we found a little frothy blood, but the roan got away.

Big irregular gouts of dark blood mean a shot somewhere in the abdominal cavity, and often this blood will be mixed with the contents of the stomach or intestines. A gut-shot animal will die eventually, but if it is badly frightened it can travel a long way. A determined and experienced tracker can recover an animal so wounded, but it is not easy.

A shot through the body cavity behind the diaphragm makes an animal sick and miserable. Animals shot in the liver seem to be in great pain. They are reluctant to move and generally die before long, as the liver is full of blood vessels and they bleed heavily. But the animal wounded only in the abdominal cavity can, if pushed, travel a long way and is often very difficult to recover. On two occasions I have seen animals lose everything back of their diaphragms and yet travel. A big buck mule deer I shot dragged his stomach and intestines along the ground behind him for about 100 yards before he fell. He was dead when I got to him. A desert bighorn ram shot by a friend I was hunting with had his abdomen laid open by a .300 Savage bullet as he ran directly away from the hunter down a canyon. He ran out on a flat and when he jumped a barrel cactus the protruding stomach caught in the thorns and was jerked out. The ram ran between a quarter and a half mile before he fell dead in a sandy arroyo.

Clear, uniform blood of medium color in splashes almost always means a muscle wound that does not penetrate the body cavity. Animals so wounded are generally not found, and most of the time they recover. In India in 1955 I took a shot at a tiger at night from a machan. I could not see the tiger as it was behind some brush but the Indian boy in the machan with me said he could. I took it for granted that he had enough judgment to put the bright center of the flashlight's beam on a vital spot on the tiger. I put the intersection of the crosswires in the middle of the bright spot and touched off the .375. The tiger took off like a runaway truck horse.

The next morning the lad and I found blood and tracked it all day by a splash here and a spot there. Along in the late afternoon, absolutely dead beat, I came around a bend in a narrow canyon high in the hills. There was my tiger. He was lying there facing his backtrack by a little spring. All day he had been resting with the flesh wound in his cheek against cool sand and taking a drink now and then. He took one bound and was in heavy jungle before I could get into action. If I had been carrying my rifle at ready I could have got him, but I was unprepared since the last blood I had seen was black and dry and had been on the rocks for hours. The tiger of course recovered from what was little more than a scratch, but I'll bet he never came back to another kill. Another thought: if that tiger had been feeling mean he would have got *me!*

Other evidence besides blood can be found that will indicate the location of the wound. Sometimes bits of bone from a broken leg will be found. Once I was helping a companion trail a wounded deer and I found some teeth. He had shattered the poor creature's lower jaw. Luck was with us and we managed to locate and finish the buck.

Tracks will show if a leg is broken, and the height of blood on high grass and bushes will show how high up on the body the wound is. If there is blood on both sides of the trail, it is obvious that the bullet has gone clear through. Evidence that the animal has fallen and got up again shows he is hard hit and not long for this world. The first moose I ever shot was in very heavy timber. He gave no sign of being hit, but I didn't see how I could miss an animal as big as a horse at a few yards. I followed his track out of the timber into a swampy muskeg meadow. There I could see where he had fallen to his knees. He was lying in waist-high willows not many yards beyond. He staggered to his feet and I shot him again.

Now and then an animal shot through the lungs will survive, particularly if a small-caliber bullet that does not expand much is used, or if a bullet blows up and does not give much penetration. In 1962 I had a report on an elk killed that had been wounded a year or two before but had survived. Some of the lung tissue had actually grown out through a three-inch hole in the rib cage and was lying against the skin. However, this is a very rare exception. A shot through the lungs, even with a fairly light caliber, will usually collapse the lungs or drown the animal in its own blood. If the character of the blood shows a lung hit, the animal 99 times out of 100 will be quickly recovered.

In all cases, if an animal falls but is not dead and the hunter can see to shoot again he should do so. It is far better to expend an extra cartridge or two and spoil a little meat than to lose the whole animal. When an animal is hit it is in great pain and shock. For a short time it doesn't think of much else. If an animal is knocked down or lies down with a gut shot it will usually lie there for a little while until some of the shock wears off. For that reason, I believe it essential to go immediately to the animal—or to the spot where the animal was standing. If the animal is there and still alive, it should be shot again and put out of its misery.

It is dangerous to try to cut the throat of an animal that is still living.

I had to learn that the hard way. In northern Arizona about in the early 1930's, I took a shot at a magnificent mule deer with a .30/06 at about 300 yards. The buck sagged at the front quarters and I suspected a lung hit. I shot again and afterwards found I had broken a leg.

I found a little bright, frothy blood, followed it and found the buck down and at the point of death. Since this was one of the finest mule deer heads I had ever seen, I wanted to get it mounted. I decided against shooting him again. I took out a pocket knife, walked up to the buck, felt around until I found the carotoid artery—and jabbed in my knife. Instantly that dying buck came alive. I threw myself on his head, held an antler in each hand. The buck did not get his front feet off the ground, but he got his hind feet under him and dragged me in a 50-yard circle. When the rhubarb was over I was a bloody and dusty mess.

If the hunter arrives at the spot where the animal went down and finds it gone, he should follow very quietly and carefully on the blood trail. If the animal is lung shot he'll find it in from 50 to 150 yards and he'll usually find it dead. If it is gut shot or has a broken leg, it has been my experience that if the hunter does not find the animal within a quarter of a mile he is in for a long, bitter, and often fruitless chase. It is the tendency of the animal to get away from the spot where he has been hurt. Then if he does not receive further fright, he lies down and watches his back trail. If left alone the loss of blood may so weaken him that he will be easy to approach. On the other hand, he may recover sufficiently as the shock wears off so that if frightened he may be able to get up and travel a long way.

The first few hundred yards on the trail, then, is of crucial importance, and every effort should be made to slip up on and finish the animal in the first spot where he lies down. If there are two hunters one should do the trailing and the other should go quietly to one side, keeping in touch and taking great pains to watch the wind.

As the hunters follow the trail they should look ahead and take special care to note spots where an animal might lie down. It is the instinct of a wounded animal with any choice in the matter to pick out a thick patch of brush or otherwise conceal himself. If the tracker sees the trail leading toward such a patch, he should try to circle it and see if the tracks come out. If they don't he has the animal located. He should always approach a spot where he thinks a wounded animal is lying in such a manner that he can shoot if it goes off.

It is not true that a wounded animal always travels downhill just as it likewise isn't true that a whitetail deer always drops his tail when struck by a bullet. However, it is generally true that a wounded animal dislikes climbing, particularly if he has a broken leg and has been struck in the lungs and often he will lie down a little way up a hill.

Once my wife, a friend, and I were hunting whitetails in southern Arizona. My wife and I were on one side of a hill, my friend on another. I heard a couple of shots, and then my companion came over the sky-line and announced that he had wounded a deer. It afterwards turned out that he had shot it in the abdomen and also had broken the left hind leg high.

We tracked the deer around a bare, grass-covered nob, and I could see that the tracks were leading to a brushy draw where there was a little spring. On the other side of the draw was a steep hillside thick with yellow gramma grass and spotted with a few evergreen oaks. It struck me that the buck would be lying down toward the head of the draw, as there he had both cover and water. I felt that he wouldn't want to climb that steep open hillside, and that if he didn't lie down in the draw, the only other thing he would do would be to travel down the draw. I asked my wife and the other hunter to sit down on the hillside so they could shoot the buck if he came out. Then I went down below the spot toward which the buck's trail was headed. I found no blood so I was reasonably sure he was above me in the draw. I circled the hill and came to a point above the head of the draw from the other side. There was no blood trail cross-ing the saddle above the draw.

I sat down with my rifle across my knees to see if I could see the buck. I had been there perhaps five minutes when a crow came floating along downwind. At a point about fifty yards from me, he wheeled around, announced that he had seen something interesting and lit in a tree. I moved about thirty feet and I could see the buck's head. He was lying there watching my wife on the opposite hill.

Every effort should be made to locate and finish an animal the first time he lies down. If it becomes apparent to him that he is being followed, his fear gives him a new shot of adrenaline, his wariness in-creases, and he is much more difficult to come up to. A friend of mine of wide hunting experience tells me that not once in forty years of hunting has he ever followed a wounded animal more than a quarter of a mile and recovered it. He says that if he does not get the animal the first time it lies down, experience has taught him that it is no use to follow further.

I think he is unduly pessimistic, but I agreed that if the animal is not located and finished in his first bed, the job of trailing it down becomes at least ten times more difficult. If an animal is spooked out of the first spot in which it lies down, it is best to wait a half hour before taking up the trail once more.

A wounded animal becomes tremendously thirsty, and if it is able and if not pushed too hard it will generally head for the nearest water. Many years ago, when much writing was being done about the deadliness of the high-speed .22s on deer, I took a pop at a Sonora whitetail with a 50-grain bullet from a .22/.250. When I shot, the buck fell and rolled down into some brush below a cliff. I was so certain that it was dead that I approached carelessly. I heard the buck going out ahead of me but did not see him. I trailed him about 300 yards, but there was little blood and the country was nothing but a pile of broken volcanic rock where even a mouse would make noise. I found the buck the next day. During the night he had gone to a pool in a narrow little canyon, had had a drink, and had then laid down for his last sleep. The light varmint-type .22 bullet had blown up on the ribs and had made a hole about the size of an egg high in one lung. The buck had slowly bled to death.

Precautions with Dangerous Game

If the wounded animal is potentially dangerous, the hunter on his trail should be doubly careful. Gut shot, a grizzly, a lion, a tiger, or a leopard is angry and vindictive and can move just as fast as if he were unwounded. With a leg broken low he is angry and can move about as fast as if he were uninjured. A chap I knew was killed in Angola in the late summer of 1963 by an unwounded lion, but this is a rare exception. Most hunters killed or mauled by dangerous game come to grief when following up wounded animals.

My own experience in following up wounded dangerous game is very limited. In the first place, I have had no vast experience on dangerous game; and in the second, I almost always make certain that I place my first shots well enough so that the animal won't give trouble. I have trailed two tigers, both merely scratched, and one of which I located. I once followed the blood trail of a lion into tall grass but the lion had been shot through the heart and was stone dead. One other time I followed up a wounded grizzly but that bear had no more fight in him than a rabbit. The only grim experience I ever had with a grizzly came from a nervous guide who was convinced that the bear was dead and forged on ahead. The bear let out a roar and took after the guide. Fortunately I was close enough to shoot it, but the experience strengthened the tender regard I have for my own hide.

Almost always those who are killed or mauled by dangerous game have been following wounded animals. The cemetery at Nairobi, Kenya, is sprinkled with the graves of gay young Britishers who got too close to wounded lions. Dozens of white men have been killed by wounded tigers in India, and I know of one woman hunter killed by a tiger. Wounded tigers have even jumped up on elephants and killed hunters in the howdahs. I'd make a rough guess that ten or twelve people are killed or badly mauled by grizzlies every year from Montana to Alaska. A few years ago a grizzly killed both a hunter and his guide in Alaska, and within recent years a grizzly killed a hunter in Montana.

Without knowing much about it except what I have read, I'd make a guess that the world's most dangerous animal is a wounded tiger and right after him comes the lion. Both lions and tigers are tremendously faster than grizzly or brown bears, they have much better eyes, and they are more used to killing things than is the omnivorous bear. Since they are smaller, they can conceal themselves better. Baron Werner von Alvensleben, Mozambique white hunter, tells me that charging lions come on so fast that he does not believe they can be stopped with a rifle if they are not crippled and make a determined charge from within fifty yards. The only sure medicine is a load of heavy buckshot in the last instant.

In India, where many wounded tigers have to be followed up every year, I believe the art of tracking down a wounded dangerous animal is more highly developed than anywhere else. The secret of not coming to grief is never to be surprised. There the trail is followed slowly and carefully. If possible there are two men, one with a heavy rifle and the other with a 12-gauge shotgun charged with buckshot. The "guns" never attempt to trail, but keep their eyes ahead and alert.

If the blood trail goes into a brushy nullah (draw) a man is always sent up a tree to look it over. If he cannot see into it well, he is given a shotgun with birdshot to fire into the thick places so the tiger will betray his presence by growling. The man after a wounded, dangerous animal should remember that his primary mission is to locate the animal and not blunder into it and get himself charged and possibly mauled or killed. Whether the animal is tiger, lion, grizzly bear, or leopard, the first step is to locate the animal within a certain area so that it cannot move without being seen. Then the thing to do is to let the animal make the next move. Either it will come out with the hunter expecting it and ready to shoot, or if it is far gone it will die.

Americans habitually take the most horrible chances with grizzlies, blundering along in heavy willows after infuriated bears and in cover too thick either to fight in or run in. Dangerous animals, even if unwounded, hate to be chivvied around. Often lions will charge even when unwounded if they are pushed out of their cover a couple of times. The San Franciscan, Joe Shaw, was killed by an Angola lion in the late summer of 1962 simply because he and his white hunter followed the lion from cover to cover when the lion wanted to lie up and go to sleep.

Americans who follow up wounded bears should keep in mind the Indian example. Never should they approach dangerous cover without the utmost care. If a spot looks bad they should circle it to see if the bear has come out. If he has not they should throw stones into the cover, shoot into it, and otherwise get the bear to betray his exact location. Never should they attempt to follow an animal at dusk. It is better to wait until the next day. By then the animal may have stiffened up so he can be approached safely—or he may have died.

Once in late afternoon, my old Yukon guide Field Johnson and I waited for a grizzly to come out and feed on berries on a sandbar. When he did so I started shooting and the bear headed for the heavy forest in our general direction. The bear wasn't down and stone dead until I had fired four shots. Just then Field said, "Look at the other bear!" Way out in the bed of the Generc River another bear that had been frightened by the shooting was galloping off. My blood was up and very foolishly I swung ahead of the bear and shot. It went down, then slowly got up and headed into thick willows.

My .30/06 was now empty. I opened the little leather cartridge box I carried at my belt only to discover that I had picked up the wrong one. It was full of .270 cartridges.

Wanting to appear a brave and hardy fellow, I told Field what had happened. "Give me your .30/30," I said, "and we'll go get the bear." The closer I got to where the bear had disappeared, the more foolish I felt. My hair was standing on end and I was devoutly hoping the bear was miles away. Field's brown face was a sickly yellow.

Just then a flock of ptarmigan exploded at our feet. My heart almost stopped beating. I looked at Field and Field looked at me. "Let's come back in the morning!" we both said at once. We did and found the grizzly dead.

Every hunter owes it to the game he hunts to do all he can to avoid wounding it, and if he does inadvertently wound he should do everything he can to follow it up. He also owes it to himself to stay out of trouble. To accomplish this, his best weapons are care and common sense.

10 | *Hunting Mule Deer*

The mule deer got his name because of his outsized ears. These are noticeably larger than those of the whitetail and very much larger than those of such game animals as the mountain sheep, the antelope, and the Rocky Mountain goat. The mule deer is a Westerner which has never ranged east of the Mississippi River, but early explorers found the deer in what is now Nebraska and the Dakotas.

Used to the large conspicuous "fan" which the whitetail deer tosses up when he is frightened, the early explorers saw at once that the mule deer was a different animal. Since he did not have the conspicuous white tail and since the opposite of "whitetail" is "blacktail," they first called the mule deer the blacktail. However, his tail is not black. It is small, black on the tip, and mostly a dingy white like his rump patch. Later explorers ran into the true blacktail deer, which is found west of the summit of the Coast Range on the Pacific Coast. It has a tail that is black on top and about midway in size between that of the whitetail and that of the mule deer. Neither the mule deer nor the blacktail tosses his tail up like the whitetail when he is frightened. Except for the tail, the Columbian blacktail looks just about like the mule deer except that on the average it is smaller. Generally considered nowadays a variety of the mule deer, the blacktail is found from about the latitude of San Francisco north to the coast and islands of Southeast Alaska. Whereas the mule deer is generally found in fairly dry, semi-open country, the blacktail is always found in heavy brush and forest.

In Arizona as late as the 1930's, some hunters swore that there were two kinds of mule deer in the state—the mule deer and the blacktail deer. Since they had heard both terms, they invented deer to fit them. Actually there are two subspecies of mule deer in Arizona—the Rocky Mountain mule deer in the high mountain and plateau country of northern Arizona and the desert mule deer in the south.

The range of the mule deer extends from the Dakotas to southern California and from northwestern Mexico to northern British Columbia, and in the case of the related blacktail, to the Alaska Panhandle. As is the case with any species found over such a wide variety of country and climate, the mule deer varies to some extent in size, in coloration, in habits, and in the type of country where he is found.

I have hunted mule deer on the coastal deserts of Sonora a few feet above sea level. Here it is extremely hot in the summer and very dry. In many desert areas the mule deer get along without open water and obtain all their moisture from dew and from the sap in the browse they eat. I have also hunted mule deer above timberline in Alberta and British Columbia, country of lush feed, of icy streams, of heavy snowfall and bitter cold. I have hunted mule deer on sagebrush flats in northern Arizona and in Wyoming, on open grassy hillsides in Idaho, in semi-open forests of yellow pine, alligator bark, juniper, and oak in Arizona, and in winter range of one-seeded juniper, bitterbrush, and piñon.

Since the mule deer have adapted themselves to many different types of country and many different climates, it is difficult to say just what mule deer country is. Generally speaking, the mule deer likes country that is rougher, more arid, and more open than the country preferred by the whitetail. Throughout most of his range the whitetail shows a decided preference for brush, but mule deer are often found in country almost as open as that in which mountain sheep range. One of the finest mule deer I ever shot was lying beneath a lone juniper in northern Arizona. There was not another tree within a quarter of a mile.

The mule deer isn't as cunning as the whitetail. Seldom will he lie tight while the hunter is walking within a few yards of him, as a whitetail will. Once a whitetail makes up his mind that the immediate neighborhood is unhealthy and he had better leave it, he goes flat out and puts geography behind him with great rapidity. The mule deer, on the other hand, doesn't make up his mind so fast, and even after he moves he is apt to stop for one last look just before he crosses a ridge. I have often stopped fleeing buck mule deer by whistling at them or by yelling.

Because they tend to live in more open country and because they are less wary animals, the mule deer were quickly shot off by market hunters, meat-hunting homesteaders, and even hide hunters when the West was opened up to extensive settlement in the 1870's and 1880's. My own

Jerry O'Connor proudly displays a good desert mule deer he shot in the Rincon Mountains in southern Arizona.

111

maternal grandfather began his ranching career in northern New Mexico in the 1870's. Every time he crossed the line into Trinidad, Colorado, for supplies he took a wagon load of mule deer to trade for flour, beans, molasses, and whatnot. One market hunter I knew used to kill deer for Winslow, Arizona, butcher shops; but he put aside his handsomest bucks to sell to travelers who came through on deluxe Santa Fe trains bound for California. He hung these big bucks in front of the station, each with a red apple in his mouth and with a $50 price tag. The travelers bought them, put them in the express car, and took them on to Los Angeles.

I shot my first mule deer in 1914 when I was twelve years old, and at that time deer were very scarce all over the West. Oldtimers like my grandfather took it for granted that the decrease in deer was natural and that eventually they would be exterminated. Deer were so rare that in the little Arizona town where I grew up, anyone who actually killed a deer was something of a local celebrity.

But the buck law was passed, and eventually hunters began to pay some attention to it. The bag limit was reduced to one buck annually and most hunters began to respect that regulation too. Private and government predatory animal hunters thinned down the mountain lions, those great enemies of the mule deer. Probably the years just before the outbreak of World War I were the low point in mule deer numbers over the West. By 1920 in Arizona the more astute observers began to realize that they were seeing more deer and more deer sign than they had been used to seeing.

The Kaibab National Forest north of the Grand Canyon in Arizona had been set aside as a mule deer preserve under the administration of Theodore Roosevelt. At that time it was badly overgrazed by cattle and the deer had been shot down by Indians and by Mormon settlers, who took so many deer out of that high plateau that they called it Buckskin Mountain. When the reserve was established most of the cattle were moved out and the lions that abounded there were hunted hard. Presently the Forest Service began to report that there were too many deer in the Kaibab and they were destroying their own forage.

The notion that there could be too many deer was to most people at that time as absurd as a statement that a woman could be too beautiful or too virtuous, that air could be too pure, or that an automobile could be too safe. The Forest Service wanted to open the Kaibab to hunting. The state of Arizona opposed it. While officials wrangled, the deer increased and the range deteriorated. The forest was finally opened and has been opened ever since. However, tens of thousands of deer died of starvation during bad winters, and in 1966, a half century after the situation began to be critical on the Kaibab, the range has not completely recovered.

O'Connor congratulates his wife on a big buck she shot on the brakes of the Snake River in Idaho.

The Kaibab was one of the first and the best known of the mule deer explosions in the West. Since that time the animals have become too plentiful in many areas, and when this happens game departments try to get hunters in to take off the surplus by long seasons and generous bag limits. In Idaho there are usually a good many two-deer areas, and at various times Colorado has allowed the taking of three mule deer in one season. The deer are very prolific, as healthy does produce two fawns a year. As this is written, Wyoming and Montana have for several years had special licenses for deer—$20 or $25, whereas the general big-game license is $100. In addition, these states do not require a nonresident to hunt with a guide.

In some areas it is practical to combine a hunt for antelope with one for mule deer. In others mule deer and elk can be taken in the same territory. Generally, though, the best elk country is seldom good mule deer country, as the individual elk eats much more than deer, is larger, stronger, and can browse higher.

Mule deer can be still-hunted on foot, and in very rough or very brushy country this is the most successful means. I have had more fun hunting mule deer on horseback in semi-open country such as the winter range of the Kaibab than any other way. In many areas the hunter can ride along trails until the buck he wants jumps out. Then he can get off his horse and smoke him up. In some parts of Wyoming there are many mule deer in the brushy coulees and they often run out onto open sagebrush plains. There the use of a 4-wheel drive vehicle like the famous Jeep is entirely practical. Jeep hunting is also done in the rolling winter range when snow drives the deer down in some parts of Colorado. I have even hunted mule deer from boats on the Snake River. The boat hunter cruises up and down the river until deer are spotted. Then the boat is beached, and he jumps out and opens up.

A big buck mule deer has the largest and handsomest head of any North American deer. The typical head is dichotomous (which means that it is evenly branched—and not with all the points coming off of one main beam like the antlers of the whitetail). In the West it is the custom among the native hunters to count the points on one side and not to count the brow tine or eye-guard, which is smaller in mule deer antlers than in whitetails and sometimes is absent altogether. What a Westerner would call a 4-pointer would be a 10-pointer in the East.

The best mule deer heads come from areas where the soil is impregnated with bone-building minerals. Arizona's North Kaibab, a plateau composed of limestone, has produced some tremendous heads. The Canadian Rockies are largely limestone and have produced some very fine mule deer heads as well as excellent sheep heads. First class heads have come from Idaho, New Mexico, Colorado, Washington, Wyoming, Montana, and the Mexican states of Chihuahua and Sonora. The present (1966) record typical mule deer was shot in Wyoming. Who shot it and when no one knows. The present non-typical record mule deer head is from Alberta and was shot in 1926. However, the Nos. 2, 3, and 4 were all taken in the 1960's.

In order to grow an exceptional set of antlers a mule deer needs not only plenty of food rich in minerals but plenty of time. It is rare that fine heads come from heavily hunted country where bucks are shot off the moment they grow antlers conspicuous enough to see 100 yards away. At one time many bucks with handsome antlers were taken in the lava bed country of northern California, but for a generation now hordes of hunters have shot off anything that showed an antler. Bucks simply have not been allowed to mature.

The antlers of the mule deer reach their greatest size in the typical form when the buck is from six to eight years old. After that the antlers generally begin to freak. Sometimes they grow many points. Sometimes they flatten or "palmate," and such antlers are responsible for the stories one hears of crosses of mule deer with moose or caribou. Often the bases of the antlers get very rough and warty.

To me the handsomest and most spectacular heads are those with wide spreads and many points. In the early days of Kaibab hunting in the 1920's many such sets of antlers were taken. I saw one such Kaibab head in Kanab, Utah, that had a spread of 45 inches. The widest spread I have ever got was 37½ inches, the longest beam 29¾ inches, but the head was narrow and rather homely. One of the handsomest heads I have ever taken was shot on the Salmon River in Idaho. It is now in my trophy room. It has 8 points on each side and the spread is 34½ inches. The best desert mule deer head I have ever collected was shot in December, 1941, on the coastal desert of Sonora. It is a very handsome and massive head with 7 points on one side and 6 on the other.

Buck mule deer that grow these exceptional heads are not stupid. When the hunting season is on they head for country that is not overrun with hunters and they lie up where it is almost impossible to approach them without being seen. Since they often bed down for the day just under rimrocks, these wise old bucks are often called "rimrockers." They are hard to get at. The hunter who tries to approach them from below is quickly seen. The buck will slip out, find a notch in the rimrock, and go over the top. The hunter who tries to approach these smart old bucks by hunting at their level around under the rim through the brush that usually grows there makes too much noise, and if he gets a shot at an old rimrocker it is usually a snap-shot at a vanishing rear end.

I have successfully hunted deer like this two different ways. One, if the terrain permits, is to ride or walk from 200 to 300 yards below where the rimrock joins the talus slope. I go 100 yards or so, then stop to look and glass. Generally the mule deer isn't as cool as the whitetail. This business of stopping makes him nervous, as he thinks he has been seen. He'll then get up and try to sneak off. With luck the hunter can see him and go into action.

Another good way to collect one of these old bucks is to hunt from above. The deer usually lie down in spots where they can look through thin brush, where they can see but are not apt to be seen. They think of danger as coming from below but not from above. Often they are in plain sight of a man above them. If the hunter is in such a position that he can see anything that moves over a considerable area, he can often push old rimrockers out of their beds by dropping stones. Any deer (even a smart Arizona whitetail) can take just about so much of the racket. When their nerves are shot the real smart bucks try to sneak out, but some simply panic and run for it.

Another spot greatly favored by smart old bucks is the end of a

On these open grassy ridges above the Snake River there are many mule deer.

wooded point. They like to lie down there just inside the brush or timber so they can see anything below them and generally smell anything below on the rising air of the warm hours. They can usually hear anything coming down the point toward them through the brush or timber. Then they simply fade away. One stunt practiced by smart old bucks is to start

116

off a point on one side, then go around the point in the brush or timber
and escape on the opposite side. I remember one old northern Arizona
buck that pulled this little stunt on me twice on the same point. I'd catch
a glimpse of him as he took off to my left. I thought the natural thing for
a buck to do would be to go straight off the point, but I found from his
tracks that he had circled the point, had got back of me, and had thus
escaped. Twice I followed him hoping for a shot. The third time I ran to
my right, stopped on a trail on the other side of the point and waited. In
a few seconds he came trotting quietly along right toward me.

The smart old bucks will almost always stay in high, rough country
much later than will the does, fawns, and young bucks. They do not come
down into lower, softer, and easier country until snow pushes them out.
On the Mogollon Rim in Arizona the old buck mule deer used to stay
high in snow that would drive bull elk down to the low juniper flats.

Except during the rut, old bucks do not associate with the does. Often
I have seen a little spike or forkhorn buck of the vintage of the year
before still running with his mother and her current fawns. But before
the rut mature bucks are generally found in small groups—two or three.
The association of a young buck with an old one is quite common. Many
times very old, very large bucks live all alone just as old mountain rams
sometimes do. One of the best bucks I have ever shot was an old solitary,
blind in one eye. I knocked him over during the Thanksgiving weekend
when the rut among the Rocky Mountain mule deer of northern Arizona
was in full swing. He was so old, however, that he had apparently lost his
interest in does. His neck had not swelled and his venison was sweet and
so tender you could just about cut it with a fork. This was the buck with
the 29¾-inch beam I have mentioned before.

Another very fine loner, one with a magnificent head with a 37½-inch
spread, was lying by himself on a steep open hillside under an isolated
juniper. I doubt if I would have seen him, as I had thought of this almost-
bare hillside as being too open for deer. I tied my horse on top of the
ridge above him and about 300 yards away, ate my lunch, smoked a
cigarette, glassed the whole country except the ground beneath that
juniper. Then I untied my horse and started to lead him down that steep
hillside. Apparently that old buck had been getting more and more
nervous, and when I started down the hill he couldn't stand it any more.
Out he came. I opened up on him and rolled him over on the second or
third shot.

Often in the winter when deer are concentrated in the low country by
the snow, several bucks will be seen together. But why they should gang
up in good weather before the rut I have no idea. Nevertheless it happens
sometimes. The largest herd composed entirely of bucks I ever saw was
near Slate Mountain northwest of Flagstaff, Arizona. This is beautiful

O'Connor with a good trophy mule deer shot in northern Arizona in the early 1930's. This buck had a 37½-inch spread.

and interesting country. All of it is of volcanic origin. The San Francisco Peaks a few miles to the east are what was left of a tremendous volcano and so are the other high mountains in the area.

The hills that dot the area are all cinder cones. Ancient yellow pines with red boles and whispering needles grow among the cinders and lava but mostly the country is spotted with junipers. There are stands of cliff rose and open grassy meadows where antelope ran. The country slants off north toward the Grand Canyon, and from any of the cinder hills a deer hunter could see the crimson slash of the great canyon topped with the purple timber of the North Rim.

I had been out there alone a few days before and had seen one very fine buck that had faded from view before I could shoot. The next time I came back I took my wife with me. As we drove across an open park we saw a herd of perhaps fifteen or twenty antelope wheeling across the yellow grass as light and swift as a flock of birds.

My wife is one of the best game-seers I have ever known. Quietly she said: "I see three bucks. They just ran into the draw over by the cinder hill." Since I was watching the antelope then I thought she meant she had seen three buck antelope.

I drove on west past the draw, which ran north and south along the eastern side of a cinder cone about 400 feet high. I stopped the car. My wife and I got out, rifles in hand. I slammed the door.

"Look," said my wife, "there are those bucks I saw and some more!"

I glanced to the right and my astonished eyes saw a herd of about thirty big bucks running up and around the cinder cone. They were so close together that with their forest of antlers they reminded me of movies I had seen of herds of migrating caribou.

I thought that if we could get to the top of the cinder cone we would get a shot. I yelled for my wife to follow me and took off. It was about a 400-yard run to the top. When I stopped just under the crest my chest was heaving and my heart was about to jump out of my mouth. I paused for a few seconds to get my wind back, turned and motioned for Eleanor to join me. She had run out of gas about 100 yards below me and she shook her head.

Cautiously I walked the next few yards to the crest. The minute I stuck my head over, two superb bucks took off below me, traveling in those long, rubbery bounds mule deer often use when they are surprised or when they are going down hill. My chest was still heaving but I had no choice but to sit down and open up with my .30/06. At the foot of the hill there was a dense little thicket of oak, pine, cliff rose, and juniper. Two bucks went in but only one came out.

The one I had nailed with my .30/06 was a big mature buck with a large but not particularly exceptional head. I had a tough time getting

This mule deer has horns in velvet. It was an exceedingly large one. The picture was taken many years ago in the Kaibab of northern Arizona.

him loaded into the car. When we got home I strung him up in the garage, skinned him, quartered him, and after I had let the quarters age in the cool shade for a few days I took them down to the cold-storage plant. The four quarters weighed, with about one-third of one ham cut away to get rid of bloodshot meat, 176 pounds. I believe this is the heaviest deer I have ever shot. I believe he would have weighed somewhere between 225 and 250 pounds field dressed and not far from 300 on the hoof.

With more and more hunters taking fall trips and extending their gunning experience a bit, I get a good many questions about the suitability of various cartridges for mule deer. Apparently the word has got around that mule deer are large, tough, and hard to knock off.

The mule deer averages larger than the whitetail, but from all I can find out the largest mule deer are no heavier than the biggest whitetails found in Maine, Michigan, and favored localities elsewhere. The heaviest mule deer I have any authentic dope on weigh, field dressed, from about 300 to possibly 350 pounds. But deer that large are very rare exceptions. I have never killed a buck anywhere near that heavy. I once saw an enormous buck shot by another hunter that I am sure was a good deal heavier than the largest I ever shot. It may have dressed out at over 300 pounds, but it was not weighed. The two heaviest bucks I ever killed weighed about 175 in the quarters, and that would give them a field-dressed weight, I imagine, of somewhere between 225 and 250.

I have seen many mule deer weighed, and I have never hunted in an area where a 175-pound buck wasn't a good big buck, and a buck that went 200–225 wasn't an exceptionally big buck. The last large mule deer I shot was a good one. He weighed 189 pounds field dressed. I have heard rumors of bucks that field dressed at over 400 pounds. If such creatures exist, they must be very rare. I have checked up on many stories of such monsters, but when I get specific information it always turns out that the weights were estimated.

However, there isn't any doubt that the average mule deer is larger than the average whitetail. Some subspecies of whitetail will run heavier than some subspecies of mule deer, but for the most part the mule deer is the larger animal.

The mule deer is also generally shot at longer ranges than whitetails. Over most of the whitetail country of North America, the average shot is under 100 yards, since whitetails usually like thick cover. The mule deer as we have seen is generally found in more open country and a typical shot at one is across a canyon.

In Idaho, in the canyons of the Snake and Salmon rivers, mule deer are commonly seen on grassy, open hillsides, and I have picked them up with binoculars at over a mile away. I believe the longest shot I ever made on a mule deer was with a scope-sighted .270 on a hill overlooking the Salmon. That buck must have been around 400 yards away.

Rifles and Cartridges for Mule Deer

The smallest cartridge I ever used on mule deer was the .22 Long Rifle. With it I have bushwhacked a few deer for meat in Mexico. The most powerful rifles I have ever used on them have been the .300 Weatherby Magnum with a 150-grain bullet at about 3,350 and a .35 Whelen with the 250-grain bullet at about 2,450. I wouldn't take an oath on it, but I believe that I have shot more mule deer with a .30/06 than with any other caliber, but besides those I've mentioned I have used a .250/3000 Savage, a .30/30, a .35 Remington, a .256 Newton, a .32/40. I have shot almost as many mule deer with the .270 as I have with the .30/06.

Probably more mule deer have been killed with .30/30's than with rifles of any other caliber, and properly used at moderate range by good shots the .30/30 is plenty of rifle. However, the .30/30 has also wounded more deer than any other cartridge.

It has been my experience that the .30/30 is generally used by two classes of hunters. In the hands of those who knew the country, knew how to get fairly close to game, and who were good shots, the .30/30 was entirely adequate for deer. I have seen many deer killed by .30/30's, and with good shots at ranges up to 200 yards or so, the deer never got far.

But because the .30/30 was the first popular and successful smokeless-powder cartridge, because ".30/30" was almost synonymous with the term "deer rifle," and because there were tens of thousands of old .30/30's in the West, rifles and carbines of that caliber were often used by poor shots and poor hunters. They didn't know the limitations of their rifles, didn't know how to sight a rifle in, didn't know how to assume a steady position, and never did any shooting except during deer season. In the hands of such persons, .30/30's wounded more deer than they killed and got a bad reputation among the more knowledgeable riflemen. On dozens of occasions I have seen .30/30 hunters standing on their hind legs and blasting away at deer 500 and 600 yards away. If the animals were wounded, most of the fault lay in the hunters, not in the cartridges.

I wouldn't advise anyone to buy a .30/30 as a mule-deer rifle today, since there are many more suitable cartridges. I have probably killed more mule deer at over 200 yards than under, and even out at 200 yards, the .30/30 is losing much of its authority. Most .30/30's I have seen in the field are sighted in for about 100 yards, and the 170-grain bullet will drop about 30 inches at 300. This is probably the reason the .30/30 has such a reputation as a leg breaker.

At 200 yards the velocity of the 170-grain .30/30 bullet has fallen off to 1,630, and at 300 yards it is 1,410. At these velocities, most .30/30 bullets do not open fast enough to produce enough shock to put an animal down with poor shot placement. It is exceptional when any bullet kills an animal in his tracks with a gut shot, but the faster-stepping bullets sometimes actually do kill and will often knock an animal down and keep him there until the hunter can get up for a finisher. The .30/30 and other rifles of its class seldom do, particularly at ranges at which mule deer are shot in the West.

I remember one time many years ago when I was hunting mule deer with a .30/30. I came over a ridge just as a big buck walked between a couple of big yellow pines and stopped with his head and chest behind a massive tree trunk. I was excited and impatient. I should have waited until the buck exposed his chest, but I was too jittery. Aiming as close to the tree trunk as I dared, I cut loose. Off went the buck. I missed it on the second shot. I spent several hours trailing that gut-shot buck. I blamed the .30/30. I should have blamed myself.

The mule deer is the principal big-game animal of Arizona, the state where I was born and where I was always hunting something until I moved away in 1948. It is likewise the most numerous game animal in all the Western states. For many years, more .30/30 rifles were in use in Arizona than any other caliber, but there were also quite a few .25/35's and .32 Specials. Old Krags in .30/40 were likewise popular because, for many years, they could be purchased from the army through the National Rifle Association for about $3.50. During the 1920's and 1930's, a great many .30/06 rifles began to appear in the hunting country. Some of these were Remington Model 30's and Winchester Model 54's, and later Model 70's, but a great many were 1903 Springfields which could be bought through the N. R. A. for about $30, in the case of the regular military rifle, to between $40 and $50 for the famous N. R. A. sporter, a rifle with gilt-edge sporter barrel, a sporter stock, and a Lyman 48 receiver sight. The best shots in the state were the hep characters who did some hand-loading, belonged to civilian rifle clubs, and who hunted with those N. R. A. sporters.

After the middle 20's, the Model 99 Savage in .300 Savage caliber began to appear in the mule-deer country, along with an increasing number of 270's. Oddly, 7 × 57 Mausers were often seen and had an excellent reputation when used with the now-obsolete Western 139-grain open-point bullet. The .250/3000 had a following in those days, and later the .257 also did.

As early as 1930, a few daring souls started putting telescope sights on mule-deer rifles. However, scopes were few and far between until Bill Weaver brought out his Model 330 along in the late 1930's. In 1931, I hunted mule deer in the Kaibab National Forest north of the Grand Canyon. There were two Californians in our camp. One of them was Clark Gable and the other some citizen who had a Springfield with a telescope sight. He attracted far more attention than the movie star. Within a few years, however, scopes began to be common.

Since 1948 I have lived in Idaho, where there is a large mule-deer herd. From what I've seen, I'd say that the .30/30 is still the most popular deer cartridge among those who are not rifle nuts and who live back in the hills. With town dwellers, particularly those who reload and have considerable interest in the rifle, the .30/06 is No. 1. So far as store-bought rifles go, the .270 is probably second in popularity to the .30/06, but within the past few years a good many .308's and .243's have appeared in the hunting country. High-velocity enthusiasts have bought many .300 Weatherby Magnums, and there is considerable interest in the new .264 Winchester and the 7 mm. Remington Magnum. For whatever the reason, the excellent .280 Remington has not become popular. All over the West, the scope sight is now just about standard. I would guess that at least 75 percent of the more expensive factory big-game rifles are equipped with scopes within months after purchase.

Because mule deer are so often shot at fairly long range and are hunted for the most part in hills and canyons and often from horseback, the ideal rifle for use on them is quite different from the proper weapon for the whitetails of the Eastern brush and forest. The ideal weight seems to be about eight pounds with scope sight. A twenty-two-inch barrel is a good compromise for carrying on foot and in a saddle scabbard. A 4X scope is about right. It combines good enough definition so that antlers can be seen at considerable distance, and yet such a scope has a wide enough field so that it can be used for fast-running shooting. I prefer such a scope on a good solid top mount such as the Redfield Jr., the Buehler, or the Weaver top mount.

I am a bolt-action man myself, partly because I cut my eye-teeth on the old Model 1903 Springfield, partly because I am a handloader, and partly because, generally, a good tuned-up bolt-action rifle gives a bit better accuracy than rifles of any other type.

However, those who like other actions have a wide choice—the Remington Model 760 pump action, the Remington Model 742 and Winchester Model 100 semiautomatics, the Savage Model 99 and Winchester Model 88 lever actions.

Flat trajectory is a necessity for the open-country rifle, and for that reason the mule-deer cartridge should have a muzzle velocity of at least 2,700 foot-seconds. Bullets should have reasonably good sectional density and should weigh at least 100 grains in .24 and .25 calibers, at least 120 grains in 7 mm., .280, .270, and .284 calibers, at least 150 grains in .30

caliber. Bullets of inferior sectional density lose their velocity quickly and give poor penetration.

The average mule deer isn't a big animal. The largest bucks, as we have seen, put on considerable venison, but the average young buck or doe probably won't weigh much more than 140–150 pounds. I have had to follow up many well-hit mule deer in the past because some of the bullets I have used, particularly in the .30/06 in the old days, didn't open up fast enough. My own experience has been that I get quicker kills with the lighter, faster bullets—the 150-grain in the .30/06, the 130-grain in the .270, the 139-grain in the 7 mm., the 100-grain in the .257. I have shot enough deer with both the 150- and the 180-grain bullets in the .30/06 to know that the 150 grain gives a far higher percentage of instant kills.

The bullet that expands quickly on impact has another very real advantage in that, when hit with one, an animal almost always shows plainly that it is hit. It sags, stumbles, falls, gives a perceptible flinch, whereas the animal hit with a slow-opening bullet often gives no immediate sign of being hit, even with a well-placed shot.

Some years ago I took a poke at a small buck mule deer on the Snake River. I was using a .270 sighted in for elk with a famous, controlled-expanding 150-grain bullet. The buck appeared to be something over 300 yards away, so from prone position I held the horizontal crosswire even with the top of his shoulder. The buck gave not the slightest sign of being hit. I was about to shoot again when it went down. Out at over 300 yards where the velocity has fallen off, a bullet expands much less violently than it does at 100 or even 200, and a bullet that does well at short range often opens up too slowly out yonder.

Because of these longish ranges, the rifle should be sighted in for mule deer for the longest possible range that will not cause midrange misses. That means the bullet should strike about 3 inches high at 100 yards. So sighted, the .270 with the 130-grain bullet, the .280 Remington and the .284 Winchester with 125-grain bullets, the .264 with the 140-grain, the .300 H. & H. Magnum with the 150-grain, the .300 Weatherby Magnum with the 180-grain, will strike the point of aim at about 275 yards, and a dead-on, center-of-the-chest hold will get venison to over 300.

With the same sighting, the .30/06 and .308 with 150-grain bullets, the .257 and the .243 with 100-grain bullets, and the 7 mm. with the 139-grain bullet are on at between 240 and 250 yards.

The .300 Savage with the 150-grain bullet and the .30/06 and .308 with the 180-grain bullets are on at from 200 to 225 yards.

All of these figures are approximate, plus or minus an inch or two, depending on variations in powder charge, on barrel length, and on the height of the scope above line of bore.

As a final tip on mule-deer shooting, I'd say that with a rifle so sighted for maximum range, the smart thing to do, even though the deer appears to be way out yonder, is to hold dead on for the first shot. Most people tend to overestimate rather than underestimate range, and I have missed more deer by overshooting than by undershooting.

11 | *Rifles for the Brush*

I saw the buck as I was plodding back to camp late one winter afternoon in northern Mexico. A long and unsuccessful day on a sheep mountain had left me weary and heavy-footed, but the moment my eye caught a vague movement on the other side of an ironwood tree about seventy-five yards away I began to perk up. The shadowy form shaped itself into a desert buck with antlers that looked as if they carried five points to the side.

He was facing toward me as he browsed, but since there wasn't much cover I was afraid to try to sneak around the tree to get a clear shot. The best stunt seemed to be to take a crack at him from where I was. I picked a thin place in the brush, and squeezed one off.

As luck would have it, the 150-grain Remington Bronze Point bullet hit a limb of the tree just in front of the buck, cut it off cleanly, and dropped a fork right across the old boy's shoulders. The bucking exhibition he gave trying to get rid of it would have shamed a rodeo horse. I couldn't shoot again for laughing, and for all I know that deer's still running.

I didn't need the buck very badly, and his capers struck me as funny. But what brush can do when it gets in the way of a bullet that's headed for a hunk of big game can sometimes be very unfunny.

One hot day in Africa, Syd Downey, Myles Turner, and I were stalking a greater kudu bull—the beautiful big, gray antelope with spiral horns that's considered by many to be Africa's finest trophy and one of

127

the hardest to come by. The bull moved, came toward us through the brush, and stopped about 100 yards away. All I could see was his head; his body was concealed by at least twenty yards of thin, hard-limbed brush. He was eyeing us suspiciously as we crouched on the ground.

Resting the .300 Weatherby Magnum for a steady hold, I put the intersection of the crosswires where I figured his shoulder should be, and cut loose. He jumped as if someone had stuck a pin in him, whirled, and was gone. At dawn a couple of days later, I caught an even bigger bull out in an open field and popped him. But I still remember my bitter disappointment at that muffed first chance.

The deflection of bullets by limbs, twigs, and even blades of grass is something which has plagued hunters for years. Deflection was a problem even in the days of blunt, heavy, lead bullets. As velocities have risen and bullets have tended to become lighter and sharper pointed, the problem has become more serious.

My grandfather, a Kentuckian who migrated to the Rocky Mountains in the 1870's largely because of the excellent hunting there, used to tell me how he missed a mountain lion he'd carefully stalked because his bullet struck a small branch on its way. His rifle was an old Model 1876 Winchester, but what caliber it was I can't say. All the Model 1876 rifles, however, were chambered for cartridges firing heavy bullets at low velocity.

The lion that got away wasn't the first animal to be saved from a bullet by a branch or twig, nor was he the last. Daniel Boone no doubt used the deflection alibi many times, and our great-grandchildren will do the same.

I've done a good deal of experimenting to find out what factors contribute to bullet deflection. I put up a target behind brush thin enough so it can be seen, then shoot at it with bullets of various weights and shapes and driven at various velocities. I've shot everything from spire-point .22 caliber bullets at velocities around 4,000 feet per second, to rifled slugs and .38 Special wadcutters. I've tried shooting 100-grain .270 bullets through brush, and also 500-grain full-jacketed bullets from the potent .458 Winchester.

Among the more important factors contributing to bullet deflection are the shape of the bullet, its weight, velocity, construction, and spin.

The shape of the bullet's point is exceedingly important. The sharp, or spitzer, point is the most efficient at minimizing velocity loss in long-range shooting. Most bullets loaded in high-velocity cartridges are spitzer or semi-spitzer in shape. But this same sharp point is the worst possible form for getting through brush. The blunt point of the old-fashioned soft-nose bullet is a far better deal, and the nearer the point comes to being flat, the better.

A friend of mine, who used to do a lot of elk hunting in jackpine country, swore by flat-pointed bullets for his old .33 Winchester. When he could get them, he preferred the full-metal-case, or solid, bullets. With those, he said, he didn't have to pay any attention at all to intervening brush and limbs. The half-brother of the .33, the .348, likewise had a fine reputation as a brush cartridge.

After doing a lot of experimental shooting through brush, I've concluded that a heavy bullet absolutely flat and square on the point would be about the best possible form for this use. Shooting with wad-cutters in a .38 Special seems to bear me out. Many African elephant hunters who have to drive bullets through several inches of spongy bone to reach the brain are of the same opinion.

It takes no genius to understand why the heavier bullet is more likely to plow through obstacles without turning aside. A 200-grain bullet, all things being equal, is more reliable in the brush than one weighing half as much.

High velocity is desirable for long-range shooting since it is indispensable for flat trajectory. For brush and forest shooting, high velocity is a handicap because the faster a bullet is moving the more likely it is to deflect if it strikes something. I'll string along with those who like the quick kills given by relatively light, fast-moving bullets for deer-size animals. But a deer has to be hit before he's killed, and the light, fast-stepping bullet is not exactly ideal in the brush.

A velocity of 2,400 to 2,500 feet per second gives as flat a trajectory as anyone could possibly need for brush and semiopen forest. Even 2,200 feet per second at the muzzle gives a sufficiently flat trajectory for forest shooting. An iron-sighted .30/30 sighted to put the 170-grain bullet 2 inches high at 100 yards is at point of aim at 150 yards and only 4 inches low at 200. That trajectory is plenty flat for forest and jungle use, and even satisfactory for the open bush of East Africa where a 200-yard shot is a long one.

The 220-grain .30/06 bullet, the 300-grain .375 Magnum bullet, or the 175-grain 7 × 57 Mauser bullets are on at around 175 yards and only slightly low at 200 yards when sighted to print 2 inches above iron sights at 100. Nice thing is that bullets moving at below 2,500 feet per second are less likely to deflect than those going faster.

Stoutly constructed bullets properly shaped hang together and stay on course through brush better than more fragile ones. It's not uncommon to have a bullet with a soft jacket and a soft lead core arrive at the target in two or more pieces—even though its shape may be good and its velocity not excessive. Once years ago I loaded some 170-grain soft-point .30/30 bullets in .30/06 cases to give about 2,600 feet per second. That was too much speed for bullets designed to expand at 2,200. One such bullet I shot at a buck through brush broke on a small limb and hit the animal in two pieces. Another was so well opened up when it hit a mule deer that the entrance hole was about three-quarters of an inch wide.

I've mentioned the chap who hunted elk in heavy timber with full-metal-case .33 Winchester bullets. I've known other cool, careful shots to shoot full-jacketed round-nosed bullets on all game in the brush in 7 mm. Mausers and .30/40 Krags. This is illegal in many states. The old Peters belted bullet with its strong construction and flat nose was fine for brush, and so is the Remington soft-point Core-Lokt bullet.

The more stable a bullet is—the nearer its center of gravity to the center of the bullet—the better it is in the brush. A short, sharp-pointed bullet—the .30-caliber 150-grain Remington Bronze Point and others like it—is an unstable form and easily turned from its course. In brush it will glance away from a twig, and after it strikes flesh it will tumble and dart hither and yon instead of following a straight course to the vitals. Before World War II I did a lot of jackrabbit shooting in southern Arizona with a 2-R Lovell, and one of my loads was a 45-grain spire-point bullet that traveled about 3,150 feet per second. I've often seen that bullet deflected from its course by blades of grass. Once I took a crack at a coyote standing behind a prickly pear cactus. The speedy little bullet blew up on one of the flat, moisture-filled leaves and apparently showered the coyote with bits of lead and fragments of jacket. He took off so fast he whizzed.

I've always felt that spin had a good deal to do with bullet deflection. A spinning bullet should show the same tendency to fly away from an object in the direction of the spin as a billiard ball does. The bullets for old black-powder arms were short, blunt, and heavy, but perhaps one of the principal reasons they got through brush well was that their rate of spin was relatively slow. The rifled slug for shotguns doesn't spin at all but flies point on because it is heavier in front. Because of its shape, weight, and *lack of spin,* it is one of the best of all missiles at close range in brush.

Factors which contribute to bullet deflection, then, are sharp points, fragile construction, high velocity, unstable form, high rate of spin, and light weight. Factors which contribute to the reliability of bullets in brush are blunt or flat points, moderate velocity, strong construction, stable form, and slow spin.

With this in mind, it's easy to see that bullets designed for varmints and for long-range, big-game shooting are about the worst possible for woods shooting. Unless the hunter can find a hole to shoot through, light varmint bullets like those for the .222 Remington and the .22/250 are worthless in brush, and high-speed, big-game bullets like the 130-grain for the .270 or the 150-grain for the .30/06 or .300 Magnum leave a great deal to be desired.

A hunter who may have to shoot through brush to put a bullet where he wants it should use the slower and heavier bullets available to him. In the .30/06, the 220-grain bullet is more reliable in brush than the 150- and 180-grain bullets; the 150-grain factory-loaded soft-point at about 2,800 feet per second is better in the .270 than the 130-grain. Likewise, 180-grain bullets are the best bets in the .300 Savage and .308; the 117-grain in the .257. The handloader can name his own medicine in bullet weight, shape, and velocity.

But even relatively slow, heavy, and ruggedly constructed round-nose bullets will deflect. I remember taking a crack at a lesser kudu bull in the brush of Kenya's northern frontier district. I don't believe he was forty yards from me, maybe not over thirty. I could see his shadowy form through the brush, and the ivory tips of his horns above it. This time I had the .300 Weatherby stuffed with 20-grain Remington soft-point Core-Lokt bullets which I had loaded to about 2,700 feet per second. I felt that this big, rugged bullet should be able to plow through the brush and get to the kudu. It did, but when I examined the animal I discovered that the bullet had deflected so badly that it had keyholed or turned sideways, when it struck. Since bullets tumbling over and over in air or traveling sidewise aren't to be recommended for accuracy, I probably would have missed the kudu entirely if it had been much farther away. Some bullets are better in brush than others, but all will deflect—even the 300-grain bullet for the .375 Magnum.

A man who does most of his hunting in jungle, forest, or brush will do well to pick a rifle using cartridges with fairly heavy bullets at moderate velocity. The good old .30/30 with its 170-grain bullet at 2,200 feet per second isn't a bad brush rifle, and the .35 Remington throwing a 200-grain bullet at the same velocity has been so satisfactory that it simply refuses to die. The 200- and 250-grain bullets in the .348 Winchester also did well in brush, and the .444 Marlin with its 240-grain bullet should likewise be excellent.

The now obsolete .35 and .405 Winchesters that used 250- and 300-grain bullets, respectively, were favorites for brush hunting of elk and big bears. Some brush hunters used to swear by the .401 Winchester self-loading cartridge, now also obsolete. The .375 Magnum with 270- and 300-grain bullets is good in brush, but of course the big Magnum is unnecessarily severe for anything in the deer class. With its 250- and 300-grain bullets the .338 Winchester is in the same class as the .375.

But, alas, there's no such thing as a perfect brush cartridge. At least I've never seen one. Even the round-nosed, heavy, and relatively slow .35 Remington bullet will show a good deal of deflection and evidence of keyholing when shot through brush. So will the 300-grain bullet of the .375 Magnum. A 220-grain .30-caliber bullet is far better than the 150-

grain bullet of the same caliber in getting to the target in a relatively straight line, but as my experience with the lesser kudu shows, even that bullet can do some plain and fancy departing from line of aim.

So about all a brush hunter can do is use the most suitable bullet for his rifle, one that's round or flat nosed, strongly constructed, and moderate in velocity. Even then he should try to pick a hole in the brush. If he can't, he'd better mutter a small incantation to the Red Gods and hope for the best. Of all the alibis for missing game, the one that blames the brush for deflecting the bullet is still the best I know of.

12 | *The Art of Sheep Hunting*

My first sheep hunt was a complete victory—for the sheep. It took place in the early 1930's in a rugged limestone range in the northwestern Mexican state of Sonora. The range was called in Spanish the Sierra del Viejo—or the mountain of the old man. As it turned out the name was highly appropriate because the experience aged me considerably.

The range was not particularly high. I doubt if the loftiest peak is over 3,500 feet above the Gulf of California, which I could see about forty miles to the west. It is cut with sharp ridges, precipitous canyons, and it is solid limestone eroded until it is as sharp as a coarse file. At a distance the range looks gray and bare but actually it has considerable desert growth—cacti in various forms, a dwarf tree called the torrote prieto, which looks and smells like a diminutive pepper tree. There is another odd plant there called by the Mexicans the sangren grado. When it is broken the white sap turns black in the sun like silver nitrate and the plant is supposed to be a cure for all manner of odd and loathsome diseases.

With its gray rocks, its shouldering cliffs, and its outlandish plants, the Sierra Viejo looks like the surface of some other planet. But it is sheep country. Two companions and I had stopped at the last water, a ranch called Pozo Ascerno, where a blindfolded burro traveling in endless, patient circles pulled rawhide buckets of cool, clean water from a

133

Bill Rae, editor of *Outdoor Life* (right), with guide and very heavy Dall ram shot in the Yukon.

deep well. A vaquero there told us he had seen sheep in the sierra only a few days before.

The three of us were novice sheep hunters. Although we fancied ourselves skillful deer hunters we had neither seen nor hunted sheep. We were young, tough, reasonably good shots, and used to climbing. We got to the foot of the mountain just before sundown and set up our cots under a dilapidated shed at an abandoned mine. The next morning we divided the range between us, split up, and began our climbs.

Rain had fallen a couple of days before and I wasn't far up the mountain when I saw my first sheep tracks. They were larger than those of the deer and more blunt. I found droppings that had been made within twenty-four hours.

The sign raised my blood pressure. I fancied that I had but to top the first ridge and I'd see sheep in the next canyon. At that time, in my innocence, I imagined that hunting sheep was something like hunting deer, and that presently a ram would come bursting out of some of the thin brush in the little draws.

All that morning I continued to encounter sign. I climbed clear to the

134

highest ridge. From it I could see the blue Gulf beyond Puerto Libertad fringed with little red hills, which I later found were also sheep country. I could see thousands of square miles of flat desert, gray and brown, threaded with white arroyos. Thrust up from the desert floor were other sheep ranges like the one on which I stood.

I worked north along the ridge. Now and then I paused to hurl stones into the head of some canyon under the impression that I could by that means spook out a ram. I saw sign, droppings, big blunt ram tracks in the occasional patches of soil. Now and then in a saddle I'd see where sheep had pawed out beds. Droppings were sprinkled around and some of the tracks looked quite fresh.

But hour after hour passed and I saw no sheep. It was wintertime, but down in Sonora the sun can be hot even in December. My wool shirt made me itch and sweat and now and then I'd stop to take a drink from my canteen. Around 1 o'clock I stopped by the mouth of a little cave just under the ridge. I ate my sandwich, took a few more sips of water. There was a lot of sheep sign about and presently I noticed that the floor of the cave was deep in dung. This was the first time I had realized that when caves are available sheep go into them to stay dry, keep cool, or to get out of a chill wind.

Then along about 3:30 my heart jumped right out of my mouth. On a ridge about a half-mile away, three animals were silhouetted against the skyline. They could be nothing but sheep. In my innocence I had no binoculars, but I did have a German 4-power scope on my rifle. I got them in it. They were sheep, all right—and rams. I could see the curl of their horns against the sky.

I looked at them with interest and they looked at me with interest. In fact they seemed content to look at me as long as I looked at them.

The thing to do, I knew, was to stalk them. Sheep and I were on the right side of the main ridge. I decided to cross the ridge, work along it out of sight and in the direction of the sheep. Then I'd come over the ridge. They should then be about 200 yards away from me.

Heart pounding, I executed the stalk, but when I poked my head over I saw no sheep. This was an odd circumstance, but they were nowhere in sight. An hour later I saw them again. Once more they were on a ridge. Once more they were about a half-mile away. Once more they looked at me with vast interest.

Dusk had fallen by the time I got back to camp. All of us had seen sheep. We'd had a little bad luck, we thought, but tomorrow it would be different. We hunted two more days. Each day we saw sheep. Always they were on the top of a ridge and too far away to shoot at. When our water ran out, we retreated with sore feet, aching legs, and worn-out shoes to a ranch about thirty miles away where we hunted deer. We knew some-

Moose Johnson, famous Yukon guide, packing the head of the best Dall sheep O'Connor ever shot. This head was for a time No. 12 in the world's records.

thing about deer and had some luck. My two companions got down off the mountain that last day, filled with cactus thorns and frustration and convinced that sheep hunting was a sucker's game. As far as I know neither of them has ever again in his lifetime set a foot on a sheep mountain. But I came down fascinated by the country and the game and resolved to get myself a desert ram if I had to wear my legs down to the knees to do it.

So in my dumb and untutored way, I continued to hunt for sheep whenever I could sneak away from my job. I tried taking Mexicans as guides. Some of them had undoubtedly killed sheep and they all talked a good sheep hunt, but presently I realized that they had killed sheep simply by accident.

Eventually it dawned on me that the reason I saw those sheep on the skyline and about a half-mile away was that the sheep had seen me first. I also realized that if I were ever going to become a sheep hunter I'd have to see them before they saw me. Because the sheep always saw me before I saw them, I realized that the eyes of sheep must be a good deal better than the unaided eyes of human beings. I therefore went in hock for an excellent pair of 8 x 30 Bausch & Lomb binoculars.

My first desert ram was actually a fluke. A Mexican friend and I had seen in the soft sand of an arroyo the tracks of a ram and two ewes. They turned up a big canyon, so the Mexican took the ridge on one side and I the other. For once I had a break. The sheep saw the Mexican, did not see me. They came tearing around the head of the canyon under the rimrocks, the ram in the rear. I could hear the stones rolling before I saw them, and when the ram showed up I shot it at about fifty or sixty yards.

By the time I nailed my second ram, I was becoming a sheep hunter. I realized that the principles of sheep hunting are really very simple. The hunter must see the sheep before the sheep sees him. Then he must select a route where the wind is right and where he can stay out of sight of the sheep. Then he sneaks up and shoots the sheep. Just like that!

I found my second ram very early one morning in a range called the

Field Johnson, Yukon Indian guide who was mauled by a grizzly later, with O'Connor's first Dall sheep. The head measured just under thirty-nine inches.

Sierra San Francisco. He and two slightly smaller rams were moving slowly up a mountainside, pausing now and then to nip a bit of browse. They were about a mile away and I never in the world would have seen them if I had not been using binoculars.

For a wonder I had enough sense to watch them to see what they were going to do. After about a half hour they stopped on a point under a high ridge and decided to bed down in the pleasant sunshine to get some warmth in their bones after a frosty night. They pawed the stones out of their beds and presently they lay down. By that time I had enough experience with sheep to know that unless they were disturbed they'd lie there until about noon. Then they'd get up and browse a bit, probably not far away, and then lie down again until the shadows started lengthening in mid-afternoon.

Slowly and carefully I sneaked out of sight. I went around the long way, worked up the ridge behind them. I had marked the point on which they lay by a peak of peculiar shape. I had seen the rams shortly after 7 and it was not long after 11 when I reached the ridge.

For a few minutes I lay behind it, getting my wind back and fighting off an attack of the shakes. Then, keeping my head behind a little bush, I peeked over. Two rams lay on the point less than 200 yards below me, facing away from me and looking out over the vast empty desert plain. I wondered where the other ram was. Presently I saw a movement behind some brush to the left of the point. He had got hungry and was having a little snack.

All of the rams were old. One had a heavy, close-curled head, with horns broomed so they were two or three inches wide at the points, as I could tell when he turned his head to the right one time. The other had perfect points but horns that dropped down. When I got a good look at the feeding ram I could tell his head was not as heavy as those of the other two.

It might have been sporting if I had whistled so the rams would have stood up. But I didn't. I very carefully aimed right in the middle of what sheep I could see, which happened to be right at the root of the tail, and squeezed off the shot. The 7 mm. Mauser bullet paralyzed the ram's rear end. Another shot finished him.

I felt that day that surge of triumph only the sheep hunter knows. I was alone high on the mountain with a beautiful trophy of one of the world's finest and rarest game animals, I had seen this sharp-eyed and wary creature before he saw me, had stalked and taken it fairly in his own high and desolate mountains.

Below me lay the vast and empty desert already swimming in mirage from the hot winter sun. I heard a swish of wings and a cruising buzzard with bare obscene head and glittering inquisitive eye swept by. Others

The author with a good Stone sheep shot in northern British Columbia. This ram was very old, had a close curl like a bighorn, and the horns were heavily broomed from rubbing them against rocks.

were gliding out of the blue. I covered the carcass with brush to keep the buzzards away, and taking the head, the scalp, and the backstraps, I began the long rough hike back to my little camp under a palo verde tree. The next day my camp boy, Ramon, and I would go back for the meat.

Since that long ago day in the glittering winter sunshine of Sonora, it has been my great good fortune to hunt other kinds of sheep in other kinds of mountains—the snow-white Dalls of the arctic and subarctic ranges of Alaska and the Yukon, the gray-faced, black-bodied Stone sheep of the northern British Columbia Rockies, the chunky dark-brown bighorn of southwestern Alberta and southeastern British Columbia, the Barbary sheep of northern Africa and the lively little Persian red sheep and the larger red-bodied, white-necked urial of the mountains of Iran.

The wild sheep of the world probably originated in the high mountains of central Asia. Adapting themselves to climate and terrain they moved through the ages from mountain range to mountain range in the near East, where they became the small "moufflon" of Turkey, Iran, and of the islands in the Mediterranean Sea. Those that crossed the Mediterranean basin during the Ice Age, when it was a vast swampy valley filled with mountain ranges that eventually became islands when the water of the melting ice caps swept through the Straits of Gibraltar, evolved into the odd audad, or Barbary sheep. This is a large animal as sheep go. He has smooth horns, a long fringe of hair along his brisket, and his hide is medium brown. He dwells in the Atlas Mountains of North Africa and ranges clear down into the southern Sahara wherever there are cliffs and rocky hills.

In the Himalayas there is another off-beat sheep, the Bahral, or blue sheep, which like the audad has goatlike affinities. The horns are also similar. Another sheep-goat is the tur of the Caucasus. The white-necked urial, a handsome sheep of medium size with a red-brown body, is also found in parts of the Himalayas.

The largest of the world's sheep and the finest horns are found among the various members of the *Ovis amon,* or argali, tribe in Central Asia. These are very large sheep. Some of them weigh as much as 400 pounds. One subspecies, the famous *Ovis poli* of the Pamir plateau, has horns that are sometimes as much as six feet long, and the great argali of Mongolia have horns that measure as much as nineteen inches in circumference at the base. All of the argali have white neck ruffs, reddish-brown bodies, legs long for sheep.

In Eastern Siberia there are two varieties of sheep, the Kamchatka bighorn and the Clifton's bighorn, which are large sheep but smaller than the largest argali. Closely related to the wild sheep of North America, they are gray sheep with large areas of white.

During the Pleistocene period, the ancestors of the North American sheep migrated across the land bridge in the Bering Sea to Alaska. They were split by the great ice sheet that covered the Canadian Rockies and those of the northern United States. South of the ice, the sheep evolved into the brown bighorn and the smaller desert bighorn. North of the ice they became the snow-white Dall and the black-bodied, gray-faced Stone sheep. Then as the ice receded the brown sheep worked north to occupy the Montana and southern Canadian Rockies. At the same time the sheep that had been north of the ice moved slowly south to a point where they were stopped by the great Peace River.

Over the world these various kinds of sheep merge one into the other. In Iran there are areas where the little red sheep and the medium-size urial intermingle, and on the border of Russian-Iranian Turkistan the sheep are at once the largest of the urial and the smallest of the argali. The type locality of the Bokharan argali is over in Russian Turkistan not far away.

In ranges off the Pamir plateau, it is difficult to say whether the sheep are *Ovis poli* or Mongolian argali, and in the southeast Yukon and northern British Columbia the white Dall sheep and the black Stone come together and the sheep cannot honestly be assigned to either subspecies.

Over this vast crescent of sheep country that extends from the mountains of Lower California and northwestern Sonora in Mexico up

This is a situation that often develops on a sheep hunt. A bunch of rams are lying around the point. One of them gets suspicious and comes around to take a look at the stalker.

through the Rockies to Alaska, across Asia into Africa, the sheep all have similar habits. They all like much the same country. The man who learns how to hunt sheep in the rocky hills of the Sahara would immediately feel at home in Sonora, and he who has mastered the art of sheep hunting in Alberta would know how to go about it in the fabled Altai range of Outer Mongolia.

Sheep are very adaptable animals, as is shown by their tremendous range. By nature they are mountain animals that are grazers rather than browsers, but in some areas they have learned to browse almost exclusively. They are never found far away from rough and rocky canyons, ridges, and hillsides, since they escape their enemies by taking to the rocks. However, they are not cliff animals like the North American white goat or the incredible ibex of Asia and northeastern Africa. Instead they prefer to feed in big grassy basins and on rounded hills adjacent to rough country. When they are frightened, they generally but not always head for rough country. When the white men first invaded the Great Plains of the West they found bighorn sheep in the cliffy brakes of the Missouri River, in the low but rough Badlands of the Dakotas, around rough little buttes clear out onto the plains. A small area of rough country for refuge will enable sheep to live far from high mountains. This will protect them from their natural enemies, the big cats and the wolves, but not from human beings with rifles.

In many areas sheep live on gently rounded hills over which a horse can be galloped, but always not far from rough country. In Mexico and the southwest, sheep live in very rough and rocky but low mountains, but they often come clear down into the flats to feed and then cross level open country to go from range to range.

The North American and eastern Siberian sheep are stocky animals with short, powerful legs, but the central Asiatic argali and urial have long legs, tend to live in less rugged country. They can run like antelope and take to the rocks only as a last resort. Often wild sheep and wild goats are found in the same country both in North America and Asia, but the sheep always keep to the easier terrain and the goats to the cliffs. A sheep would break its neck in country where the goat is at home. But still there is something recognizable about sheep country. The old sheep hunter in a strange place will suddenly say: "Ah, that's a sheep mountain!" Generally he is right.

Wherever wild sheep are found they have similar habits. During the breeding season rams and ewes are together. The wild sheep is neither polygamous or monogamous. He is promiscuous. During the rut he is excited and battles his fellow rams but shares the ewes. Rams do not collect harems the way elk do, nor stay with one female as long as she is in heat the way a bear, for example, does. During the rut the sheep fight, mate, and frolic with gleeful promiscuity. The wild sheep is one of the most concupiscent of males. One ram can cover a half dozen ewes in a few minutes, and wherever wild sheep are hunted the natives look upon the powers of rams with awe and admiration and believe that eating their testicles (mountain oysters) adds to one's ardor.

In most northern latitudes the height of the rut is in December so that the lambs will be born in May, but in the deserts of the southwest it is in September so the lambs will be born during the winter rains when feed is good. But once the rut is over, the rams have no interest in the ewes. They form bands and go off by themselves. No self-respecting full-grown ram would be caught dead around his frisking lambs.

Sometimes rams are found on the same mountain with ewes and lambs before the rut, but if they are it is pure coincidence. Often they spend their summers many miles from the ewes, generally in higher and rougher country. One time when I was hunting Stone sheep in the high Rockies of British Columbia, I must have seen around 200 big rams but only *one* ewe. What that solitary ewe was doing on a mountain with sixty rams, miles from another ewe, I'll never know.

In addition rams tend to sort themselves out into age groups and generally if one sees a couple of young rams, a middle-aged ram, and an old ram together it is a sign that there are few sheep in the country. Wherever he is found the wild ram is old at twelve, generally dead at fourteen. The big trophy heads come out of these groups of old rams, these Colonel Blimps of sheepdom. The trick of trophy hunting is to find such bunches.

Now and then a very old ram is found all alone, and these lone rams are usually very good ones. Probably as their teeth start to go and they develop pyorrhea, they are subject to toothache and are mean and unsociable. Possibly they are slow and weak and the stronger rams bully them. The heaviest desert ram I ever shot was a solitary one. The sign told me he had been living for weeks in and around the crater of a cinder cone in the Pinacates of Sonora. His teeth were in bad shape and his horns broomed back so far I could not tell for certain how old he was. He had been living on winter wheat and was butter fat. The heaviest Dall sheep I ever saw was likewise all alone. He had found a grassy basin where he had plenty of feed and could water in a cool little rill.

Rams are generally up and feeding at the earliest light. Sometimes they go to water, but a sheep is a dry-country animal able to go for long periods without water. They feed until around 9:30 or 10 o'clock and then head for their bedding ground. Favorite places are shale slides with a rocky cliff behind them. Then they can see out over a wide area, and if anything comes for them they can outrun it on the slide.

Another favorite spot is in a saddle on a ridge. Then they can look

This is a little sheep cave where the desert sheep go to get out of the hot sun or the rain.

down on two sides. Still another favored spot is a point that projects out from a ridge giving an angle of observation from three sides. Often they bed down at the heads of big basins where they can see for long distances and run over the top if anything comes from below.

Sometimes a bunch of rams will choose a bedding ground where they simply cannot be stalked. Bad spots are a saddle between two knife-edged ridges, the top of a shale slide right at the foot of a high cliff, or an isolated peak. One of the most tantalizing of my sheep hunting experiences was getting a spotting scope on a bunch of seven big rams, several of which had heads that surely must have gone from thirty-eight to forty-four inches, that were bedded right on the top of a little volcanic hill exactly in the middle of a great basin above timberline in the Yukon. For a half a mile in any direction there wasn't enough cover to conceal a weasel. In a case like that all the sheep hunter can do is to drool and wait for the rams to move.

The sheep's principal means of protection is his wonderful eyes. A stationary object doesn't mean much to him, but he can see moving objects at incredible distances. I have seen sheep watching something and have been unable to see it with my naked eye, just barely able to make it out with 9-power binoculars. Many times I have located rams with binoculars only to discover that they had seen me first and were watching my every move.

144

Sheep have good noses and anyone who stalks sheep should watch the wind. However, in any mountain country the wind is notoriously fickle. Often some vagrant shift in the wind will mean a ruined stalk, and sometimes it may appear that a sheep is getting the hunter's wind when actually he is not at all. Some sheep hunters will swear that sheep cannot smell better than human beings, but many times I have deliberately given them my wind. They always react.

Locating shootable rams is half the battle, and patience and the ability to use binoculars are the sheep hunter's most valuable assets. The beginner stands up on his hind legs, jauntily sweeps the country with his binoculars, then announces there isn't a damned thing in sight. The old-timer selects a good vantage point where he will not be conspicuous and sits down. At first he looks the country over carefully with his naked eye to be sure there is nothing in plain sight and to pick out the likely-looking spots. Then he goes over the country piece by piece with binoculars.

Often he will watch something that might be a bedded sheep for several minutes. If he doesn't see it move, he'll look somewhere else and then come back to it. In the late summer and early fall hunting season, the white Dall sheep are the easiest to see against the green of basins and the gray of slide rock. The dark Stones with their white necks are also not difficult to pick up at long distances. The toughest job of glassing is for the brown bighorns and desert sheep, as they generally blend with the terrain. Many of the desert sheep mountains are thinly brushed so that the outlines of the sheep are broken up and identification is difficult. Often in the early fall, bighorn rams will bed down in the scrubby trees right at timberline, and it is then extremely difficult to locate them.

When the rams are in timber, one has to look for parts of sheep—a horn, a white rump patch. Once in Wyoming I watched something that might be a horn or might be an oddly shaped limb in a patch of timber at the head of a lofty Wyoming canyon. When whatever it was moved, I knew it was a horn. An hour later when feeding time came, about a dozen rams materialized out of that patch of scrubby arctic fir and whitebark pine.

Another time in Alberta, an Indian guide and I saw some suspicious-looking objects on a grassy slope over a mile away. They were brown and about the right size for rams. We could even fancy we saw white rump patches. They might be rams or they might be stones that had broken off the cliff and rolled down the slope. We had no spotting scope so I laid my 8-power binoculars on a log and watched. Presently I saw one of the objects move. They were sheep all right!

The sheep hunter should have a first-class binocular of about 8 or 9 power to locate sheep, and he should also have a high-power spotting scope to size up the heads once the rams are located. I like a prismatic spotting scope of about 20–25 power with a little tripod stand. With such a glass one can look over a head and decide if it is shootable at a mile.

Unless the sheep are fairly close by and the stalk can be completed without much elapsed time, I do not like to stalk feeding rams. Often sheep feed in one place and bed in another, and if the stalk is a long one, the hunter may arrive to find his rams gone. Then he must relocate them and try another stalk with the chance that while he is trying to find them again, they'll see him first. Then he is dead.

Particularly if it is getting anywhere near the time for the rams to bed down, I watch them and see where they bed before I begin the stalk. Then I work out the route by which I can approach them, planning it so the wind is in my favor and I can come on the sheep from above. Mountain game always expects danger from below and seldom looks up. I have tried stalking from below but I have never had any luck. Once the sheep are bedded they generally stay in the same place for five hours or so unless they are disturbed.

In the last stages of the stalk, great care should be taken to look carefully over any new piece of ground before proceeding. There are two great dangers. One is that the sheep themselves may have moved a little. Maybe it got too hot in the sun, too cool in the shade, or they decided the shale around the point was softer. Sometimes they will move, generally not far, but enough to catch the stalker by surprise.

Another danger is the so-called sentinel ram. Often a sheep will become uneasy. Maybe a bunch he was in got shot up at one time or a wolf rushed some sheep from above. Anyway, a ram may detach himself from the group, come back up on the ridge from which the hunter plans to approach. Before he begins his final stalk, the hunter should glass his approach and make certain the coast is clear.

When I was young and dumb I had some sad experiences at a time when I knew I was within a couple of hundred yards of sheep and the worst was behind me. One time a big bunch of rams had moved. I was traveling fast, blundered right into them where they should not have been. Another time, instead of going high and coming down on a bunch of rams, I tried to stalk them from the same elevation, didn't look my route over carefully enough, and spooked a young ram that had gone off from the main bunch to reconnoiter. In both cases, haste and carelessness wrecked my sheep hunt.

But, let us suppose, the stalk has gone well. The rams have stayed put. The wind hasn't shifted. The hunter has controlled his desire to sneak up over the ridge and peek at the rams every few minutes. No sentinel ram is out.

Finally the hunter has only a few yards to go. Hours ago he planned to come over the ridge, by a dead tree in line with some gray slide rock. This is the tree; there is the slide rock. The hunter lies under the ridge until he gets his wind back. Then, keeping his rifle in front of him, he slowly edges up to where he can see below. If all has gone right the rams, all unsuspecting, are waiting at the rendezvous.

What if they are not where he has seen them last? If he has not shown himself and the wind has not changed they should be close by. If he cannot see them immediately he has no reason to panic. Once I made a long stalk on some white rams, but when I crawled up to the spot where I should have been able to see, they were not there. For five minutes I looked and looked. No rams. I crawled a few feet farther ahead, thinking they might have moved to the right or left up under the rimrock. Suddenly I caught a movement directly below me. It was the top of a horn not thirty yards away. I sneaked forward. Five big rams were directly below me, so close that if I had been so inclined I could have spat on them—so close I almost hated to shoot the largest.

The final step in the ram hunt before the actual shooting is to pick out the best head. Generally, old bighorns, or any sheep with close-curled horns that grow close to his eyes and block his side vision, have horns that have been broomed off blunt. Horns that are heavy, broomed, curve below the point of the jaw and come up even with the bridge of the nose or above mean an old ram with an excellent head. An old-timer from eleven to fourteen years old is always a good trophy. On the other hand, perfect points, tapering horns, horns that do not go below the point of the jaw mean a youngish ram and a poor head. No genuinely ardent and experienced sheep hunter would be caught dead taking home a ram like that.

Nor does a complete curl always mean much. Often Stone and Dall sheep have flat curls that do not go below the point of the jaw, yet come well above the bridge of the nose. These are poor heads from young rams. I have seen such heads that wouldn't measure thirty-six inches. In any species of North American sheep, the head of an *old* ram broomed off at the points and heavy throughout its length is a fine trophy. If it goes between thirty-seven and thirty-nine around the curl it is a very fine trophy. If such a head goes forty inches or over, it is a head to celebrate in song and story. Because fewer Stone and Dall sheep have close-curled horns, more of the old rams have heads that are broomed little or none at all, as the horns do not then block their vision. It is far easier to get a Stone or Dall with a forty-inch head than it is to get a forty-inch bighorn.

If the stalk has gone well and the head carefully picked out, the shooting of the ram is generally so easy that it is anticlimactical. The great sport of sheep hunting is in the stalking, not the shooting. More sheep are shot under 200 yards than over. Shots are generally at station-ary targets and are easy. Long shots generally mean a poor stalk, bad luck, or an excited hunter.

Be it desert sheep or bighorn, Dall or Stone, blue sheep or *Ovis poli*, the old trophy ram, one of the world's grandest game animals, deserves a quick and painless death. The hunter owes it to his quarry to lay those crosswires on the chest cavity and squeeze that trigger!

One of the most interesting, yet at the same time one of the goofiest stalks I ever made for a wild ram took place in Mexico a long time ago.

I was camped with some friends by a little well in northern Sonora. Many years before, the well had been dug by a cattleman, but it was abandoned when it was discovered that the flow of water was too slow to take care of more than a few cattle. It did produce enough water, however, to take care of the needs of a few horses, and as a consequence I often took horses in there from a ranch about twenty-five miles away and had many fine hunts in the surrounding country.

The primary object of the trip on this occasion was to take a few desert mule and whitetail deer, but in my wallet I had a museum permit for one ram. One of my companions, a retired army colonel, likewise had a special permit. When we got the camp supplied with venison, the colonel and I decided to see if we couldn't find a ram or two.

Ten or twelve miles from the well was a range of rugged hills and mountains of red volcanic rock. It was called the Sierra Los Mochos, or the mountain range of the cuts. Many years before some Mexicans and Papago Indians had ambushed a party of cattle-stealing Seri Indians there. They cut the heads off of those they killed and carried them back to show to some ranchers who had offered them a reward for every Seri they bumped off. Hence the name. Once when hunting sheep there I came across the scene of the slaughter. Weathered human bones were scattered through the rocks but there wasn't a skull in the lot.

The colonel had never hunted sheep but I had done considerable sheep hunting at the time, and since I had always seen sheep in Los Mochos I volunteered to show him a ram.

So early one morning the colonel, a Mexican cowboy named Zefarino, and I left camp for Los Mochos. We saw some desert mule deer and one very fine whitetail buck as we rode over that morning, but since the object was a ram we passed them up.

By late morning we had tied our horses to some palo verde trees behind a little ridge, and I sat down in a spot where I could glass the peaks and ridges in several directions. This was one of those lucky days; within a few minutes I had detected a moving animal just under a ridge about a mile away. It was partially hidden by low, thin vegetation, but I was just about sure it was a sheep.

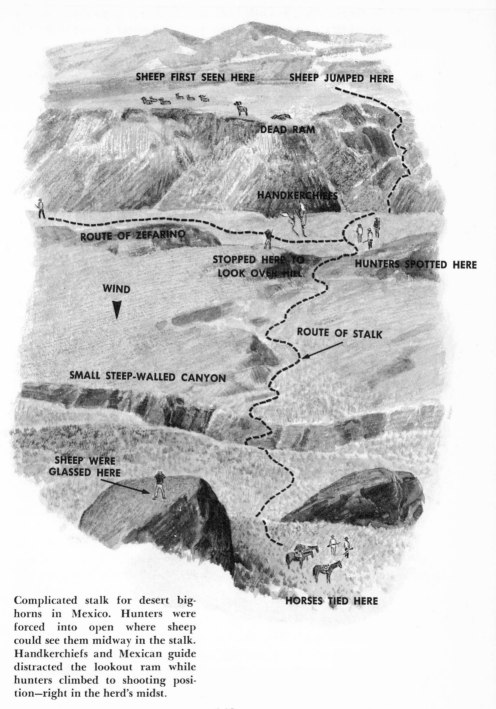

SHEEP FIRST SEEN HERE   SHEEP JUMPED HERE

DEAD RAM

HANDKERCHIEFS

ROUTE OF ZEFARINO

STOPPED HERE TO LOOK OVER HILL

HUNTERS SPOTTED HERE

WIND

ROUTE OF STALK

SMALL STEEP-WALLED CANYON

SHEEP WERE GLASSED HERE

HORSES TIED HERE

Complicated stalk for desert bighorns in Mexico. Hunters were forced into open where sheep could see them midway in the stalk. Handkerchiefs and Mexican guide distracted the lookout ram while hunters climbed to shooting position—right in the herd's midst.

149

Then it walked up and stood against the skyline and I could see the curling horns of a ram. A spotting scope to size up the head would have come in handy just then, but I did not have one. With a 9X binocular I eventually found about a dozen sheep and showed them to the colonel and to Zefarino. It was in late November, and at that time in Sonora most of the rams are still with the ewes. They join them in late August or early September for the breeding season (which is earlier in the desert than it is farther north) and generally stay with them until the ewes start dropping their lambs in February and March.

As I watched, the sheep fed slowly over the ridge. I was sure they would lie down on the other side. It is characteristic of wild sheep all over the world to get up and feed a little about midday and then bed down once more until the shadows lengthen and it is supper time.

The herd, I decided, would probably lie down in the shade on the other side of the ridge, and the reason they were moving their beds was that it was rather warm on the southern exposure where they had been lying. The sheep went over the crest near the head of one of the canyons that cut the mountain into an H. The thing to do, I decided, was to go around, come up the canyon that opened to the east. The herd, I thought, would be at the head of the canyon that ran west. We would be able to come slowly over the saddle that separated the heads of the two canyons and the sheep would be below us.

When I first outlined the plan to the colonel, he proposed that we ride for the first part of the stalk. I objected on the grounds that just before us lay a narrow but steep canyon difficult to cross with horses and that if we were on horseback we'd be both noisier and more conspicuous. But the colonel, who wasn't as young as he once was, was not happy. Nevertheless I won my point and led out with the protesting colonel and Zefarino bringing up the rear.

The first part of our stalk was easy. Intervening hills kept us out of sight and the going was not difficult. Finally we came to a low ridge. Between it and the mountain where we had seen the sheep was an open valley about 300 yards wide. Crossing this would be the critical part.

Keeping myself partly concealed by low, thin brush I crawled up to the crest of the ridge and carefully glassed the entire mountainside to make sure that none of the sheep had stayed behind. Finally I was convinced that all had gone over the crest. I gave the signal and we started across the open valley. The colonel was still grumbling because we hadn't taken the horses. He did not like to walk.

Then it happened. We were halfway across the valley and in plain sight when a young ram popped up on the ridge, instantly spotted us. If he became badly frightened and ran he would spook the herd and our hunt would be over.

I decided to try a ruse. Long ago I had discovered that although sheep have marvelous eyes they can't count very well and that they are more interested in moving objects than stationary ones. I took out a white handkerchief and a large red bandana, tied them to the long flexible stems of ocotillo. They flapped there madly in the breeze.

I then instructed Zefarino to walk away from us up the valley paralleling the mountain. The ram now had too much for his mind to comprehend—three men, one moving and two stationary, two flapping handkerchiefs. Making myself as inconspicuous as possible I watched him with the glasses. When Zefarino was about 400 yards away, I could see the ram was looking at him and thinking of nothing else.

The colonel and I walked slowly away until we got into an arroyo leading to the mouth of the canyon. Then we ducked out of sight. The last peek I took at the ram showed me that he was still concentrating on Zefarino and the handkerchiefs. I was sure he was so befuddled that he would never miss us.

The rest of the stalk seemed as if it would be easy. We had to work up that narrow steep canyon, sneak over the saddle, and from there we should see the sheep. The sides of the canyon were composed of heaps of boulders, some as small as baseballs and some as large as small houses. I had been hunting Stone sheep for six weeks in northern British Columbia earlier in the fall and I was in fine condition. I leaped from rock to rock silently on soft rubber soles. But the colonel was having a tough time. He was slipping, sliding, and out of wind. He was still angry because I had not allowed him to ride.

I was near the saddle and too far ahead of the colonel, who was out of sight around a bend in the canyon when his patience became exhausted. He was deaf and like many deaf people he spoke loudly.

"Wait a minute, Jack," he bawled suddenly. Then he added: "Damn it. Back at the ranch I have horses that would gallop up this canyon!"

That did it. The sheep had not followed my scenario. Silent on my rubber soles I had sneaked right into the middle of the herd. They were lying in the rocks all around me, and when the colonel's voice boomed out they all jumped up. From where I stood I could see three shootable rams and seven or eight ewes and young sheep.

"Rams, rams! Hurry, colonel, hurry!" I howled.

But the colonel couldn't make it. One ram was leaping over the rocks headed for the ridge above me and about to get out of sight. I took a crack at him in the middle of a jump with my .30/06 and he disappeared behind a big rock. Two other rams were humping up the opposite side of the canyon, but by the time the colonel, heaving and scrambling, came into sight, only ewes and young sheep were in sight. I waited for the colonel to join me, but by the time we got together, Zefarino, who was a

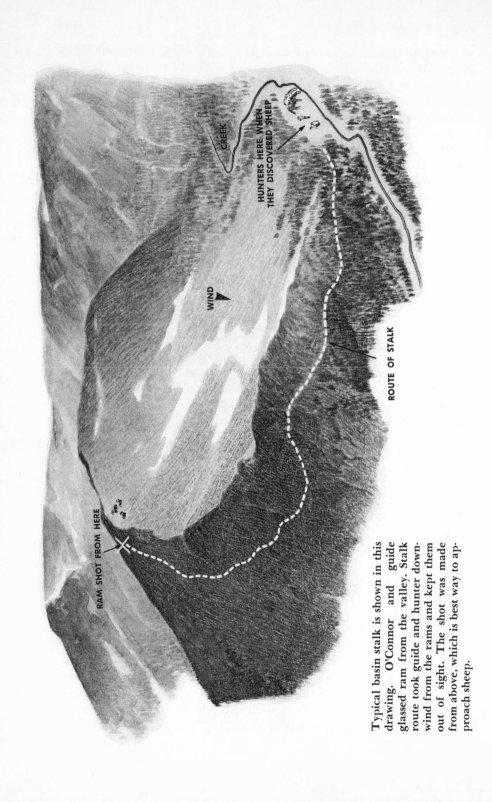

CREEK

HUNTERS HERE WHEN THEY DISCOVERED SHEEP

WIND

ROUTE OF STALK

RAM SHOT FROM HERE

Typical basin stalk is shown in this drawing. O'Connor and guide glassed ram from the valley. Stalk route took guide and hunter downwind from the rams and kept them out of sight. The shot was made from above, which is best way to approach sheep.

magnificent mountaineer, had run up the other side of the mountain, had come over the ridge and had found the dead ram.

To me this was one of the most interesting stalks for rams I have ever made, one filled with complications and suspense, good luck and bad. I was lucky to find the sheep so quickly with glasses, lucky that my ruse worked. The sentinel ram, Zefarino told me, stayed put staring at him and the handkerchiefs all the time the colonel and I were completing the stalk and took off only when he heard me shoot. We were unlucky in that this ram had come back over the ridge and had spotted us, unlucky that the herd had come across the saddle into the head of the east canyon, unlucky that the colonel started talking at the critical time.

If the sentinel ram had not popped up, if the sheep had not moved into the head of the wrong canyon, and if the colonel had kept his mouth shut, the stalk would have been of the routine sort such as I have often made.

The finest North American sheep I have ever taken, a superb Yukon Dall, came as the result of a very easy and uncomplicated stalk and an easy shot. The whole business was so simple, so cut and dried, that if I had not done a good deal of sheep hunting before that I would have thought that the taking of a fine trophy ram was always child's play.

My guide and I hadn't gone more than a mile from camp when we saw to our right a beautiful and sheepy-looking basin. We got off of our horses to glass it and almost immediately discovered three Dall rams lying down well over a mile away. I set up a 20-power spotting scope to look the heads over. The rams were just fair and I was about to decide to go on when I made out part of the head and the base of the horns of another ram. He was partially concealed by a hollow in the ground. Since the small part of the horn I could see looked very massive, my guide and I decided to take a closer look.

We had one very steep, rocky stretch to get our horses over, but we managed to lead them over it. From then on we rode in a big circle that kept us out of sight of the rams and the wind right. When we finally tied our horses to some arctic willow above timberline we had an easy stroll to a point on the ridge directly above the rams. They lay there gazing out over the vast empty basin, never suspecting that danger lay behind and above them. The big ram when measured for the Boone & Crockett Club competition had a curl of 43⅝ inches and a base of 14⅞. He won second place in the competition that year and was No. 12 in the 1952 record book.

The toughest time to stalk sheep is during the rut when the rams are with the ewes and the bunches are large. In the United States sheep seasons are early in the fall, when the rams are bunched by themselves and their flesh is at its best, but in Asia and in parts of Canada the sheep

Oscar Brooks of Mexico City and London with one of the finest rams ever taken in North America. This ram was shot in a little range right in back of the town of Piti Quito, Sonora.

season extends into the rutting time. I have hunted sheep in Mexico when the rams were with the ewes, and the last time I was in Iran the Kopet Dagh urials, beautiful rams with red-brown bodies and snowy-white necks, were bunched with the ewes.

During the rut the rams are too busy fighting and chasing the ewes to keep a very sharp lookout, but the ewes never let their love life make them forgetful of danger. When thirty or forty pairs of eyes are on the lookout a stalk is difficult.

My last and best urial ram came as the result of a stalk during the rut that was done all wrong. I had no faith in it, but got a ram only through luck. The herd of perhaps sixty sheep containing seven big rams was fighting and frolicking on the side of a hill above a deep canyon. Down-wind from them and to the left was a juniper-filled draw by which we could approach out of sight. My shikaris wanted to go up the draw and then work around the hill on the level with the sheep.

I suggested that we go farther to the left up the main canyon, then climb the hill a half mile to the left of the herd and come at them from

154

behind and above. As the shikaris had planned it, the stalk seemed to be very risky to me. I was against coming from below so close to the herd. I was afraid that the junipers might conceal a stray sheep that would spook the others, and I was afraid that we would be seen on our horizontal approach and have to shoot at running rams if I got a shot at all.

My plan would have taken much longer but it looked to me like a sure thing. The shikaris' plan was faster but riskier. With profound misgivings, I strung along with the shikaris. All went well until we got to the junipers at the head of the draw. Then a ewe came boiling out and headed right for the big bunch. I knew that all the sheep would run the moment she came in sight.

I ran after the ewe as fast as I could travel, and, sure enough, when I saw the rams they were taking off. I had about two or three seconds to pick out the biggest ram of the bunch, stop, switch off the safety, swing ahead and shoot. As it happened I was lucky, the ram was about 150 yards away and I didn't swing far enough ahead. I did hit him, however, but too far back. He ran about 100 yards, fell off a cliff, and was dead when the shikaris got to him.

The sheep hunter should do all he can to prevent bad luck from haunting him, but the best-planned stalks can go sour by pure chance. The urial hunt I have just described was not unlucky—merely poorly planned. The desert bighorn hunt I told about was well planned but haunted by bum luck. Once I was stalking a desert ram when a cruising crow floated down a ridge, saw me, let out a squawk of surprise and spooked the sheep. Another time I was in the final stages of a stalk when some rotten granite let go, started a rock slide, and scared my prospective victims out of the country.

But there can also be good luck. If the ball hadn't bounced just right I would never have got that big urial, for example. Another time I was lying behind the ridge watching a dozen rams in a big basin. They were about a quarter of a mile away—too far for a certain shot. I was wondering how in the devil I could approach them. Suddenly they all got up and walked purposefully right toward me. The best Stone sheep I ever shot was moving away from my companion, whom I had not seen for some hours. He could have run in almost any direction but he chose to come within range of my rifle and I nailed him.

To me hunting the mountain ram is the most exciting of all sports. One reason is that sheep are found in wild and beautiful country, where the hunter is up in the air with the eagles and the sheep themselves. I know of no more beautiful country than some of the rough and strangely lovely mountains in Sonora right above the blue Gulf of California or the big timberline basins in Alberta.

Another reason the true sheep hunter never tires of his sport as long as his legs and his wind hold out is that stalking sheep sustains the thrill and excitement longer than most other types of hunting. A man may see his ram feeding not long after sunup. He may then watch it until it beds down. His stalk may take hours and cover miles of territory. It may be eight or nine hours from the time he gets his glass on a trophy ram until he gets a shot—if indeed he does get a shot.

And all that time he is in a high pitch of excitement, living a month in each five minutes. A real-gone sheep hunter will pass up the biggest grizzly that ever walked if he thinks shooting it will spook a forty-inch ram. A real sheep hunter would rather take a forty-five-inch ram than a ten-foot tiger, an elephant with hundred-pound tusks, a moose with a sixty-five-inch spread.

Some try sheep hunting and don't like the brutal climbing, the lung-tearing effort, the hours of uncertainty while the stalk is in progress. But once a hunter is hooked on sheep, the only things that can stop him are wobbly legs, a bum heart, or broken bones. There is no other hunting quite like it!

13 | Rifles and Cartridges for Wild Sheep

I had done a great deal of reading on the subject of proper rifles and cartridges for sheep hunting before I made my first trip for desert bighorn in the early 1930's. The phrase "long shots at sheep and goats" occurred like a refrain in everything I read. Much was made of the need for flat trajectory. I pictured myself perched on a knife-edged ridge shooting at a ram on another ridge at least 500 yards away. At that time the only real sheep hunter I knew was a skinny and tough little character who by profession was a mining engineer but who was by preference a desert rat, a prospector, and sheep hunter. He liked nothing better than to disappear into the harsh and barren desert mountains of Arizona and Sonora to look for gold and copper mines and to hunt sheep. In his day he had got some very fine rams, and although he claimed he had got them all in northern Mexico, I strongly suspect that in those lawless days he did a good deal of his hunting illegally in Arizona.

I was astounded to discover that his sheep rifle was a Winchester Model 94 carbine with a 20-inch barrel and in .25/35 caliber, about as evil looking a firearm as I had ever seen. Not a vestige of finish remained on the stock or barrel. The bore, however, was mirror bright, and later when I hunted with him I found him to be an excellent shot.

"Hell's bells," he told me when I tried to pump him about sheep rifles, "the trick of sheep hunting is to find the damned things. Once you've done that you can knock them over with just about anything."

He showed me his binocular—a big, much-used Hensoldt roof-prism job which I believe was a 10 × 50.

"Give me a good glass," he said, "and I'll hunt sheep with a .22. I don't care much about the caliber of the rifle just so long as it's light!"

I took his advice about Mexican sheep country, but I had my own notions as to suitable sheep rifles. I considered him a hopeless fuddy duddy. I simply could not believe him when he told me that he generally killed his rams at 150 yards or less. Sheep, I had read time and time again, were always a long-range proposition, and potting a sheep at short range was immoral if not actually illegal.

I had expended a good deal of sweat and effort before I got my first ram, as I had to learn the hard way that in sheep hunting a good binocular and the ability to use it is more important than the rifle and cartridge and generally, but by no means always, more important even than shooting skill. I also learned that two or three extra pounds in the weight of the rifle seem like twenty or thirty at the end of a long rough day.

When I had finally learned by trial and error enough about sheep hunting to get myself a ram, the shot that did the business was not from ridge to ridge across a big canyon but at maybe fifty or sixty yards. The rifle I used was a 7 × 57 Mauser that weighed about seven pounds with iron sights and a sling, and the load was that formerly put out by Western Cartridge Company—a 139-grain open-point bullet at a velocity of about 2,800 foot-seconds in a 22-inch barrel. Except that I would now have a low-mounted 4X scope on such a rifle, I don't know of a much better combination today.

In the course of a good deal more desert sheep hunting, I was fortunate enough to knock over some more rams. An occasional shot was at from 200 to 300 yards, but for the most part the ranges were modest. Before I learned the facts of sheep hunting I shot at and missed some rams at from 400 to 600 yards, but once it dawned on me that the way to hunt sheep was to see them before they saw you and then sneak up on them, I didn't do much missing. In a fairly extensive experience in hunting all four varieties of North American sheep, and in addition the African Barbary sheep and a couple of species in Asia, I have never wounded and lost one. The vast majority of the rams I have taken have been at modest ranges and have been killed with the first shot.

After all the build-up one reads about "long-range shots at sheep and goats," it is difficult to realize that the average ram is taken at no great range. The best bighorn I have ever knocked over was somewhere around 100 yards away. The best Dall I have ever taken a crack at fell somewhere around fifty or sixty yards from the muzzle, and the last desert bighorn I knocked over was probably about thirty-five yards away.

On my last overseas sheep hunt, I shot three urial rams (the Iranian legal limit) and an ibex. One urial ram was shot in his bed at about sixty-five yards, one runnning at maybe ninety yards, and another running at what looked like 150. The ibex billy was sharply down hill at probably less than 200. I missed another ibex billy by shooting just over his back as he bounded over the rocks. I didn't remember to hold low. The only long shot I made on the trip was on a fine urial ram that had been wounded by a companion whose scope was out of adjustment. It was getting away with a broken leg at about 400 yards.

All this is not to say that long shots are never taken at wild sheep. Sometimes the long shot is the only way the sheep hunter can get the ram he wants. It is always wise to be prepared for such a shot. The best Stone ram I have ever taken—and one that was No. 10 in the 1952 and 1958 record books—was shot at what I thought at the time was not much over 200 yards but which from the drop of the bullets must have been around 300. A good Persian red sheep I knocked over (and again judging from the drop of the bullets) must have been something over 300. In the Yukon at a time when two rams were allowed on a license I shot a pair from the same bunch, one at a bit over 300 and the other around 50 yards farther.

Most sheep country is cut with canyons that will keep the sheep hunter out of sight while he is stalking, and generally sheep can be approached from behind ridges. The beginner is tempted to blast away at long range as soon as he spies a shootable ram, but the old-timer generally tries to get reasonably close so he can make a sure thing out of it. In some areas, however, sheep are found in rolling country with wide canyons and big basins. When they are, the sheep hunter must take his shots at greater range than he would if he had found them in more cut up, steep, and broken country. Some of the red sheep country of the Middle East is like this, and in North America I have seen both Stone and Dall sheep in rolling hills where a close stalk was very difficult. Some of the urial country of Asia is rolling ground with round hills and shallow basins and draws, not unlike some of the antelope and mule deer country in Wyoming. Friends of mine who have hunted *Ovis poli* of the Pamirs of Central Asia tell me that those great sheep with their five- and six-foot horns are likewise found in this same sort of terrain, but at tremendous altitudes of 16,000 to 18,000 feet.

Above all, the sheep rifle should be reasonably light and handy. A good weight with a scope is about 8 pounds, although some can weigh as little as 7½ pounds. Often the sheep hunter has to take some fearful treks. One time in Sonora I left camp at 4 o'clock in the morning, climbed around in rough country all day, and got back to camp by starlight after midnight. I was a very tired hombre when I finally fell down half dead on my cot, and I would have been a lot more tired if I had been carrying a 10½-pound instead of a 7½-pound rifle. The day I shot my largest Stone ram my guide Frank Golata and I left camp as soon as we could see, shot the ram somewhere between seven and ten miles from camp, and about 3,000 feet above it. We finally got in loaded with head and meat well after dark.

In Asia, where hunting is generally done with a regular task force of gun bearers, tiffin boys, and shikaris, the weight of the rifle could be of no moment because the hunter generally has someone to carry it for him. The same thing is true in the sheep hills of Africa's Sahara Desert, as an American hunter there would usually have a gun bearer to lug his musket through the wait-a-bit thorn and rocks in that fearful heat.

Back in the days when the British ruled India and British officers and civil servants used their leaves to hunt blue sheep, urial, and *Ovis amon* in the high rugged mountains of Kashmir and Tibet, they always had stooges to carry their rifles. Consequently British hunting writers often recommend rifles that are heavy and long of barrel. If they had been forced to carry those cannons themselves they would sing another tune.

In the United States, Canada, and Alaska the sheep hunter almost always carries his own rifle, even if he has a guide. The guide will probably carry a spotting scope, maybe some lunch, and generally his own binocular. But the hunter lugs his rifle.

If the sheep hunter doesn't have a guide, he often carries a rucksack with some food, maybe some water, a camera, skinning knife, and various oddments. In many areas it is a good idea to plan to spend a night up high right with the sheep instead of going back to camp and then climbing another day. On several occasions, when getting to ram country meant either a long ride or a tough climb, I have carried enough water, some grub, a tin can, and some coffee with me so I could lie out all night and be with the sheep when they were feeding in the early morning.

The point of all this is that the sheep hunter shouldn't burden himself with more rifle than necessary. A pal who hunted sheep in Alaska one time tells me that each day he had to stumble five miles through muskeg and then climb from 2,000 to 3,000 feet before he got into ram country. He said the super-accurate ten-pound rifle he carried almost killed him. This chap, as far as I know, was so soured by the experience that he never again went after rams.

The sheep rifle should be as light as good accuracy permits, and it should also be handy. I generally use a twenty-two-inch barrel, but there is no particularly good reason why the sheep hunter couldn't use a barrel as short as twenty inches. A short barrel cuts down on the velocity a bit, but has little if any effect on accuracy. Often it is necessary for the sheep hunter to strap his rifle across his back so he can climb a cliff or along a ledge with both hands. Then he doesn't want a long barrel that will catch on the overhanging rocks. In the rugged Swiss and Austrian Alps, the chamois hunters always use short barrels. You couldn't run fast enough to give me a sheep rifle with a twenty-six-inch barrel.

In many areas, a .243, 6-mm. Remington, and the old but good .250/ 3000 and .257 are plenty of cartridge for sheep. All of them have sufficient killing power and trajectory flat enough for 300-yard shooting—and anyone should generally think long and hard before he tries to shoot a sheep at greater range.

However, in many areas the sheep hunter may encounter caribou, moose, and even grizzly bear in and around ram country. In fact I know of no better way to get a grizzly in the mountains of Canada during the fall than to hunt sheep. Sooner or later, the glasses will turn up a grizzly, as at the time rams are being hunted the big bears are often above timberline poking around for ground squirrels and marmots. Some Yukon sheep I had glassed at great distance led me to one of the last grizzlies I shot. After an exhausting climb, my guide and I got right up among the sheep but found no suitable heads. However, we did see a traveling grizzly and nailed him.

In areas where grizzlies are apt to be encountered, the sheep hunter should carry a rifle with somewhat more authority than one of the .24's or .25's. About the minimum caliber I'd want to take on a grizzly with is the fine little 7 × 57 Mauser. The .30/06 is, of course, an excellent caliber for either sheep or grizzlies, and so is the .308—with the further advantage of being available in self-loading, pump, and lever-action rifles, if the sheep hunter happens to be allergic to the bolt action.

I have shot more rams with .270 caliber rifles than with anything else, but I have also used the .30/06 extensively as well as the 7 × 57 mm. I have shot one ram with the .257 and one with the .348. Whatever caliber is chosen, it should be used with a fast-stepping, quick-opening bullet—the 140-grain in the 7 mm., the 150-grain in the .30/06, the 130-grain in the .270, the 125-grain in the .284 Winchester and .280 Remington. Such bullets give flatter trajectory over practical sheep ranges than do the heavier ones of the same caliber and they also are better at killing or disabling the animal with poorly placed hits. If luck is good and the stalk successful, sheep are generally cold turkey. Now and then, however, a sheep will have to be shot on the run or at long range and shot placement may not be good. Then that extra shock from a fast, rapidly opening bullet comes in handy.

Through long, successful and affectionate use, I lean toward the .270, but there is no one best sheep cartridge. I have known good sheep hunters who use everything from the .25/35 to the .375 Magnum. One Britisher I read about made the long trip to Alaska and took everything from white sheep through caribou and moose to brown bear with a double .450/400. I can think of a great many other rifles I would consider more suitable for sheep, but the lad brought home the mutton.

Let's take a look at calibers some fine sheep hunters have used. The late Bill Morden, who hunted sheep extensively in North America and then in Asia for *Ovis poli* and other wild sheep, used a .30/06. So did my old friend the late Grancel Fitz. The Roosevelt brothers carried .375 Magnums on their trip to Central Asia for ibex and argali back in the 1920's. The famous Charles Sheldon, the first man ever to collect all varieties of North American sheep, used a 6.5 mm. Mannlicher with a 160-grain bullet at about 2,200 foot-seconds. Col. Harry Snyder, who has done a vast amount of hunting for bighorn, Stone, and Dall sheep, likes the 7 × 64, a German cartridge that is almost a dead ringer for the .280 Remington.

Prince Abdorreza Pahlavi, brother of the Shah of Iran, has most often used a 7 × 57, but in the summer of 1965 he used a .270 on the great sheep of the Altai and Tien Shan along the border of Siberia and Outer Mongolia. In 1966 he used the same rifle in Ethiopia for the rare Walia ibex and mountain nyala. George Parker, authority on desert sheep and one of the hunters who has taken all varieties of North American rams, has used a .257, and a 7 × 64, and a 7 mm. Magnum. Herb Klein and Elgin Gates who successfully hunted *Ovis poli* in 1959 used .300 Weatherby Magnums. Felipe Wells, a crack desert sheep hunter and old amigo of mine, has used a .25/35 and a .30/06.

I'd say that both the .300 Weatherby and the .375, fine cartridges though they are, carry unnecessary power for sheep, and their recoil in a rifle of weight suitable for sheep hunting would bother many. In most cases the little 6.5 Mannlicher-Schoenauer would be adequate, but the man using it would be handicapped on the occasional long shots.

For my money the standouts in the field are the .280 Remington and the .284 and .270 Winchesters. With their 125- and 130-grain bullets they are flat shooting, deadly, and generally very accurate in a tuned-up rifle of light weight. Recoil is light, even in well-stocked 7½- and 8-pound rifles, and yet they are powerful enough for the moose and grizzlies one is apt to run into in sheep country. Another nice thing about them is that light rifles of these calibers can be obtained right over the counter in the Winchester Model 70, the Savage Model 110, and the Remington Model 700.

The sheep rifle should have a sling, and about a 4X scope on a good top bridge mount. Some hunters like a variable-power scope so that if a long shot presents itself they can crank up the power. It sometimes happens that the hunter will pick the best ram out of a bunch with binoculars at considerable range, and then if they move he can't distinguish the head he wants with the scope on his rifle. Then it might come in very handy indeed if he had a variable-power scope and was able to jack the power up to 7 or 8 for better definition.

How much sheep hunting I'll do in the future I do not know, as an automobile accident has left me less nimble than I used to be. But whenever I go out for the noble rams I'll take one of a matched pair of Model 70 Winchester featherweights in .270 caliber. One has a Redfield Bear Cub 4X scope, the other a Leupold 4X, but otherwise they are identical. Each has the now obsolete Tilden mount and each is stocked in French walnut. I sight them in to hit on the nose at 275 yards with the 130-grain bullet at 3,140, and if a long shot is necessary a hold on the backbone is good for a solid hit to about 400 yards. If I am in grizzly country I take with me a few cartridges loaded with the 150-grain Nosler bullet at around 2,950, and either of them will put this heavier bullet to the same point of impact as the lighter ones to 200 yards. There are other combinations just as good for sheep, no doubt, but I can't think of a better one.

14 | *Elk: The Greatest Stag*

Charlie and I made our little jack camp late that September afternoon right at timberline up there in the Wyoming Rockies. We unsaddled our two riding horses, took the loads off our pack mules. In a few minutes our little tent was up, the panniers and pack boxes lined up neatly. Our eiderdown robes were unrolled on their waterproof tarps, the air mattresses were blown up, and a fire was blazing. A tiny brook fed by a snowbank below a cliff over to our left tinkled fifty yards away, and we could hear the melodious song of the horse bells as our stock bounced off in their hobbles to feed on high bunch grass that grew tall and rich up there on the plateau two miles above the sea.

The teapot was on. The Dutch oven was heating. Charlie was slicing round steak off a hindquarter of the bighorn ram I had shot a few days before. I hung the ram horns in a timberline tree, unrolled and spread out the salted scalp and the hide of a black bear to let them air and dry. I unwrapped the rest of the sheep meat, hung it up to chill during the night.

All that day, while we had been traveling from the ram range to this spot, Charlie's favorite early-season elk country, it had been bright, sunny, almost hot; but now as the sun sank the thin air turned suddenly and surprisingly cold. The fire felt good and so did my down jacket.

We were having our nightly drink of bourbon and creek water from icy tin cups as we waited for the teapot to boil and the Dutch oven to heat up when Charlie stiffened.

"Hear that?" he asked.

164

"No, what?"

"Bull elk," he said. "Listen!"

I moved away from the crackle of the fire to hear better. Now I got it. From down in the wooded basin below us came the "bugle" of a bull elk. It was a high, long-drawn-out whistle, surprisingly thin and birdlike.

"Young one," said Charlie. "Spike probably!"

Then an answer: "Eee-oh-wah—eek!" It started out hoarse and deep, then for a moment it sounded a bit like the bray of a donkey and ended with an almost hysterical shriek.

"There's an old one," Charlie said. "He sounds like one hell of a big elk, an old six-pointer. He's down there with some cows and the sound of that damned little spike whistling like that gets his goat. We'll have to look him over tomorrow. Maybe he's your big head . . ."

Perhaps I had been too busy to notice it before, or perhaps it was the sound of the bugling bulls working on my imagination, but now I began to smell elk—the thick, rich, faintly repugnant, faintly stimulating odor of those great round-horned deer in the rut.

"Charlie," I said, "I *smell* elk!"

"Hell, I've smelled elk ever since we got to camp here. Boy, we're in elk country! There's a big elk wallow up there toward the snow and the bulls have been horning the devil out of these trees. You watch. Tomorrow morning we'll be up to our tails in elk!"

As a usual thing Charlie was up as soon as the day began to silver on the eastern horizon. Every day on that short trip I had awakened to find Charlie's sleeping robe empty, to hear the crackle of the fire in front of the tent, see its red leaping flames and Charlie silhouetted black against them. But that morning both of us were late in awaking. We had traveled about twenty long, rough miles the day before and we'd been very tired when we hit the sack. When we stuck our heads out of the tent, the sun was over the horizon, clear and bright, and the heavy white frost was beginning to melt into glittering opalescent beads on the grass.

"Hell and damnation!" Charlie said as he jumped out of bed. "We should have been out on the ridges an hour ago. We're late!"

When I had pulled on my clothes I went outside to find the grass glittering white with frost and our little creek frozen over. I got the fire going with frozen frosty wood while Charlie brought in the stock, removed their hobbles, gave them their morning feed of oats, and tied them up. I had hardly finished mixing the flapjack batter and started frying the bacon when the coffee started to boil.

As becomes a good guide, Charlie, as soon as he had finished his chores with the stock, had gone up on the hillside with his binocular, a battered old 10 × 50 Hensoldt roof-prism job as half as long as your arm but beautiful optically. Presently, I heard him whistle.

"Hey," he said, "bring your glass and come here!"

I dived into the tent, grabbed my binocular, and joined him.

"Look clear across the basin. See that big gray rock just above that patch of green timber? Put your glass on it and see what I see!"

The glass showed me a whole line of elk moving slowly along, spots of brown and tan against the frost-cured yellow grass. They were over a mile away, but bringing up the rear was a particularly large animal that from its size and the way it carried its head was undoubtedly a bull.

"Want to get the spotting scope?" I asked.

In a moment Charlie was back with it. We set the 20-prismatic scope up on its little stand on a grass hummock, and in a moment I had found my elk. It was a bull all right, a big six-pointer. His image was tiny but clear and I could see his great antlers sweeping back to his hips. Once as I watched I saw him stop and horn a little timberline tree and another time I saw him lift his head to bugle.

"Big son-of-a-gun!" Charlie said when I turned the spotter over to him. "If we hadn't been so doggoned lazy we'd have had him down by now, the rascal. They've been up feeding since dawn. Now they're looking for a basin to bed down in."

High up there in the Wyoming Rockies, the annual rut, the mad moon, of the elk was just beginning. When we had first hit the high country a week before to locate rams, big bulls had been in bunches all over the tops of the great plateaus. Sometimes we saw lonely singles but more often they were in herds of from three or four to a dozen. To those who think of elk as forest animals it would have been a revelation to see those great bulls high above timber at from 10,500 to over 11,000 feet up on those open, rolling mountaintops. They had spent the summer in country as open as the caribou barrens of the far north, and indeed I could almost imagine I was in caribou country.

We had both thought that after we had the bighorn ram behind us there would be nothing to getting an elk. All we'd have to do, we thought, was to ride around those open mountaintops, stopping every time we came to the top of a rise. Then we could glass the country, find the bulls, take our pick. We had found where the rams were hanging out—a long flat-topped point jutting out from the plateau. Nowhere was it more than 400 or 500 yards wide. On three sides it fell away sharply to purple timber and silver streams far, far below. The rams fed on the high rich grass on the top of the plateau, watered in a little lake. During the day, the various bunches took their ease around the heads of the canyons. For some reason there were no elk at all on this one particular plateau.

Getting the ram, once we had the bunches located, had been easy. Charlie and I had found him late one afternoon, too late to stalk and too far away to shoot. The next morning he was with a bunch of lesser rams

Early season elk country right at timberline in Wyoming.

and within 200 yards of where we had last seen him. Once we had him located again, we dropped back on the other side of a ridge, sneaked down it, and came out through scrubby white-bark pine to within 200 yards of him. One shot was enough.

Then we went elk hunting. But we saw no elk. A few days before, bulls had been all over the lofty plateaus. Now there wasn't a one. We found fresh tracks, fresh droppings, torn and battered little timberline trees where they had been cleaning the velvet from their great antlers. We found wallows, still rank with their scent, dappled by their cowlike tracks. No elk. The mysterious chemistry which guides them had told them that now was the time to drop into the big timbered basins just below the high plateaus where the cows had spent the summer raising their calves.

So we rode around the head of the big basin that morning. Now and then we'd stop and glass. Once we saw a couple of spike bulls traveling. Probably they had been run away from one bunch and were looking for another. Another time we rode almost on top of a lone five-pointer that had been bedded in a thick tangle of stunted alpine fir. Finally we got clear around to the other side where we had seen the traveling elk that morning.

"Here are the big bull's tracks," Charlie said, leaning over. Then, a moment later, "He's herding the cows over into the next basin, I think. They'll brush up there for the day."

167

When we got to the top of the ridge, we tied our horses out of sight, got up to where we could look into the basin, and began to use our binoculars. Below us was a beautiful basin where a canyon headed. Most of it was open, but a little creek, partly fed from a spring at the head and partly dependent on a big mass of last winter's snow at the upper end, ran through the bottom. For about 200 yards on each side the timber was thick and heavy. That was probably where our elk were.

Suddenly Charlie stiffened.

"I see some elk," he said.

"Where?"

"Way hell and gone beyond the head of this basin. See? Way up just under the rimrock. They're lying down in the willows. I can see their heads and the tops of their backs."

Again we set up the spotting scope. They were elk, all right, about six cows and a bull.

"That isn't the first bunch, is it?" I asked.

"I thought they'd be in this basin below us," Charlie said. "Maybe they went through it and wound up over there."

We took turns looking at the bull, trying to figure out how we'd get at him. About the only feasible way was to go back to our horses, ride clear to the head of the basin by which we had camped, get out on the ridge somehow, and then come at him from above.

Charlie was at the spotting scope, sizing up the bull's head as well as the job can be done from more than a mile. All the time he was muttering half to himself and half to me: "It's got to be that bull, but his head doesn't look as heavy. Hey, another bull showed up! His nibs got up and chased him the hell out of there . . ."

While Charlie was manning the spotting scope, I was idly glassing the thick timber in the basin below us. Suddenly I saw a tan form appear for an instant in the field. Then it was out of sight. I continued to look, and finally I made out the camel-like head of another cow lying down.

"Hell, Charlie," I said, "there are elk right below us in the basin."

He left the spotting scope and began using his binocular.

"I see one," he said. "I think that's our bunch all right. That big bull over there didn't look too much like the one I saw last night. Horns too damn thin!"

Then from the opposite rim we heard the shrill challenge of a young bull elk. From right beneath us came an answer, hoarse, defiant, hysterical.

"Hear that?" Charlie asked. "The old boy's down there. Now we'll have some fun!"

We made a long circle back over the ridge and down to cross the ridge once more and enter the canyon below the elk and get out of sight. Then

Charlie Peterson, Wyoming guide, packing out the massive head of an elk O'Connor shot in September.

we squatted down with our backs to some trees. The wind was in our favor. The bull could hear us but could not smell us.

Charlie put his bugle to his mouth and whistled.

Immediately an answer came. The bull was not more than 300 yards away. An answer also came from the other bull we had heard whistle from above not long before.

"Damn that other bull!" Charlie said. "I hope the big one comes our way."

He waited a couple of minutes then bugled again.

Once more an answer came, this time nearer, hoarse, defiant, a little like the bray of a donkey.

"He's coming, the son-of-a-gun!" Charlie said, grinning.

Next we heard him thrashing and whacking at some trees as he worked himself up for combat. He was nearer now.

We were sitting at one end of a little swampy meadow with an elk wallow in the middle. The timber on the other side was thick and the bull was not far in it. We could hear him thrashing at limbs with his horns, grunting.

Then Charlie said, "By golly, I think I can see him!"

But I could not. Charlie whistled again and the bull gave a raucous answer ending on a high-pitched whistle. Then he burst out of the timber, stopped for a moment to look wildly around for his adversary. His eyes were little, red and mean. The hair stood up on the back of his neck and I could see a thin amber stream as he urinated. I could also smell him, rank with musk.

Slowly I lifted the rifle. I put the intersection of the crosshairs right on his brisket, right on the sticking place, as he stood there. The rifle roared and the tiny 130-grain .270 bullet sped true to the mark. For an instant, the bull stood petrified with surprise, mortally stricken, the hunted now instead of the hunter. Then he turned to flee, came crashing down. He was dead before we got to him.

Then the whole basin was alive with frantic cows. They couldn't smell us and they hadn't located the echoing and re-choing sound. A couple of cows came tearing out toward us. They almost ran over their fallen lord, swerved when they were just past us and caught our wind. They climbed frantically up the ridge and over.

I was watching the elk, when I heard Charlie say: "Give me that damned gun!" He grabbed it out of my hand. I saw him get into a good sitting position. I looked at the point where the rifle was directed and saw a fat juicy spike bull trotting along the opposite side of the basin. Probably this was the bull we had heard whistle not long before. Confused and apprehensive by the sound of the shot, he was taking out—he knew not where.

"How much shall I hold up?" Charlie hissed.

"Lead him but don't hold very high," I said. "He's only about 350 and I'm sighted in for 300!"

Charlie's first shot was behind but perfect for elevation. The next time he shot farther ahead with a swinging muzzle, and the elk collapsed as if the ground had been jerked from under him. It looked like a broken neck and so it proved.

"Well, now," Charlie said, grinning all over. "Our little play party is over. You've got that stinking old bull with the big head and I've got my eating meat . . . We'll skin and quarter them today, chill them out tonight, and tomorrow we make tracks back to the road."

I never see a bull elk whistled up but what I think of the way a well-born Englishman who had just killed his first bull described it. He was greatly impressed. "The great lustful beast," he told me, "came rushing and roaring through the woods like a soul in torment . . ."

Elk can be still-hunted in timber just as whitetail deer are hunted. In the very high, open country like the Wyoming Rockies in September they can be glassed and stalked. They can be jumped and shot on the run. But of all the ways of converting a bull elk into steaks, roasts, and chops, this business of whistling them up during the rut is the most exciting.

As far as suspense goes, the only things that can compare with it are the stalking of a great mountain ram, listening to a good pack of hounds work a mountain lion, or seeing a first-class bird dog trail up, circle and pin a wary cock pheasant in a stubble field. By the time an old belligerent bull comes bursting out of the timber, the most blasé hunter is as taut as a violin string.

The elk is a great trophy animal. Of all the family of *Cervidae,* which begins in the British Isles with the European red deer and extends clear across Europe and Asia, the American elk is the largest of body and carries the finest antlers. Just as our whitetail deer was named for the familiar British red deer, and the unique pronghorn was named for the antelope of Asia and Africa, so the "elk" was given the name of the Scandinavian animal we call *moose.* More properly he is called by the Indian name of wapiti, which has never caught on in the United States but which is universally used for the animal in England and which is also very popular in Canada.

Like the mountain sheep, the moose, the Rocky Mountain goat, and the caribou, the elk or wapiti is geologically a relatively recent immigrant from Asia. A pocket of Asiatic relatives of the American elk, the wapiti of the Tian Shan mountains of China, are so nearly like the American animals that a casual sportsman probably would not notice any difference. The late Pleistocene invaders from Asia spread over a large part of the United States in the course of their thousands of years of wandering. There were elk from New York and Pennsylvania west to Vancouver Island, all over the Great Plains, in the higher mountains of Arizona and New Mexico—all over the United States except for the gulf country of the South and the deserts and isolated desert mountains of the Southwest. To the north elk were found clear up into the northern British Columbia Rockies, something which few people were aware of until the Alaska Highway was built.

Any animal as large, as conspicuous, and as productive of eating meat as the elk was bound to be hunted—and hunted hard. He was hunted for meat, and he was also hunted for his hide. Even worse, he was slaughtered for his teeth. Thousands of big bulls were shot down so their "tusks" could be taken. Then their carcasses were left to rot.

It is difficult for many of today's elk hunters to believe that elk were once animals of the open plains like the eland of Africa, yet the explorers Lewis and Clark found them in large herds on the prairies of Montana, Wyoming, and the Dakotas. However, market hunters shot off the elk of the open country and the range was converted into wheat farms and cattle ranches. There were always some elk in the mountains, but climax forests of evergreens do not furnish much game food. Elk did not become plentiful in the forested mountains until the forests had been opened up by logging and by forest fires.

Today elk are found in all of the Western states, but the largest herds are in Idaho, Montana, Wyoming, and Colorado. There are a few elk in Utah, Nevada, and California, and fair herds in Arizona, New Mexico, Oregon, and Washington.

The best states for elk are good not only because they have large elk herds but because they have great areas of wilderness mountain country not accessible for motor vehicles and because they are also relatively thinly populated. Washington and Oregon have large centers of population and rather small elk areas, much of which are accessible by road. The result is that in those states the woods in elk country are crowded during the open season.

Many hundreds of elk are killed annually by hunters who have driven into elk country and have camped by a road, but the hunter who packs in has a much better chance of success. Elk and deer are very different animals. If a deer is shot at he runs around the hill and hides out in the brush. A frightened elk will travel five or ten miles. There may be plenty of elk near a forest road when the season opens, but once the country is bombarded the first day most of the elk move farther back. I constantly get letters from hunters in the East and Middle West who know nothing about elk, who know nothing about high mountain country, and who don't have much money. They want to drive out to Idaho, Wyoming, or Montana, camp along a road and knock off an elk. I always advise them to postpone their trips until they can afford guides and outfitters. Some out-of-state road hunters do come West and do return with elk meat and elk antlers, but the overwhelming majority spend a lot of money, a lot of time, wander around the country, and return empty handed.

In some areas in the Western states the elk season opens between September 10 and 15. To me this is the most interesting time to hunt elk because the meat of the bulls is then prime and because it is about the time the bulls begin to bugle, to fight, and to round up their harems of cows. The old bulls in late August and early September are sleek and fat. Their meat is tender and delicious. After they have been in the rut for ten days or two weeks, they have got rid of most of their fat and their meat is strong and tough. By October 1, when the elk season opens in many areas, the meat of an old bull that has been fighting, worrying, herding his cows for nearly a month is about as palatable as shoe leather. By the first part of November the old bulls are generally through with the rut and their flesh is beginning to recover.

About the only thing that can be said against early-season elk hunting is that in some areas the weather can be rather warm until October, and in warm weather the elk generally stay in heavy timber and are hard to see. In addition elk meat is more difficult to keep in warm weather than it is in cool. However, in the high altitudes in Wyoming and Montana around timberline the mid-September weather is generally delightful. Sometimes there will be an unseasonable snowstorm then, but usually the days are bright and clear and there is frost at night. In those high altitudes the thin air does not long hold the warmth of the sun, and as soon as the sun begins to sink it gets cold. It is wonderful weather to hunt in, to sleep in, simply to be alive in. Much of the Idaho elk country is lower and warmer early in the season.

Precisely what controls the onset of the rut in elk no one knows exactly. The Indians say that elk, moose, and caribou begin to rut at the time of the first full moon in September. Others say that the rut starts with the first hard frost. In 1964 my wife and I hunted elk in the high country off the South Fork of the Shoshone River out of Cody, Wyoming. For whatever the reason, the elk did not start bugling until about the 18th of September. On the hunt described in the first of this chapter the elk were bugling by the 12th. In 1956 I was hunting elk in Wyoming in high country near the area where my wife and I hunted in 1964. We made camp in a big canyon and that night it rang with the bugling of elk of all sizes and ages. This was early in October.

On the Mogollon Rim in Arizona I have heard elk bugling toward the last of August, and I have heard the thin, birdlike whistles of spike bull elk in Arizona as late as the last of November. In Europe and Asia the red deer, those Old Country relatives of the elk, roar early in September, just as the elk here generally do.

Elk "bugles" are sold in sporting goods stores throughout the elk country. One season I called up two bulls by using a child's tin whistle which cost about twenty-five cents in a dime store. The last bull I saw whistled up responded simply to a whistle made by the mouth alone. I have never shot an elk that I myself have whistled up by mouth but I have got bulls to answer me.

All elk calls are supposed to sound like the whistle of a spike or five-point bull. The younger the elk the shriller and thinner the whistle. The bugling of old bulls sounds like the braying of a donkey mixed with whistles and grunts.

The old bulls collect harems of cows. They strive mightily to keep other bulls away. Nevertheless young bulls particularly spikes (yearlings) and five-pointers (two-year olds) are always hanging around the harem. For this reason the defiant whistle of a young bull enrages an old one and he will come to run the bold interloper off. He knows he is big enough and heavy enough to whip any spike or five-pointer, and the young elk know they are no match for the lordly six-point herd bulls.

My advice to anyone trying to call up a bull is to try to make the whistle as natural as possible but not to make it too loud. The elk have ears better than those of human beings and I have seen bulls come to a hunter's bugle from a quarter of a mile when I could not hear it at 100 yards. And the hunter attempting to call up a bull should not whistle too often as it has been my experience that prolonged and repeated whistling from one spot makes a bull suspicious.

However, at the proper time an old bull is not difficult to call up. He will answer anything that sounds somewhat like another bull. He will even bugle when he hears a packtrain on the trail as he thinks it might be a herd of elk in charge of a bull he might be able to whip. One time I was riding along a trail through heavy woods just before the elk season was to open. Suddenly my horse shied and I looked up to see an enormous six-point bull bearing down on me with his eyes glaring and the hair on his neck standing straight up. I had to yell at him to turn him back. Even then he was not quite convinced that our horses were not a herd of voluptuous cows held captive by a mean old bull. He hung around back in the timber within 100 yards. He would whack the trees with his antlers and now and then he would bugle. Sex had driven the old boy off his rocker.

Bull elk do some very wild things during the rut. My wife's first bull was shot at about 9,000 feet in Wyoming. We were headed back to camp when along a tongue of timber that ran through the middle of a mountain valley we saw a bull elk hurrying toward us. We were on horseback in plain view. I think that crazy bull saw us, since elk have excellent eyes, but seeing us didn't seem to bother him. As he continued to hurry along toward us, we dismounted, quickly tied our horses, and sat down with our backs to trees. The bull disappeared in the timber and then came trotting out about 150 yards away. A 160-grain bullet from my wife's 7 × 57 put him down.

The weather is an extremely important factor in elk hunting. The fall of 1965 was a very poor season for elk throughout the West, not because there were not sufficient elk but because the weather was unseasonably warm. The elk stayed in the cool shade of heavy timber where they were difficult to see and almost impossible to approach. They fed at night, very late in the afternoon, very early in the morning. That season my wife and I hunted in an area off Idaho's Selway River where we had both shot elk previously with no difficulty. We hunted hard for seven days and did not fire a shot. There were sufficient elk in the country, but for most of the time it was unseasonably warm and the elk simply were not moving. Then the weather changed and from that time on it was either raining or the clouds were so low that up in the hills it would have been impossible to see an elk fifty yards away. In the entire week my wife

O'Connor with a good but not remarkable bull elk shot just above timberline in October in Wyoming.

and I saw only two bulls. They were about a mile away feeding in an open mountain meadow. The wind was wrong and we would have had to go the long way around to get to them. There simply was not time.

Today elk are mountain animals and the weather moves them up and down. Heat will send them into the coolness of high timbered basins and sidehills. Storms will likewise push them down into timber. Heavy snow that covers food and makes getting around difficult will drive them clear down into the warmer river valleys where the snow is not so deep. The notorious firing line near Gardiner, Montana, is a spot where the elk come out of Yellowstone Park when driven by deep snow. There citizens wait when the word gets around that the elk are migrating; then whenever a herd crosses the park boundary the heroes open up.

A light "tracking" snow early in the season is the hunter's delight. Then it is easy to locate elk. But these tracking snows sometimes get out of hand. Once some friends and I packed back into Idaho elk country on the last day of September, the day before elk season was to begin. That night a howling blizzard developed. At the end of three days the snow was almost three feet deep and there wasn't a track to be found. The elk had moved down about 2,000 feet. We got out as well as we could.

Once in Wyoming a storm came up at about the same time of year. I was getting ready to pack back into the mountains about twenty-five miles when it hit. For two days the wind howled, snow pelted down, and it was bitterly cold. Then a warm wind blew out of the west. The sky cleared, and the snow began to melt. But the snow in the timber in the dark cool canyons and the heavy basins was protected from the warm wind and had not melted. The big open grassy basins above timberline were full of elk. A companion and I each got a magnificent bull the first day we hunted. In one basin I saw about sixty elk and of these at least twelve were big six-point bulls.

Where elk are not molested they often feed until mid-morning and are afoot and feeding by 4 o'clock in the afternoon. If they are hunted hard or if the weather is warm, they finish feeding not long after dawn and do not resume until almost sundown. It behooves the elk hunter in country where there is much competition to be out at dawn when the elk are feeding and moving. Often it is productive to find a lofty perch to watch from. Then if the hunter sees an elk not too far away, he can make his stalk. If it will take him more than a half-hour at the most he should hold off and try to determine where the elk beds down for the day. Then he can begin his stalk with the assurance that his elk will probably stay put until he gets there.

When several people are hunting elk it is often profitable to put two or three in spots from which they can see over a considerable area; then the others can go around and work slowly through a basin or up a canyon. The elk will sneak out ahead of the drivers, and the hunters on the lookouts will get shooting.

The best elk I ever shot in Idaho came from a drive of a sort. My wife sat on a rocky point overlooking a basin and I on a hillside about 400 yards away from her. Between us was a saddle through which a nervous elk pushed out of the basin would probably travel. By the time I saw the bull I later shot the driver had already gone through the basin and was sitting with my wife on the point. But he had made the bull nervous. Apparently it planned to cross through the saddle into the next basin.

I first became aware of the bull's presence when I saw, perhaps 125 yards away and sharply below me, a magnificent set of elk antlers moving through a very thick patch of snowbrush. The antlers moved slowly to the edge of the patch, and then I believe the bull saw my wife and Dave Christensen sitting up on the rocky point. The antlers turned, started diagonally back as if to go around the hill on my right. They had traveled perhaps twenty or thirty yards when the bull went through a spot where the brush was thinner. For the first time I could see some elk

The author and guide Dave Christensen with the best elk the former ever shot in Idaho. The bull has seven points on one side, six on the other. The horns are quite heavy but not especially long.

hide. I shot offhand, aiming for the lungs just to the left of the spine and behind the shoulder. The bull went down when the 150-grain 7 mm. Remington Magnum bullet hit him. He never moved. He had a fine head with seven points on one side, six on the other.

An elk grows his first antlers in his second year when he is a long yearling. These are spikes, but often these spikes are quite long—two feet or so. His second set has five points to the side. Generally his third set, when he is a long three-year-old and in his fourth year, has six points to a side, but these first six-point antlers are short and thin. The size of the antlers increases until the sixth or seventh pair. Then they start to become smaller and are often freakish—with more than six points to the side, with irregular points, and sometimes with crown formations on the top like those developed by some species of Old World red deer.

The best way to be able to judge a set of elk antlers when you get a bull in the scope is to compare it mentally with other elk heads. Anyone

O'Connor with a good but not record six-point bull elk.

interested in learning to judge trophy elk should look critically at every live elk and every mounted head he sees until he has a basis for comparison. A really good elk head looks big immediately. It should appear to go high above the bull's back—with the top portion about as high above the elk's back as the back is above the ground. The antlers should appear massive, the points long, all well defined.

The moment the hunter sees a record-class set of antlers he should know it, whether it is on a live animal or not. When my wife and I were hunting in Alberta with Fred Huntington Jr. in 1961, we came in late one afternoon to find Fred there with a big grin on his face. He pointed to an enormous elk head. Instantly I said, "There is a head that will go up in the records." I was right. It is No. 36 in the 1964 Records of North American Big Game. Several years ago I was in Grangeville, Idaho, when a friend who runs a sporting goods store called to me and told me he had something to show me. It was an elk head with nine points on one side and eight on the other. Before I had touched it with a tape I said it would be in the first ten in the records. It is No. 4. The big ones *look* big.

178

It is the ones we are not sure of that never measure as well as we hope.

A score of years ago it used to be said that elk no longer grew antlers like the ones they had back in the days before farmers and cattlemen had taken over their winter range. This may be true to some extent, as the pioneers were not trophy hunters and undoubtedly many record-class heads of all kinds were simply left back in the mountains. Rich Britishers were the first hunters who were interested in anything but elk meat (which they could eat) and elk teeth (which they could sell). In the late 70's, the 80's and the 90's Britishers made the long journey to the American West and brought back the noble elk heads which today decorate the manor halls of England.

But with luck and perseverance today's elk hunter has a good chance for an outstanding trophy. In the 1964 edition of *Records of North American Big Game,* the No. 1 head was shot in 1915 and the No. 2 in 1890, but of the other heads in the first ten one was shot in 1912, but the others were taken between 1946 and 1950. Of the rest in the first twenty, one was shot in 1936 and one in 1874, but the others were taken in the 1950's and 1960's. This goes to show that the modern hunter still has a chance and it also shows that there is a much greater interest in trophies today in the United States than there was thirty and forty years ago.

Of the elk heads in the first ten, one comes from Colorado, four from Montana, one from Arizona, two from Alberta, one from Wyoming, one from Idaho. I'd guess that the hunter who wanted nothing more outstanding then a good, average trophy bull would stand as good a chance as any in Wyoming or Montana in some area adjacent to Yellowstone Park as he would see more elk and have more good bulls to look over. The man wanting to get a head well up in the record class would probably have more luck in wilderness areas in the Alberta Rockies. The elk there have good feed in limestone mountains. They are not hunted hard and have time to grow up. Some areas, because of the character of the soil, never produce outstanding elk heads. Some never do because the elk are shot down and not allowed to mature. But an area of rich soil, plentiful elk, and light hunting will always produce good trophies—if the hunter has patience and knows a good set of antlers when he sees it.

15 | *Medicine for Elk and Moose*

Every year in the West thousands of elk are shot with everything from the .25/35 to .375's and even .458's. Probably more elk are killed with .30/06 rifles than anything else, but the .270 is also popular as is the .300 Savage and the .308. Now and then some eccentric, usually one of the nuttier gun nuts, takes to the boondocks with a .375, and in the small Idaho city where I live there are several .338's in the hands of elk hunters.

All of these cartridges and many others kill elk well if they are pointed right and poorly if they aren't pointed right. A gut-shot elk is just as gut-shot with a .375 as with a .25/35, and an elk with a leg broken by a .460 Weatherby will go just as far as if the leg had been broken by a .243.

I have read many times the specifications for elk cartridges. The authors list minimum bore diameters, minimum bullet weights, minimum amounts of residual energy at 100 or 200 yards. One authority says that elk should not be hunted with a cartridge with a bullet of less than .33 caliber or weighing less than 275 grains. Another sets 250 grains as the low limit for the elk bullet. Yet another says the bullet should have a sectional density of at least .270 and should deliver at least 2,500 foot-pounds of energy at 100 yards.

If an elk hunter is filled with euphoria by going after the big deer with a .458 I am all for him. If he wants to make a reasonably honest dollar by knocking off an inspirational essay on elk rifles, I can under-

180

stand his problem as I have felt the cruel pinch of want myself. I draw the line only if he expects me to take the stuff seriously.

The most important pieces of equipment the elk hunter can take into the hills with him are shooting skill and common sense. Like any other game, elk are killed neatly and cleanly by putting well-constructed bullets in the right place. They are wounded by putting any bullets in the wrong place.

First, let's take a look at this odd creature, the elk. To those used to hunting deer he is an astonishingly big animal. It takes a very large buck deer to weigh 200 pounds field dressed, but bull elk that dress out three times as much are fairly common. Even a spike bull elk makes the largest deer look small, and to the uninitiated a big bull looks as large as a good-sized horse.

The bones of an elk are larger and heavier than those of a deer and the walls of the rib cage are thicker. Lightly constructed varmint-type bullets that will go through the ribs of a deer and kill like dynamite are apt to expand too rapidly on the ribs of an elk and give insufficient penetration.

Another little item is that an elk (particularly a frightened elk) is harder to kill in his tracks than deer, sheep, antelope, or other animals of that size. An elk with a bullet in the brain or with a broken spine will go down as quickly as a jack rabbit, but often an elk will travel farther than a deer when well hit through the lungs even with a good bullet from a powerful rifle.

I shot at my first bull elk on the Mogollon Rim in central Arizona in 1934. Another hunter had been shooting at this bull and the great deer came by me under a full head of steam. I shot at him a couple of times, saw hair fly, but he ran out of sight.

I found hair cut off by the bullet but no blood. I could see no tracks because the bull was running over volcanic rock called malipai in Arizona. After searching aimlessly I gave up. A few days later, after having killed another bull, I blundered into the one I had shot at. He had traveled somewhere between 250 and 300 yards and was lying in a little grove of Gambel oaks. He had two .30/06 bullets through the lungs, and if he hadn't been so frightened he probably wouldn't have gone fifty yards.

If I had known as much about elk as I do now I would not have given up so easily, but that was the first legal elk season Arizona had had since the native Merriam elk had been exterminated in the early 1890's. We native Arizonans then thought of elk as being as hard to knock down as Cape buffalo. Many were lost that first year because some of us didn't have enough sense to follow them up.

Another little detail in which elk differ from deer is that because elk are larger, bullets seldom will go clear through them—even on broadside shots through the rib cage. The hide of an elk, like that of most animals of its size, is thick and rubbery. By the time the bullet has gone through rib cage, lungs, and more ribs it is well expanded and has pretty well lost its ambition. It generally cannot penetrate the hide and is found rolled like a ball under the hide on the far side. Often the presence of the bullet can be detected, as it makes a little lump. This is a common occurrence even on animals smaller than elk and with heavy bullets. The handsome big-maned lion I shot in Angola in 1962 stopped a 300-grain .375 Magnum bullet. I found it as a lump between hide and ribs—and a lion is a lot lighter than a bull elk.

As a consequence, a lung-shot elk that runs from 50 to perhaps 150 yards is apt not to bleed much and occasionally one does not bleed at all. The entrance hole of the bullet is generally high and there is no exit hole. Generally a lot of blood of medium color is the sign of a surface muscle wound.

The elk is large and fairly phlegmatic. He does not react to a shot the way a deer does. Often a fatally hit elk that will be dead in minutes if not seconds will show no sign of being hit. I once shot an elk about 250 yards away across a canyon. I was absolutely sure of my shot, but because of some quirk of wind or terrain I did not hear the bullet strike. Neither had the elk flinched nor given any sign of being hit. Instead he had walked slowly into some brush. Because I was convinced I had hit the elk, I went over to the spot where he had been standing and found him stone dead within forty yards.

I hope I have not given the impression that elk are difficult to kill, as they are not—if the shots are well placed and good bullets are used. They may not collapse in their tracks as quickly as deer do, but well-placed shots that get inside generally lay them down without much fuss. I have shot in all about eighteen or nineteen elk but I have also shot a fair number of African greater kudu and roan antelope, both of which are about the size of elk and are just about as difficult to kill.

The big bores (.338, .375, .358 Norma Magnum, .416 and such powerful medicine) have two advantages over rifles of smaller bore with lighter bullets when used on elk and moose. First is that their strong, heavy bullets will generally break the shoulder blade whereas lighter bullets may not. This is a very academic advantage as the average elk hunter never uses the shoulder shot and couldn't locate the shoulder blade with the aid of three bloodhounds and an anatomical chart. The other very slight advantage is that the heavy bullets *may* kill or disable with a rear-end shot. However, this is questionable. Long ago I learned it was folly to shoot at the rear end of large animals. I have never seen any bullet that can be depended upon to go through the heavy rump muscles of an elk, up into the abdominal cavity and on into the lung area. A round-nose solid will do it but expanding bullets generally will not.

The disadvantages of the big bores are that they are heavier and more unpleasant to carry, kick more and are more difficult to shoot accurately, and kill little if any quicker than smaller calibers with the same shot placement. I am a firm believer in big bores where they are needed and have done quite a bit of shooting with them. But elk hunting is not one of the spots where they are needed.

Many hunters with limited experience in elk hunting believe in all honesty that rifles of considerable power should be used on elk. Generally they arrive at the notion through a piece of bad luck or poor shooting. After my first elk hunt I was convinced that a real cannon was the only answer for elk because, as I have related, the first bull I shot at got away wounded to die. But this was just one of those things.

The third elk I shot was about seventy-five yards away when I put a .270 bullet through his lungs. He ran about thirty yards in a semicircle and fell dead. Another elk was at very long range, but when a 130-grain .270 bullet took him through the lungs he wobbled around on rubbery legs for a few seconds, then collapsed. I began to think that one did not need a cannon for elk.

Once I was hunting with a friend in heavy timber on a dark, drizzly day. I heard my pal shoot about 100 yards away and went over to see what had happened. He had taken a poke at a big bull with a .30/06. The bull was facing him, almost fell when he shot. We found blood but to me it looked as though it was from a flesh wound. We tracked the elk by the blood until the rain washed it out. We never found the elk. My pal is convinced that if he had been using a heavier rifle he would have got the elk. I am convinced that the bullet only grazed the bull, made a flesh wound, and that he wouldn't have killed the elk if he had been using a .50-caliber machine gun. I may be wrong, but I do not think so.

The elk is a tough and courageous animal, and when thoroughly frightened he will carry on with very severe wounds. In this respect he is more difficult to stop than the larger moose. Often moose will lie down and will allow themselves to be approached and finished with wounds so superficial that they would not slow down an elk—or even a deer.

I have lost only two wounded elk in almost thirty years of off-and-on elk hunting. One was the frightened bull I have already described. The other was a bull I gut shot with a .270 at very long range. The wound made the bull sick. He took a few steps and lay down. A companion and I started down the hill toward the elk. I was only recently off the sick list from a ruptured tendon in a leg, but my companion was young, and tough and frisky. He forged ahead of me and when he was about 100 yards from the elk, he opened up on it with a revolver—and missed it.

The elk took off, got into a miserable tangle of down timber, and when darkness came on we were forced to give up the trail.

A great many elk are lost, but almost always the reason lies in human error—and not in insufficient power in the rifle. Too many hunters blaze away at elk at long range and from unsteady positions. They shoot at the whole elk instead of trying to hit a particular and vital spot. Unless the elk turns a double flip or gives some other unmistakable sign of being hit, they do not go over to look for blood. Even if they do find blood, many hunters give up too soon and go look for another elk. As a consequence of this careless shooting and careless tracking many elk go off to die. I have heard various estimates of losses of wounded elk, some as high as one elk escaping wounded for every two brought in. What the actual loss is, no one knows for certain.

The best place to shoot an elk is in the lung area just behind the vertical line of the foreleg. If a good bullet is placed solidly in the lungs, the elk seldom goes very far—maybe 50 yards, maybe 150. The heart of an elk lies low in the thorax between the front legs when the animal is viewed from the side. I never shoot for the heart. One reason is that a heart shot kills an elk little if any quicker than a good solid lung shot. Another reason is that the heavy leg bones may blow the bullet up without hitting the heart. If I can, I like to put the bullet high in the lungs. Shock transmitted to the spine from the high lung shot will very often knock an elk down in his tracks and he'll bleed to death before he gets to his feet.

One of the finest bulls I ever shot was about 250–300 yards away and below me at a slight angle. I put a 150-grain Nosler .270 bullet to the left of his spine so the bullet would range forward through the left lung into the right lung. The bull dropped instantly and as far as I could tell was stone dead before I could get another cartridge in the chamber.

On another occasion I was hunting elk with a pal. He shot a five-point bull, and I was watching it when I became aware that a juicy spike was running along a hill broadside about 150 yards away. I swung along with it, fired, and the young bull slid on his nose. Another high lung shot.

The neck shot is deadly if the spine is hit, but if it is missed the animal may get up and take off when the shock wears off. Some who hunt in heavy timber like head shots, but a head-shot elk is a pretty messy sight and there is always a possibility of shooting the jaw off and losing the elk.

In many places elk are shot either at very close range or at long range. In much of Idaho's elk country, for example, the animals are taken across wide canyons at ranges of from 250 to 400 yards or in timber on the same side of the canyon at from 25 to 75 yards. Early in the season in Idaho the elk tend to hole up in heavy timber during the daylight hours and the successful elk hunter has to sneak around upwind and be as quiet as a mouse.

One chap tells me that he has shot three elk with a .44 Magnum revolver, none at over fifty yards. For this sort of shooting, almost any rifle using a strong bullet that will do a fairly decent job of getting through brush is all right. In the West hundreds of elk are killed every year with .30/30's and .32 Specials. One old-time Montana elk hunter I knew swore by the now obsolete .33 and .35 Winchester cartridges loaded with solid bullets. He told me he could shoot through a fair-sized tree with either and get an elk. For brush hunting, the round-nose 200- and 220-grain bullets in the various .30-caliber rifles are fine.

Shooting at longer ranges is something else. Then the medicine is a rifle for a flat-shooting hard-hitting cartridge. I have killed more elk with .270 rifles than with anything else, and I have had good luck with good 150-grain bullets loaded to between 2,900 and 2,975 at the muzzle. My pet handload is the 150-grain Nosler in front of 58.5 grains of No. 4831 for around 2,950 foot-seconds in a 22-inch barrel. I have also shot elk with a .30/06 and 180- and 220-grain bullets, and with a .300 Weatherby with the 180-grain bullet. My wife has had good luck with the 7 × 57 and a handload with 160-grain bullets driven at about 2,650.

Actually the world is full of good elk cartridges. The .30/06 is the most popular of all and a good one. I have read many times that any .270 bullet bounced off of elk, but I have killed quite a few elk very dead with one shot when using that cartridge. John George of Lewiston, Idaho, who once owned a piece of a hunting lodge and did a lot of guiding, has killed a great many elk in his day. His favorite cartridge is the .270 with the 130-grain bullet. A Colorado game warden who in the course of duty had to shoot hundreds of marauding elk liked the .270 with the 130-grain bullet better than anything else he used.

I have never shot an elk (or any other animal) with a .264 Magnum, but I don't see why it should not be fine elk medicine with the 140-grain bullet. Les Bowman, the Cody, Wyoming, guide and outfitter, was lent a couple of 7-mm. Remington Magnum rifles before they were on the market. He considers the cartridge to be about as good elk medicine as one can get. He tells me he finds the 150-grain bullet to be a quicker killer than the 175-grain. That was also my impression from using the caliber on one seven-point bull and on elk-sized African antelope in Mozambique and Angola in the summer of 1962.

If the elk hunter can use one of the more potent magnums without getting gun shy, there is no reason why he shouldn't. The new .300 Winchester Magnum, the .300 Weatherby, the .308 Norma—all are fine elk medicine with the 180-, 200-, and 220-grain bullets. The .338 Winchester, the .358 Norma, and the .375 H. & H. Magnum do very well in the hands of those who like them and can shoot them—as indeed they should!

However, there is no real necessity for any of these heavy cartridges, as elk are killed neatly with much less powerful cartridges. Les Bowman, who during his many years as an outfitter saw several dozen elk killed annually, says he saw more elk wounded with the magnums than with less powerful rifles because the hunters placed their bullets less well.

I'd say that anyone using a .243 or a 6 mm.–.244 on elk would be somewhat undergunned, but the old 7 × 57 with 140-, 160-, or 175-grain bullets, the .270 with any bullet from 130 to 170 grains, the .284 Winchester with the 150-grain bullet, the .280 Remington with 150- and 165-grain bullets, the .300 Savage and the .308 with 180-grain bullets are all perfectly satisfactory. The .30/30 and the .32 Special are all right for moderate ranges in the timber, but poor for cross-canyon shots because of their rainbow trajectories.

Whatever caliber is chosen, the elk hunter should use strongly constructed bullets—and not bullets of the softer type that are sudden death on varmints and on deer. Among good ones are the Noslers, the Speers, the heavier Hornadys, the Remington Core-Lokts, and the Winchester Power Points.

But the important thing with these big deer is to be sure that the first shot goes into the vital heart-lung-shoulder area. The man who doesn't shoot until he knows his bullet is going to hit in the right place won't have much trouble killing elk cleanly. On the other hand if he blazes away into the brown on running animals, through brush, and at ranges beyond his skill he'll have a tough time killing elk with anything he can fire from the shoulder.

16 | *How To Handle a Grizzly*

In the spring of 1950, the late Field Johnson, a Yukon Indian guide with whom I hunted on several occasions, was out in the bush near the Indian village of Champagne. He had his beat-up old .30/30 carbine with him and he was probably looking for a moose. Suddenly something struck him a tremendous blow that sent his .30/30 flying and knocked him end over end. He was dazed by the blow, but an instant later he realized he was being mauled by a grizzly. He also knew that his only chance to survive was to feign death—and he did. Presently the grizzly decided Field was dead, so he dug a shallow hole and buried him.

Field was bruised and bleeding and in great pain, but he lay there for about an hour. For a time he could hear the bear shuffling around and sniffing. Then all was quiet. He decided that the grizzly had gone, pushed up through the loose earth and brush that was his grave, lurched to his feet, and started off.

But the crafty bear had been hiding nearby, silent and vindictive, waiting and watching to make sure the hated man was dead. With a roar he was on Field again. Once more he knocked him down with a tremendous blow. Then he chewed on him some more. Again Field played dead, with less difficulty this time, because he had spells of unconsciousness from pain and loss of blood. This time the grizzly decided to bury him in a better place. So he took him by the feet and dragged him a half-mile. Then he dug another and deeper hole and covered Field with brush and loose earth.

When Field regained consciousness he could tell that many hours had passed. He was weak, in desperate pain, and burning with thirst. He once more staggered out of his grave, knowing that if he was to live he must have help. This time, the grizzly, certain that he had done his job and that Field was dead, had gone. Field managed to make it to the Alaska Highway, got a ride into Whitehorse, and with the aid of sulfa and penicillin and skillful surgery he pulled through. In spite of good medical care, the terrible ordeal eventually proved too much for him. He went insane and eventually died. He was one of the nicest guys I have ever known.

It is fashionable among hunters who have been very lucky or who have had a very limited experience with grizzlies to scoff at the notion that the grizzly is dangerous and that he has come honestly by his scientific name *Ursus horribilis*—the horrible bear, or his early popular name, the grisly (or terrible) bear.

A northwestern guide and outfitter I know hoots at the very notion that a grizzly can be dangerous. His grizzly hunting experience has been in the states of Wyoming and Montana, where most grizzlies have learned that in spite of their enormous strength and bulk they are no match for white men. Generations of mother grizzlies have taught their cubs that the rancid, sickening smell of human beings means danger, fire and thunder, sudden unexplicable pain. For more than a hundred years white men with rifles have waged war on the American grizzly, with rifles, with dogs, with traps, and with poison. Grizzlies that have survived south of the Canadian border have learned that the white man is his one dangerous enemy.

But this wasn't so in the old days, just as it isn't so in the wilderness today. When the first beaver trappers and mountain men invaded the domain of the grizzly more than a century ago, they found him a very tough and aggressive customer indeed. In the open plains country of what is now Nebraska and the Dakotas, in the foothills of the mountains, and in the high Rockies themselves, the grizzly was the lord of the land, afraid of nothing, just as the lion was on the plains of Africa. Occasionally a big bull buffalo might give a grizzly a tussle, and now and then perhaps a hunger-mad pack of wolves would try to drive one of the great bears away from a kill; but getting accidentally gored by a buffalo was an occupational hazard and one blow from a grizzly's paw would knock a wolf halfway out of the country.

With their puny bows and arrows, the Indians were no match for grizzlies and let them alone. The big bears probably thought no more about the Indians than they did of the bighorn sheep, spry, nimble, elusive, that haunted the rough country. If a grizzly came upon a helpless bighorn lamb, he'd no doubt eat him; but since the ewes bore their young in rough rocky places the soft-booted grizzly did not care for he seldom encountered one. Likewise the Indians lived in large congregations, smelled bad, and were surrounded by dogs and fire. The grizzly didn't bother them except, perhaps, to take a kill away from a hunter now and then.

White men had long been familiar with the shy, timid, furtive black bear of the Eastern woods, and they soon found that the grizzly was another animal entirely. One wrote: "The reddish bears (grizzlies) are mischievous creatures for they fall fiercely on the huntsman, whereas the black ones fly from them." They recorded that the Indians considered the hunting of the black bear a safe and enjoyable pastime, but that the grizzlies played too rough.

If a grizzly smelled something in camp that he wanted, he simply walked in and took it, just as the polar bear is apt to do today. If he could take it without a fuss, so much the better. If he couldn't he was willing to fight. Those early beaver trappers who were the first whites to invade the Rockies, had to kill many grizzlies to protect their meat, a job which soon taught them that their long Kentucky rifles with their small bores and small, light balls were no match for grizzlies, just as they were no match for the buffalo. The grizzly, as much as the buffalo, was responsible for developing the heavy big-bore "plains rifle," like the famous Hawken.

Heavy rifles in the hands of good, cool shots, even though they were muzzle loaders, made the chances of a grizzly distinctly poor in the case of a mix-up. After the Civil War, when powerful lever-action repeating rifles were developed, the grizzly lost what little chance he had against the big muzzle loaders.

Under ordinary circumstances, a cool, well-armed man who is alert and cautious has no need to fear a grizzly. The blow of a modern bullet is as terrible as that of a grizzly's paw, and it can be delivered repeatedly and from a distance. In his dim, animal way the grizzly knows this and the first reaction of the grizzly who lives in settled country today and has been harassed by man is to bolt the moment he smells a human being.

Nevertheless the grizzly anywhere is still a dangerous animal, along with his first cousin, the Alaska brown bear (which is simply a fish-fed grizzly), the only really dangerous game animal in North America. A good shot with a powerful rifle ordinarily isn't in much danger, but the danger is always there. No better hunter than Field Johnson has ever lived, yet he got mauled by a grizzly.

It is rare that the big-game hunter who is out after grizzlies gets into trouble. He is armed. He is looking for grizzlies, and he usually has a guide. He has binoculars that enable him to locate the bear before the bear sees him.

But even the best grizzly hunt can go wrong—and that's one of the reasons grizzly hunting is fascinating. Take the case of a New York surgeon who hunted grizzlies in the Yukon in 1949. He wounded a grizzly and he and his guide went into the willows after it—a wonderful way to get into trouble. The grizzly was lying in wait. He charged the doctor and knocked him down before he could do more than shoot at it from the hip. He had the doctor's right hand in his mouth, tried to chew on it, and the doctor said, "Well, here goes my career." The guide killed the bear and pulled the doctor out from under the great bleeding carcass intact except for some terrible bruises which an Indian told me were "as black as black-bear hide." One thing had saved the doctor's hand—and probably his life. A shot had broken the bear's jaw and he couldn't bite.

Perhaps the most dangerous grizzly of all is the sow with cubs, and the majority of the killings and maulings I have heard about come from someone, usually unarmed, blundering into a female who thinks her young are menaced. One pathetic instance happened in the 1930's in Alberta. A Canadian homesteader and his little girl were picking berries in the summer, when they encountered an old female with a cub. The bear showed fight so the man told his little daughter to run for home and that he would hold off the bear while she got a good start. The little girl got home all right and told her mother that daddy was having a fight with a grizzly. Taking a rifle the courageous pioneer woman went to the rescue, but she found her husband mauled and dead, a spruce limb with which he had tried to fend off the bear beside him.

On the other hand, an acquaintance of mine got out of a similar scrape much more fortunately. He was photographing big game in Yellowstone Park when he saw a female and her cub eating berries in an open meadow. He stalked them, set up his movie camera, and was letting her roll when mama decided he meant no good and charged. Using the camera on the tripod as a club, he waited until the bear was on him, then crashed it against her skull. She staggered back, then looked around, saw that her cub was getting away, and followed it. The photographer's hide was intact, but his expensive camera was a total loss.

Another bad situation is to find a bear over a kill, particularly if the man has the wind on the bear and cannot be smelled. The eyesight of bears is very bad. They are exceedingly myopic, and I am sure that at more than fifty yards or so they see only masses and outlines. They are also undoubtedly color-blind. Once when I was stalking a grizzly the bear changed his position and saw me in plain sight at no more than 200 yards. He watched me for thirty seconds, perhaps, and then, not the least disturbed, he lay down again. A friend of mine ran across a pair of caribou-hunting grizzlies and drew them up to within twenty-five yards by holding his arms up over his head in imitation of caribou antlers.

Now let us suppose that a human being blunders onto a bear at a kill. The bear is hungry and excited. He has blood in his nose and this impairs his sense of smell. He is on the alert for a rival who may try to take his kill from him. He looks up and sees a human being *standing in an upright position that grizzlies themselves assume in order to see better.*

"Ah," says the bear to himself, "here's another grizzly trying to chisel in on my kill. I'd better deal with him!"

So the bear charges what he has taken to be another bear, and before he has realized his mistake he may have killed a human being.

A hungry grizzly will come toward the smell of fresh blood to see what he can promote. One Alaskan had killed a moose and was dressing it, when a tremendous blow from behind knocked him clear over the moose and against a tree on the far side. His assailant was a grizzly who had seen him bending over the kill and had thought he was another bear. The instant he had *smelled* his opponent he had fled, but the man, though badly bruised, was lucky to be alive.

Once in the Yukon I had shot a big bull caribou and had finished taking off the head and scalp and dressing him when I spied a black speck that looked like a burned stump, except that this stump was moving and my guide and I were far above timberline where there simply were no stumps. It was a big grizzly that had smelled the blood and was hot-footing it toward the kill. He was a grand silvertip, and the hide of this bear who delivered himself is now hanging on the wall of my study. On another occasion in the Yukon I had shot a fine snow-white Dall ram. Snow was falling and low-hanging clouds covered the ice-sheathed peaks as I slowly picked my way down the steep shoulder of a great mountain through rocks and shale. I was carrying the head and scalp, a load of meat, and my rifle and binoculars. I was desperately weary and miserably cold and wet, and the only thing I could think of was to get to my little tent far below to change clothes, to get warm, and to make some hot tea.

Suddenly right behind me I heard a growl. I turned around and there, not more than twenty-five yards away, was a big grizzly. He had smelled the blood and had come to see what was going on. When he got to where his poor eyes did him some good, he had stopped, puzzled. This was very wild country and I doubt if that bear had ever seen or smelled a human being before.

For an instant that bear and I looked into each other's eyes. My hair rose on my neck and my heart skipped a couple of beats. Then I yelled: "Get out of here, you — — —!" At the sound of my voice the bear almost turned a back somersault, and the way he got out of there looked exactly like one of Walt Disney's scared and fleeing bears. I dropped the head and meat, ran to a little ridge where I could watch him run. I didn't shoot. Right then I wouldn't have traded a cup of hot tea and a pair of dry socks for all the grizzlies in the Yukon!

Food + grizzly + human being that the bear thinks stands between him and food is a bad combination. Ned Frost, the famous Wyoming guide and grizzly hunter, was badly mauled by a grizzly once when he was lying in his tent asleep in his bedroll. There was some bacon in the tent and the grizzly felt that Frost stood between him and the bacon. Frost, by the way, hunted grizzlies probably more than any other man when there were many of the great bears in the Rockies of Idaho, Montana, and Wyoming. He believes that when the number of hunters, the number of animals, and the number of maulings are taken into consideration, the grizzly is more dangerous than the African lion. About this I am doubtful—and have hunted both species.

Going into cover after a wounded grizzly is a dangerous thing to do and most northern guides do not relish it in the slightest. Frantic and furious with pain, frightened and desperate, the wounded, cornered grizzly is a tough and vindictive opponent. Theodore Roosevelt, who was an enthusiastic and experienced grizzly hunter back in the days when the big bears were still plentiful in the Rockies of the United States, records several instances of maulings in his excellent book, *Hunting the Grisly*. In one case a grizzly mauled a cavalry trooper so badly that he died, in spite of the fact that both the bear's front legs were broken! Roosevelt himself might never have lived to become President of the United States, as he was charged by a grizzly he had stumbled onto and lived to write about it only because he was a quick and accurate shot.

Some years ago in Alberta, an American sportsman wounded a grizzly and he and his guide followed the bear into cover. The bear charged, got the guide down, and was mauling him when the sportsman put the muzzle of the rifle to the bear's head and killed him. The sportsman got the almost unconscious guide on a horse, managed to get him back to camp, and eventually out of the bush to a hospital. He recovered.

One of the weirdest instances of an aggressive grizzly I have ever heard of had happened in the Yukon only a couple of years before I was told about it. A party outfitted by the late Jean Jacquot of Kluane Lake was on the trail with a full outfit of packhorses. Through some trick of the wind, a female grizzly did not hear the approach of the pack train, and the whole outfit rode right up on her as she and her cubs were feeding on berries. The old bear charged right into the pack train, scattering horses right and left. A hunter from Texas in the party killed her within twenty feet of the muzzle of his rifle. In the majority of cases a grizzly would have run off under those circumstances, but there are enough exceptions to make for occasional excitement in grizzly country.

An amazing piece of information about grizzlies is contributed by the late F. W. "Bert" Rigall, a pioneer rancher and outfitter in Twin Butte, Alberta. Back in the 1890's, he told me, there was a great smallpox epidemic among the Stoney Indians who lived in the Rockies of south-western Alberta and southeastern British Columbia. When a village would get heavily infested, the Indians who were not yet stricken would ride off and leave the dead unburied and the dying to their fate. Grizzlies found they could invade the tepees to feed on the dead and dying. They got a taste of human flesh, and the next step was stalking and killing live and healthy Indians. So dangerous did those bears become that the tribe completely abandoned the country. When Rigall first settled there he found the trails all grown up and the older grizzlies still man-eaters. He stopped two unprovoked charges within a few feet.

The grizzly is a tough baby, but all reported charges by grizzlies are not charges by any means. The average hunter who goes up against one is in a pretty jittery frame of mind, and if the bear comes toward him he tells the folks back home that he was charged. This may be true and it may not be.

In the first place, all bears see poorly. Let us say that our grizzly is busily and innocently digging up a ground squirrel in a big lonely basin above timberline when suddenly he feels searing pain and hears the crashing report of a rifle. Panic stricken, the grizzly flees, but right in the direction of the hunter. The fact that the grizzly isn't charging doesn't make this entirely free from danger. He might suddenly see the hunter and take a swipe at him as he goes by. If he does, there is a badly hurt hunter.

Once up in northern British Columbia, Frank Golata and I went into a patch of scrub willow to kick out a grizzly another hunter had wounded. The bear spied me first and went straight toward the guide, who in turn was running backward trying to throw a cartridge into the chamber of an unfamiliar rifle. I ran to the side so I could take a pop at the bear without hitting the guide. I shot and the bear turned away and out of the willows onto an open hillside. The guide, who by this time had the rifle working, put a couple of shots into the seat of the grizzly's pants, but did not stop him. I sat down, took careful aim, and killed the grizzly as it ran broadside by me.

Was that grizzly charging? I don't think so. I think he was simply running from me and Frank happened to be in the way. Nevertheless he *might* have taken a swipe at Frank as he went by, and when anyone is swiped by a grizzly he knows he's been swiped!

Above all things, the grizzly hunter should avoid shooting at a bear on a steep hillside above him, as a wounded bear will always roll down hill. One dude I know saw a bear from the pack train. It was about 300 yards away and 400 feet directly above the outfit. He piled off, shot the grizzly. Bawling and growling the great beast came catapulting right into the midst of the panic-stricken horses. It took the guides the rest of the day to gather up the packs and find the horses.

Once in the Yukon I got my binoculars on a grizzly in an open basin about a mile away. I stalked him and finally ended up at the bottom of a little glacial creek about seventy-five yards from the bear and perhaps 100 feet below him. I didn't like the situation. I was too close to him and he was above me. My first two shots broke both shoulders and down that hill he came, propelling himself by his hind feet, roaring, bellowing, bawling. I knew I had the situation in hand, but I must admit that I was scared!

With the hide off, the carcass of a grizzly looks like the naked body of a grotesque and tremendously powerful man. The great ropes of muscle show where the bears get their strength. They can crush the head of a moose or a buffalo with one blow, literally powder the backbone of the largest steer. I once saw a rather small female grizzly uproot the stump of a dead timberline tree with one smooth, effortless pull. Apparently she did it as easily as a tractor would have done. Grizzlies have been known to carry away the entire carcass of a bull elk that would weigh from 700 to 800 pounds, and to drag that of a bull moose for a mile—and a big bull will weigh 1,200 or 1,300 pounds. When a grizzly puts his mind to it, he can break open the door of a trapper's cabin as if he were an animated battering ram. For his size, he is one of the most powerful beasts that walks this earth.

And how large does a grizzly get? They are by no means as large as their cousins the monster brown bears of Kodiak Island or the Alaska Peninsula, which sometimes are reputed to weigh 1,500 pounds. Now and then a wild grizzly may weigh a thousand pounds, and I have seen one that I would guess might weigh between 850 and 900. The average *big* male grizzly will weigh from 500 to 600 pounds and the females from 300 to 400. A hide that will square eight feet is a very large one, and one that will square nine feet is tremendous—larger, probably, than the average hide of an Alaska brown bear. The average adult grizzly's hide will square about seven feet.

At one time grizzlies ranged from Alaska clear into northern Mexico, from California out into the great plains. Now they have been almost exterminated in the United States, and only a few remain in Wyoming, Montana, and Idaho. There are some in the wilder ranges of northern Mexico. In the Canadian Rockies they are fairly plentiful, and the natives of the Yukon Territory believe the grizzlies there to be increasing. They have taken a pretty bad beating in many parts of Alaska, but they are still plentiful. Over most of the Canadian Rockies, the hunter who packs back on a thirty-day trip in the fall can pretty well count on seeing one or more. He ought to have about a fifty-fifty chance to get one. The most grizzlies I have ever seen on one trip was in the area north of Jasper Park along the Alberta–British Columbia boundary. Between us, Jack Holliday, my companion, and I saw thirty-three altogether, or more than one a day. The most grizzly sign I have ever seen was along the head of the White River in the Yukon. There tracks were so thick along the sandbars of the rivers that it was difficult to put a foot down without stepping on a track!

Probably the majority of the grizzlies killed by sportsmen are shot in the fall when they are come upon by accident while the hunters are above timberline hunting for sheep or caribou. For a short time after the berries are gone and before the bears go into hibernation, they spend much time in timberline basins digging marmots or ground squirrels. They are easily seen then and not too hard to stalk.

The grizzly hunter's chances are better in the spring than at any other time of year, as the bears are then hungry and ranging far and wide to get something with which to fill their shrunken stomachs. They hunt for winter-killed elk or moose or for goats or sheep killed in snowslides. Grizzlies have excellent noses and the smell of overripe flesh in the springtime will bring one on the double.

A favorite method of getting bears, either grizzlies or blacks, is to bait them. The guide gets two or three old crow-bait horses, herds them back into the hills, then shoots them in spots where a traveling grizzly would be apt to come near enough to smell them. Then when it is found that a bear is feeding on a carcass, the guide brings the dude back, puts him in hideout located where the bear will not get his wind. When the bear comes back for a snack the dude bushwhacks him.

However, there are dudes and dudes. One chap I knew got so engrossed in a pocket book he had brought along to while away the time that he did not look once at the bait while a big grizzly was finishing up what was left of a horse a little over 100 yards away. Yet another leaned his head back on a log and slept soundly while a female black bear with two cubs had a banquet on a horse he had paid the outfitter $75 for. In both cases the guides had gone up on a hill to watch for the approach of the bears. The moral of this, I suppose, is that for the guide the client is as big a problem as the bear.

Because of the grizzly's liking for ripe meat, the hunter in the North who has to leave part of a carcass in the hills should make it a point to go back to it now and then. With luck he may find a grizzly on it.

Bears commonly feed on the slides where the snow melts off and fresh vegetation comes up. Hunters locate the bears with binoculars, then stalk them. That sounds easy but it isn't. The bear may be seen a mile or two away. By the time the hunter flounders through deep drifts, climbs through thick timber, the bear may have moved off—or he may have heard the hunter and left. Hunting grizzlies in the spring is cold, wet, difficult, and often heartbreaking, but it is the surest method of getting that trophy.

Suppose, just to see what it's like, we go on a spring grizzly hunt. About the middle of May you meet your outfitter at some little railroad station in the Canadian Rockies and pack back into the mountains anywhere from a couple of days to a week. Nights are still very cold and snow lies deep under the trees and in the high passes. Days are bright and fairly warm though, and now and then you hear the thunder of a slide where thousands of tons of snow have broken loose and tumbled down into a valley.

Every day you and your guide climb 1,500 feet or so to a vantage point overlooking several old slides where the snow has melted and vegetation is coming up. When your binoculars show you a grizzly on a slide the stalk begins. You drop off the mountain from which you have been watching, cross the raging creek, then climb through trees, brush, and snow to a point from which you can shoot at the grizzly.

More often than not, the grizzly is gone when you get there. Perhaps he has heard or smelled you—and in the mountains wind can shift often and unpredictably. Perhaps he has simply filled up and gone off to lie down in the timber. If the bear is gone and you cannot find him nearby, the only thing to do is to try to find another bear—and make another stalk.

Eventually, you'll creep those last few yards through the snow and timber, putting each foot down as carefully as if you were walking on TNT, and when you come out you'll see old *Ursus horribilis* rooting around from thirty to 100 yards away. He is big, massive, blocky, 500 pounds of bone and muscle in a shaggy coat of long, dark-brown hair silvered or yellowed along the backbone. You see the hump on his back, the concave forehead that distinguishes the grizzly from the black bear.

He is a big tough fellow and for a moment as you stand there watching him, your breath catching in your throat, you wonder why you're a grizzly hunter anyway, why you've spent all this time, money, and effort for a shot at an animal that may knock your head off. . . .

"Shoot!" your guide whispers.

The grizzly stops feeding, raises his big shaggy head. It's now or never. The crosshairs of the scope wobble around. Sometimes they are on the bear's shoulder, sometimes not. Finally you touch off the shot. It's too high. You see a shower of silvery hair sail into the air. The grizzly whirls, starts up the slide blindly. Now that the chips are down, you're able to shoot almost automatically. The next time you fire you hear the solid plunk of the bullet and the grizzly goes down on his nose. He struggles to his feet. You shoot once more and this time the bear is down for good.

Now the guide grabs your hand. He jumps up and down in celebration.

"Your first grizzly—a big old he-bear," he shouts. "You did fine after that first shot . . . Well, let's go over and skin him!"

But you'd rather not. Your legs are very weak, so you sit down on a log at the edge of the slide, smoke a cigarette, and watch the bear. Now you have forgotten the weary miles by pack train, the camps pitched in slush, the fruitless stalks through snow and timber. You're a grizzly hunter!

17 | *Caribou: Beautiful But Dumb!*

Often when I see a big bull caribou I am curiously reminded of a gal I knew when I was in college. She was tall, square-shouldered, high-breasted, with long, lovely legs. Her olive skin was dusky velvet and the roses blooming beneath the skin of her cheeks did not come from rouge. The wavy hair she wore in a long bob was jet black, and her large eyes beneath arching, unplucked brows were deep serene blue. She was, I believe, the most beautiful girl I have ever seen. Had Helen of Troy been immortal and half so lovely the Greeks and the Trojans would be fighting yet.

But at college they called her One-Date Kitty. Whenever a new boy in school first laid eyes on her he gasped in astonishment. Then he rushed toward her with glad cries. But our new boy seldom asked Kitty for a second date. She was exquisite, but she was appallingly dumb. She talked in monosyllables, went to sleep in movies, read nothing she didn't have to read, had no ideas, felt strongly about nothing. Beneath the exquisitely contoured bones of her skull rattled the brains of a chipmunk. Her tiny commonplace soul dwelt in that glorious structure like a mouse in a cathedral.

And so with the caribou.

The cows are drab enough creatures, but the big bulls are the most strikingly beautiful of all American game animals. In the fall just before

198

the rut their gray-brown bodies gleam as sleek as the hide of a seal, their powerful white necks shine in the sun, and their fantastic, palmated, many-pointed antlers rise above beautifully moulded heads with long, handsome faces, and flaring nostrils. When they are frightened they raise their little white tails and go off with a high, springing trot so graceful as to make the gait of the finest horse seem lumpish and clumsy.

A handsome, high-stepping, beautifully antlered creature, the bull caribou, but Oh Lord, how dumb! He has a dull and infantile curiosity and a mind of almost incredible indecision. His eyes are as poor as those of a grizzly bear, and when he does see something, he won't believe it until he smells it. Then when he does smell it and trots off in a high-stepping panic, he'll forget what it was he smelled, wonder why he is running, and come back for another whiff. Then he'll go into his act all over again. As the tainted air strikes his nose, he'll jump into the air, hoist his tail, and trot off. It is a wonder that this strange, dumb, and unpredictable beast has survived from the Pleistocene, and indeed he is the first game animal killed off in an area when wolves grow thick and he is helpless before heavy hunting pressure.

Just before and during the rut, when I have mostly hunted them, bull caribou are seen at their worst. They are blinded by desire and overwhelmed by a hopeful and bumbling lust. Once in the Yukon my Indian guide and I were slogging our weary way down the bar of Count Creek. We had packed our saddle horses with sheep trophies and meat and were leading them. Our one pack horse was heavily laden with bedrolls, tent, and gear and he was desperately gaunt and weary. We had been for a week above timberline where the only thing the poor plugs had to eat was unpalatable and unnourishing willow. Head down, almost staggering as he walked, the pack horse lagged farther and farther behind.

It was in the midst of the rut and all day we had seen caribou dotting the rolling uplands scarlet with frost-turned arctic birch flaming below ice-sheathed peaks. Two or three times we had almost walked into caribou traveling on the bar, but they had run off and watched us. We hadn't bothered them, nor they us.

Then late that afternoon I heard a thunder of hoofs and turned around to see a wild-eyed white-maned bull bearing down on our poor innocent pack horse. The hope in his heart and his poor feeble vision had convinced the bull that our horse laden with a mountainous pack covered by a white pack cover was nothing less than a hot little number among lady caribous. As you can imagine, Baldy the pack horse was never so insulted in his life. He lashed out with his hind feet and a hoof cracked against the carbou's jaw like a rifle shot. Baldy then fled in one direction, the caribou in another. If ever a guy got slapped it was that bull! During the balance of the day, we continued to pass caribou, and whenever we did Baldy would snort and roll his eyes. During the rest of the trip he never strayed far from the other horses and from then on he was definitely anti-caribou.

On another occasion I found a bunch of Dall sheep three or four miles away feeding in a high saddle perhaps 2,000 feet above camp. I had no spotting scope and with ordinary binoculars I could not tell the age or sex of the sheep. As my companion and our one guide had located a couple of big rams the previous afternoon and had ridden off in another direction to try for them, I decided to saddle a horse, ride as far as I could, then make the climb and look the sheep I had located over.

When the country got rocky I tied my horse and took out on foot toward the saddle. On my way up I saw, on the other side of the canyon, a couple of cow caribou and a calf. Then well below them I saw a big bull. I paid no attention to them, but they saw me and followed along on the other side of the canyon gaping at me.

Finally I labored up into the saddle where the sheep had been feeding. Tracks told me that they had been ewes and lambs but I was high and I could see into a couple of beautiful basins. I lay down and began to use my binocular.

Suddenly I heard a snort not thirty yards behind me. It was the caribou! They had come to see just what I was. I rolled over, grabbed my camera, and sat up. As they circled to catch my wind, I shot pictures. Every time they would smell me they would hoist their ridiculous white tails and go bounding off. Then when they got one hundred yards away or so, they would forget just what it was they had smelled and come back. Again and again they went through the performance. When I left them to climb a peak so I could look into more basins they were still there.

Late in the afternoon when I got back to the place where I had tied my horse, he was gone—and with him the lunch in my saddlebags. He had uprooted the willow bush to which I had tied him and had left in a hurry. The tracks told me the reason—he had been investigated by a bull caribou. When my weary legs got me back to our miserable jack camp, my horse was there, still trembling, still snorting and rolling his eyes.

The first big trophy caribou bull I ever saw was in the Big Smoky River country of Alberta. My guide and I had put in a rough day trying to shoot a moose, as I have related in the chapter on woods hunting. But the bull moose weren't having any. We'd climb a thousand feet or so up the side of a mountain, then sit there with the glasses until we would locate a shootable moose below us in the timber. Then we would make the stalk. But never did we get close to the moose, as the combination of shifting vagrant breezes and dry twigs underfoot always warned the great bulls so that they slipped away like giant black shadows before us. Three times we had come to the spot where a moose was to await us only to find him gone.

So we sat there on the shoulder of the mountain above timberline trying for the last time in that fading day to pick up the flash of white moose antlers in the thick timber along the silvery creek a half mile below us. Behind us lay a cold dank basin, overshadowed by a great snow cornice. Nothing grew in the cold wet shale but a few intricate and tiny arctic flowers and scattered patches of lichens, but all that day we had been seeing in it a herd of perhaps a dozen cow and calf caribou. It was the coldest and most miserable spot in the mountains and for that reason those arctic reindeer had chosen it as a resting place.

Below us, the canyon widened and swept away. It was carpeted with moss and grass as lush and velvety as an English meadow and the thick-clustered little alpine firs marched up the slope in a hard clean line as abrupt and clear cut as a hedge. Then two thousand feet below, my binocular caught a flash of white moving among the larger trees. For a moment I thought I had seen the ivory antlers of a moose, but, no, it was some strange animal. Then whatever it was crossed an opening in the trees and I could tell it was a great caribou bull.

He was headed at an angle that would bring him much closer to us on the other side of the canyon. As I watched I could see his white neck flitting through the deep cold shadows of that sub-arctic forest like a moth in the dusk. He grew nearer and nearer until finally he pushed through the last of the stunted little arctic firs and trotted soft and silent along that clipped-lawn greensward above timberline, headed apparently for the little herd in the basin. How lovely, how exotic, this creature looked! He was sleek and powerful and his towering palmated antlers rocked above his snowy neck as he moved.

I slipped my left arm through the loop of my sling, got my left hand hard against the front swivel. Then I eased a cartridge into the chamber of my rifle.

"Is he any good?" I whispered to my guide.

"Pretty damned good," he said. "Better take him. You can take two more on the B. C. side if you think you want something better."

As he said that the crosshairs were following smoothly along with the intersection just even with the bull's brisket about one-third of the way up the body. I was squeezing the trigger so gradually that I was surprised when the rifle recoiled and a long jet of orange flame shot from the muzzle. The bull stopped as if he had run into a wall. For a moment he stood there like a graven statue. Then, almost imperceptibly, he began to lean. In a moment he was rolling down the side of the canyon.

I wanted to stay by the side of this big bull marveling at the wonder and beauty of him. He was sleek and glossy and almost as large as a bull elk! But it was rapidly growing dark, and my guide and I had to skin it, cut it up, and load our two saddle horses with head, hide, and meat. When, long after dark, we staggered into camp with the trophy I was as proud as a man who had just knocked out the heavyweight champion or has managed to date a reigning Hollywood beauty. Actually, as further experience taught me, I had no great reason for pride. In spite of his impressive and exotic looks, a big caribou trophy should rank far lower than the commoner but more intelligent elk and even below a good whitetail buck.

Caribou antlers, the crowning glory of these strange beasts, are built on the same plan, yet no two are exactly alike. One thinks of caribou heads as always being palmated, but a few are almost as without palmation as those of an elk. The most characteristic thing about all antlers is the "shovel," which projects out over the face. Usually there is a spike and a single shovel, which may be from as little as three or four inches in width to as much as sixteen or eighteen inches. Rarely double-shovel heads are seen but these are trophies much sought after if the rest of the head is good.

The *bez* formation projects above the shovel and may have several distinct points. About half way up the main beam of the antler there is a single point projecting backward. At the top of the beam the antler palmates and several points come off. Formerly, heads were rated in the record book by length of main beam alone, and some of the top heads were long spindly things with not much more of the characteristic caribou palmation than elk antlers. Now they are rated by a complicated formula that emphasizes massiveness and palmation—and that is as it should be.

Of the main types of American caribou—woodland, mountain, and barren ground, the mountain caribou are the largest and heaviest animals and the barren ground have the largest and finest antlers with the greatest amount of palmation.

I have seen, among at least 300 trophy bull caribou that I have looked over, only two heads with double shovels. One was lying down in timber above me as I was riding along a river bar in the Yukon. He got up not more than 150 yards away and stood for a moment, plainly revealing his massive double-shovel head while I fell off my horse and made a grab for my rifle in the scabbard. I had hardly got my hand on it, though, when he faded into the scrubby timber and disappeared. I never saw him again.

The other double-shovel bull I saw was right on the crest of the Rockies, so precisely on the British Columbia–Alberta border that it would have taken a surveyor to find out in which province he was lying. The story of my failure to get him illustrates a caribou characteristic.

But to begin. My guide, Isaac Plante, a Cree Indian, and I had picked him up with binoculars at about a mile and since he looked good, we worked to within perhaps 400 yards of him. His head was hanging down like that of a drowsing horse and his great antlers hanging forward. We were a couple of thousand feet above timberline, and all around us lay great sweeping upland basins thick carpeted with alpine moss and grass and lichens and splotched with dazzling patches of snow. On the horizon sharp ice-sheathed peaks were boldly white against a sky of Kodachrome blue. The rut was about to begin and caribou were everywhere, some resting in the snow fields, some feeding, some moving aimlessly about.

Stalking this big bull seemed child's play and my guide and I were closing the range when suddenly he threw up his head and took off, trotting away from us at right angles with great sweeping, rubbery strides. That was that. Disappointed we found and shot another bull, good but not as good as the one that ran away. We were finishing the skinning when I happened to glance up, and here came my double-shovel bull headed straight toward us, head up, antlers back, nostrils flaring. He passed within thirty yards of us, still driven by some mad and mysterious urge. All caribou, particularly during the opening of the rut, are subject to these aimless panics, these pointless running fits, and often these are the only difficulty of the stalk.

The caribou is a circumpolar animal found not only all over the northern fourth of North America but in the northern portion of Europe and Asia. The reindeer of the Laps is simply a domesticated European caribou, a good deal smaller than the average North American caribou, but a caribou nevertheless. Swedish and Norwegian sportsmen hunt the wild reindeer in subarctic mountains and glaciers of their countries, and from the pictures I have seen of those European examples of the family, I doubt if the average hunter could tell a wild Scandinavian reindeer from a British Columbia caribou. In Alaska, where European reindeer were introduced to help the Eskimo economy, the wild caribou bulls interbred at every opportunity with the domesticated animals.

A few caribou have in historic times drifted into northern Montana, Idaho, and Washington, but with the exception of those in Alaska, they are almost entirely Canadian animals found all through the highest mountains of British Columbia, in the northern Alberta Rockies, in the

Yukon, throughout the barren grounds, and even on the islands in the arctic sea.

Actually they are arctic animals and they are seldom found except in spots of the arctic, whether it is above timberline along the crest of the Rockies or on an island washed by the polar sea. They are never found far away from their caribou moss, that whitish lichen which is their favorite food, nor from the glaciers and everlasting snow. The coat of the caribou is one of the warmest of nature's garments, and a caribou will die of heat stroke where a man is freezing in long, wool underwear and wool shirt. The favorite winter sleeping bags of Eskimos and northern hunters are made from caribou skins.

In the Canadian West, from the Smoky River country of Alberta to the Arctic ocean, it is in the late summer and early fall, when the caribou are hunted by sportsmen, rare to see the animals away from the everlasting snows. When they have fed and want to lie down, they find a snowpatch somewhere.

Our literature had conditioned us to think of the caribou as an inhabitant of the open, gently rolling barren grounds; but probably more caribou are shot by American sportsmen in high mountains than anywhere else. In some areas, caribou actually live above the mountain sheep. In one section of the Alberta Rockies where I hunted many years ago, the bighorns were found quite low on rocky slides and in rough canyons, whereas the caribou dwelt far above them on the tops of snow-splotched mountains. In the Stone sheep country of northern British Columbia the big Osborn caribou are found right up among the sheep in the great basins above timberline and it is not uncommon to see caribou grazing on one side of a basin and Stone rams on the other. The caribou cannot negotiate the rocks the way a sheep can but it can get over surprisingly rough country for an animal so large and heavy.

The great enemy of the caribou is the arctic wolf, which for a decade around the time of World War II were on the upswing of a cycle. Just after the last big war, wolves about exterminated caribou in the McKinley National Park in Alaska and in many other areas in the far north. In the area of the Yukon around Pilot Mountain where I hunted in 1950 and which was at one time famous caribou country, the animals have absolutely been exterminated and the only reminders of them are the bleaching bones and antlers of old wolf kills. In another Yukon area where I have hunted the wolves have not quite killed the once-abundant herds off. A few caribou still remain there. They live timorously on the tops of the highest mountains and to see one is an event. That they were once very plentiful is shown by the bones that are strewn over the mountain sides and by deep game trails now grown up in grass.

The Eskimo and the Indian and the pioneering white trapper and prospector are great caribou killers, who thin them out near towns and villages to eat on themselves and to feed to their sled dogs. The caribou is the beef of the far north, an animal which like the cottontail rabbit is easily killed and is destined to feed others, be it wolf or man. I have shot a good many caribou in my day and I have seen many others shot. Once I saw a bull absorb fourteen poorly placed shots that struck him around the edges—in the belly, in the flanks, in the legs, low in the neck. The poor beast staggered around until the lousy marksman that was shooting at him managed to break one front leg and one hind leg. Then he was helpless. One well placed shot through the lungs with any reasonably adequate rifle will almost always bring down the biggest caribou within a few yards. Although he is almost as large as an elk, he has far less vitality, apparently little if any more than a whitetail deer. I have dropped big bulls almost in their tracks with one shot at from 300 to 400 yards. I do not think a caribou is any more difficult to kill than a deer. Eskimos and Indians shoot them with varmint cartridges like the .22 Hornet, the .218 Bee, and the .222. At one time I had shot sixteen caribou with twenty shots fired. A rifle of the .270–.30/06 class is more than adequate.

In fact the caribou is so easy to stalk and so easy to kill that almost the only thrill connected with hunting him is being in the grand mountain country where he lives. Unless meat is necessary, there is no excuse for a sportsman to shoot anything except an exceptional bull.

Actually, the greatest sport for the caribou hunter is to photograph the animals. They are photogenic and so is the country in which they they are found, and the necessity of getting within camera range gives much more spice to stalking them than getting within longer shooting range.

Years ago I was using a binocular one day high on a ridge in the Alberta Rockies near the head of Copton Creek when I picked up the antlers of a big bull caribou just sticking over a rise. My companion, Jack Holliday, and I got the wind right and with no special pains we stalked to within thirty or forty feet of him as he lay there gaping idly at the beautiful timberline basin that lay below him. I shot two or three stills, but my companion with the movie camera grew restless because the bull wouldn't move. I picked up a pebble and hit him on the fanny with it and shot a good picture as he pranced panic-stricken away. If you want to make an easy reputation with the home folks as a red-hot stalker and animal photographer, just operate on caribou. The massive, palmated, many-pointed antlers of a big bull will attract lots of attention in the trophy room, but good movies of the same bull will attract even more.

As I write this in 1967 the hunter must go north of the Peace and Stikine Rivers in British Columbia before he encounters caribou in great numbers. There used to be thousands of them in the Smoky River country of Alberta, but roads made the area fairly easy of access and resident Alberta meat hunters shot them off. I shot my first caribou as I have related in this chapter in 1943 right at timberline along the Alberta–British Columbia border. At that time this was the finest mixed-game country I have ever seen. On that 1943 trip we saw several hundred caribou, thirty-three grizzly bears, thousands of goats, thirty or forty mature bighorn rams, and somewhere between 200 and 300 ewes, lambs, and young rams. We also saw a dozen or so bull moose and a fair number of mule deer.

I had always entertained romantic memories of the area, so in 1961 I returned with my wife and my daughter Caroline, who had just grad-uated from college. This wonderful wilderness, one of the most beautiful in North America, was ruined. A road had been bulldozed out right to the Smoky River past the old Indian village of Grand Cache. Hunt-ers from the Edmonton vicinity would drive by automobile to Grand Cache, rent a few horses from the Cree Indians there, cross the Smoky River on a bridge built by a company operating a coal mine. They were then right in my old wilderness country.

The country was full of winter cat trails up the creeks made by outfits exploring for oil, and all the campsites were littered with tin cans, cigarette packages, cardboard cartons, old comic books, and broken crates. We saw a few very spooky bighorn sheep, one very large bull moose, one mule deer doe, about thirty or forty goats, but not one grizzly or caribou. I heard rumors of a "big grizzly" an American hunter had shot but the "big grizzly" turned out to be a three-year-old cub. The meat hunters had pounded the game hard, shooting small rams, ewes, even lambs for meat if they had the chance. Elk had increased as the elk along the Smoky area are found mostly in the timber and are very smart animals. I have no idea what had happened to the goats. Surely they must have got some disease, as goats are poor eating and hunting them is hard work.

But of all the game along the Smoky, it was the poor, dumb caribou that had been most shot up. When the road to the Smoky was opened most of the meat hunters that came in were used to shooting moose and deer, species in which the females have no antlers. Since cow cari-bou have little spindly antlers the meat hunters mowed them down. Knowing these hunters would shoot cows anyway, the Alberta game department opened the season on the Smoky to any caribou. Unless things have changed for the better, the Smoky River caribou must cer-tainly be extinct today.

As I have intimated in this chapter the caribou is a pathetically easy animal to stalk. Most animals that evolved in open country have very good eyes. The wild sheep, the old world gazelles, the pronghorn antelope, the horse—all see well indeed. But the poor caribou's vision is bad indeed. He sees only moving objects and those at no great distance and not very well. But his nose is excellent. In stalking caribou the animals are usually located with binoculars at a distance. The hunter then walks or rides toward them, taking pains to travel upwind or crosswind so the caribou will not smell him. However, even if the caribou do get a whiff of human scent and run off they'll probably forget what frightened them and come back for another look as they are curious. They are very easy to hunt once they are located.

If caribou are scarce as they are in many parts of the Yukon, they are usually located by glassing. Early in the season when flies and gnats are still out, they often stand in saddles where the wind will keep the bugs away. A bull caribou with his gray-brown body and white neck has about the same coloring as a Stone sheep but when he is resting he stands with his head down. His silhouette is unmistakable. When it is warm early in the season the caribou are found around glaciers and snow patches and beside streams of icy water. They cannot stand much heat. The bulls begin to rut, according to the Indians, with the coming of the first full moon in September, and if anything is dumber than a love-sick bull caribou I have yet to see it. About the last week in August the bulls start getting rid of the velvet on their great antlers, and they are usually difficult to find at that time because they are then down below tree line "horning" the trees to clean off their antlers. Seen at this time the parts of their antlers freshly cleaned of velvet are bright red and strips of velvet hang from them like moss from a Mississippi live oak.

With their antlers cleaned off, the bulls come up above timberline to take part in the annual rut. A caribou is eccentric enough at any time, but during the rut he seems demented. The only hazard of stalking at that time if ordinary care is used is the danger that the chosen bull will get the notion that there may be a cute but lonesome little cow caribou over the next mountain range and take off in that direction. To his love-sick brain everything may be a cow caribou. On one occasion, the day before caribou season opened, my son Bradford and I were riding with a packstring above timberline. I had just commented that this certainly was caribou country when we saw a couple of big bulls at a distance. We were headed in their direction and presently they saw us. Here they came at a trot, convinced that our heavy-laden pack horses were all lady caribou. They'd trot within about thirty yards, catch our man smell, hoist their little tails and trot off. Then they would forget what had frightened them and come trotting back.

Anyone who wants to shoot a bull caribou for meat should do so as early as possible. Before the rut a fat old bull furnishes tender and delicious meat. But once the fever of the rut comes on them they quit eating and within a few days their meat is strong.

With their warm coats, their big feet, and their indifference to cold the caribou are arctic and subarctic animals, and during the Pleistocene era, which ended only 10,000 years or so ago, they ranged far south in the United States and were favorite game for the cave-dwelling Cro-Magnon hunters of France. But as the earth warmed up, the glaciers and the arctic flora receded, and the seas filled again from the melting ice caps, the caribous followed their environment north. Patches of the arctic have lingered in high mountain country, and some of the same plants are found in southern Colorado, northern New Mexico, and on the San Francisco peaks in Arizona as are found above tree line in the far north. I understand that ptarmigan, the arctic grouse, have even been seen in northern New Mexico.

Caribou have been found in the boreal zone wherever there are continuous stretches of it as along the great peaks in the southern Canadian Rockies. But when their habitat goes the caribou go. Much of the year they are dependent on caribou moss, which in the Hudsonian and boreal zones has grown for tens of thousands of years and in places is two and even three feet thick. In many parts of Alaska careless hunters, trappers, and prospectors have let fires start in the moss. Some of these have burned for years and have devastated great areas. Without the moss the caribou cannot exist.

Right after World War II there was a big flap in Alaska about wolves killing off the game. A great deal of wolf control was done and probably because of this some game biologists think many parts of Alaska have a surplus of caribou. Alaska in 1967 allowed three caribou in some areas. The Yukon has no surplus of caribou, as the herds in the territory have been heavily preyed upon by wolves, and neither has the Northwest Territories. Throughout the Arctic there is no bag limit or season on caribou as the Eskimos and Indians of the Far North live on them.

For purposes of record keeping the Boone and Crockett Club recognizes three species of caribou—woodland, mountain, and barren ground. Each of these is divided into several subspecies. Woodland caribou are found in eastern Canada and Newfoundland and have ranged in Maine and northern Minnesota. The mountain caribou are found in the Canadian Rockies from the American border to the Yukon line, but as we have seen in this chapter they have been badly shot up in the more accessible parts of their range. American hair-splitters have assigned the big Osborn caribou of northwest British Columbia's Cassiar to the barren-ground species but the trophies are listed with mountain caribou. The barren-ground caribou do not average as large as mountain caribou but they have very large antlers.

In the Yukon the trappers and Indians say there are two kinds of caribou, the native resident caribou, which they called "mountain caribou" and migratory caribou, which they classify as barren ground. They say the resident caribou are not migratory but stay in a relatively small area. Now and then, they say, a big herd of barren-ground caribou comes along and sweeps away with it all the native "mountain" caribou. In northern British Columbia the mountain caribou spend their summers above timberline near glaciers and snow patches. In the winter they move down to the scrubby spruce forests for shelter from the subzero cold and howling winds. The barren-ground caribou found in the far north beyond tree line migrate back into the trees for the winter months. They travel in great herds, swim well and since they swim well and the hollow hair of their coats makes them float like corks they cross lakes and rivers easily.

One of the last encounters I had with a bull caribou was in the Halfway River country of northern British Columbia on the way back from a Stone sheep hunt. My guide and I were engaged in the worthy enterprise of trying to stalk and shoot a grizzly bear. As the first step we climbed 1,500 feet or so up the side of a big round-topped mountain so we could use binoculars on other high country that lay spread out before us like a map. From where we were perched we could see a dozen little unnamed lakes and one large one named only casually after an old packhorse called Puss. It was well along toward the middle of October and a long succession of bitterly cold nights had pretty well stripped the leaves from bug brush and willow, leaving the once-brilliant colors worn and faded, as soft as those in an old and cherished Paisley shawl. The previous night had been clear and the glowing, changing northern lights had written fantastic patterns in the black sky, but a storm was on its way. Driven by some lofty wind, long gossamer filaments of clouds trailed across the gray-blue sky.

Although the big rounded mountains all went above timberline to rolling open pastures of grass and moss and lichens, we were really in the foothills far from the tumbled peaks and craggy cliffs of the main Rockies. Beyond the high hills we could see flat and endless spruce forest, smoky purple, threaded with little glistening streams and gleaming with tiny nameless lakes. Far away, through a notch in the hills and just against the horizon, we could see with our binoculars a white, straight cut in a hillside that marked the path of the Alaska Highway.

We could look down on the hilltop pastures across the wide, flat blue of the big lake below us, and presently my guide said softly, "I see a bunch of caribou."

For a moment I watched them. There were eight animals and even at three or four miles I could tell one was a big bull. Then I shifted the glass to another spot and saw what we were looking for—a little restless black dot that was a bear.

We shifted then to the 20-power spotting scope. It was a grizzly all right. We could see his hump, the yellowish hair along the top of his back. Apparently he was in a blueberry patch and was having the time of his life. He would feed a while in one spot, then he'd move to another twenty or thirty feet away and go to it.

"Well," I said, "let's go get him!"

Forty-five days in the mountains, forty-five days of climbing for sheep, hiking along lousy trails, pulling floundering pack horses out of muskegs had made us tough. We plunged down the hill from which we had been doing our glassing, pushed fast through the two miles of swampy muskeg around the east end of the lake, then labored up the steep side of the mountain where we had seen the grizzly—and the caribou. Our plan was to go up on one side of the grizzly, then come over a hump above and behind him and knock him off.

When we got on top, the first thing we saw was the herd of caribou— five cows, two calves, and a glorious, white-necked bull. They were only about 250 yards away, and I paid no attention to them except to note that the big bull had seen us and had pranced up to the top of a little knoll, where he stood frozen like a beautiful statue.

The very last stage of our stalk, we discovered, would take some doing, as we would have to go noiselessly through a belt of scrub arctic birch before we could come out above the grizzly. The leaves were all dry and if we made any noise we were sunk. A grizzly has poor eyes, but a good nose and ears like a bat.

With our hearts pounding and every rustling of the dry leaves sounding like a rifle shot, we edged forward through the brush, nearer and nearer to where the bear should be. We'd come to the end of the brush and to the top of the rise and find the bear within fifty yards and perhaps within twenty-five yards.

Then it all happened.

We heard a crash of dry bush and a pounding of hoofs and looked around to find that damned bull caribou right on top of us. He had approached silently over the soft moss and lichens and we hadn't heard him until he hit the brushy, rocky ridge. Keyed up as I was, I was startled half out of what wits I possess.

I was looking around at the bull, hating him, when my guide hissed, "The bear!"

The grizzly had heard the racket and had come to investigate. There he stood as erect as a man, his great shoulders and massive, hairy head over the rise. Before I could even switch off the safety he was gone. I jumped to my feet, took after him, tripped in the brush and fell. When I scrambled up again the bear's hind end was disappearing into the timber.

In the meantime the big bull caribou had trotted around until he got our wind. Then he jumped and took off. In a moment he couldn't quite recall what it was that frightened him so, and he came bumbling back. He stood there about seventy-five yards away, his head up, his nostrils flaring, his snowy neck in sharp contrast with his seal-brown body—so beautiful and yet so dumb. His head was one of the best I have ever seen, long, massive, heavily palmated.

"Shoot the stupid bastard!" my guide said. "He's got it coming and anyway that's a fine head!"

But it was as difficult to stay mad at that bull as it would be not to forgive a beautiful woman. Slowly I got to my feet.

"Hell," I said, "let's glass the next canyon and maybe we can see another grizzly."

For the realization had suddenly struck me that unless I got very hungry I had killed my last caribou. Hunting them was too much like wrestling with a crippled midget or playing Twenty Questions with an imbecile. I wanted that bull to stay up there atop the mountain looking photogenic and doing dumb things. The wolves would get him eventually, of course, but for my part I wanted no piece of taking him off.

18 | *Medicine for Antelope*

An antelope hunt is one of the first Western expeditions usually made by Eastern and Midwestern sportsmen. It isn't an expensive hunt; the antelope hunter doesn't need a pack train or even a horse. The great antelope state of Wyoming doesn't require nonresident antelope hunters to have a guide, and an antelope license costs out-of-staters only $25.

Every summer I get letters from many antelope hunters—the majority of them second-timers. Usually, the first time a man hunts pronghorns, he takes along the deer rifle he's been using in his native woods. Often he finds it unsatisfactory, and *then* he writes.

Antelope and whitetail deer are entirely different creatures. The whitetail is an animal of woods and brush, and he's generally shot at offhand and within 100 yards. The pronghorn is an open-country animal —the only real plains game we have in this country now that the buffalo has become a creature of parks and preserves, and the elk, once found on the plains, has been driven to the mountains.

In Wyoming, mule deer are increasingly becoming plains animals, but they're not plains game in the sense that pronghorns are, since they're usually found around broken hills and brushy coulees. The only other examples of true plains game on this continent are caribou and grizzlies of the arctic prairies.

Ordinarily it doesn't take a deer hunter long to find out that the rifle

212

The late Dr. Elmer Braddock with a good but not extraordinary Wyoming antelope. This is about a fourteen-inch head.

which is just right for brush shooting at whitetails isn't precisely what the doctor ordered for shooting in wide open spaces. When antelope are found in country broken with draws and ravines, they can be stalked, and fairly close shots can often be taken. Then the deer rifle is all one needs. But most antelope are killed at fairly long range.

I've hunted them in Mexico, Arizona, and Wyoming, and my shots have averaged longer than those taken at any other animal. I've probably shot about as many antelope as I have mountain sheep, which also are generally thought of as a long-range proposition, but my shots at antelope have averaged much farther. I've killed more mountain sheep at under 200 yards than over, but I probably have shot more antelope at over 250 yards than under that distance, and I've nailed a few at 400 yards or over.

Antelope and mountain sheep have the finest eyes of any American game animals, and, if anything, the eyes of the antelope are superior to those of the sheep. I've found that if a hunter sticks his head over a ridge, sheep usually won't notice it if he doesn't move. But spooky antelope will almost always notice a hunter's head as soon as he pokes it over a ridge, even though he may not move it. The careful stalker can get closer to sheep than to antelope because sheep country is generally rocky and broken with sharp ridges and deep draws, and he can approach under cover. Antelope country is mostly level or gently rolling, and sometimes it offers little chance for a close stalk.

Under these conditions, about the toughest animal in the world to stalk is a smart buck antelope with a big head that has been bombarded for a few seasons. Stalking him is tough and irritating, for he'll often stand and stare at a hunter from 500 or 600 yards away. If he sees you a long way off he feels safe enough but if you disappear into a draw or coulee he jitters around for a few minutes and then takes off.

In some areas having limited numbers of antelope and short seasons, antelope hunts become rat races. Hundreds of hunters in automobiles descend on animals that haven't been disturbed for almost a year. Then the air is full of dust and bullets, the plain covered with speeding cars and fleeing antelope. Under those conditions it does no good to stalk a fine trophy, for it often happens that when the hunter is halfway in his stalk a pickup truck will come barreling over a rise and spook the buck. Either that or someone will open up on him at 800 or 1,000 yards. The best way to hunt antelope under such carnival conditions is to sit down, take it easy, and let someone run one over to you.

But stalking trophy antelope in big country not overrun by hunters is a grand experience. The hunter will see a lot of antelope (sometimes 1,000 or more a day) and have a lot of disappointments, but when he makes a successful stalk on a first-class buck he'll never forget it.

Eleanor O'Connor with a very good Arizona antelope shot on Anderson mesa south of Flagstaff.

This antelope had probably about a fourteen-inch head. It was shot on a bitter-cold day in Wyoming. Carrying an animal like that is hard on the horse because it puts him off balance.

Antelope aren't heavy animals. Size varies with climate and range, but I doubt the average mature buck will field dress at much more than 110–125 pounds. In central Arizona and New Mexico, where antelope seem to average larger than in other areas, I imagine an exceptionally heavy buck might field dress at 150 pounds. I've heard of a few that went 145 pounds or a bit over.

Antelope don't offer much area to shoot at. On a straight line from top of the shoulder to bottom of the chest, the average buck will measure about fourteen or fifteen inches. The largest I ever measured went seventeen inches. A good, full-grown buck mule deer will generally measure about eighteen inches with very rarely one a bit larger. In trying to estimate range on an antelope, I assume that a bragging-size buck is about sixteen inches thick. Keep that measurement in mind.

An antelope, then, isn't large and he's generally shot at fairly long range. The combination makes him hard to hit. Many times I've seen antelope hunters take careful shots at standing animals and have the bullet fall short by yards. Judging range on antelope is often tough because, for me and I believe for most hunters, it is difficult to estimate correctly the distance across an open plain.

Rifles and Cartridges

The ideal antelope rifle, then, would use a cartridge with high velocity and flat trajectory that would reduce as much as possible the hunter's range-judging difficulties. The hunter should also use a bullet that expands fairly easily, as the relatively frail rib cage and light bones of antelope don't offer much resistance. Fatally hit antelope often run great distances when struck by heavy or ruggedly constructed bullets that don't open up quickly.

An antelope that hasn't been disturbed is not difficult to kill with a well-placed shot from almost any adequate rifle, but a frightened antelope can carry away a lot of lead if that first shot doesn't put him down. Years ago in Sonora, I shot the bottom part of a buck antelope's heart off but he ran over a quarter of a mile before going down. Another time, I took a crack at a buck running over a rise. Though the bullet slit open his belly cavity, he ran several hundred yards. I saw a friend hit a running buck behind the shoulder with a tough-jacketed .30/06 bullet. Because the bullet didn't open fast enough, the buck ran more than 200 yards before showing any signs of being hit. Then he began to stagger, and in a few seconds went down. A bullet that's excellent on elk or moose generally doesn't open up fast enough for antelope, and it doesn't give a high percentage of instantaneous kills even with well-placed shots.

Two of the best antelope bullets I've ever used were of open-point construction—the 150-grain bullet for the .30/06 and the old Western open-point 139-grain for the 7 × 57 Mauser. I've never seen either bullet fail to kill antelope stone dead in their tracks with well-placed shots. A friend has had fine luck with the 130-grain Speer soft-point spitzer in 7 × 57 loaded to a muzzle velocity of about 3,000 feet per second. The few antelope I've shot with the various 130-grain bullets in .270 at a muzzle velocity of around 3,150 feet per second haven't known what hit them.

Up to 250 yards or so, the .243 Winchester, the 6-mm. Remington, and .257 Roberts are good antelope cartridges with 100-grain bullets, and the wildcat .25/06 with 100- or 117-grain bullets should be just about ideal. Les Bowman, the Wyoming guide and outfitter, tells me that he considers the .243 Winchester and the .244 Remington with 90- and 100-grain bullets to be the most effective antelope medicine he's run into—because of their light recoil, their flat trajectory, the quick expansion of the bullets and consequent killing power.

Bullets that give rainbow trajectories are poor antelope medicine, no matter how constructed. They're simply too hard to hit with. A hunter with a .300 Savage or a .308 Winchester should use 150-grain bullets, and the man with a .300 Magnum should use the fast-stepping 150-grain bullet. Cartridges in the .30/30, .32 Special, and .35 Remington class have killed thousands of antelope, but they've also missed and wounded thousands.

For my dough the old .270 is still one of the greatest open-country long-range factory-produced cartridges in the world for light and medium game. With its combination of a bullet of good sectional density at high velocity, great accuracy, and relatively light recoil, it's close to unbeatable. The only cartridges that shade it a bit are such smallbore magnums as the 7-mm. Remington and the .270 and 7-mm Weatherby Magnums. I haven't used the .280 Remington on antelope, but everything I've said about the .270 should apply to it. While we're on the subject, there are no flies on the 7 × 57 with proper bullets either.

Despite their high velocity, bullets made for varmints in big-game calibers should not be chosen for antelope. They're so lightly constructed they sometimes blow up. I once had one go to pieces on a buck antelope's shoulder. It put the animal down but didn't kill it. In addition, they have poor sectional density and drift badly in the wind. I wouldn't select the 87-grain bullet in .25 caliber, the 100-grain in .270, or the 110 in .30/06.

Telescope Sights

I've made some long shots on antelope with 2½X scopes, but I much prefer the 4X, and if the hunter has a 6X he will find it useful. Actually, an 8X or even a 10X is a lovely instrument for long standing shots. For running shooting, though, the field isn't wide enough. The 4 and 6X scopes are about right.

To the serious antelope hunter, if he is a crack shot who is willing to use a rest and knows the trajectory of the cartridge he uses, another gimmick worth several times its weight in platinum is a reticle which will make the judgment of range easier. A useful one for me was a 4-minute dot in a 2½X Lyman Alaskan, and on several occasions it saved me from some bad errors in judgment.

Let's suppose you see a buck standing broadside and find that your 4-minute dot exactly covers him from top of shoulder to bottom of chest. You can estimate, then, that he's about 400 yards away. If the dot covers only about three-quarters of his chest area, the dot is subtending about 12 inches and the buck is about 300 yards away. A range-finder reticle with two horizontal crosswires is available in Weaver scopes. The space between the two wires subtends 6 minutes of angle. If the chest area of an antelope almost but not quite fills the space between the crosswires, it's a pretty safe guess that he is about 300 yards away. The flat top of a post reticle, which generally subtends between 4 and 6 minutes of angle, can also be a range finder.

None of these, of course, measure range exactly, but their use will save a hunter from his worst bobbles. The brilliant white on an antelope makes him look closer than he is when the sun is bright, and when the sky is overcast he tends to look farther away. When he's sharply above or below me, he generally looks farther away than he is. An antelope on the skyline looks closer.

To minimize the effects of poor range judgment, it's smart for the antelope hunter to sight in to put the bullet 3 inches above line of scope sight at 100 yards. With rifles like the .270 with a 130-grain bullet, the .285 or .280 with the 125-grain bullet, or the .300 Winchester Magnum or the 7-mm. Remington Magnum with a 150-grain, he's on the button at about 275 yards and only slightly low at 300. If he knows the animal is beyond 300 yards but is doubtful about the range, he can hold even with the top of the shoulder and be fairly certain of a hit up to about 400 yards.

Range and Trajectory

Anyone planning an antelope hunt should give some study to his rifle's trajectory and should memorize it. If he is a forgetful type, it isn't a bad idea to write down on a little card the extent of the drop at various ranges, and then to attach this to the stock with transparent tape. The dope for a scope-sighted .30/06 with a 150-grain bullet at over 2,900 feet per second would read like this: 100 yards +3; 150 yards +3½; 250 −0; 300 −5; 350 −12; 400 −23; 450 −37; 500 −55.

Suppose our hunter sees a fine buck standing broadside at what he decides is 400 yards. His bullet, he knows, will drop about two feet at that distance, and he likewise knows that the antelope is probably about sixteen inches thick from the hairline at the top of his shoulder to the bottom of his chest. If he holds the width of the antelope's body over the top of his shoulder, and his guess as to the range is right, the bullet will strike in the chest cavity. But he should shoot from a rest and he should *squeeze* that trigger!

Eastern varmint hunters make deadly antelope shots, and men used to picking off chucks at 350 yards won't find it difficult to hit antelope that are over 400 yards away once they get used to the bright light and the strong wind characteristic of most antelope country. But such crack riflemen know enough to take a rest and they are also able to judge wind.

Back about 1953 I was hunting antelope with friends near Gillette, Wyoming, when four or five bucks ran out of a coulee and stopped on the side of a low hill at which I decided was 500 yards away. I was using a .270 with a 130-grain bullet loaded to 3,140 feet per second, and my dope said I'd get a drop of about thirty inches between 275 (the distance for which I had the rifle sighted in) and 500 yards. A frisky wind was blowing, so I held twelve inches or so into the wind and 1½ times the depth of the buck's chest above the top of his shoulder. At the shot the buck went down. My allowance for elevation was right, but I hadn't allowed enough for the wind and my bullet was too far back. He needed a second shot. A pal who claimed his paces were exactly one yard said the antelope fell 485 yards away.

Shots like that may sound wild-eyed to those whose experience has been limited to 100-yard shooting in brush, but they're easier to make than running shots on antelope at much shorter ranges. Particularly where an area is heavily hunted and the antelope are milling, there's a great deal of temptation to try long running shots. That is generally something to avoid. A really frightened antelope can travel at fifty and even sixty miles an hour and requires a fantastic amount of lead—even with a swinging rifle.

As an illustration, when I was hunting with Fred Huntington near Cody, Wyoming, one fall, I took a crack at a running buck at what afterward turned out to be 285 paces across ground as level as a billiard table. The reticle of the scope sight was moving apparently as fast as the antelope, and it seemed 2½ lengths ahead when the musket went off. I'd thought I could kill that buck before he got out of sight, but much to our mutual astonishment I cracked him right behind the shoulder on the first shot. I guessed exactly right, flinched just right, or did something just right. Anyway, I got the antelope, and I'm resolved never to hunt antelope around Cody again since I want to preserve my reputation.

A fast-stepping, flat-shooting bullet, a good scope, and careful sighting all go a long way toward making an antelope shoot successful. Plains hunting is a great experience, but you need the right tools. You also need some judgment, and you need to know how to shoot!

19 | *Planning the Big Game Hunt*

By trade I am a gun editor and a writer of hunting tales. As a consequence I get many dozens of letters a year asking me for advice on where to hunt and what outfitter to choose.

I always do my best, but very often my best isn't very good because my correspondents almost never give me the essential information on which any realistic answer must be based—how much money the hunter has to spend, how much time he can afford to devote to the hunt, how old he is and what sort of physical condition he is in. It is also very helpful if a correspondent tells me what trophy he wants above all others. I should also know if he is really not a trophy hunter but simply wants a pleasant vacation in beautiful country with clean water and fresh air and a certain amount of shooting.

Possibly it is unfortunate, but the man who wants to hunt in a strange and distant country for animals he had not hunted before must absolutely have a certain amount of two commodities: time and money. If he has unlimited time he can make do with less money. If he has unlimited money he can cut down on the time. But he has to have some of each. He also must have a certain amount of physical stamina.

Back in the 1930's I used to do a great deal of hunting in northern Mexico. I had very little money but I had a fair amount of time. More important I knew the country, the game, how to travel and camp under

221

desert conditions, and I could speak enough ungrammatical Spanish to get by. In those days the handful of outfitters in northern Mexico charged from $25 to $50 a day for a desert hunt. I was a university professor then, and I was picking up some extra money by writing. I could no more afford an outfitter than I could have afforded to buy my wife a mink coat or a diamond tiara. I had to be my own guide and outfitter.

The hunt on which I took my first desert bighorn probably didn't cost me over fifteen or twenty dollars. I bought gasoline, groceries, a Mexican tourist permit, a car permit, and two quarts of cheap bourbon whisky. I gave the Mexican officials at the border one quart when I went in hoping to create good will and the other quart when I came out so they would not inspect my car.

On another occasion my wife, my son, and I spent ten days in Sonora, shot a very fine mule deer, two whitetails, many doves and quail, ate well. We bought one Mexican hunting license, gasoline, food, hired a Mexican vaquero to show us around and take care of the horses. All told we spent $75. I remember another Sonora hunt, where I was a sort of an unpaid guide and outfitter. Two friends who had never hunted in Mexico went with me and we split the expenses three ways. We hunted ten days and I doubt if we spent over $35 each.

I have the deepest of sympathy for the man who wants to hunt in far places for the rarer types of game but who does not have enough money to finance a trip. I know exactly how he feels since I spent much of my life in exactly that boat. For many a long year I had to confine myself to the poor man's big-game hunting—what I could drive to in an automobile. I would hunt on foot, pack my game out on my back. I shot deer, antelope, turkeys, and a few black bear. I shot my first elk when I was thirty-three, my first ram about the same time. I did not hunt out of the Southwest and northern Mexico until I was forty-one. I then took a wonderful thirty-day pack trip into the Alberta Rockies.

In the chapter on pack trips I have mentioned "spot packers" who take hunting parties and their equipment back into the mountains, leave them to set up their camps and hunt, and then return on a pre-arranged date and pack them and their meat out. This is a good and inexpensive elk hunt for those who have their equipment and know how to hunt elk. The man without the equipment or knowledge of the country should make a deal with an outfitter to meet him at the road and pack him back into the wilderness area where a camp has been set up and guides and horses are waiting.

A good poor man's hunt as this is written is for antelope and mule deer in Wyoming or Montana. In some areas it is possible to take both species from the same camp. I have hunted Wyoming antelope by making a motel my base and eating my meals at a restaurant. Guides are not required for mule deer and antelope and the licenses are moderate.

The game departments of most Western states, Alaska, and the Canadian provinces encourage nonresident hunting as the nonresident pays a much higher fee than the resident, spends much more money otherwise, and is generally more law abiding. Anyone interested in making a hunt in a particular state should write to the game department at the state capital and request information on fees, seasons, and regulations, and ask for a list of outfitters. Some states do not require nonresidents to hire guides. Others do for any big-game hunting. Some require the nonresident to have a guide for certain wilderness species but let him hunt on his own for others. Regulations and license fees change from year to year and it would be futile to publish such material in a book of this sort—a book which I piously hope will continue to sell for several years.

States and provinces that require hunters to have guides do so not to shake them down for more money but to keep them from getting lost, starting fires, getting killed by grizzly bears, dropping dead of heart attacks and otherwise wrecking the country and rushing to their own destruction like so many lemmings. The Idaho county in which I live is adjacent to a large, thinly populated county much of which is rough, wild, and full of elk. Every fall hundreds of nonresident hunters swarm in driving campers, pulling trailers, sometimes towing jeeps. They get lost, they shoot each other, they drop dead of heart attacks, they fall off of cliffs, they get stuck in the mud, isolated by snow storms. The poor taxpayers of this poverty-stricken county have to dig them out of the mud, haul them through the snow, try to find them when they are lost, pack out the carcasses of those who have been shot or who have died of heart attacks. No wonder many states demand that nonresidents employ guides!

In planning a trip the hunter should consider his available time as well as money—and sad to say time is almost as scarce a commodity with many of us as money. Nevertheless sufficient time is so important that a trip should be postponed just as quickly because of a shortage of time as it would be for lack of money. My wife and I once flew into a wilderness area in Idaho to hunt elk. We had arranged to be there a week. We thought that sufficient time as previously in the same area we had knocked off bulls the first or second day. The night we arrived rain began to fall. When we awoke the next morning it was still raining and the clouds were so low that up in the hills where the elk were you couldn't see fifty feet. When our week was up we had hunted part of one day. The storm was over and it was clear and beautiful the day we flew out, but we could stay no longer as the outfitter had other hunters coming in.

Let us suppose that the hunter is making his first hunt in Alaska or northern British Columbia. He would like to take home several trophies —a respectable ram, a caribou, a moose—and a grizzly if he is lucky. He arranges for a two weeks' hunt. Let us suppose that he has to pack in for three days. He has lost six of his fourteen. Then perhaps he is unlucky and runs into a four-day storm. He now has only four hunting days left! He may get what he wants but chances are he won't.

If it is possible for the hunter to fly right into a hunting area and to start hunting the next day, and if he will be content with taking one species and happy if he gets two, a ten-day hunt might be sufficient but fourteen days would be better as it would give more leeway in case of bad weather and bad luck. I would hesitate to go on an expensive pack trip where several days' packing were involved for less than twenty-one days and thirty days would be better. The outfitter who books quickie hunts is foolish. The man who goes in for seven days and who spends a minimum amount of money expects just as much as the man who books for thirty days and tosses away a bundle. The short-timer gets just as angry if he gets skunked through no fault of the outfitter as if he had spent three months and $10,000 on his hunt. The short-timer depletes the good trophies in an area and profits the outfitter hardly at all. I know of many cases where hunters have tried to make quickie and cheapie trips, have had some bad luck and have not got what they wanted. When they return they always run down the outfitter to their friends and even write indignant letters to shooting editors.

I would not take a pack trip even for one common species for less than ten days. Two weeks is better. In 1964 my wife and I packed in for elk in Wyoming for ten days. The weather was lovely but the elk started bugling late. My wife shot her bull the last few minutes of the last hour of the last day. We packed up and hit the trail for civilization the next morning. With any luck and straight shooting the hunter of brown or grizzly bears in the spring should get himself a trophy in a couple of weeks. I have never hunted polar bears, but those who have tell me that with the enormous amount of territory that can be covered by plane it is seldom that more than from two to four days of actual hunting is necessary. However, the weather is apt to be bad and any polar bear hunter should plan to spend more time if he has to.

Not only should the man planning a trip out of his own state set aside enough time and enough money but he should be certain that he is physically equal to the hunt he is undertaking. The average hunter deceives himself more about his physical condition and his ability to walk and to climb than he does about anything else except his shooting and hunting skill.

The hunter can go on an African safari, hunt antelope from a jeep on the plains of Wyoming, make a boat hunt for brown bears in southeast

Alaska or an airplane hunt for polar bears in the arctic as long as he has enough strength to pull a trigger and sign a check. However, some types of hunting are for young men or for middle-aged men who have kept up their exercise, have limited their cigarettes, and have refrained from unseemly bouts with the fork and the bottle.

There are some types of hunting that even soft young men simply cannot hack. Many years ago I had a friend who was a target enthusiast and a magnificent rifle shot. At that time I was about thirty-five. I was six feet one inch tall and I weighed 170 pounds stripped. I was a very tough guy. My friend was twenty-two, five feet eight inches tall and weighed about 185 pounds, mostly blubber. One April we drove into a campsite in Sonora about three miles from a good sheep mountain. We could get no closer by automobile. It can get pretty hot during the day in April on the Sonora desert. My pal always started out with a two-quart canteen. We had a Mexican with us and we kept another Mexican in camp to look after things, gather and cut wood, and keep an ironwood fire burning under the frijoles. My pal could never make it. When we were a half mile from camp he would start drinking water and by the time we had started up the mountain he would be out of water and he and the Mexican would return to camp.

In some places in the Yukon and northern British Columbia it is (or was) possible to ride right up into sheep country, but generally sheep and goat hunting requires hard climbing, and there are few middle-aged and elderly men who are equal to it. Most hunting for bighorns is either at very high altitude or in very rough country or both, and hunting desert sheep (something I have done plenty of) is the toughest hunting I have ever run into except for ibex in the Middle East.

Even the middle-aged man in fairly good condition and not over-weight is a lot better off with a horse to take the wear and tear off of his legs and to haul him up the hills. That is why such men should take a second look at hunts where they are flown into a lake and then have to climb for sheep and stumble through miles of muskeg and frost hummocks after moose and caribou. It is far better to go without a sheep or caribou head than it is to drop dead of a heart attack on some lonely Alaskan mountain side.

The paragraph above is addressed to the hundreds of men who have led successful if well-fed and sedentary lives. I know many of them. They have made plenty of money. They retire. They decide that now that they have plenty of those two necessary commodities, time and money, that they will take up big-game hunting in a fairly serious way. One friend of mine was greatly overweight and walking was a chore for him. He stayed on a horse when he should have been off. The horse fell on him and hurt him badly. Another had a heart attack on a British Columbia sheep mountain. He pulled through but he now does no hunting where a horse or a safari car cannot furnish legs and wind.

Generally the man on a big-game hunt enjoys it more if he has a companion along. But companions can make or break a trip. The pal you play a round of golf with once a month or the chap you toss off a fast one with before you catch the 5:28 may wear very poorly on a hunting trip, and the longer the trip lasts the worse he may wear. The best (but also an exceedingly expensive) way to know a woman is to live with her a few years. Many a glamour girl has turned into a virago and slattern once she has conned her husband into that walk down the aisle and has a legal hammerlock on him. And many a pleasant companion in the bar or on the golf course has turned into a real jerk on a hunting trip.

I could tell some tales that would break your heart but I'll make it brief. One citizen I went on a week's deer hunt with disappeared as if by magic every time there was water to fetch, wood to gather and cut, food to cook, or dishes to wash. When a meal was ready he reappeared as mysteriously as he had vanished. Another hombre always managed to corner the choice morsels. If one member of the party had managed to shoot the heads off of a couple of blue grouse he always contrived to grab them both. "Well," he would say, "there are four of us and two grouse really aren't enough to go around. Since I am particularly fond of blue grouse I might as well take them both!"

Many a beautiful friendship has gone on the rocks during a long hunting trip. Many people are jealous and bitterly competitive. They resent it if a companion shoots a bigger elk, gets a better sheep head, kills more quail with fewer shots. Others simply cannot stand a long trip. They get bored, restless, and depressed. They gripe about the food, snarl at their companions. Many men are intrigued by the ideas of the wilderness and of big-game hunting. They like to plan trips and to brag about them when they are over, but the actual hunt bores the hell out of them. The wilderness is too quiet, the crystal-clear water in the mountain streams is insipid and tasteless as compared to the reconstituted sewage laced with chlorine to which they are used. They miss the smell of garbage and gasoline fumes. The mountains look foreboding, the silence of the forest depresses them. They quarrel with their companions just to have something to do. This ailment has variously been called cabin fever and safari fever. It is easy to laugh at but it is a very real malady.

For a long trip, one true and tried companion that has been through the mill seems to work best. If a man's wife likes to hunt and is willing to go along this is ideal, but there is nothing worse than some spoiled and pampered wench who goes along simply to keep the old man under surveillance and who is afraid of bugs, is allergic to horses, and has a tendency to hangnails, stone bruises, and saddle sores. My own storm and strife has hunted whitetail deer with me in Sonora and sheep in the Yukon, pheasants in Oregon, tigers in India, and goats in Alberta. We still get along.

I'd rather read about a large hunting party than go out as a member of one. I once knew six men who went on an African safari together. They quarreled bitterly the entire trip and returned hating each other. If there are three hunters on a trip, two tend to gang up on the third. The more hunters there are in a party, the more noise they make, and the quicker they shoot up the country and run the game out. If there are four hunters on a pack trip, provision should be made to split the party up if necessary. As I write this a friend and I are planning to hunt in Bechuanaland with our wives. We will have two complete outfits so we can separate or come back together as the spirit moves us.

Selecting a good country and a good outfitter requires a good deal of staff work. Some very good outfitters advertise in the Where-To-Go pages of the hunting and fishing magazines, and so do some very poor ones— although the magazines try to get rid of dishonest and incompetent outfitters. Some very good outfitters get all the business they want without advertising at all.

The best way I know of to locate a good outfitter who operates in good country is to talk to a friend who has been out with him. If this friend fared well, saw enough game, and was well taken care of and happy you probably will be too.

Another method is to keep a sharp eye out for stories in outdoor magazines on country in which you are interested. When you see one you can write to the author in care of the magazine. To some extent this is an imposition, but most hunters like to talk about their heroic feats and are glad to pass on what knowledge they have acquired. Since conditions change rapidly it is best to get the hottest information available. It is well known that I lived for many years in Arizona and made many hunting trips into Sonora. I still get inquiries about hunting in both places, but I made my last big-game hunts in both states in 1947.

State game departments have lists of outfitters which they send out to inquirers. They are pretty coy about writing letters recommending one outfitter rather than another but when someone calls them up on the telephone they will usually sing.

I think the man planning a hunting trip should always decide what trophy he wants most, then go to a country where his chances are good and hunt hard for it. He should make his wants plain to the outfitter he engages. He should, for example, write: "I want above anything else to get a shot at a large grizzly bear. If I get no other shooting I will be satisfied." Then the outfitter knows where he stands. The man who wants a grizzly, a moose, a goat, a black bear, a ram, a caribou, some trout fishing, and some fine grouse and ptarmigan shooting often does not get much of anything.

On my trips into the mountains of Canada I have always asked to be sent into country that produces large rams. If I have got nothing else I have not protested. However, in the course of hunting sheep I have generally encountered moose, caribou, grizzlies, and sometimes elk. All too often a man's appetite is too big for his money or his time. Just before I wrote this I received a letter from a man who wanted in one fourteen-day trip to get a moose with a spread of at least sixty-five inches, a forty-inch ram, a trophy caribou, and an Alaska brown bear. This would take a bit of doing. I can think of only one area where there are white sheep and *any* brown bears, and most brown-bear country has no sheep at all.

To produce good trophies a country must furnish plenty of rich food and animals must be allowed to live long enough to grow large heads or attain maximum body size. It takes from six to eight years to produce an antlered animal with a trophy head, from eleven to thirteen years to produce a record-class sheep head, perhaps fifteen years to produce a large bear. Game with extraordinarily large horns and antlers comes from country where the soil is rich in nutrients from underlying lime-stone and some types of igneous rock. Bears grow to great size in those portions of Alaska where there is access to rich and abundant salmon and where they have time to get old and heavy. The Kaibab forest north of the Grand Canyon in Arizona used to produce tremendous mule deer heads, as the vegetation there is rich in lime and at one time the country was difficult to get into. Now the plateau is hunted hard and few bucks are allowed to become old enough to grow big heads.

The country around the heads of the Muskwa and Prophet Rivers and adjacent areas in northern British Columbia has produced most of the great Stone sheep heads, including the world's record, as the mountains are mostly limestone and the country used to be remote. When I hunted there in 1946 it took me fourteen days on the trail just to get in. Now, however, the outfitter in the area has scratched out a landing strip in the valley of the Muskwa. His clients can fly in from Ft. St. John in a couple of hours instead of a couple of weeks. In 1965, I understand, he had fifty hunters in three camps during the season. Most of the rams simply do not get a chance to grow really big.

In selecting an area in which to hunt, the man wanting some meat to take home or simply a hunting trip should look for a place where game is plentiful. Game departments are always delighted to give out information on these "hot spots," as in these days of interference with the balance of nature browsing animals often become so plentiful that they damage the range.

The head hunter should strive to go to areas which are currently producing big horns and antlers, large bears, or whatever he is after. The best source of information for this is the Boone and Crockett Club, c/o Carnegie Museum, 4400 Forbes Avenue, Pittsburgh, Pennsylvania, 15213. The club publishes folders listing the prize-winning trophies and picturing many of them. These give the name of the person who shot the trophy, the area in which it was shot, and the name of the guide. These folders are published for each contest and can be obtained for $1 from the club. Everyone interested in trophy heads should have a copy of the book, *Records of North American Big Game.* The last edition, as this is written, was published by Holt, Rinehart & Winston in 1964. It can be obtained through bookstores and Abercrombie & Fitch, Madison Avenue at 45th Street, New York, usually has it in stock. It costs $15.

In corresponding with prospective clients the outfitter naturally puts his best foot forward. I am told that the percentage of clients who actually book hunts as compared to those who write in is comparatively small. In this exchange of letters the outfitter is sizing up his prospective client—his intentions, his experience, how well heeled he is. The prospective hunter should likewise size up the outfitter as well as he can. As a first step he should ask the outfitter for the names and addresses of clients who have gone out with him within the past year or two. He should then write to these men and ask them what sort of trophies they got, how much game they saw, how the food and equipment were.

When an agreement for a trip is under way, the client should have in writing exactly what he is to receive and exactly what he is to pay. If there are any extras he should know about them and he should also ask what the custom is in tipping help. If two hunters are to have a guide apiece, a cook, and a horse wrangler, for instance, this should be specified.

Two hunters I know contracted for a twenty-one-day hunt for general game in Alaska. They were to fly in to camp and to fly here and there for various trophies. The outfitter was charging them a nice bundle. When they got to camp they were astounded to discover that there were nine other hunters there, that there was one cook for eleven hunters, and that the outfitter picked them up a pair at a time and dumped them off with a guide above timberline. Then they hunted back down a ridge toward camp. One of the hunters was so unhappy over the deal that he stopped payment on his check and there was a lawsuit.

A hunting trip with an outfitter is a business deal and parties to any business deal are happier when everyone knows exactly what everyone else is supposed to do. If the hunter is going to have to share his camp or the services of a guide or an airplane with another hunter that is something he ought to know. If the guides, the cook, and the horse wrangler all expect to have their palms crossed with rupees he should know that. If the outfitter generally charges extra to crate and ship trophies or to haul him out to the spot where he meets the pack outfit the client should know that too. On the other hand, the dude should understand that he has contracted for a twenty-one-day hunt at $70 a day and that if by chance he should have to leave because he became homesick, his wife ran off with an adagio dancer, his house burned down, the stock market crashed, he decided his hunting partner was an unbearable creep, or he got all his game and grew weary of solitude and fresh air that he still owes the outfitter the sum total of $1,470 less the earnest money he has paid.

In a quarter century of dealing with outfitters I have had good trips and bad, good outfits and lousy ones. Most of the outfitters I have dealt with have been honest and conscientious. Some of the honest ones have been excellent and systematic organizers, but some have been poor organizers. One man who had good horses, good tents, good guides, and who knew the country skimped on food to the extent that my companions and I had to send a guide with two pack horses to the nearest trading post for more grub. Another honest outfitter who did not skimp simply could not handle his help and tried to do all the work himself. Yet another outfitter was a congenital liar, who would rather lie than tell the truth when the truth would have served his interests better. If I would ask this man if he thought I had any chance in his territory to see a pink elephant with large green eyes and a purple tail, he would assure me he had seen seven such animals in an isolated valley and that they were actually survivors of the Ice Age. The funny part of it was that I was leery of this character when I was corresponding with him and leerier when I met him. I went with him simply because at that time he was the only outfitter in an area I wanted to hunt in. Beware of the outfitter that promises the moon, who says he will guarantee you a forty-five-inch ram, a sixty-five-inch moose, and a grizzly that squares ten feet. Beware of the outfitter who has the earmarks of the con man and the hot-air artist. Beware of the one who is out for a fast buck and who is trying to mass produce hunting. Investigate your outfitter and his country even more carefully than you investigate your new automobile. Then get everything in writing. You and your outfitter will both be better off.

Outfitters seldom investigate clients, but they ought to do so more often. If they did they would save themselves a great many headaches. The best advertisement an outfitter can have is a happy and satisfied customer who will show off his trophies and brag about his trip to his friends. The poorest advertisement he can have is the sorehead to whom nothing is right.

As I write this I have just returned from a thirty-day safari in Bechuanaland. While I was there I advised my outfitter–white hunter to return the deposit of a hunter he had booked and to refuse to take him on safari. That particular guy is poison. He cannot climb. He cannot walk. He is a poor shot and a poor sport. He always quarrels with his hunting companions and his guides and when he arrives back home he never fails to write a long letter to the game department of the state or province where he has hunted denouncing his guides and outfitters as lazy drunks, crooks, and incompetents.

There are poor outfitters, lazy guides, and sorry camp cooks; but there are also lazy, greedy, and ill-natured clients—clients who would be unhappy if they shot nothing but world records, were fed on steaks from corn-fed steers, pompano with grapes, and were entertained each night by dancing girls.

I write this in September, 1966. Along in the spring, a chap called me from the Middle West. He and a companion wanted good trophy white rams, he said. If anything else came along, so much better, he said, but their primary objective was to get trophy Dall sheep. I suggested an outfitter and an area. I said that if he and his companion could climb, were willing to work, stayed in the country three weeks, and didn't shoot indifferent sheep, they should have an excellent chance to get rams with forty-inch curls or better. I said there were a few caribou in the country, and that if conditions were right they should see a good many moose and grizzly bears but if conditions were not right they might not.

A few days before I wrote this I heard once more from this chap. He was bitterly unhappy. He had shot a ram with a curl of $40\frac{1}{2}$ inches. His companion had shot one that went $41\frac{1}{2}$. In addition his pal had missed an easy shot at an even larger ram because his rifle had a bad scope mount. They had shot two moose, a grizzly, and two caribou, one of which had a double shovel. They were furious and said it was one of the poorest trips they had ever been on. They were angry because they both had not got grizzly and because their best moose didn't have a sixty-inch spread. They said their guides were lazy and the country overhunted. They felt that because of their unsatisfactory hunt, the outfitter should give them a free trip the next fall! Either that or their money back! Exactly what these two people expected I have no idea. Any time a man hunts sheep anywhere in North America and gets one good old ram with a thirty-eight-inch curl or better he has done very well. If he gets a ram with a head of forty inches or over he has been lucky indeed and anything else he picks up is gravy. I have been hunting sheep for three decades and I would have been very happy with the bag that either of these men got!

Just as there are many excellent outfitters and likewise many poor ones there are also good and bad clients. The good client does not expect the impossible from his guide and outfitter. He knows that neither has any control over the weather or the vagaries of the game animals themselves. The good client is in good enough condition so he can do the necessary walking and climbing. He can see game when it is pointed out to him. He can shoot well enough to hit animals properly and he has enough judgment not to blaze away at animals he cannot hit well. He does not quarrel with his companions and the guides, and he does not blame anyone for his own shortcomings. He has enough intelligence to realize that his guide probably knows more about hunting a particular animal in this particular area than he himself does, since the guide has hunted there before and he has not. This good client is ethical and decent enough not to ask his guide to forget about a poor trophy he has taken so he can go on looking for a better one. When the time comes to settle his accounts the good client does not groan and moan if the weather and his luck have been bad. He knows that both may be better next time.

20 | *Binoculars for Hunting*

To the hunter a good binocular is just about as important a piece of equipment as his rifle. For some types of hunting the proper binocular is actually more important than the choice of a rifle. The hunter finds many uses for binoculars—so many that I would not think of going out after any big-game animals without a glass. With his binocular, the hunter can tell a buck from a doe, a deer from a horse or cow, a human being from a game animal. He can judge horns and antlers. He can inspect the terrain he is going to make a stalk over. With a binocular he can even peer through brush to make out things he could not see with the naked eye.

The hunter of mountain game depends on his binocular to find the game and often picks it up with his glass when he could not possibly detect it with the unaided eye. I wouldn't say the hunter of mountain sheep and goats is helpless without a binocular, but he is certainly greatly handicapped.

A binocular is also exceedingly handy in the brush. Just after the last war, I was guiding my son Bradford in Sonora. That morning I had shot a big buck desert mule deer. We gutted it and had hung it in a tree and had then continued on to a chain of low hills of decomposed granite with a great deal of brush and an occasional granite outcrop. After we had tied our horses, we hunted quietly along from draw to draw, from basin to basin.

About a mile from the horses one particular basin looked very good indeed. It was brushier than most and it was all tracked up with the heart-shaped tracks of the handsome little Arizona whitetail. I sat down, took out my 9 × 35 Bausch & Lomb binocular and started going over the brushy basin foot by foot. Presently I found what looked like the ear of a deer. I watched it for a few seconds, and then I saw it twitch. Presently the deer turned its head and I could make out the antlers of a very nice buck. Little by little as I watched I could make out the body. Our buck was lying down, at peace with the world, not over sixty yards away and below us.

With some difficulty I pointed the buck out to Bradford, who was then thirteen and who had shot his first buck the previous fall. Brad put a .257 bullet through the buck's ribs. It sprang to its feet and tore through the basin in great style but collapsed just as it topped out on a saddle.

Perhaps the most important thing the binocular does for the hunter is that it enables him to tell a human being from a game animal. Some years ago a friend of mine had an experience which shook him up badly. He was hunting elk in an area where both cows and bulls could be taken when on the other side of a draw and across a creek he saw an elk bedded down in the brush just above a creek. At least he *thought* he saw an elk. He could see the tan of the body, the dark brown of the neck. From where he sat, it wouldn't be much of a trick to put a bullet into it. Through the 2½X scope on his rifle the elk was still an elk but there was something slightly phony about it, something that made him pause. Luckily he had an 8X binocular with him. When he put it on the elk, he saw that what he had almost shot was a weary hunter who had eaten his lunch, taken a drink of creek water, and then had lain down under a bush to rest his weary legs. He was dressed in a yellow buckskin jacket and brown trousers, a pretty foolish garb for an elk hunter. The colors were correct and my amigo's imagination had simply filled in the details.

I once had a similar experience. I was hunting in Sonora on the mainland near Tiburon Island with a Seri Indian guide. The Indian could speak only about three words of Spanish, no English whatsoever, and I could speak no Seri. Apparently the guide found my company dull and before long he took off. Presently, about 300 yards away across a canyon I thought I saw a whitetail deer. It was moving erratically through the thin brush with the tail flipping up and down in true whitetail fashion. I put the glass on it and found that my "deer" was the Seri guide, who was down on his hands and knees chasing a land turtle. The tail was his breech clout.

How Binoculars Work

There are various types of binoculars. Those called "field glasses" and "opera glasses" do not have prisms. Instead they are small paired tele-

Prism binoculars "fold" the light paths, thereby achieving a long focal length in a short tube. This system also allows for a wide separation of objective lenses, which increases the stereoscopic effect and permits more accurate judgments of range by giving better depth perception. *Courtesy Bausch & Lomb.*

scopes. Sometimes these field glasses are made with bulging sides to make them look something like prism binoculars. These glasses are generally inexpensive, but their fields of view are small and their optical quality is not suitable for serious work. Sometimes these are made with plastic lenses and are actually toys instead of serious optical instruments.

Prism binoculars are much better optically than field glasses—and they are also much more precise, complicated, and expensive. I am no optical engineer, but according to Robert and Elsa Reichert's good little book, *Binoculars and Scopes,* the optical systems of all prismatic binoculars consist of an objective lens, two prisms, at least one field lens, and a positive ocular lens. The objective lenses are those in the front toward whatever is being looked at. The ocular lenses are those immediately next to the eye. The "field" lens is between the ocular and the prisms. Good prism binoculars today have all air-glass surfaces coated with magnesium fluoride. This can be seen on the outside surface of the objective and ocular lenses as a tint ranging from straw color to deep purple. This hard coating process was perfected in the United States during the last big war. Coating improves the optical quality of an instrument by preventing loss of light when it travels from air to glass and from glass to air. According to the Reicherts, the loss of light in an uncoated prism binocular is from four to five percent for each uncoated air-to-glass surface. In a standard porro prism glass there are ten air-glass surfaces and in some wide-angle glasses there are twelve. Some good European binoculars have all internal air-glass surfaces coated, but not the external surfaces since some firms have not perfected hard coating. Some cheap imported binoculars have only the outside surfaces of the objectives and oculars coated as these are all the purchaser sees.

Binoculars are referred to as 6 × 30's, 7 × 35's, 10 × 40's, etc. The first figure stands for the magnifying power, the second for the diameter, in millimeters, of the objective lens. The relationship of power to diameter of the objective lens determines what is called "relative brightness." This is getting pretty far out in left field, but the diameter of the exit pupil (the little circle of light you see in the center of the ocular lens when you hold the binocular out at arms length) equals the diameter of the objective expressed in millimeters divided by the power. The figure for relative brightness is this squared. Thus the diameter of the exit pupil of a 6 × 30 binocular would be 5 mm. and the relative brightness would be 25. It can be seen that a 6 × 30, a 7 × 35, and an 8 × 40 would have the same relative brightness. On the other hand, my favorite mountain glass, the superb Bausch & Lomb 9 × 35 has an exit pupil of 3.8 mm. and a relative brightness of 14.4. The eye cannot make use of the light from the exit pupil if the pupil of the eye is closed down smaller than the diameter of the exit pupil. On a bright day the field through a 9 × 35 with its exit pupil of 3.8 mm., and its relative brightness of 14.4 seems just as bright as that seen with a Bausch & Lomb 7 × 50 with its exit pupil of 7.1 and its relative brightness of 50.4. In poor light, however, when the pupil of the eye opens up, the 7 × 50 is much brighter.

A 7 × 50 binocular is large, rather heavy and bulky. The B. & L. 7 × 50 weighs 42 ounces, for example, whereas the 6 × 30 of the same make weighs 19½ ounces and the 9 × 35, 26 ounces. Such glasses as the 7 × 50 and the 8 × 56 are often called night glasses and they are much used on ships where it is desirable to see as well as possible at night and in poor light.

A wide field of view is desirable in a binocular if it can be obtained without awkward bulk and weight. Field is expressed in two ways—by the angle and by the diameter of the field seen at 1,000 yards. For example, the angular field of a B. & L. 8 × 30 is 8 degrees and 29 minutes and the linear field 445 feet at 1,000 yards. That of the 7 × 35 and the 9 × 35 glasses of the same make is 7 degrees, 17 minutes and 381 feet at 1,000 yards. The wider the field, the more the user is able to take in and see at one time. A wide field is very useful at a football game, for example, when the user wants to have both passer and receiver in the field at the same time.

Some special wide-angle binoculars are made. During World War II a very remarkable 6X wide-angle binocular called the Sard was made for B-29 crewmen to use in spotting enemy fighter planes. A partner of mine on an Alaskan brown bear hunt had one of these Sard 6X wide-angle glasses. The field was so tremendous that looking through one was like looking through a window. However, such a glass is of very limited use in the hunting field. The prisms must be very large and the whole glass is large, heavy, and bulky. It was a fine instrument for spotting smart old Alaska brown bears coming out of the woods to the beach in the subarctic twilight, but it was too heavy for most use. Bushnell imports a 7 × 35 wide angle with a 577-foot field at 1,000 yards. Because of the necessarily large prisms it weighs 32 ounces as against 26 ounces for the 7 × 35 Bausch & Lomb. The Sard I mentioned above is much heavier.

A prism binocular is a complicated piece of optical equipment composed of many pieces of different kinds of glass precisely ground, coated, and carefully adjusted. A good glass is a lifetime investment and a joy to own. A poor one is a pain in the neck. The lenses and prisms in the good binocular are securely fastened and stay put. Poor prism binoculars do not use highly corrected lenses and precisely ground prisms and the prisms are not securely fastened.

Many years ago I bought my first binocular. It was of off-breed European make. It looked nice and shiny, just as good as the Bausch & Lomb and Zeiss 8 × 30's that cost twice as much. I bought it and thought I had saved myself about $35. At that time the Zeiss and Bausch & Lomb 8 × 30's sold at retail for about $70.

I noticed that using the binocular gave me a headache. I found that it was out of alignment and my eyes were straining in an attempt to fuse the cockeyed images. I sent it East to an optical company to be realigned. Then the elements in one ocular lens separated. Finally, when I had spent as much as I thought I had saved, I gave the glass away and I went in hock for an 8 × 30 Bausch & Lomb.

Most binocular purchasers are not very knowledgeable about optics, and about all they can do to protect themselves is to buy a glass bearing one of the famous names in quality binocular manufacture or a glass by an American importer who is willing to give a written guarantee with what he sells. Traditionally the manufacturers of top-quality binoculars are Bausch & Lomb of the United States, Ross of England, Hensoldt, Zeiss, and Leitz of Germany. Before the war, the Zeiss plant was at Jena, which is now in communist East Germany. The Zeiss binoculars currently sold in the United States are made in West Germany by a company formed by Zeiss executives and engineers who fled from the Reds. I believe Zeiss also controls the Hensoldt company. Leitz makes the famous Leica camera, binoculars, and other optical goods. British Ross binoculars used to be— and I presume still are—of absolutely top quality. The better prism binoculars made in Japan are good. They are usually copies of Zeiss and Bausch & Lomb designs. A Japanese prism binocular with a good guarantee is generally a good buy.

Selecting a Binocular

There are various types of binocular construction. Most are of the porro prism type like the standard glasses made by Zeiss and Bausch & Lomb. With this type the distance between the objective lenses is greater than between the oculars. This increases the stereoptic effect. Hensoldt roof prism binoculars are less bulky than binoculars of the porro prism type. They are often mistaken for field glasses because of their straight tubes. Their lack of bulk makes them easy and comfortable to carry around the neck, but they do not have the same stereoptic effect as those with porro prisms. Leitz has within the past two or three years put on the market a new series of binoculars called "Trinovids." They have a new lens system something like that of the Hensoldt roof prisms. These are light, compact, and of top quality optically. They are made in 6 × 24, 7 × 35, 8 × 32, and 10 × 40.

Prism binoculars can be divided into three classes: the little pocket glass that is light, handy, and can be carried in a shirt pocket, the standard-size glass of from 6 to 10X and weighing from about 18 ounces to about 26 ounces, and the heavier, bulkier special purpose binoculars—wide-angle jobs, extra-high powers, and night glasses.

The little pocket binoculars such as the little 6 × 25 Bushnell are handy to carry along to check the antlers on a buck, to help identify the other hunter across the ravine, to see if the patch of white in the brush on the other hill is a piece of paper or your bird dog on point.

The standard prism binocular is an all-purpose job. With it the hunter locates game he could not see with the naked eye, sizes up trophies, sees that the patch of tan in the timber on the other side of the canyon is an old decayed stump and not a bedded elk. Probably the most useful all-around power is the 7X with the 35-mm. objective, a size which Bausch & Lomb made popular. The U.S. Army has long specified 6X binoculars on the grounds that more power made the wobble annoying. However, those who buy high-grade binoculars for hunting are riflemen who know how to hold things reasonably steady. They can use more power.

The woods hunter never needs more power than 6 or 7X. For his purposes field and brightness are of more importance than magnification. The man who does most of his hunting in open country should choose a glass with more power. I have used an 8 × 30 Bausch & Lomb a great deal and likewise an 8 × 32 Hensoldt. I prefer them for use in the West to glasses with less power. These are good for general open-country hunting, but I think a reasonably light and compact glass of higher power is even better. My favorite sheep-hunting glass is an old 9 × 35 Bausch & Lomb I got in 1946. I have glassed all varieties of North American sheep and some foreign species on three continents. For a combination of weight, definition, handiness, and durability it is hard to beat. I have never hunted with the 10 × 40 Leitz Trinovid, but it should be excellent. Of the very good sheep hunters I have known, one swore by the 10 × 50 Hensoldt Dialyt roof prism, another by a 10 × 50 Zeiss, several by the B. & L. 9 × 35. For general all-around hunting, however, the 7X is exceedingly useful. The people at Bausch & Lomb tell me that their best-selling binoculars are the 7 × 35 and the 9 × 35. The B. & L. 8 × 30 is a good bet as an all-around glass. I hunted sheep, deer, and antelope with one for years. Also very good are the other 8X jobs like the Zeiss 8 × 30B and the 8 × 32 Leitz Trinovid, and 8 × 32 Hensoldt Dialyt. Zeiss makes two 8 × 30B glasses. One, the 8× 30B "Dialyt" is a roof-prism binocular something on the order of the Leitz Trinovid. The other 8 × 30B is a porro prism glass, small, light, compact—a most excellent all-around glass, particularly for the wearer of spectacles. All of the Zeiss "B" type binoculars have folding eye cups of synthetic rubber. Unfolded they put the pupil of the eye of the person who does not wear spectacles the correct distance from the ocular lens. The eye cups folded down put the eye of the spectacle wearer close enough to the ocular so that he gets the full field.

These beautiful little binoculars cost as this is written in 1967 something over $200 in the United States. In Germany and at duty-free airport shops in Europe they can be bought for about $115. In addition Zeiss makes two other "B"-type binoculars with folding rubber eye cups—a 7 × 50 and an 8 × 50. Both are on the heavy side but they are superb optically and unsurpassed for use in poor light, at dawn and dusk. The Zeiss 10 × 50 is an excellent glass for picking up detail at great distances, but it is somewhat heavy to carry on a mountain hunt. The Zeiss 15 × 50 has too much power to be hand-held. It should be used on a tripod.

Spotting Scopes

The use of a big, high-powered glass is quicker and handier than taking the time out to set up a spotting scope, and most of the time something like my 12X will suffice. However, at extremely long range there is no substitute for a spotting scope. The famous deer-hunting guides of Scotland use draw-tube scopes of high power, hold a stick in their left hands, rest the glass over their wrists. Many American hunters try to rest spotting scopes on stones or logs and use them that way. I have found

At long ranges there is no substitute for a spotting scope. The scope should be supported by a collapsible tripod, as is this one being used by Bill Rae, Editor of *Outdoor Life,* while watching distant sheep in the Yukon.

that because of the much greater steadiness a small collapsible tripod such as is used by the small-bore target shooter is the most satisfactory. The tripod should be made of steel. Those of aluminum I have tried are too flimsy. Scope and tripod are a bother to take along, but when they are needed they are worth their weight in gold. In the Yukon in 1945 my guide and I once located a bunch of rams so far off the 8 × 30 I was using told us only that they were rams. We spent the whole day stalking them, almost broke our necks, then discovered that of the fourteen not a one had a trophy head.

Excellent prismatic spotting scopes are made in this country, and the same optical qualities that enable those who use them to pick up a .22 caliber bullet hole in the black at 200 yards also make it possible for the

240

hunter to count the points on the antlers of a mule deer or estimate the curl of a ram's horns at a mile. Power of from 20 to 24 is about right. With higher power the field is too small and except under perfect conditions mirage becomes too much of an annoyance. But they should be used only for sizing up heads after animals have been found with a glass of lower power and wider field.

Use and Care of Binoculars

Binocular users who wear spectacles all the time should either order binoculars with shallow eyecups or they should make sure that the binoculars they acquire have some provision for positioning their eyes properly in relation to the ocular lens. With standard eyecups the eye of the spectacle wearer is too far from the ocular and some of the field is lost—like trying to see through a knothole in a fence with the eye too far away. Some of the Bushnell binoculars have adjustable eyecups for the spectacle wearer. The Leitz Trinovids have eyecups that can be screwed off, leaving shallow cups for the spectacle wearer. Bausch & Lomb and other manufacturers of high-class binoculars will furnish shallow eyecups.

Binoculars should be carefully focused. Generally they are made in two different styles—one to focus centrally by turning a wheel to rack them back and forth and the other to focus each side individually by rotating the oculars. The binocular with individual eyepiece focusing can be made more nearly dust and moisture proof and with a glass with a considerable depth of focus this is probably the best idea. My son Bradford has now inherited my 8 × 30 Bausch & Lombs. These have individual eyepiece focusing. Each eyepiece is marked in diopters, plus and minus. I knew what my correct settings were. Before I started to use the 8 × 30's I would glance at the eyepieces to see if they were at the proper setting.

On the other hand, the 9 × 35's and other glasses with less depth of focus are handiest with central focusing. In order to allow for differences in the individual's eyes the right eyepiece of central-focusing binoculars is adjustable. To focus, the right eye should be closed and the focus for the left eye established by the central wheel. Then the left eye is closed and focus for the right eye made by the adjustable eyepiece. In focusing, the glass or eyepiece should be racked out on the long (+) side, then turned slowly in until what is being viewed is needle-sharp. Then the user should stop. Focus slightly on the plus (+) side will not strain the eyes, but focus on the short (−) side will cause eyestrain.

The handiest way to carry a light binocular when hunting is to suspend it from a strap around the neck. The strap should be just long enough so that it will go over the head. If the hunter is crawling on hands and knees or wants to protect the glass from rain, he can simply put it inside his shirt. Light, compact binoculars like the Leitz Trinovids, the Zeiss 8 × 30B, and the Hensoldt Dialyts are nicely carried this way. The porro prism glasses are bulkier but can be managed. The really heavy ones are best carried suspended by a strap over one shoulder in a hard leather case. In Kenya the British white hunters leave the carrying straps long and carry their binoculars uncased under their left armpit.

The user of binoculars should hold them as still as he possibly can. The higher their power the steadier he must hold them. I constantly see pictures of hunters jauntily looking through binoculars held with one hand, using them from horseback, looking through 20 and 25X spotting scopes held offhand. Just seeing such pictures makes my head ache. Looking through a wobbly binocular is like trying to read fine print when traveling in an automobile over a rough road. You simply cannot see detail that way and you hurt your eyes.

The skillful user of binoculars sits down. He rests his elbows on his knees and holds his binocular firmly with his index fingers extended around the eyepieces and resting against the bone above his eyes. He will use his glass offhand for a quick check but for serious work, for picking up obscure detail he sits down. For the very finest work, he will focus his glass as sharply as he can and rest it on a stone or a log. Once I lay watching seven brown boulders high on a grassy side for an hour or more. From the way they were distributed I suspected they were sheep but they were around two miles away. I put my 8X binocular on a log, lay behind it and watched. Presently one of the stones got up and began to move around. As it turned out they were all rams.

If I had been using a 12X glass I probably could have told that they were sheep immediately. Possibly I could have with a 10X. Nowadays most serious sheep hunters take along a prismatic spotting scope of from 20 to 25X to size up heads, to find out what faraway objects are. The spotter simply cannot be used offhand. It can be laid on a log or a stone but it is better to take along a small tripod.

The hunter trying to locate game in open mountain country with binoculars should above all things be thorough and patient. In Tanganyika in 1959 my white hunter John Kingsley-Heath and I, along with three gunbearers, glassed a brushy basin inch by inch for three hours and saw almost nothing. Then a magnificent bull kudu that had been lying out of sight in the brush over a half mile away got up to stretch. His head went sixty inches around the spiral, one of the best heads ever to come out of Tanganyika. Once in the Yukon my guide and I saw two smallish rams about a mile away. We set up a spotting scope and with it I could see part of the horn of a third ram over a rise. What we could see of the horn looked heavy so we made the stalk.

The best way to carry a light binocular is to suspend it around the neck with shoulder strap. Here George Edzerza watches game as he guides Bradford O'Connor in northern British Columbia.

When using binoculars the hunter should hold them steadily. He should sit down and rest his elbows on his knees. His forefingers should be steady against his forehead.

I have often heard people remark on the wonderful eyes Indians have. I do not think their eyes are better than anyone else's, but they know what to look for. A distant white spot that the inexperienced white man would not glance at the second time interests the Indian because he knows it might be the newly cleaned horns of a bull moose. The inexperienced hunter pays no attention to some off-white spots far across a canyon but the Indian takes another look as he knows they may be the rump patches of a herd of sheep.

The inexperienced user of binoculars takes a quick glance at a hillside or a basin and announces that there isn't a damned thing in sight. The experienced man first looks an area over with his naked eyes to see if there is anything in plain sight. Then he focuses his binocular and gets to work, examining the country bit by bit. He watches likely-looking spots particularly—points and saddles where sheep might bed down. He makes note of any suspiciously shaped object or of anything that is of game color. If after watching it for a while it does not move or resolve itself into an animal, he examines something else and comes back to it.

244

Once in Wyoming I noticed below me in scrubby timberline trees something a bit off-color and of odd shape. Presently I began to wonder if it were not part of the horn of a bighorn ram. Time and time again I came back to it. Presently I saw it move and I *knew* it was the horn of a ram and in a little while I could make out the head. Presently the ram stood up, walked out onto a little grassy sidehill and started to graze. Other rams that had been bedded down in the scrubby little trees stood up and before long a bunch of eight or ten rams was feeding. If I had not been persistent in watching that suspicious looking object, if I had got up when I saw nothing after a few minutes of glassing, I would have never dreamed there were rams in that particular basin. If that suspicious object is an animal it will eventually move. I once saw a large brown stone with yellowish moss on the top turn into a large grizzly. I have seen stones turn into bighorns, snow patches into goats, logs into elk. But alas I have seen many logs, stones, and spots of snow that never turned into game no matter how long I watched them.

When the hunter ships his binocular by plane, train, or automobile, he should see that it is well protected from rough treatment. I nest mine among my clothes in a strong wooden pack box or fibre pack pannier.

When traveling by horseback the hunter should carry his glass or keep it in its case in the saddle bags. Many a binocular has been lost because it was tied to the saddle horn and a limb yanked it off.

A good binocular is a pretty durable instrument, but it should not be thrown around like a camp ax. In camp it should be hung in a tree, placed on a pack pannier or otherwise put out of harm's way. When the lenses are cleaned dust should be first blown off and then a soft clean handkerchief or lens tissue should be used. It isn't a bad idea to send the binocular back to the maker once every five or six years so that it can be cleaned and the collimation (alignment) checked.

Anyone who loves the outdoors will probably get more use out of a binocular than he will out of any other possession. In the long run even expensive binoculars are cheap to own as they last a lifetime if given decent care. When I got my 9 × 35 back in 1946, it retailed with tax for about $200. A lot of money, you say? Let's see what it has cost to own it. I write this in 1966, twenty years later. I have used it on varmint hunts, big-game hunts, at baseball and football games, for bird watching. With it I have looked over many thousands of head of big game all over the world and located trophies I would not otherwise have seen. I sent it back to the maker once for cleaning and checking. It is as good now as it was the day I got it, and so far, if I divided the original cost by the number of months I have owned it, the cost would be less than $1 a month. Good optics are about the best investment a hunter can make.

21 | *Skill and Judgment in Shooting*

Back in the late 1940's I had a somewhat acrimonious exchange with another writer. He had taken a backhanded swipe at me for using what he called "inadequate" calibers (the .30/06 and .270) and for "never giving the game a chance." He scorned such pipsqueak calibers, he wrote, and he had nothing but contempt for those who sat down before they shot, who used slings, who took rests.

For his part, he went on, he shot only off his hind legs and if the game wasn't on the move he always yelled to get it going. Because he was such a sporting fellow he liked what he described as the great killing power of heavy bullets of large diameter.

I replied that everything he wrote proved that he was a hunter of scant experience because the more experience a hunter had the more effort he made to take every possible advantage and to place his bullet exactly right. No matter how good a shot he is the veteran hunter would rather shoot at a standing animal than one that is running. If he has done a great deal of shooting he has undoubtedly made some spectacular shots on running game but he does not kid himself that he can hit a moving target as well as he can a stationary one. He *knows* he can't. He likewise knows that "giving the game a chance" by taking a risky shot, such as one offhand at a running animal, when it is possible to sit down and wait for an animal to stop, he is actually giving the animal a chance to go off wounded. This experienced hunter also knows that the largest,

246

heaviest, and fastest bullets are no substitute for good shot placement. No one needs to tell him that an animal that has a leg broken or has been shot in the guts with a .300 Magnum, a .338, a .375, or a .458 is just as leg-broken or gut-shot as it would have been if it had been hit with a .243 or a .25/35. He knows that caliber is no substitute for good shooting.

I once saw a Western game department's estimate of wounded and lost game in one state. The figures were staggering. For every ten ante-lope brought in by hunters, they estimated, five got away wounded to die. For mule deer and elk the estimate was a little less. What really rocked me was the loss of bighorn sheep. At least three rams were left rotting in the mountains for every ten brought home, the experts said. The bighorn is a rare and wonderful animal, and a good bighorn head is the most valued of all American big-game trophies. Many hunters have waited for years to draw a permit to hunt bighorn in this Western state, but excited and careless hunters are wounding these fine animals and letting them go off to die.

Various interpretations have been placed on these figures for wounded game. Some say that this game is lost because of the use of inadequate calibers. Others say the game is wounded and lost because hunters are too inexperienced to know if they have hit an animal or not and too lazy to go over to see if they can find blood, hair, or some other sign of a hit. There is such a thing as using rifles of inadequate caliber, of course. I once knew a backwoodsman who hunted the plentiful deer in his area with a now-obsolete cartridge called the .22 Extra Long. I also saw a kid who was hunting elk with a .25/20. The .22 would probably let a lung-shot buck get away fairly often and the .25/20 certainly is not the medicine for elk. I also agree that the toll of wounded and lost game would be greatly reduced if hunters would only take the trouble to go over and look around in the area where the animal was they think they might have hit.

I remember an experience of my own. My wife and I had been hunting whitetails in some hills in southern Arizona near the Mexican border. She had got a big four-point buck, and as the ridge we were taking back to camp was steep and rough I simply laid the buck across my saddle, cut a slit in his belly skin and buttoned it to the horn, and tied him down with the saddle strings. These Arizona whitetail are small deer. This was a large buck as the Coue's whitetails go but I doubt if he weighed more than 110 pounds field dressed.

I was leading my horse, carrying my .270 by a sling over my right shoulder. My wife was riding. To my left was a steep, rocky side canyon. Suddenly a handsome whitetail came tearing out of the brush below and started up the opposite side of the canyon not over seventy-five yards away. He startled me half out of my wits, but I dropped the reins, unslung my rifle, and took a crack at him just as he reached the top. He took a tremendous leap—and disappeared.

The sides of the canyon were very steep, very rocky. I was tired. I doubted if I had hit the buck and my wife was sure I hadn't. We went in toward camp. The farther we went the more the doubts began to gnaw on me. That buck was really moving, but he was quartering and was not very far away. Actually it was not the toughest shot in the world and the crosswires had looked good when the rifle went off. Why had that buck jumped? At the time I had assumed that the bullet had burned him with ricochets from rock or bullet jacket. But was that the reason?

By the time we got to camp I was full of doubts. I hung my wife's buck in a tree, got back on my weary and protesting horse, and rode up the ridge. The buck had just made it out of sight. He lay there stone dead.

Was I justified in taking that shot? I think I was. The buck was not far away, running at an easy angle, and I had dropped into a sitting position. At that time I was shooting a great many running jackrabbits and at that distance and under those circumstances I would never miss one more than by a few inches. The fact that I was tired and the canyon meant an unpleasant climb had warped my judgment.

I probably owe that buck to the fact that I had trained myself to sit down if a sitting shot were possible and to sit down instantly. If I had shot at that buck offhand I might well have missed it. The experienced big-game hunter never shoots offhand if he can kneel, never kneels if he can sit, never sits for a long and difficult shot if he can shoot prone, never shoots without a rest if he can take one. He doesn't believe in giving the game a chance to go off wounded. He takes every advantage and his ideal is to place his shot as exactly as is possible under the circumstances and to kill quickly and painlessly with one shot.

And neither does the experienced hunter take a long and doubtful shot if he can make a stalk and take a short and certain one. I am sure that more pronghorn antelope are wounded and lost in proportion to those brought to bag than any other North American game animal. The reason for this is that antelope are open-country animals and are easily seen. Then the hunters get excited and start blasting off. I have seen hunters blazing away offhand at running antelope from 400 to 800 yards away. I have actually seen antelope missed by as much as 50 yards and maybe 100 yards. Now and then someone does kill an antelope by this wild shooting, but he is far more apt to wound than to kill.

The sooner the big-game hunter learns to pass up the shots he is not reasonably sure of, the more certain he is not to leave wounded animals in the woods and hills. It is almost always possible to get closer to open-country animals like sheep, antelope, and caribou, and consequently it is seldom necessary to take a long and chancy shot. I saw the last antelope I knocked off at perhaps 600 yards. It was a fine buck who had with him a harem of about a half-dozen does. They were in a little grassy basin where a spring-fed stream had its source. I could have shot from below and at about 500 or 600 yards. I might even have hit the buck but the chances were against it. Instead, I stalked the antelope just as if I were after a ram. I went around and came at him from above at the head of the basin and shot at about 100 yards. It was a one-shot kill and he did not move.

It is almost always possible to stalk close to sheep if the hunter sees them first and does not disturb them. Sheep are rough-country animals and the hunter can keep a ridge between himself and the game. If the hunter cuts loose at long range he is apt to miss or wound and whatever happens he'll chase the rest of the band out of the country. The man who bases his shooting on the hope in his heart has about as much chance of success as the person who invests the grocery money in a ticket for the Irish Sweepstakes.

Let's look at it this way. The man who *hopes* he can hit almost never does. The man who *thinks* he can hit often makes a good quick kill but sometimes wounds. The man who *knows* he can hit almost always does a neat job and almost never wounds.

Even if a shot is an easy one, the experienced hunter does not like to leave anything to chance. The first African lion I ever shot had been feeding on a bait. His sign was so fresh that Don Ker, my white hunter, decided he had only moved off when he heard the hunting car. With a Dorobo tracker we decided to circle around to see if we couldn't find the lion. When we saw him he was about 125 yards away, sitting up in the tall grass and looking back in the direction of the bait. The grass was too high for me to sit or kneel. I am certain I could have killed the lion offhand, but since he had not seen us, I crept quietly over to an ant hill about thirty feet away, took a rest, and shot the lion in the neck. The old hunter knows that in all the world there is nothing like a good rest and the sight of a steady front bead or aiming reticle against the target to calm a man down and head off an incipient attack of buck fever.

No two game-shooting situations are exactly alike. When one arises the hunter feeds the factors present into the computer of his intelligence and experience and comes up with the answer. If he has been around enough and does not panic he generally comes up with a pretty good decision. Let's take a couple of examples:

In 1959 my white hunter and I were hunting in the direction of some lion roars we had heard just before dawn. Suddenly a lioness poked her head out of grass about 2½ feet high. Then a maned lion stood up and looked at us. Behind him the grass was six or seven feet tall. The lion looked to be between 125 and 150 yards away. I started to sneak quietly over to an ant hill to take a rest. The lion started galloping diagonally toward the high grass.

I fed the following facts into the computer. I get an enormous kick out of lion hunting and I wanted a lion. I had invested $75 in a lion permit. Lions were not plentiful and this might be my only chance. But on the other hand a wounded lion is the most dangerous animal in Africa. This lion was headed for tall grass. If I wounded the lion, getting it would be dangerous and someone might get killed—maybe even *me*. On the other hand, I had shot many non-dangerous animals under those conditions and had indeed shot many running jackrabbits about that far away. The .375 was swinging and the crosshairs looked very nice as they rolled along just in front of the lion. Apparently my computer said to shoot, as the rifle went off and the lion gave the quick, heavy growl of the wounded cat. Luck was with me that morning. The bullet had gone right through the heart at a distance we found to be 140 paces.

I am a fairly decent rifle shot, but I am quick to admit that in this case I took a very grave chance. I got away with it that time. Someone else might not have been so lucky!

On another trip my wife and I with a white hunter and gun bearers tracked a big lion that had killed and eaten a kudu. We jumped him in an open meadow in the bush. He took off running almost directly away at about 200 yards. It was my wife's turn to shoot. She hoisted up my .375 and looked for an instant at the crosswires against the lion's fanny. Her computer told her not to shoot. It was, I believe, a pretty good computer!

An important factor in the wounding of game is the willingness to take a chancy shot by shooting from an unsteady position when there is time to assume a steadier one. Another is this business of shooting at long range when it is possible to get closer. Yet another is the common fault of aiming at the whole animal and consequently shooting him in the middle. These are all faults of the inexperienced hunter.

I remember a magazine story about three people on their first sheep hunt. They must have had a real jackleg outfit because all three were together with one guide. They saw a bunch of seven or eight rams (all "legal" but immature) bedded down in the shale at the foot of a cliff across a basin and about 500 yards away. They all opened up on that bunch of rams and kept on shooting while the confused sheep milled around. Eventually three were seen to go down and the last of the rams disappeared over the top. There was a dead ram for each of the rejoicing hunters, but no one knew who killed what, whether each had killed a ram, whether one hunter had killed all the rams, or anything else. How many rams that got away were gut-shot or had broken legs, the writer did not say—and probably neither knew nor cared.

This struck me as being pretty sloppy hunting and careless shooting. Under such circumstances it is almost always possible to stay out of sight, to sneak around, and to come on rams at close range and from behind. If they had done that, each hunter could have had a good look at the rams and would have had the opportunity to decide coolly if he wanted one of them or not. Then if he did he could have shot his ram cleanly without bombarding the whole countryside, and he would have had the satisfaction of knowing that it was his trophy and not someone else's.

An Alberta outfitter of great experience once told me that the best mountain big-game shots he took out were New England woodchuck hunters. The poorest, he said, were those who went deer hunting once a year but who never popped a cap between seasons. Many of these last, he told me, tried to do their shooting offhand and couldn't keep all their shots in a 3-foot group at 100 yards. He said they did not have any idea how to assume a steady sitting position, how to use a sling, how to use a rest, or where to aim on an animal.

The New England woodchuck hunters, however, had long since discovered that to hit the small animals they shot at they had to assume the steadiest position available. They knew how to use slings. They knew how to use the sitting position and how to shoot from prone. They knew how to take advantage of a rest. They placed their shots because they were used to shooting at small marks quickly and at estimated distances.

This outfitter always asked his dudes if they had done any varmint hunting and breathed a sigh of relief when he heard that they had. He knew he probably wouldn't have to follow up any gut-shot caribou, rams with broken legs, or wounded and indignant grizzly bears. I can still remember how he beamed with approval when he saw me rest the fore-end of my rifle, held by my left hand, on my binocular case when we had crawled up to the top of a ridge for an easy shot.

The skillful, experienced, and knowledgeable white hunters of Kenya have long since learned that the human being on his hind legs is a mass of jumping muscles and quivering nerves and a darned poor platform for steady shooting. Even for relatively short and easy shots they encourage their clients to shoot from rests—over that hunter's friend the termite hill, over limbs of trees, or even, if nothing more substantial is available, with the fore-end of the rifle rested on the white hunter's shoulder. With a good rest anyone used to squeezing the trigger should be able to keep his bullets within a 6-inch circle at 200 yards—or within a 9-inch circle at 300. Many can do better. With such shooting, game simply does not get away.

Offhand is the position necessarily used for quick, unexpected shots in forest and brush or in grass too high to sit down in. It is the most flexible of positions, but is no position to use for anything except close-range

Bradford O'Connor takes a shot from sitting position while the guide spots for him. He would have done better on a long shot if he had gone forward to the stone just ahead.

shooting. Even a very good shot can miss or wound a standing deer 50 percent of the time from offhand at 200 yards. No one should use the offhand position if he has an opportunity to assume any other. Nevertheless anyone ambitious to become a good performer on game should practice offhand shooting.

Sitting is the queen of the hunting positions. It is the only one to use on an open hillside. It is much steadier than offhand and also steadier than kneeling. It is more flexible than prone and better for running shots. From the sitting position without a sling a good shot should be able to keep almost all of his shots in a 12-inch circle at 200 yards with most of them in 8 inches. Shooting from sitting with a sling the good shot should be able to put his bullet every time in the chest cavity of a standing deer at 300 yards. Much of the time it may be neither necessary nor feasible to take the time to get into a tight sling, but if there is time the sling is an enormous help to steady holding.

For hunting, the usefulness of prone is limited. Often it cannot be used on a level plain because grass and weeds get in the way. It cannot be used from a hillside when shooting downhill or across a canyon. It is a natural position to use from the top of a ridge. When used in combination with a rest it is the steadiest of all positions.

No one who wants to hit his game exactly right and kill it cleanly should spurn the use of a rest—any rest, just so it is solid. When using a rest the rifleman should remember that resting forearm or barrel on anything hard will make the shot fly high. I have used stones for rests and I have cushioned them with my left hand, with hats, with jackets. I have shot many antelope by laying a down jacket over the top of a sage brush. I have shot far more mountain sheep at under 200 yards than over, but I once laid a binocular case and a jacket for a rest over a hummock of earth and vegetation and shot a ram at what from the drop of the bullet had to be about 400 yards. I would not have shot at that ram without a rest. The longest shot I have ever made on any game animal was on a big bull elk. I sat on one stone, used a higher one padded with a down jacket for a rest. It was as steady as a shooting bench.

Even on a short shot like this it is well to sit down and place the shot exactly.

The buffalo hunters of the 1870's were probably as skillful as any game shots that ever lived. They habitually used forked sticks for rests. They could adapt them to various heights for sitting or prone by putting the legs closer together or farther apart. These "runners" were real pros, and there is much we can learn from them. They never shot at a running animal if they could help it. They always shot from the steadiest position they could assume. They carried rests with them and used them constantly. They tried for exact shot placement, and their ideal was one buffalo for one bullet.

They didn't get flustered. They didn't blaze away unless they were just about certain that they could put the bullet where they wanted it. They knew that one bullet in the right place was worth two dozen around the edges.

Those who take shots they are sure of, shoot from the steadiest possible positions, place their bullets exactly, and don't panic when the moment of truth arrives. They don't have to chase much wounded game—and they don't get mauled by wounded lions and grizzly bears!

Long-Range Shooting

There is something about long-range shooting that fascinates many hunters and riflemen, and the less they have hunted and shot the more fascinated they are. I think that it is because the notion of shooting down an animal that is far, far away is like toying with a dream of omnipotence. It is as if the hunter were Jove and was striking down a sinner with a thunderbolt.

Every year I get dozens of letters from people who are obviously rank beginners. They want me to give them drop tables so they will know how much to hold over with their pet calibers up to 1,000 yards. Holy jumping catfish! How many of these poor innocents have ever *seen* an animal at 1,000 yards, much less have tried to hit one with a rifle?

They get their notions from all kinds of far-out writing and from tall tales passed by word of mouth. In 1963 or 1964 an advertisement for a bullet company appeared in many magazines. It told how some hero had used a Whoosis bullet to slay a Dall ram at 1,000 yards. Not 990 yards or 1,010 yards, but exactly 1,000 (one thousand) yards. The implication of the ad was that anyone who used Whoosis bullets could knock off Dall rams at 1,000 yards. This chap used a .30/06 with a load that required that if anyone hit something with it at 1,000 yards when he was sighted in for 200 yards (as is the common practice with the .30/06) it is necessary that he hold about 38 feet above it. How this citizen knew his ram was exactly 1,000 yards away the ad did not say. Nor did it say how he was able to hold exactly 38 feet high.

Such fantastic stuff is not exceptional. I read about lads who kill grizzlies at 500 and 600 yards and think nothing of polishing off *running* sheep, deer, and antelope at 600 yards. One catalog contains several dozen testimonials by customers who have knocked over everything from addax to zebras at fantastic ranges—450, 575, 600 yards, 800 meters, and so on. The less experience a hunter has the more apt he is to write such guff and the less experience another has the more apt he is to believe it.

The experienced rifleman, the man who has shot from the various positions at cold, unemotional, revealing paper targets and has learned the sad and depressing tales they tell him, reads about these wonderful performances with a tolerant smile or a howl of rage, depending on his personality. He knows that bullets are more uniform, that barrels are more accurate, that magnum cartridges give a little flatter trajectories, and that hunting scopes are better than they used to be. But he also knows that human beings are the same twitching, trembling, and palpitating platforms they have always been, and that the human carcass was not specifically designed for precision shooting.

Our experienced rifleman and hunter knows likewise that if game is so far away that elaborate calculations must be made if it is to be hit, it is too far away to shoot at. Nevertheless, the unsophisticated really adore gadgets and gimmicks which enable them to get the exact range—to zero in on some poor unfortunate herbivore a couple of townships away.

Some of them make me wonder whether I am bereft of my reason or whether I am simply the victim of a cynical practical joke. Some years before I wrote this, a citizen published a card showing silhouettes of whitetail deer as they would appear broadside at various distances if the card were held out at arm's length. The card (so help me!) showed deer as they would appear at 50 (!), 100, 150, 200, 250, and 300 yards. All the hunter had to do was to find himself a whitetail buck, get it to stand broadside while he held the card out at arm's length and compared the various silhouettes with the size of the actual buck. Then when he gets that straight, he lets the deer have it.

How anyone who has ever hunted deer could with a straight face try to peddle anything like that is beyond me. In the first place, just imagine a whitetail buck standing patiently around at 50 and 100 yards while he was measured for size. In the second place, even the humble .30/30 can be sighted in so that a dead-on hold in the center of the chest will catch a deer with no allowance for drop up to 200 yards. In the third place, a modern scope-sighted rifle for a high-velocity cartridge like the .270, .280, .284, .30/06 with the 180-grain bullet, 7-mm. Remington Magnum, .264, the .300 Winchester Magnum, or the Weatherby series all have flat enough trajectories so that if properly sighted in they have practical point-blank ranges of from 300 to 350 yards. With the middle-aged .270

sighted in with a scope for the 130-grain bullet, a hold at the top of the shoulder would drop a bullet into the chest cavity of even a medium-sized deer to about 375 yards—and 375 yards is a long way off. In the fourth place, deer are not all exactly the same size.

Another card that someone hoped to peddle had a series of holes in it, each subtending six feet at various ranges. To the card you were supposed to attach a string exactly thirty inches long if I remember correctly. Then you were supposed to hold one end of the string to your eye so the card would be exactly thirty inches from it. Then you were supposed to find something where the deer was that was exactly six feet high. Then you compared whatever it was with the various holes and when you found one that fitted that was the range. It would be convenient for the card user if he had a friend exactly six feet tall and then he could send him over to stand beside the deer.

Another system is to use two horizontal wires in the top portion of a variable power scope, turning the power selector ring until the deer fits between the two wires. Then you glance down at the bottom of the scope and read off the lowest figure in the scale etched there. This will tell you how far away the deer is IF he is a standard-size mature buck measuring eighteen inches from shoulder to chest and accommodating enough to stand still broadside while this is going on. Then, if you are a foresighted fellow, you refer to a drop table for your particular load and for the distance for which you are sighted in. This could be written on a piece of paper and fixed to the buttstock of the rifle with scotch tape or something similar. This last idea is an ancient one of mine which I ran in *Outdoor Life* magazine a generation ago when I was more enamoured of long-range shooting than I am today. All of these schemes depend on patient deer, deer of standard size, *and* the hunter's being able to rest the rifle on something while the measuring is going on. My own notion is that all this is more intriguing than practical.

Comparing the depth of an animal's body with a scope reticle of known value is an old method of range estimation. As handy a reticle for this as I have ever had was a four-minute dot in a 2½X scope. Comparing the apparent size of the dot with an animal from shoulder to bottom of chest was a pretty good way to get an approximate notion as to how far the deer was away. At 300 yards, for example, such a dot would not quite cover an antelope from shoulder to chest, as a full-grown buck antelope will measure about 16 inches, an average whitetail about the same, a mule deer about 18, and a Rocky Mountain billy goat or large ram 22 to 24. A spike bull elk, a cow elk, or a bull caribou will measure 24–26 and a big bull elk around 30–32. A big bull moose will measure about 40 inches. These figures are, of course, approximate as animals even of the same age and same species vary considerably in size.

I used to use this dot reticle to help me estimate range—and generally I found out that the animal was not as far away as I had at first thought it was. Animals look smaller when viewed from above or below, smaller on dull days than on bright, smaller against a blending than against a contrasting background.

A good deal of the malarkey one reads about long-range shots comes from the guides. A city dweller who has paid any attention to distances is usually a better judge of range than the guide. He is used to known distances—a city block, the length of a football field, the distances from tee to green on a golf course. The more unsophisticated guides simply do not think in such terms and hunting country is not marked off in 100-yard units. They think of distances in terms of how long it would take them to get there. Such terms as "100 yards," a "quarter of a mile," etc. mean nothing to them. Furthermore, the guide wants to keep his dude happy and he likes to tell the client what the guy wants to hear. That is why 400- and 500-yard shots are so common in the Rockies and why ten-foot lions and ten-foot, six-inch tigers are so common in Africa and India. It also explains why so many grizzly bears weigh 1,000 pounds.

A conversation between Dr. J. Rupert Jones, eminent surgeon, and his Indian guide would run about as follows. Dr. Jones has just knocked off a grizzly:

Dr. Jones: He is down, Johnnie. You think he is dead?

Guide: Yes, maybe so, he dead. If he don't get up no more he sure dead.

Dr. Jones (glowing with pride) : That was a hell of a shot, Johnnie.

Johnnie: Good shot!

Dr. Jones: That was a long way! How far do you think it was?

Guide: Pretty far. Long way.

Dr. Jones: About *how* far?

Guide: Pretty damn far, far like hell!

Dr. Jones: About 400 yards, you think?

Guide: Sure. Long way. Pretty far—400 yards.

Actually the bear was about 160 yards away when the doctor opened up, about 180 when it went down.

They reach the defunct bear. Since the bear is not breathing the doctor assumes it is dead.

Doctor: Pretty big bear!

Guide: Yeah, pretty big.

Doctor: How much do you think he weighs?

Guide: Don't know. Pretty damned big!

Doctor: Think he'd go 1,000 pounds?

Guide (who has no idea how much 1,000 pounds is and who has never in his life seen a grizzly or any other game animal weighed, but who wants to be agreeable) : Yes, maybe so. Maybe weigh 1,000 pounds. Big bear!

Doctor: Ever see a bigger one, Johnnie?

Guide: No, big bear. Great big bear.

So when the good gray doctor returns to his practice glowing with health and pride the following story appears:

"Dr. J. Rupert Jones, Central City surgeon, returned this week from a three-week big-game hunt in the Yukon. Among other prize trophies, Dr. Jones collected a grizzly bear that weighed 1,000 pounds, according to Johnnie Lame Horse, famous Yukon guide. The guide said the bear was shot at a range of 400 yards and said that it was the largest grizzly he had ever seen in 35 years of guiding and trapping in the Yukon Territory."

Actually the grizzly was a large one. It would have weighed between 450 and 500 pounds.

So let's lay down a few rules about long-range shooting.

A long-range shot should never be taken if there is a reasonable chance of getting closer.

A long-range shot should never be taken if the rifleman feels doubtful of his ability to make a good, solid, well-placed hit.

A long-range shot should never be taken if the hunter cannot get into a solid position—prone with sling, from a rest, etc.

A long-range shot should never be taken at any dangerous animal—a brown, grizzly, or polar bear, a lion, a tiger, a leopard, a Cape buffalo.

A long-range shot should never be taken at an unwounded, running animal.

A long-range shot should never be taken if the animal shot at can get out of sight so quickly that it would be difficult to ascertain the effect of the shot.

A long-range shot should not be taken if the range is so great that a hold on the top of the shoulders will not drop a bullet into the chest cavity.

These rules may seem ultra conservative to many, and I must admit that there have been times when I did not follow them myself. However, the more I hunt and shoot and the more I see others shoot the more convinced I am that they are wise and sensible rules and if they were universally adopted the number of game animals that get away wounded to suffer and die would be greatly reduced.

22 | *Where To Hit Them*

Early one frosty October morning many years ago I was hunting mule deer on Arizona's high plateau north of the Mogollon Rim. It was very lovely country at around 7,500 feet above sea level, a rolling land of big yellow pine, Gambel oaks, alligator-bark junipers. In those days it contained many turkeys, some deer, a few black bear, and myriads of tassel-eared Abert squirrels.

The sun was just coming up as I sneaked quietly along upwind, half frozen but full of excitement and anticipation. I had just topped out over a ridge and had stopped to look over new country when on the other side of a draw below me I saw a big buck take a few steps as he came out from behind a bush and then stop with his head and chest concealed by a big yellow pine.

I was carrying a Model 94 Winchester carbine in .30/30 that day. I raised it and waited for the deer to come out. But he did not. He stood absolutely still. He had probably heard something and had stopped to listen. The buck wasn't over 100 yards away, perhaps not over sixty. The smart thing for me to have done was to have waited until the buck came out so I could lay a bullet behind his shoulder.

I hadn't shot many deer at the time and I quickly became jittery and anxious. I decided to shoot at the rear half of the deer and hope for the best. I aimed carefully right in the middle of what deer I could see and cut loose. The buck took off and I missed him with my second shot.

With the help of a companion, I finally found that buck late in the afternoon, many hours later, and finished it off. The meat from the harassed, feverish creature was no good, but at least we ended its suffering.

That night around our smoky campfire we held a post mortem and decided that the .30/30 was an inadequate deer cartridge. From the depths of our inexperience we were convinced that if I had been shooting a .30/06, a .30/40, or a .256 Newton, a wonder of the day, that buck would have gone down with the gut shot—or at least it would not have gone far.

Our conclusion was wrong. The correct one would have been that O'Connor, the guy behind the .30/30, was an inadequate deer hunter, nervous, impatient, and lacking in judgment. If I had just waited for the buck to come out from behind the tree I could have shot him through the lungs and he probably wouldn't have gone fifty yards.

Many years later I took a running shot at a little Thomson's gazelle on the plains of Tanganyika. A Tommy is a frail little antelope about the size of a coyote. This little creature was running and a bit over 100 yards away. My rifle was a .300 Weatherby Magnum that moved the 180-grain bullet along at about 3,150. But I didn't lead the Tommy enough. The bullet struck too far back. It blew out everything back of the diaphragm, but the little fellow got up and took off. I had to run him down and shoot him again. And this with a cartridge that with a proper bullet placed right has taken rhino, buffalo, and even elephant!

In my day I have seen a lot of game shot—everything from small gazelles and deer to creatures as large as Alaska brown bear, moose, Cape buffalo, and elephant. Almost never do I see an animal well hit in a vital area get away or even go far, and seldom do I see an animal poorly hit that doesn't cause trouble.

I read many tales of animals hit in the lungs and yet escaping, but these yarns are so completely at variance with my own experience that I simply cannot believe most of them. I put them down as the alibis of poor shots and unsuccessful hunters or the fantasies of hobby-riders.

A score of years ago, one chap, who was an advocate of heavy bullets of large diameter, wrote that he saw another hunter put six or seven 180-grain .30/06 expanding bullets through a deer's lungs before the deer went down. Another chap wrote that he saw a mountain sheep hit several times through the lungs with the old Western 139-grain open-point 7-mm. Mauser bullet. Then the ram had to be caught and held by the guide while the hunter shot it twice more. Still another character told me he had shot an antelope five times through the lungs with the 130-grain .270 bullet—and the antelope had got away and he had never found it.

As one who has used the bullets and calibers in question I simply cannot swallow those tales. If an animal is hit through the lungs with almost any reasonably adequate bullet, he seldom goes far. If he does give the hunter a chase or gets away, it is because of poor bullet action. Either the bullet does not open up or it expands too rapidly and does not get inside.

Poor bullet action almost always comes either from selecting the wrong bullet for the particular game being hunted or from poor bullet construction. Once in French Equatorial Africa I forgot that I had my .375 Magnum loaded with solids and put one of them right through the lungs of a big roan antelope. The bullet, of course, didn't open up at all and we never caught up with the bull. This is the only animal I can remember having lost in Africa.

On a trip in Mexico when the .257 Roberts first came out back in the middle 1930's, I had a tough time making quick kills on mule and whitetail deer because the bullets I used were too strongly constructed and didn't open up quickly enough. Later when I shifted to bullets which expanded better I had no trouble getting quick kills with the .257, even on large mule deer.

Often hunters select for deer bullets that are designed for much heavier game. Then they do not get quick kills even with powerful rifles. Many of the 220-grain .30-caliber bullets, which are fine for moose and big bear, are not very satisfactory deer bullets. Some of the "all-around" controlled-expanding bullets have been made too stout in such calibers as the .30/30 and the .32 Special for small, light animals and do not put the creatures down as quickly as the softer old-fashioned soft-points with softer jackets and cores.

When hunting bullets were stepped up in velocity from around 2,000 feet per second to 2,700–3,000, many of them were too soft, went to pieces too quickly, and often didn't drive deep enough into an animal for a quick kill. I once took an offhand shot at about 125–150 yards at a nice plump buck standing broadside. The 150-grain .30/06 bullet exploded on his ribs and his lungs looked as if they had been hit with a charge of shot. The buck was killed in his tracks, but if the animal had been larger (an elk or moose, let us say) or the shot had been taken at an angle, the penetration would have been insufficient.

Actually, however, most bullets of American manufacture are so good that they almost always do their job pretty well and on a surprising variety of game. One fall, hunting in British Columbia, Arizona, and Sonora, I shot with the 130-grain Silvertip bullet of the .270 a moose, a grizzly, a caribou, a Stone ram, a desert ram, one whitetail deer, two mule deer, and one javelina. In all cases I considered the bullet action adequate.

The point I am trying to make is that the most important factor in killing power is the placement of the bullet. The second most important factor is bullet action—depth of penetration and rate of expansion. Compared to these two factors, bullet weight, bullet diameter, and even velocity don't have much to do with the price of potatoes. The specific caliber is the least important of all. Favorite questions put to gun editors are: Which is a better killer, the .30/06 or the .280 Remington, or the .264 Winchester or the 7-mm. Remington Magnum? The answer is, of course, that any of those calibers is perfectly adequate for about anything it would be turned against if the shot is well placed and the bullet does its part.

To kill an animal relatively quickly a bullet has either to disrupt the nervous system or to stop the vital processes. A shot in the brain will, of course, kill instantly. So will a shot in the spine forward of the shoulders. Shots in the shoulder-heart-lung area sometimes kill instantly, always (if the bullet does its part) kill quickly. No animal shot through the heart can live long, and any animal will die quickly if much lung tissue is ruptured, as the lungs are collapsed or he very quickly drowns in his own blood. No animal can travel with both shoulders broken, and a shot through the spine back of the withers anchors an animal.

Except on elephants, which have very poor eyesight and are generally shot at very short range, brain shots are not a good idea. For one thing the brain is relatively small, and a shot that misses the brain can eventually cause an animal's death without immediately disabling it.

I have a friend who was cuffed around by a head-shot grizzly. Luckily the bullet had broken the bear's jaw, but at that the bear would probably have killed my amigo if the guide hadn't shot it. Another friend of mine was badly mauled after he had tried to stop a wounded lion that was charging him. The bullet missed the brain and did not stop the lion. His gun bearer rushed in, grabbed the rifle, and killed the lion. Once I put a 275-grain .375 caliber soft point into the bridge of a lion's nose below the eyes. The lion required another shot.

Even if the brain shot works, the result is a nauseating mess. In Mexico one time Carroll Lemon of Tucson and I were hunting whitetail deer. A buck had been lying in waist-high chaparral and he took off running hard with only his head showing. We each shot at the same time. The buck went down. One of us had hit him through the brain and the other had put a bullet through one ear. The head of that beautiful creature looked like a bag of mush. The horns were askew and the eyes bulging. It was a sight to turn the stomach.

The neck shot is better, but I bear no great love for it. As it happens my own luck with neck shots has been quite good for the most part. However, it is easy to miss the spine, as it is a relatively small target and often the exact location of the spine is a bit obscure. I knocked my first lion down with a neck shot with a .375 Magnum. But I didn't hit the spine. The lion was leaping around like a chicken with his head shot off. He needed another shot to settle him. A neck-shot animal will often drop and then recover and get away. One method of capturing wild horses is to shoot them through the muscles of the neck above the spine. This stuns them and they are then tied up before the shock wears off. Not long before I wrote this I saw a Rocky Mountain billy goat shot low in the neck and he wasn't even knocked off his feet.

Just as most skilled and experienced game shots always try to shoot from the steadiest possible position—from prone, from sitting, from a rest—they also generally aim for the largest vital area: the front one-third of the body forward of the diaphragm. These experienced shots always take aim at one particular spot—for the heart, for the shoulder, or center for the lungs.

The often-given directions for the shoulder shot—to hold on the foreleg one-third up from the body line on a side shot is very good advice, but if the bullet strikes there it isn't going to break the shoulder. If it hits bone it will break the leg high, cut the blood vessels above the heart, rupture the lungs. It is a fine place to hold but *not* if the hunter wants to break the shoulder blade.

The heart of a game animal lies very low in the thorax between the front legs when the animal is viewed from the side. Aim taken behind the forelegs won't do the animal any good but it won't hit the heart. A heart shot is fatal, but often not as quickly fatal as one might believe.

For dangerous game the best shot is through the shoulder blade. Aim for a broadside shoulder shot should be taken about one-third of the way down from the withers and very slightly behind the line of the foreleg. An animal with both shoulders broken is helpless, and generally the impact of a heavy bullet on the shoulder blade will knock an animal flat. I'd guess the reason is that the shock is transmitted to the spinal column.

If one shoulder is broken a large, heavy animal like a rhino, an elephant, or even a brown or grizzly bear is almost helpless. If the shoulder is missed, the shot is still a good one. It will rupture the lungs or break the spine.

If, however, the bullet goes to pieces on the shoulder blade, an animal can hobble away. Fast-expanding bullets which are deadly on shots into the lungs through the rib cage often break up on the shoulder. In Africa I had a 150-grain .30-caliber bullet go to pieces on the shoulder of a bull roan antelope and I once had the same thing happen in the Yukon on a caribou. For non-dangerous game I see no particular point in the shoulder shot, as such a shot wrecks a lot of edible meat, whereas a shot through the rib cage into the lungs spoils no meat except lung tissue and that is not ordinarily eaten.

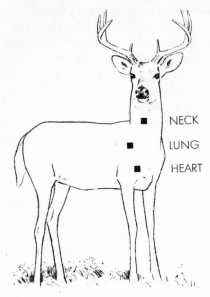

NECK

LUNG

HEART

Front quartering position.

Rear quartering position.

NECK

SHOULDER

LUNG

HEART

ON DEER-SIZED GAME

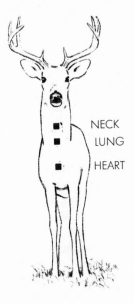

NECK

LUNG

HEART

Front position.

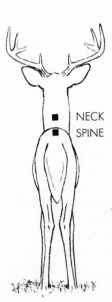

NECK

SPINE

Rear position.

So far we have assumed that our game animals have been standing or moving slowly and that they have been broadside to the hunter or slightly quartering. It would be very pleasant indeed if animals always presented themselves like that.

Unfortunately they do not. They are often found facing the hunter, quartering, or standing hind-end to. This complicates matters but the hunter should try to put his bullets up into the vital chest area no matter what the angle. As good advice as I have ever heard is on an animal quartering away to shoot for the opposite shoulder. Best shot on an animal facing the hunter is to aim at the point where the neck merges into the body.

On a rear-end shot, a bullet at the root of the tail will paralyze and disable the animal. A bullet right between the hams will generally drive clear through up into the lung area and kill quickly.

The faster an animal is moving or the farther he is away, the more complicated the placement of the shot becomes. I have heard of riflemen who thought nothing of breaking the neck of a standing deer at 500 yards, and who could always place their shots on running game animals at 250 and 300. I have never seen such a paragon operate.

Many years ago a very experienced and skillful deer hunter wrote that any hit on a running animal at any distance was a good shot. As a guy who has missed jumping deer in the brush at less than fifty yards I agree with him. Anyone who doesn't string along should watch a running deer match. At from sixty to 100 yards the average "practical" hunter not only doesn't place his shot in the vital area of the plywood deer target, but the first two or three times he shoots he generally manages to hit two or three feet behind the whole deer.

No one should shoot at a standing animal any farther than experience has taught him that he can keep *all* of his shots under hunting conditions in about a one-foot circle. It takes a good shot to do that with a scope-sighted rifle from a sitting position at 250 yards, and many once-a-year hunters cannot do it at 100 yards. It takes a good offhand shot to keep all his shots in a twenty-four-inch circle at 200 yards and if he can hold in an eighteen-inch circle offhand he is pretty hot.

Under average hunting conditions all shots are not going to be well placed. When a big buck crashes out of his bed and goes bounding away through the brush and over fallen timber, most of us do not have the patience and self-control to refrain from shooting. Instead we try to get on, see the sights somewhere against gray hide, and press the trigger. Under those conditions we are not doing badly if we hit him anywhere.

With poorly placed shots we aren't going to kill him in his tracks, but all of us can do two things which will reduce the number of cripples that escape to die annually. For one thing we can all make it a point to follow

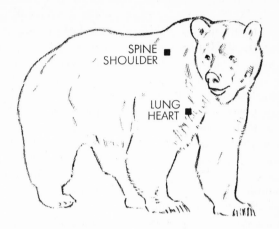

Placement of shots on grizzly bear, front quartering position.

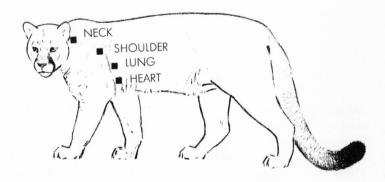

Placement of shots on cougar, broadside position.

a wounded animal until we recover him or all chance of recovery is exhausted. Too many hunters give up if they don't find a wounded animal within a few hundred yards.

For another thing we can use reasonably powerful rifles and well-chosen bullets. With a well-placed shot under ideal conditions almost any cartridge will result in a quick kill. Eskimos kill caribou, sheep, and even polar bears with .22 Hornets and .222's. Pioneer Canadian moose hunters kept their homesteads supplied with moose meat with .25/35's and .30/ 30's.

But more potent cartridges do a somewhat better job of disabling animals with poorly placed shots. A .30/06 will put a deer down more often with a poorly placed shot than will a .30/30, and a .270 will do a better job of anchoring a deer with a gut shot than will a .25/35. On shots in the hams and guts, the high velocity bullet that expands violently sometimes kills in spite of the fact that it has not struck a vital area. One should not count on this, but it happens.

I have killed two mountain sheep that were running directly away from me with shots that struck the ham and did not penetrate into the vital area. One was killed with the 7 × 57 and the 139-grain Western open-point bullet and the other with a 130-grain bronze point in a .270. The last ram I killed was running broadside at about 150 yards. I didn't lead him enough, hit him through the guts with a 130-grain Silvertip .270 bullet. He ran about 100 yards, fell over a little cliff and was dead when found.

But no one should ever count on a quick kill from a poorly placed bullet. The poorly placed bullet generally means trouble, just as the well-placed bullet means a trophy on the wall and meat in the frying pan!

23 | *The Rocky Mountain Pack Trip*

Travel by packtrain may seem slow to people used to hurtling along freeways in automobiles at seventy miles an hour or flying from New York to London in a few hours. The packtrain is one of the oldest methods employed by human beings to move themselves and their effects from one place to another. It has changed only in detail since Abraham packed his tents and gear on donkeys and horses and struck out for the Promised Land.

A packtrain is making good time if it averages three miles an hour, even on a good trail. If it averages $2\frac{1}{2}$ miles an hour and covers twenty miles in a day, it has done very well indeed. In areas of much muskeg, deep rivers, and steep mountains, a packtrain often does well to cover eight or ten miles in a long day.

The packtrain may be slow but it is sure. It can go where no wheeled vehicle can follow, no airplane can land. It is by far the best method to get into wilderness areas where game is plentiful and where there isn't a hunter beside every bush. The packtrain hunter can take a comfortable camp with him and when he arrives in the area where he wants to hunt he has a horse to take some of the wear and tear off of his legs—an important consideration for anyone on the wrong side of forty. If the hunter doesn't like a particular bit of country he can move to another where game is more plentiful. He has horses or mules to pack out his trophies and his meat.

The light airplane is faster, and it saves much time. However, when the hunter arrives at his camp he has no horse to hunt with, and because of the limited capacity of the plane his camp is apt to be sketchy. To me the most agreeable feature of packtrain travel is that it brings the hunter into intimate contact with the country. He sees goats up in the cliffs, deer bounding away through the timber. He crosses crystal-clear trout streams, sees where a grizzly has rolled over a log to hunt for grubs and where a bull elk has polished his antlers. On the trail the hunter may have the opportunity to stop and pot a mess of juicy blue grouse for the evening meal or rig up his rod for unsophisticated wilderness trout.

But today the outfitting business, like most other businesses, has been hit by cost accounting, mass production, and efficiency. Many wealthy men no longer want to spend the time to take a long pack trip. They see no point in spending eight hours a day in the saddle, clumping along at two or three miles an hour. They get no enjoyment out of seeing the camp dog tree a covey of blue grouse, of watching a herd of ewes and lambs high above timberline across the creek. To many of them the horse bells are not music and Scotch and creek water in a tin cup doesn't taste nearly as good as a drink from the bar at Dave Chasen's or at "21." I once told a big-time executive that I had spent thirty days on a Yukon pack trip, had looked over a lot of sheep, and had shot only one forty-inch ram. "Pretty damned expensive sheep!" was his comment.

Some outfitters have found that they can woo these types by sending the packtrain ahead, camping by a lake on which float planes can land or in a valley where they have scratched out a landing strip. Then the dudes can fly in and cover the ground in an hour or two that would take them many days by trail and saddle horse. They can then take off with a lighter and smaller outfit and be hunting the next day. I knew one tycoon who left a warm bed in a Whitehorse hotel early one morning, flew into a lake and landed where his outfit awaited him, ate a stack of hotcakes, and rode out after a big Dall ram his guide had spotted the day before. He shot the ram, a forty-five-incher. Since a big ram was what he had come for, he packed up, rode to the Alaska Highway with a guide and a packhorse, caught a bus into Whitehorse, paid his outfitter off for the fourteen-day trip he had bargained for, hopped a plane, and flew back to the United States. He was delighted that he had not wasted any time.

Too many hunters these days want to get in, knock something off, and get out with a minimum of fuss and "wasted" time. I like the details of a pack trip—the slow progress through the cool, fragrant air along the trail, the clean icy water in the turbulent little creeks, the delicious warmth and comfort of a down sleeping bag after a hard day on the trail.

Types of Pack Trips

There are many varieties of pack trips. Some last but a few days, are inexpensive, and the packer furnishes little. Others last from two weeks to as much as two months. They are necessarily much more expensive and the outfitter furnishes everything but the hunter's rifle, binocular, and bedroll.

In many areas, some "pack trips" properly speaking are hardly pack trips at all, particularly in the elk country of Idaho and Wyoming. There a packer establishes a camp a day's pack from the road before the elk season opens. He takes in tents for the help and the cook to sleep in, oats and sometimes hay for the horses, grub, saddles and other equipment. Then when the season opens he meets his dude hunters at the road and loads them, their bedrolls, duffle bags, and whatnot on horses and takes them "a day's pack" (generally from ten to twenty miles back from the road) into a mountain wilderness area. There each dude can unroll his bed in a tent that is already set up and which he'll probably share with a companion. He is generally furnished a saddle horse and a guide and he is fed at the communal mess tent. When he has taken his game, he is

Packstring crossing the Middle Fork of the Salmon River in Idaho, heading into big-game country. In some sections packhorses are led rather than allowed to run free.

packed out along with his meat, his trophies, and his equipment. Such a trip is not very expensive and it is usually productive. Best of all is that the dude can devote himself to hunting, has a man along who knows elk and knows the country, and doesn't have the time-consuming responsibility of cooking, horse wrangling, and so on. The man who packs in like this is generally far enough away from the roads so that the hunting is reasonably good and he doesn't have too much competition.

In some areas, the airplane substitutes for the packhorse, and the dude with his equipment is flown in to an established camp, which may be a few tents set up or may be a comfortable wilderness dude ranch many miles from an automobile road where everything has to be flown in or packed in. There are several relatively luxurious dude ranches like this in the wilderness areas of Idaho and at least one in Oregon. I have even heard of one in Alaska.

In Idaho and Montana particularly there are packers who do nothing but take the hunters in and leave them and then come back at a specified time to pick them up. In the middle 1960's the union price on this service in Idaho's Selway and Lochsa country was $150–$200 per man. For that sum the packer took all the hunter's gear into the big woods, then came back, went out to the scene of the elk kill, packed the meat to camp, then packed the hunter, meat, and outfit back to the road.

A great many fine and skillful hunters live from year to year for these hunts and in the course of time they collect very adequate outfits—their own stoves, tents, packboxes, camp dishes, pots and pans. The old hands get very skillful at camp-making and some of the camps are downright luxurious—even to the extent of having five-gallon cans with perforated bottoms suspended on limbs for shower baths. Since these hunters know the country and know elk they do not want or need guides.

The real wilderness pack trip is something else again. Instead of going to one campsite and staying there, the pack outfit will go to one area, camp, and then move on to another for another type of game or where shooting may be better. Often the outfit will travel 100 miles or more before any hunting is done.

How a Pack Outfit Works

The pack outfit is an exceedingly ancient means of traveling, so ancient that its origin is lost in the mists of antiquity. I have seen native Masais and Somalis of Africa on the move with their pack strings of donkeys and bullocks, and I have packed back into mountain ranges in Iran with native pack outfits. By American standards Old World packing is pretty terrible, and generally the only way Old World packers can keep their packs on is to have someone walk alongside every pack animal.

This packhorse is loaded on each side with a canvas and leather pannier and on top with a sleeping bag rolled in a canvas tarp. The guides are testing how the entire load balances on the horse.

Wooden panniers serve as side packs on this horse; a duffel bag rests on top between the side loads. The guide is covering the load with a canvas tarp to protect it from rain or from snags along the trail.

American packing methods originated in Mexico and spread north by the way of Arizona, New Mexico, and Texas. The Mexicans are great packers. They pack firewood in from great distances, supplies into remote mines, and ore out. They probably developed the sawbuck packsaddle from the Arab packsaddle used on camels and brought into Mexico by the way of Spain. Mexicans are hard on livestock but they know how to put things on horses and donkeys and make them stay put. Packing terms are of Mexican origin just as are many terms used in the cattle country—cinch for *cincha*, lariat for *la riata*, alforka for *alforja*, etc. In many parts of the West the canvas cover which is thrown over the pack to protect it from the weather and before the final hitch is thrown is called a "manty" from the Spanish *mantilla*, or cover.

The universal pack animal of Asia, Africa, and Mexico, the donkey, or *burro* as it is called in Spain and Mexico, is a tough, nimble little beast that is amazingly strong for its size. The Arabs brought the donkey to Spain and also to the Sudan, Somaliland, and Kenya in Africa. The little donkeys are used for packing to a limited extent in the American Southwest but almost never farther north. For the most part horses are used in Arizona and New Mexico, but perhaps the majority of outfits in Wyoming, Idaho, and Montana use mules. These long-eared hybrids are more sure-footed than horses, can carry heavier loads for their weights, can stay fat on less food, and are more enduring and less apt to panic in an emergency. However, they are useless farther north in the Canadian Rockies and in the mountains of the Yukon, as their small feet let them sink down in muskeg.

Depending on the number of people in the party and the duration of the trip, anywhere from a half-dozen to twenty or more packhorses are taken along. The most widely used packsaddle is the old-fashioned sawbuck, which, as we have seen, originated in Mexico. It is universally used in the Southwest, widely used in Wyoming. I have made many trips in Alberta, British Columbia, and the Yukon and I have yet to see another type of packsaddle used there.

The back of the horse is first protected with a pad and a blanket and then the sawbuck saddle, generally with breast strap and breeching to keep the saddle from slipping when going up or down hill, is put on. Two side packs are then put on. It is necessary that they balance because if they do not the pack is pulled to one side. Generally the weight of the side packs is held to no more than seventy-five pounds, and the packs themselves can be in the form of packboxes (sturdy wooden boxes with strips of board nailed to the sides at an angle of about 45 degrees so the rope won't slip), panniers (packboxes or little trunks with leather loops to hang over the sawbuck), kyaks or alforjas (soft canvas bags with leather loops to hang over the packsaddle). The top pack, which goes

Final step in packing a horse is tying down the entire load with a diamond hitch, a specialized lash which secures the packs and prevents them from bouncing or falling off during the trip.

right on top of the sawbuck saddle, should be something soft like a bedroll so that the hitch (squaw, single diamond, double diamond, etc.) can bite into it and not slip. When trophies are taken they are set on top of the top pack and the hitch thrown over them. This should be carefully done as many a load has been strewn all over the countryside because a sheep head slipped down and gouged a horse.

Most Idaho and some Montana packers use the Decker packsaddle—a padded contraption of leather on an iron framework which fits around the horse's body and is probably easier on the animal. Loads are two side packs hung across the saddle and carried low. This method of packing is satisfactory for good trails, but the packs hang too low for rough and trailless country.

A properly packed horse will go all day with little attention, but on the trail all hands and even the more experienced dudes keep their eyes on the packs to see that they are riding well and do not slip.

For a pack trip the best type of tent is the wall tent. Patented types with jointed aluminum poles are right for the automobile camper, but the pack outfit needs tents that are easily set up. If there is time the wall tent can be erected with a proper ridgepole between two forked poles and

This is a saddle pile. A good outfitter piles pack boxes, saddles, etc.—everything that isn't to be used in camp—in a pile and covers it with canvas pack covers and tarps to protect the gear from rain or snow.

properly staked down. If there isn't, one can make do with a rope stretched between two trees and the sketchiest of pegging.

All tents should be of white canvas as those of green or brown canvas are as dark as the inside of a cow. The dude tents should be equipped with little folding sheet-iron stoves. The heat from them is very pleasant on frosty mornings and on rainy days, and it is necessary for the drying of damp clothes. A ten-by-twelve-foot tent is about right for two people. One much smaller is cramped and there isn't room for the stove. If it is much larger it may be hard to heat.

The cook tent should be large enough so that dudes and crew can all sit down to eat at once. Most outfitters use tables made from wooden slats tied together, then rolled out and tied on an improvised frame, and covered with oilcloth. Dudes and "hands" sit on packboxes while they eat. Such tables are rickety but they work. The cookstove is sheet iron perched up on posts driven into the ground. These look pretty crude but a good cook can use them to turn out excellent bread, rolls, cakes, pies, and succulent roasts. With its comforting warmth, the smell of cooking food and brewing coffee, the cook tent is the center of camp life.

Long experience has shown that the properly balanced crew for a pack trip should consist of a guide for each hunter, a cook, and a horse wrangler. If there are more than three hunters with the resulting increase of saddle and pack stock, it isn't a bad idea to have an extra horse wrangler and sometimes a "bull cook" or cook's helper. It is the duty of the horse wrangler to get up before daylight and go out and round up the horses—the saddle horses for hunters and guides if it is to be a hunting day or the whole herd if the outfit is moving. A good horse wrangler is an exceedingly important member of the crew. If he is lazy and inefficient it means that the outfit always gets a late start on the trail and that the hunting days are short and often unproductive. If the outfit tries to get along without a horse wrangler, the guides have to do the work and they are tired and often cross. Since the horse wrangler is generally supposed to skin out the heads during the day and to rustle and cut up firewood, an outfit without one will have fewer and shorter hunting days, since the guides must perform these chores.

When the outfit is on the trail everyone packs, including the cook, the horse wrangler, and sometimes the dudes; but on hunting days the guides

The cook tent on a Yukon hunting trip. The panniers in front of the tent contain food.

should be free to concentrate on what the trip was organized for—hunting.

In many ways, the key man of the whole outfit is the cook. If he is speedy, efficient, and good natured the trip is a joy to the paying customers. Then they eat well, sleep well, and have fun, and the cook tent is a center of warmth, good cheer, nourishment, and companionship. If the cook is sloppy, dirty, inefficient, slow and ill-natured the whole trip suffers. I have been on trips where a hot delicious meal was on the table within an hour after the outfit came into the campsite, and I have been on trips where nothing in the way of food was forthcoming to hungry dudes and hands for four hours or more. Sometimes, particularly in the southern Canadian Rockies, women are taken along as cooks. Some hunters object to this, saying it cramps their style, robs the experience of something of the atmosphere of masculinity. For my part I am all for a good cook without regard to sex, color, age, or anything else. Many mountain women have been brought up in the saddle, are used to cooking on camp stoves, and are tougher than the average dude. Generally speaking they are better cooks than men, better natured, cleaner, and more efficient. Too high a proportion of male cooks that go on pack trips are drunks and screwballs that are available only because no one will hire them for regular jobs. Some women cooks, however, get no medals. One girl I had as trail cook on one long trip was having a mad love affair with the horse wrangler. Both she and her boyfriend resented the other dudes and me because our presence interfered with their love life. The wood didn't get cut, the horses didn't get wrangled, and the meals were sketchy. All in all, it was a pretty miserable trip. Not all women cooks are models of feminine virtue.

Sometimes it is best for the hunters to leave the packtrain for a few days. The horse herd of twenty or thirty animals banging bells, whinnying, and wandering through the country tends to push back the game. The sound of the axe, the curses of a dude as he stumbles over a tent rope, the smell of smoke warn the warier wilderness animals that their country has been invaded. Sometimes good hunting country doesn't have enough horse feed for the whole outfit or is too rough to take a big packstring into.

Before the war, there were relatively few outfitters in all the dude hunting country from Wyoming to Alaska, and these few were very good. Ned Frost, Max Wilde, and Bert Turner of Wyoming; Roy Hargreaves, Ray Mustard, Bert Rigall, and Jack Brewster of the bighorn country of southwest Alberta and southeast British Columbia; Jim Ross, Frank Golata, and Westley Brown of the Stone sheep country around the Prophet and Muskwa Rivers; and Jean and Louis Jacquot of the Yukon—all were famous and all knew their business. A few are still in there pitching but some have retired and some, alas, have passed to the happy hunting ground.

Since the war there has been a tremendous demand for outfitters and a host of new men have come into the field. Some are excellent organizers and some are not. At best the most honest outfitter has a tough row to hoe, and his principal headache is getting good help.

Outfitting is no bed of roses, as the outfitter has to make considerable investment in horses, tents, pack and riding saddles, pots and pans, dishes, axes, saws, and various other oddments. Some outfitters wrangle fishermen or sight-seeing dudes during the summer, some run dude ranches. Others pack for the forest service or for companies or individuals engaged in mining operations, but at best their horses and equipment are in use for only a short time during the year. Theirs is a lot of responsibility for scant reward, but those who stay in business do so because they love it.

Often the outfitters who put on the best hunts and feed and care for their dudes the best are those who either run dude ranches or who take out summer pack trips as well as fall hunting parties. They realize how generally soft and luxury loving the average middle-aged man who takes a pack trip is. Many trappers who outfit on the side are in a poor position to know what a sixty-year-old business executive from Chicago considers comfort and good food and they put on trips that are pretty grim.

Charges for a full-fledged pack trip vary enormously from a minimum of about $40 a day to a maximum of perhaps $150 a day per man. As a rule prices are lowest in the United States and in the southern Canadian Rockies. The farther north one goes the higher they are. In northern British Columbia and the Yukon the standard price in the middle 1960's was about $80 per day per man if two or more hunters went together, about $100 a day for a single man. For many reasons prices are higher in Alaska—higher food costs, higher wages, expense of wintering horses. Actually there are not many pack outfits in Alaska, as there is little country there where a horse can winter. In the Yukon and in northern British Columbia there is much country where the wind sweeps the snow off the nourishing grass and peavine and where the horses get fat and sassy even though the thermometer may plunge to sixty below.

An extended pack trip into good wilderness game country is expensive but it is an experience of a lifetime. It may cost almost as much as a new automobile. Is such a trip worth it? That's up to the individual. The shine gets worn off the new car quickly and in a few years it is a junker. The memories of a fine hunt in beautiful country have a way of staying fresh as long as a man lives.

Many sportsmen also overestimate their own capabilities. They feel that because they have hunted whitetails in New York or mule deer in

New Mexico they do not need guides in Alaska or the Yukon. They forget that every man is a dude in a new country. Fredrick Courtney Selous, pioneer South African ivory hunter and museum collector, went to the Yukon in the early years of this century for North American game. He hired a guide. The best moose hunter in Canada is an ignorant novice on a tiger hunt in the Indian jungles, and the finest sheep guide in Alberta wouldn't have much notion as to the best way to collect an African leopard or greater kudu.

And the prospective hunter should allow himself enough time. A man packing back one day into the Wyoming or Idaho Rockies, who wants only one elk and who is not too particular about the head, should be able to connect in ten days. Unless his luck and the weather are bad, two weeks should give him plenty of leeway.

Suppose, on the other hand, the hunter plans to go to the Yukon or northern British Columbia to hunt for a general bag in an area where he will have to pack in five days and out five days. He will spend a good deal of money for licenses, possibly for equipment he does not have, and for transportation. Under those circumstances, he would be mad to plan a fourteen-day hunt. Three weeks would be the absolute minimum and a month would be better. It is far better to spend some extra money and extra time and have a good hunt than to skimp on money and time and have a poor one.

The man taking his first long pack trip should not plan too large a party. Two is about right. Three is dangerous, and anything over three is for the birds. When three men go on a long trip together, one of them almost always feels left out. If four go, they are apt to divide into cliques. The greater the number of hunters in the party the sooner they stir up a piece of country, the longer it takes them to get going in the morning, the more horses they have to take.

In 1963 my wife and I went on a Yukon pack trip with Robert Chatfield-Taylor of Boston and Bill Ruger, the Southport, Conn., gun manufacturer. We had two complete outfits. We traveled together and camped together when we wanted to, separated when we felt like it.

It is possible to save a little money if two hunters go out with the same guide, but I know of no better way to get into trouble. Suppose the two hunters and the guide stalk a bunch of rams, find one with a forty-four-inch head and the others not over thirty-five. Who will take the big one? It is a problem that has wrecked many a friendship. Or suppose the two hunters are out thirty days with only one guide and see but one grizzly. Who is to shoot?

24 | *Outfitting for the Pack Trip*

Footwear

When I am making up a personal outfit for hunting in a type of country new to me, the first thing I give serious thought to is the shoes I am to wear. Long ago I found out that if the hunter is properly and comfortably shod he isn't too badly off, but if his feet are cold, wet, covered with stone bruises or if he constantly slips and slides he is a very unhappy man.

I also found out that the type of footwear varies with climate and terrain—that a pair of boots ideal for hunting sheep in the desert mountains of Arizona or Sonora are almost worthless in the sheep mountains of the Yukon or northern British Columbia. Likewise a pair of boots that do very well for hunting in the dry mountains of Wyoming will not be satisfactory for the wet mountains of Alberta. Whatever kind of boots are taken along, they must fit and be well broken in.

Because I grew up in the Arizona desert, when I made my first pack trip into the Canadian Rockies I was pretty vague as to what the country was like. I was told by my outfitter to bring a pair of "boots" with soles and heels studded with round-headed Hungarian hobnails and to bring plenty of "dubbin" to keep them waterproof. He also told me to bring a pair of Maine shoe pacs with leather tops and rubber bottoms, in case of snow, and to take along a couple of pairs of thick felt inner soles for them.

For use in the snow, the shoe pacs were all right, but for the most part I wore the boots with the hobnails. These were simply a pair of light, chrome-tanned army shoes with 6-inch tops and built on the Munson army last. I took them to a shoemaker and had them nailed and I rubbed neatsfoot oil on them thinking this would make them waterproof. Brother, was I wrong!

Wearing them I hunted high in the mountains along the Alberta-British Columbia border in a region full of little streams, wet moss and lichen above timberline, wet or frosty grass everywhere in the early morning. We ran into some snow and a good deal of rain. I was in a fine game country. My outfitter was one of the best. Everything was perfect except that my feet were wet and cold most of the time. The little streams all seemed to be from four to seven inches deep. My guide had a good pair of oil-tanned logger boots with eight-inch tops, and he could walk dry-shod through them. Every morning my feet would be soaking wet before I had gone 200 yards. Each time I cut across a shale slide I would wind up with my shoes full of stones. It was a grand trip, but no one can be completely happy with his feet freezing or his shoes full of pebbles.

A pair of boots for mountain hunting should be as light as is consistent with durability and protection of the feet and ankles. The sole should be thick enough to protect the feet against being bruised by sharp stones and to keep the transverse arch from sagging. Even a light boot should be strongly made, have a good arch, and a steel counter. The worst boot I can think of for the mountains is the light, thin-soled boot of the "bird hunter" type. These are excellent for strong, young feet and the work for which they are intended—easy walking across gentle uplands for quail, pheasants, and grouse. For walking across slide rock, through muskeg and icy streams, and for tough going generally they are no good. Once a companion of mine took a pair on a sheep hunt—against my advice. At the end of a ten-day trip he could barely hobble because his feet were covered with stone bruises and he had had to spend an hour every night sewing the soles back on.

For the dry mountains of early fall in Idaho, Montana, Colorado, and Wyoming, a good pair of light but sturdy boots with some sort of a composition sole that will not slip on dry rock, pine needles, and dry grass is the best. I like eight-inch tops, as boots with lower tops are bad to take on pebbles. I like the boots to be laced. I do not like hooks. These often get bent and they wear out the laces. A heel somewhat higher than the one worn on a street shoe helps one to dig in when coming downhill. The most awful boot is the one with continuous sole and heel. These are like wearing a pair of skis. Since there is nothing to dig in with they can cause some bad tumbles. Even if the boot is not supposed to be waterproof a bottle of neatsfoot oil or other "dubbin" will preserve the leather and make the boots somewhat water resistant.

For mountain hunting farther north around timberline in British Columbia, Alberta, the Yukon, and Alaska, the best boot is a sturdy oil-tanned "logger" boot with sole and heel studded with round-headed Hungarian hobnails and with the toe of the sole protected with a tin plate so slide rock will not wear the sole down at the toe. These boots are made to measure by various companies in the Northwest and in Canada. I have had excellent boots made by Pierre Paris of Vancouver, British Columbia, and the White Shoe Company of Spokane, Washington. These boots are fairly heavy, but they are handmade of the finest materials and will stand many years of hard use. Wearing a pair of these oil-tanned boots with eight- or ten-inch tops, the hunter can walk right across most of the little creeks with which the mountains abound. He will neither ship water nor get his feet wet. He can cross shale and slide rock without getting stones in his boots. He will not get stone bruises.

Around and above timberline where he will be hunting sheep, goats, grizzly, and caribou, there are many very steep hills covered with slick grass or with moss and lichens. The hobnails bite into these slopes even when they are frosty and partially frozen. Wearing them he can climb with ease, whereas the hunter would find the going very difficult with any other type of sole. Hobnails will also stick on wet rock, whereas composition or rubber soles slip and slide. Since the war many mountain hunters have been wearing logger-type boots with "vibram" soles imported from Europe and worn by mountain climbers. These are made with substantial rubber lugs. They should stick nicely on slick grass and moss, but how they do on wet rock I cannot say from personal experience as I have never used them. Many swear by them. With a good pair of logger boots with nailed or "vibram" soles and with a pair of Maine hunting boots with rubber bottoms and leather tops and worn with a thick felt innersole in case of snow or much rain, the hunter on a northern pack trip is pretty well fixed. If he is the careful, forward-looking type he might take an extra pair of logger boots in case one pair gets wet.

It is of utmost importance for the man planning a Rocky Mountain hunt to break in his boots before he leaves. Wearing them makes them conform to his feet. If he has a pair of loggers he should get used to the extra weight and extra height of heel. Also, he should take dubbin (boot oil or grease) with him and keep his boots well oiled.

Since the end of World War II more people have made pack trips into the wilderness areas of the mountains of western North America than ever before. They hunt from Colorado to Alaska, for everything from elk to sheep. Some are well equipped, but, alas, most are not.

"Go light but right!" is the advice often given to prospective Rocky Mountain hunters. The catch is in the word *right*. It is silly to load up with mountains of useless equipment, but it is even sillier to take too little and to spend a good part of the trip cold, uncomfortable, poorly shod. A Cree Indian guide in Alberta may start a thirty-day pack trip with a dinky little bedroll, a couple of cotton shirts, a change of underwear, and an extra pair of socks. This is not being tough. It is simply being improvident—and when the guide starts out like that he is often depending on getting extra clothes from his hunter. I have left wool shirts, wool pants, logger boots, stag shirts, and long underwear from one end of the Rockies to the other because my Indian guides did not take enough clothes and I hated to see them suffer. White guides will generally come well equipped, often better than the hunter; but Indians almost never will.

Bedding

The most essential piece of equipment on any pack trip is the bed. If it is good, the hunter will sleep well, feel good, and enjoy his hunt. If it is not, his trip is doomed. The very best bed for a land of frosty nights is a good eiderdown sleeping bag or "robe." Some have a pocket for an air mattress. Some do not. I think it is just as well to lay the bed on the mattress. For the average man the opened up size of 84 × 84 is excellent, but the large man, or anyone who likes to roll and toss about is better off with the 90 × 90. The air mattress can be full length or three-quarter length. I prefer to use the shorter air mattress which leaves my legs from the knees down on the ground. Such a mattress is less laborious to blow up, is lighter and to me comfortable enough. Others loathe the short mattresses. I take a down pillow. Some like air pillows and some hardy souls roll up extra clothes and use them to lay their heads on. The bed should contain a wool or cotton liner or a wool blanket. A liner keeps the sleeping bag from getting dirty, and when the thermometer goes down the blanket between the bed and the mattress will keep the cold from creeping up from below. Some hunters use little cots made of aluminum and with down below. The hunter does not lie on the down. It is not compressed and this keeps him warm. My wife has such a cot and swears by it.

To complete the bed the Rocky Mountain hunter needs a good waterproof canvas tarp about 8 × 10 or 10 × 10 feet in size. Often the tent will be pitched on wet, cold ground—sometimes ground from which the snow has just been shoveled. The tarp will protect the bed from the dampness, as a damp bed is worthless. Beware of plastic tarps. The green waterproof canvas tarp "breathes." The moist air from the body can get out. The plastic tarp seals this moist air in and after a few nights the sleeping bag gets wet and chilly.

The tarp also has the function of protecting the bed from snags on the trail, against rain and snow, and against getting wet when the pack-train fords a river. Anyone who has ever come into camp on a chill, dank night with a wet bed will in the future see that he has a good tarp. When the bed is on the packhorse it is wrapped in the tarp and lashed with a rope into a compact, waterproof roll. Cheap, light canvas will tear on the trail. Canvas that is not waterproofed will let moisture seep through when laid on soggy ground.

It must be remembered that the only reason down is warm is that it traps air in little pockets and this serves as insulation. A down bag laid out on bare, icy ground on an air mattress is not warm because the down is compressed. In the far north the sleeping bag is usually spread on a soft, spongy bed of sphagnum moss. The moss is soft, retains body heat. If the bed is on bare ground or sand, the hunter will sleep cold and uncomfortable even in fairly moderate weather unless he takes the time to cut spruce tips to put under his bed for insulation. The advantage of the little down cots mentioned above is that they are just as warm above sand or bare ground as they are on moss.

Packing Your Gear

Next piece of equipment to consider is something to carry the clothing and personal gear in. Most hunters take a duffle bag of some sort. About as good as any is one made of stout canvas with a drawstring at the top. Another and more expensive type opens on the side and is closed with zippers and buckles. Whatever sort of bag is chosen, it should be made of good strong canvas, because thin canvas will tear on the trail when a knotheaded packhorse forces his way through timber.

The very best deal of all, but fairly expensive, is a pair of fibre pack panniers as sold by Abercrombie & Fitch of New York. They are light, very strong and they protect fragile equipment like cameras and binoculars. They are made with straps which are used to hang them on a sawbuck packsaddle. For one trip their expense is probably not justified, as mine cost in 1947 around $80 a pair, but for the man who plans to hunt by packtrain often these or something like them are almost a must as they are perfect for packing and shipping.

There are other ways to handle the problem. One is to buy a pair of canvas and leather pack bags from some Western saddle maker. These are sometimes called "alforkas" in Idaho. They buckle down and are made with stout straps to hang on a packsaddle. These are all right as they are except that they do not protect fragile equipment like binoculars and cameras. As I write this in 1966, a pair of these pack bags can be purchased from Crozier & Son, Lewiston, Idaho, for about $40.

About 1958 I purchased a pair for my wife. I then took them to a cabinet shop and had a pair of plywood boxes with hinged lids and hasps for padlocks made to fit inside them. I had the lid of one of these boxes fitted with a mirror and a tray made that was compartmentalized for the mysterious salves, unguents, powders, and lotions that my wife takes along to preserve her looks. I then got a piece of foam rubber exactly the size of the tray. This is carried between the tray and the mirror to protect the mirror from the jars and bottles in the tray. My wife packs these artifacts with strips of foam rubber to keep them from rattling. This is a very satisfactory outfit. On a Yukon pack trip, a pack slipped and a horse managed to buck my wife's outfit off. The mirror was unharmed and not a bottle was broken.

Still cheaper is to have two packboxes made of ⅜-inch plywood with hinged lids and hasps for padlocks. Screws, not nails, should be used in their construction. The edges should be reinforced with tin strips so the boxes will not get beaten up too badly when the packhorse bumps into trees. Strips of board are nailed on each end at an angle of about 45 degrees, just as they are on camp packboxes. These retain the ropes that hold the boxes on the packsaddle. Two holes should be bored in each lid and a rope run through them and knotted at each end to form a handle for carrying. Then each box should be given two good coats of spar varnish to protect them from the weather and to make them waterproof.

On a long pack trip it is the custom to assign one packhorse to each hunter. His packboxes or panniers form the side packs, his bedroll the top pack. With panniers or packboxes he can pack all his gear before he leaves home. Then when he arrives at his designation and meets the pack outfit, all he has to do is to hang his panniers on the horse and he is all set. My own pack panniers are marked "No. 1" and "No. 2." This makes it easier to find the snake-bite medicine when camp is being made after a long cold day on the trail. It is also helpful to list the contents of each pannier and fix it to the under side of the lid with scotch tape. Then it isn't necessary to go through both boxes to find some small item like a screwdriver or a roll of color film.

Clothing

Big-game hunting seasons in the packtrain country of the American West and the Canadian Rockies open at a time when the weather is changing and last in various areas from the first of August until the last of November. The hunter may be cold or warm, wet or dry, and he should be prepared to be comfortable in all kinds of weather. On my first trip into the Yukon I was constantly dressed in long wool underwear, wool pants, two pairs of wool socks, oil-tanned logger boots, two wool shirts, and a down jacket. I was convinced I knew *all* the answers for a fall trip into the area. Next time I went I took no light clothing. It was a freak fall, warm, dry. I almost roasted in the middle of the day. On a long trip into northern British Columbia for Stone sheep I started out traveling in light underwear, khaki pants and shirt, ended the trip getting up every morning with the thermometer below zero, wearing all the wool I had, and wishing for more.

When I pack for a trip now I usually put in a couple of pairs of khaki cotton pants and a couple of khaki cotton shirts and light underwear. I may not use them but if I need them they are there. The hunter who climbs a sheep mountain in bright hot sun when he is dressed for frost and icy winds can get miserably uncomfortable.

I usually take for a long pack trip three suits of medium weight two-piece underwear of pure soft wool, three all-wool shirts like those made by Woolrich and Pendleton, and two pairs of wool trousers. The all-wool saddle pants are the best looking but the wool work pants such as those worn by lumberjacks and sold by country stores in the big woods are cheaper and just as good. These should be "stagged" or cut shorter than dress pants. Two pairs will give the hunter a change if he comes in wet and cold.

Two wool shirts will generally keep the hunter warm enough in the early part of the season when he makes a climb for sheep or goats, but on his horse he should have a heavy woolen stag shirt or a down jacket. Some hunters take Mackinaw coats with them, but to me they are heavy and bulky for their warmth. The down jacket is probably the most useful of all outdoor garments for cold weather, as it is, weight for weight, the warmest garment of all. If it is opened up so that the air can circulate one is generally not too hot. Zip it up and it is possible to survive a blizzard. I usually take with me the Skyliner model as made by Eddie Bauer of Seattle. I have worn the same style of jacket hunting mule and whitetail deer in Arizona, elk in Idaho, bighorn and antelope in Wyoming, white sheep in the Yukon, ibex and urial in Iran, kudu and lion in Africa. It is warm, windproof, relatively wetproof. Good jackets are likewise made by Woods and by other manufacturers.

For a thirty-day trip I like to take about four pairs of short socks of pure springy wool and the same number of pairs of knee-length wool socks. I then will wear the ankle-length socks underneath the long ones. Two pairs of socks keep the feet warmer and cushion them better than one.

A large cowboy-type fur-felt hat keeps sun off the face and out of the eyes, rain and snow from getting down the neck and rain off the glasses—

if the hunter has to wear them. A cap is for most purposes a pretty worthless piece of wilderness headgear, as it lets snow and rain get down one's neck and allows the ears to sunburn.

Some like to sleep in an extra suit of long underwear, but I prefer to take along pajamas—usually for a thirty-day trip a couple of pairs of cotton and one of flannelette or light, soft wool-flannel. A pair of loafer-type slippers to wear around camp is a great boon. For keeping the hands warm, mittens are better than gloves. I like them fur-lined.

Rainwear

Because of pack outfit often travels in the rain, the hunter needs some sort of a rainproof outfit. The handiest for a short time is a knee-length jacket of tough, waterproof, rubberized fabric. After the war, stores dealing in surplus military equipment sold such jackets by the thousands, often with a pair of waterproof pants to go with them. The old-fashioned oil-skin slicker is good but heavy and clumsy. Light plastic outfits are no good because they are too easily ripped and torn. Dealers in outdoor clothing can furnish suitable rainproof jackets of rubberized fabric.

Binoculars

A good binocular is almost a must for any type of big-game hunting and for the West it is just about as necessary to the hunter as his rifle. Binoculars and spotting scopes and their use are discussed in a separate chapter, but here it is enough to say that cheap binoculars are seldom bargains. The hunter's binoculars should be of top quality, of 7, 8, 9, or 10X, light enough to wear around the neck without being burdensome. For mountain hunting I'd rather have a 9 or 10X than a binocular of lower power. If the hunter has two binoculars he should put the extra pair in for his guide to use. White guides generally have their own binoculars, but I have yet to see an Indian with a pair.

Rifle and Ammo

The rifle taken on the Rocky Mountain hunt should have range enough for the occasional long shot one has to take and enough bullet weight and shocking power to roll over a grizzly. Either the .30/06 or the .270 answers the purpose nicely. So do the various .30-caliber magnums, the 7-mm. Remington or Weatherby Magnums, the new .284 Winchester, or even the 7 × 57 Mauser.

The man hunting alone should take two rifles for insurance, preferably in the same caliber in order to simplify the ammunition problem, and one of them, I am convinced, should have iron sights as well as scope available. A receiver sight with a quick-removable slide along with a scope on a detachable side mount like the Griffin & Howe is a very satisfactory outfit. If two hunters go, an extra rifle between them should be sufficient insurance. Each rifle should have a scabbard made of good stiff leather as discussed in another chapter.

As in Canada the possession of a handgun by an alien is illegal, the American who hunts there and who wants a meal of delicious blue grouse now and then must take a .22 rifle or a small-gauge shotgun of some sort. If the rifle is taken it should be remembered that hollow-point ammunition has to be used unless the bird is shot in the head or neck. I have seen grouse shot through the body with a solid .22 bullet fly a quarter of a mile. Probably more fun can be had with a cheap .410 than with anything else. In some areas ptarmigan offer high-class wing shooting and it is always more fun to knock off a bird on the wing. An inexpensive and handy meat gun is the Stevens over-and-under .22/.410. In a pinch a good shot can knock the heads off of grouse with his big-game rifle.

Generally speaking, sixty rounds of ammunition for the big-game rifles is a great plenty and should give the hunter enough to check his sights with from time to time. He might, let us say, take forty rounds for sheep, caribou, mule deer, goat and such game and twenty rounds with heavier bullets for moose and grizzly. For the .410 shotgun, fifty rounds should be sufficient and for the .22, 100 rounds of hollow points.

Best way to carry cartridges for the big-game rifle while hunting is in a little leather belt-box made to take the inside of a cartridge box. I have found that if I reinforce the factory boxes of big-game cartridges with wide adhesive tape I do not have ammunition spilled all over the bottom of a pack pannier or duffle bag.

The hunter should take a minimum outfit for caring for his weapons. I put in a jointed rod of proper size, and if one of the rifles I take has a trap buttplate I carry a pull through in it. I also take a box of cut patches and a can of gun oil which will serve to protect the bores and the outside metal. A little bottle of linseed oil to rub on the stocks after they get wet is likewise handy to have. One should not forget screwdrivers with blades ground to fit slots in guard screws and screws in the scope mounts. I periodically go over all screws to see that they are tight. Plenty of hunters, including me, have missed game because they neglected these precautions. A pair of pliers comes in handy.

Often there are days of bad weather when the hunters must sit around camp. For such exigencies I always take along a couple of books. The choice makes no difference as long as it isn't something that requires time and concentration.

As we have seen in the chapter on pack trips, a good outfitter furnishes comfortable sleeping tents with folding stoves in them for cold weather, cook tent, tents for the help, horses, pack and riding saddles, food, cooking and eating utensils, gasoline pressure lamps.

He doesn't furnish the hunter's flashlights, towels, scabbards, saddlebags, bedding, binoculars, or anything else of a personal nature. A pair of old leather saddlebags used at one time by the U.S. Cavalry is a handy thing to have. A pair can be made to order or bought ready made if the cheap ones cannot be obtained. They will carry camera, lunch, extra film, extra ammunition, and the other odds and ends that come in handy.

I know of no greater joy than traveling with a well-run pack outfit. You wind into the campsite. In a little while the cook tent is up and blue smoke is curling from the chimney; the packs are off and the horses are bouncing away in their hobbles to feed. Then the dude tents go up and the hunters unlash their beds, spread out their tarps, blow up their air mattresses.

They've made twenty miles that day, and they are tired, but it's good to sit on a pack pannier and relax. Presently someone gets some boiling water from the cook tent and brews up a hot buttered rum. Then one of our dudes notices that in the little stream near camp the grayling are jumping. He goes in and digs out the fly rod he keeps in his bedroll, and on the first cast he has a nineteen-incher.

The sun is going down now over the big rugged sheep mountains to the west and the delicious odor of country-fried caribou steak drifts out to mingle with the smell of icy water and willows and spruce. It's a great life, and a day with a pack outfit probably adds two more to a man's quota!

Checklist of Clothes and Equipment to be Taken on a 30-Day Pack Trip

2 restocked Winchester .270 Model 70 Featherweight rifles with 4X scopes on Tilden mounts with detachable slings.
2 combination saddle scabbards and carrying cases with hoods.
1 .410 shotgun for grouse.
1 saddle scabbard for guide to use in carrying .410.
40 .270 cartridges with 130-gr. bullets.
20 .270 cartridges with 150-gr. bullets.
50 .410 shotshells.
1 leather cartridge box to hold 20 cartridges to be carried on belt.
1 Bausch & Lomb 9 × 35 binocular with case.
1 12 × 60 Leitz binocular with case.
1 20X prismatic spotting scope with case and tripod.
1 35-mm. Contax camera for black-and-white film.

- 1 35-mm. Contax camera for color film.
- 1 135-mm. telephoto lens for Contax.
- 1 magazine type 16-mm. motion picture camera with 1-in. 1.9 lens and 3-in. 3.5 telephoto.
- 15 rolls medium-speed black-and-white 35-mm. film.
- 15 rolls 35-mm. color film.
- 20 50-ft. magazines color film for movie camera.
- 1 camera kit bag to be carried in saddle bags with extra film, filters, etc.
- 1 pr. oil-tanned boots with 8-in. tops and Hungarian hobnails.
- 1 pr. light waterproof boots with composition soles and 8-in. tops for dry days and trail.
- 1 pr. shoe pacs.
- 3 prs. felt inner soles for shoe pacs.
- 6 prs. wool socks, 20-in. height.
- 1 pr. "loafer" shoes for wear around camp.
- 3 suits medium wool underwear (2 piece) .
- 3 medium-weight wool shirts.
- 1 Eddie Bauer "Skyliner" model down jacket.
- 2 prs. wool trousers.
- 1 strong belt.
- Extra shoe laces.
- 1 saddle slicker.
- 1 light short rain jacket.
- 1 pair cotton pajamas.
- 1 pair flannelette or wool flannel pajamas.
- 18 white cotton handkerchiefs.
- 4 large bandanna handkerchiefs (red or blue) .
- Toilet kit with comb, razor, blades, shaving soap, toothbrush, nail file, chapstick, etc.
- 1 pr. fur-lined gloves or mittens.
- 1 wide-brimmed "10-gallon" type hat.
- 1 90 × 90 down sleeping bag.
- 1 air mattress.
- 1 8 × 10 waterproof canvas tarp.
- 1 lash rope for bedroll.
- 1 pr. fibre pack panniers.
- 1 stout pocketknife.
- 1 jointed cleaning rod.
- 1 steel tape for measuring heads.
- Cut patches.
- Gun oil and solvent.
- Screwdrivers to fit guard screws and scope screws.
- Small bottle linseed oil.
- 1 pr. leather saddle bags to tie on behind cantle of saddle.

Sample Grub List

This was the standard grub list used on thirty-day pack trips for years by Frank Golata, the famous guide and outfitter of the Stone sheep country of northern British Columbia. Golata, who outfitted out of Dawson Creek, B.C., submitted this list to hunters, then changed it according to their individual desires. This is a good representative grub list. It is always wise for the hunter to see one, as no two people have exactly the same likes and dislikes in food, and outfitters can make changes. I, for instance, loathe both canned peas and canned pork and beans, and look upon canned corn with but small enthusiasm. Such a list will, of course, be greatly supplemented by game and, in some cases, fish. This list assumes there will be two hunters, a cook, and two guides.

150 lbs. flour in 25-lb. bags
  8 lbs. corn meal
 10 lbs. minute rolled oats
  5 lbs. wheat cereal
  5 lbs. rice
  5 lbs. navy beans (or preferably frijoles)
  5 lbs. baking powder
  1 lb. soda
  5 pkgs. yeast
  5 lbs. macaroni
 24 pkgs. dehydrated soup
 12 cartons Oxo soup cubes
 50 lbs. salt for hides
 25 lbs. salt for horses
  4 lbs. salt for kitchen
 15 lbs. coffee
  3 lbs. tea
  4 lbs. sweet chocolate
 40 lbs. sugar
  8 lbs. honey
  5 lbs. maple syrup
 10 lbs. assorted jam and marmalade
 25 lbs. powdered milk
 40 lbs. butter in cans
 36 small cans condensed milk
  5 lbs. peanut butter
 16 lbs. lard
  5 slabs bacon
  6 hams

24 cans spiced ham (Spam, Prem, etc.)
24 cans sausage
50 cans sardines
24 cans salmon
24 lbs. cheese
10 lbs. raisins
 5 lbs. dried apples
10 lbs. prunes
 5 lbs. dates
24 cans tomatoes
24 cans peas
24 cans corn
24 cans tomato juice
24 cans grapefruit juice
12 pkgs. custard powder
12 pkgs. Jello
15 lbs. egg powder
 2 bottles vanilla
 1 bottle maple extract
 1 doz. lemons
 5 lbs. dried potatoes
 5 lbs. corn starch
 6 bottles mixed pickles
 3 bottles meat sauce
10 doz. chocolate bars
 1 can curry powder
 2 cans cinnamon
 2 cans pepper
 1 can mustard
 5 jars sandwich spread
 6 rolls toilet tissue
 6 bars toilet soap
 6 bars laundry soap
 1 roll wax paper
10 doz. lunch bags
10 boxes matches
 2 doz. candles
 1 bottle vinegar
 1 can molasses
 1 bottle mint sauce
 1 bottle ginger
 4 tea towels

25 | *The Hunting Horse*

One morning I started off alone for a hunt, and to make sure I'd go straight back to the camp, I took my bearings and found it was on a direct line between one of the peaks in the Picus and one in the Sierra Los Mochos. Outside of the hills and mountains, the whole country looked pretty much alike—sandy flats peppered with the tracks of deer and javelinas, scrubby desert trees, saguaro, cholla, dry sandy arroyos. Much of the time down in the brush it was impossible to see the land-marks, but they could always be located by climbing a little hill. The road from the ranch where we had borrowed the horses ended at the well. If a man went too far south and west he'd miss it—and there was not another road between the well and the Gulf of California.

When I started back that afternoon I rode up on a little hill west of Los Mochos, took my line between the two peaks and started out. About halfway to camp my horse started veering to the left. I pulled him to the right, but again he began to drift over to the left. I rode up on another little rise, checked my line again. I was right. My knot-headed horse was wrong, something I regarded as odd because horses are supposed to have an infallible sense of direction. I had to fight the horse to keep him in line. Then suddenly I encountered horse tracks and the marks of a heavy limb being dragged. The trail was in the direction my horse had wanted to travel, and I felt very foolish indeed. That day I had told my Papago horse wrangler to go out and bring some wood to camp—and here was the sign that he had done so.

My horse started to trot now and I gave him his head. In a few minutes we were in camp. I found later that I had taken a line on the wrong peak in the Picus and if I had kept going I would have missed camp by about a quarter of a mile.

I had always known that horses were pretty well equipped with built-in gyro compasses, and I had always been told that if I were ever out on a horse and lost to give the horse his head and the horse would take me home. If I hadn't been so certain of my direction, so sure of my line, I would not have argued with the horse. Since that day, more than twenty years ago, horses have occasionally thought camp was in one direction when I thought it was in another. I have been smart enough not to argue with them—and the horses have always been right.

Once in northern British Columbia my guide Frank Golata and I had been out on horseback to scout for sheep and caribou, and when we started back I suggested we give the horses their heads and see how they operated. Instead of traveling direct to camp, they followed their tracks back, taking every twist, every turn. They went over every little knoll where we had stopped to glass, around every point where we had looked into another basin, crossed every little brook exactly where we had crossed that morning.

A horse has a magnificent nose and it would have been easy to follow a trail that fresh by smelling it out. In Alberta one time my guide and I steered our horses a half mile into a tangle of down timber, couldn't find a way out. We gave the horses their heads and they worked their way into the clear always exactly on their backtrack. Sometimes before going on, the lead horse stopped and sniffed the ground.

Horses also have a remarkable memory for country. Roy Hargreaves, who for many years outfitted in Alberta, told me that once an outfit of his was lost in a snowstorm at timberline. The head guide had no idea where the trail was, but Roy had told him that if he ever got into trouble to put a steady old packhorse named Red in the lead and to follow him. So Red was put at the head of the string. He turned around, started back, worked through some timber, and started down a long ridge. Presently the guide was conscious that they were on a trail. Presently he heard running water and before long Red stopped under a tree at the campsite they were looking for. The sense of smell cannot account for this, as Red hadn't been over that particular trail or at that camp for years.

The fact that a horse will return to camp if given his head is something which anyone taking a big-game hunt on which horses are used should store away in his memory. This uncanny ability possessed by almost any Western range horse has saved many a dude hunter, and for that matter many a cowboy, from going without supper and sitting out all night in the cold.

The horse is about the most useful piece of equipment the Western hunter can have, and if it were not for the horse, many middle-aged, elderly, or out-of-condition hunters would have to stay at home. A horse furnishes the muscle, the wind, the endurance for those who don't have them. A horse also extends a hunter's range enormously. It takes a young, tough man to hunt ten miles from camp on foot and return in fairly rough and hilly country, but a twenty-mile circle is a breeze for a good horse.

Carrying in the carcass of even a smallish deer is a back breaker for a strong man but a cinch for a horse. I have carried in dozens of whitetails tied on back of the saddle with the saddlestrings. I usually carry the larger mule deer across the saddle and lead the horse.

The easiest way to carry a big buck to camp on a saddle horse is to lay it across the saddle and button it to the saddlehorn by a hole cut in the flat of the belly skin. Then the head should be pulled back to the cantle and the antlers tied securely with the rear saddle strings. Then the hunter should cut through the joints of the legs, break them so they will not catch on brush, and tie them down with the forward saddle strings. If the hunter has taken the trouble to balance the buck well he'll ride nicely to camp.

A great many horses are allergic to having a deer put on them. They jump around, making packing the deer difficult, and sometimes they lash out with their hind feet. I cure this by blindfolding a horse with a large bandanna handkerchief, then covering my hand with deer blood and rubbing it over the horse's nose and into its nostrils. If the horse still feels like kicking (and he almost never does) I tie one hind foot up with a rope to the saddlehorn. When the hunter takes off the blindfold and starts leading the horse to camp he is generally philosophical. I have even seen horses uncomplainingly carry mountain lions and black bears into camp after being blindfolded and given the blood-in-the-nose treatment.

But this magnificently powerful and gifted creature with his wonderful nose and eyes, his marvelous sense of direction is a relatively stupid animal. I am sure that the horse lovers of America will organize a posse to lynch me on reading this, but I'll stick to the sentiment. An article on my fellow native Arizonian Rex Ellsworth, the rancher and owner of one of the nation's most successful stable of race horses, quotes him as saying exactly the same thing. Caught in a barbed-wire fence, a horse will cut himself to pieces in his struggle, but the more intelligent but less appealing mule will remain quiet and wait for someone to get him out.

A horse is subject to sudden and unreasoning panics, as anyone who grew up in a small town during the horse-and-buggy era as I did can testify. When I was a lad, two or three runaways a week were routine, and they usually ended with broken buggies, torn harness, and often injured drivers and horses.

If a pack slips on a mule, that wise and cynical animal will almost always stop and wait for someone to come and fix it. If it slips on a horse, he'll go into a panic and strew everything packed on him all over the countryside. In 1956, Bill Rae, the editor of *Outdoor Life,* and I were on a sheep hunt in the Yukon. One of the packhorses was loaded with two pack panniers containing, among other things, the party's supply of whiskey. A bedroll was the top pack and above that, held on by a diamond hitch thrown over it and the bedroll, was Bill's Dall sheep head.

The head slipped and the end of one of the horns tickled the horse in an unexpected place. Off he went, frantic with terror, wild eyed, bucking, knocking other packhorses down. Bill's sheep head sailed about twenty-five feet in the air and every now and then a bottle of booze would go shooting out of a pannier like a shell from a mortar. Hooves were drumming, the guides and wranglers were yelling, and the air was filled with the popping of brush and the crash of broken pack boxes. Presently the horse had got rid of everything packed on him. The wranglers calmed him down, jury-rigged the broken panniers, and repacked him while Bill hunted down the sheep head and I backtracked the horse to the brush for the bottles. As miraculous as it may seem, none of them was broken.

Another time in the Yukon, my party had come into a campsite after a long day on the trail and was making camp on Count Creek. Two packhorses were tied to an old stump, the roots of which had rotted. A fly bit one of the horses, he jerked his head and the stump moved. This astonished the other horse. He snorted and backed away. This tilted the stump and bugged the first horse. He also yanked back. Now the stump was pulled from the ground and was suspended in the air between the two horses. Neither had ever seen a floating stump before. Wild eyed, screaming with terror, each put on all power and backed away from the stump. One of the ropes broke and the horses fled in opposite directions, throwing their packs all over the countryside. As long as we were in that camp those horses would snort and roll their eyes whenever they came near the spot where the stump had been.

A pal of mine is an ex-stunt pilot, parachute jumper, and wing walker. On his days off he used to drive race cars for relaxation. He is now a dude rancher, outfitter, and big-game guide. In his long and dangerous life he has been seriously hurt three times—and every time by a horse. His wife wears store teeth because a tame and friendly horse was in a bad mood and kicked her face in one time. Another friend of mine, one of Arizona's famous lion-hunting Lee Brothers, was killed by a horse a couple of weeks after I had hunted whitetails on his ranch. He had been out looking at his cattle all day. He got almost back to his ranch house when he decided to ride back a quarter of a mile to look at a cow. The horse had been planning on getting the heavy rider and saddle off and kept trying to turn back to the ranch. He was on a steep sidehill when he decided to buck. He lost his footing, fell on his rider, and killed him.

Outfitters generally put their dudes on calm, patient, well-broken horses, and seldom do these novice riders have any trouble with them, but even the slowest old horse can panic. Once down in Mexico my wife and I were riding out on a little afternoon hunt on a couple of pokey, half-starved old cow ponies. A half-mile or so from the camp I discovered that some dogs were trying to follow us. That morning they had spooked a couple of deer and I didn't want them along. I took after them to chase them back to the ranch. As I leaned over to whack one of them with a riata the front cinch broke. The saddle turned and I crashed to the ground like a load of bricks. With the saddle held under his belly by the second cinch, that horse really went into orbit! Kicking and squealing, he rushed around tearing down bushes and bumping into trees. In the saddle scabbard was my pet .30/06 with a superb French walnut stock by Adolph Minar of Fountain, Colorado. It stayed in the scabbard for about five quick jumps, then I saw it sail fifty feet into the air and land in a pile of rocks. From that time on Old Betsy really wore the scars of battle!

A mountain-raised horse is a marvelously sure-footed animal, but there is nothing to the old saying that a horse can go anywhere a man can go. Even a fair climber can go places where the most sure-footed of horses would break his neck. The dude hunter who goes out on horseback should always bear that in mind, and if he comes to a spot where a horse might lose his footing he should get off and lead. After all, the horse is an animal which evolved not in the mountains but out on the plains. He is by nature not a climber but a runner.

The frozen ground of icy slopes is poison for a horse. Slanting solid rock is dangerous. Perhaps the worst of all is a slanting rock slope with loose stones on it. Once I was hunting with an amigo in British Columbia with an Indian guide who was allergic to walking. We were rimming around a steep hillside. It was mid-morning and the warm sun was shining, but it had been bitterly cold the night before and shady areas were still covered with heavy frost. Ahead of us was a steep frosty stretch and I suspected that the ground under the frost was frozen. I suggested that the Indian guide get off and prepared to dismount myself. But the guide went on. The instant the horse stepped on the frozen ground his feet shot out from under him. Horse and rider tobogganed about 300 yards down that frozen glassy hill and came to rest unhurt in a nice, soft, grassy meadow.

On another occasion in Arizona a companion and I were coming in from a deer hunt. Ahead of us I saw a smooth steep slope of solid rock covered with scattered small stones and pebbles. I got off and was leading my horse when I heard a fearful clatter and here came my pal and his horse, first one on top, then the other. Luckily neither was hurt.

A horse learns by experience to handle himself in soft ground and in rough country, and a plains horse is as inept in muskeg or mountains as a city-bred man is on snowshoes. I once rode on a long pack trip in northern British Columbia a very gentle and pretty little mare called Susy Q. She was farm bred and knew nothing about the bush. I had to lead her across every muskeg we encountered. If I did not she was quickly bogged down and helpless. She learned to step exactly where I stepped. She was terrified of rough country and when we came to what she considered bad going she'd stop and tremble until I got off and led her.

A horse may be shy on brains and subject to panics, but he has a wonderful nose and magnificent eyes. On dozens of occasions I have taken game that my horse saw or smelled first. One horse I rode in Mexico associated the odor of deer with rifle fire, and every time he'd smell a deer he'd snort, roll his eyes, and jitter around. Such conduct always meant, I discovered, that deer were nearby. This horse also always ran away the instant I yanked my rifle out of the scabbard, and it was something of a handicap to wonder where my horse would wind up while I was trying to concentrate on knocking off a bounding buck. I finally solved the problem by tying a knot in the reins so short that when I hauled back and put the reins over the saddle horn, the horse would stay put. His chin was pulled right up to his neck and if he tried to move it hurt him.

A gifted packhorse a guide and I used to take along to bring back heads and meat on could spot moose and caribou almost as far away as I could see him with glasses. I could always tell when he saw or smelled a bear because he would crowd right up to the guide and me, eyes rolling, nostrils distended.

A horse likewise has the night vision of a bat, and many times horses have brought me safely to camp when it was so dark I could hardly see my hand before my face. Once in the Yukon a companion and I were seated by a little stream eating our sandwiches. Suddenly my horse's ears went forward. He snorted and gazed fixedly back into the dark shadows of some timber a couple of hundred yards away. With the naked eye I could see nothing. I picked up my binocular and with the aid of its light-gathering power I could see the head of a black bear. He was watching us from the far side of a log back in the heavy shadows of the timber. My scope-sighted .270 was leaning on a tree beside me. I could also see the bear's head through the bright scope. I squeezed the trigger and hit the bear right through the brain just above the eyes.

In parts of the West, it is possible to hunt almost entirely from horseback. The hunter simply rides around likely-looking deer country until he sees a deer. Then he gets off and starts shooting. This is a relatively easy, interesting, and exciting way to hunt. It used to be the best way to hunt for big bucks on the winter range in Arizona's famous North Kaibab forest—and I presume it still is. Generally the deer are at fairly long range and are moving. The action is fast and furious.

In rougher and more wooded country the horseback hunter rides to likely-looking areas, then gets off and hunts on foot. In many sheep mountains such hunting is possible. The best North American sheep I ever shot was a fine Dall. My guide and I located the ram about a mile away and then rode around and above the bunch of rams the big one was running with. Riding around in the open country above timberline in the Yukon and northern British Columbia, I have many times spotted caribou, moose, and even grizzlies while still in the saddle, and in Arizona and Wyoming I have piled off horses and shot elk. Once I stepped off a horse at the head of a packtrain, sat down, and knocked a fine ram off a ledge about 200 feet above me and 250 yards away.

Most dude hunters unused to riding get so saddle-sore they are miserable. The major reason for this is that the stirrups are not properly adjusted. If the stirrups are too long, the rider's weight rests entirely on his buttocks and at the end of twenty miles on the trail he is convinced that his bones are sticking through the flesh. If his stirrups are too short, his knees cramp most horribly. For trail riding, the best adjustment, for me anyway, is to have the stirrups long enough so that when I stand up in them my fanny clears the saddle by from four to six inches. They are then long enough so that knees do not cramp and short enough so that my leg muscles can take some of the shock and bumps off my rear end.

Nowadays I ride only on hunting trips, but with my stirrups so adjusted I can get on a horse and ride twenty miles the first day and be only a little sore at the end. Another thing the occasional rider should remember is to keep his back straight. If he does not, the continual jiggling of the horse will pull and twist the muscles of the small of his back and at day's end he'll feel as if he had been sawed in half.

One of the most depressing sights in nature is to see a line of dudes starting out with a pack outfit on horseback. They are perched on their horses as inert as so many bags of potatoes. Almost always their stirrups are too short. They sit there miserably with their backs bowed, their knees under their chins, their rifles either carried over their shoulders by slings or tucked away in scabbards at odd and impossible angles.

The chap planning a horseback hunt or a pack trip doesn't need to be a bronco buster or a hell-bent vaquero, but he should know how to adjust his stirrups and how to sit in a saddle.

A great boon to the hunter, this Western and Northern horse, but the hunter should never forget that he is a creature of flesh and blood and not a machine. He is magnificently strong and enduring and is equipped with marvelous eyes, a wonderful nose, and a built-in compass as good as that of the homing pigeon.

A little more advice for the horseback hunter. The rifle should never be left in the saddle scabbard when the hunter dismounts for lunch, to glass, or for any other reason. If his back is sore or the saddle happens to be uncomfortable, a horse often gets a notion to roll. A rifle or a camera that has been rolled on by an 800–1,000-pound horse has generally had it.

Some more advice on horses: Don't overload your saddlebags, as they ride right over a horse's kidneys and are apt to hurt him. A horse with saddle sores or painful kidneys is a very unhappy horse. Take along a lunch, an extra box of cartridges, some film, perhaps a camera. Don't load the poor horse down with canned goods, bottles of beer, heavy movie cameras. Tie your stag shirt or rain jacket on behind the cantle with the saddlestrings. If you have your camera and binoculars with you, it is best to carry them with straps across your shoulder. Don't hang them on the saddlehorn or tie them to the saddle with the saddlestrings. If the horse plows through some brush the straps may be broken and camera and binoculars lost.

Few occasional fall hunters are expert horsemen and they are apt to be a bit in awe of the strange monsters they are given to ride. The horse quickly senses this and will take advantage of the timid rider. A hunter should have a quirt with him, but if he does not he can cut himself a good switch. The first time his horse starts lagging or decides to pause and refresh himself with a luscious bit of grass, the rider should belt the hell out of him. Then the horse knows who is master. It is remarkable how full of ambition and energy a good quirt or a pair of spurs will fill the laziest horse.

The hunter should take care not to get kicked or stepped on. Never startle a horse. Approach him so he can see you. If he is dozing, speak to him. A pal of mine had just killed and dressed a deer. He decided to go to his horse and get a pack of cigarettes out of his saddlebags. He approached from the rear and suddenly the horse was aware of the smell of deer blood. It lashed out with a hind hoof, struck my pal on the thigh, and for a week he couldn't even hobble.

As a cowpoke friend of mine says: "Always keep an eye on a horse. You don't always know what he's going to do and he don't neither. It's always them old gentle bastards that kill you!"

26 | *The Rifle on the Horse*

Those who carry rifles around on horses feel as strongly about the proper way to do it as many feel about politics. An outfitter friend of mine and I have just about quit speaking because we disagree on the subject. Since we are both reasonably intelligent, the reason we don't see eye to eye is that his horseback hunting has been done largely in an open country with good trails, whereas much of mine has been done where man and horse often have had to plow through brush in a land of no trails.

I started riding around on a horse with a rifle scabbard hung on many years ago. I have tried various types of scabbards and I have hung them in various places. Some have worked out quite well. Others haven't. It pays anyone planning to make a pack trip or to hunt on horseback in the Western United States or Canada to give a little thought to acquiring a reasonably suitable saddle scabbard and to consider where he is going to hang it when he gets it. Sometimes outfitters furnish saddle scabbards, but when they do they are seldom right for scope-sighted rifles.

A great many notions as to what saddle scabbards should be like come from those for the flat, light Winchester, Marlin, and Savage carbines with their 20-inch barrels.

The scabbard for the scope-sighted rifle should be of heavy enough leather to give the rifle considerable protection from bumps, snug enough so that the rifle does not rattle around in it, loose enough so that the rifle can be quickly inserted and quickly withdrawn. In addition, it should cover the rifle well past the point of the comb. If it does not, riding through brush and thorns will quickly take the finish off a buttstock and often score the wood so deeply that refinishing is almost impossible.

A scope-sighted bolt-action rifle is a fine precision instrument for big-game hunting, but it is an unwieldy thing to hang on a horse. The scope makes it bulky and awkward to carry and the bolt-knob is a lethal projection which has a tendency to gouge into the horse's hide if the rifle is carried on the left side, butt to the rear or on the right side, butt to the front. For years, I carried a .270 on a Mauser action that had a flat, "butterknife" bolt handle, an excellent modification for a saddle rifle. Before the war many German sporters had these flat bolt handles and the Mannlicher-Schoenauer rifles and carbines still do. They are a bit clumsy for rapid fire, but in the years I hunted with the flat-bolt .270 I cannot remember being slowed up much by it.

Rifles with 16- and 18-inch barrels are convenient to carry on horseback, but barrels this short have a bad muzzle blast and because they are muzzle-light they are difficult to shoot accurately. If a short-barreled job is chambered for a modern cartridge using slow-burning powders, velocity loss is pretty serious. I cannot muster any enthusiasm for a saddle rifle with a barrel less than 20 inches. I think a 26-inch barrel is too long, but a 24-inch barrel endurable. For the dude hunter a 22-inch barrel is about right. With a barrel of that length, muzzle blast isn't increased a great deal and velocity loss is not serious. In addition, a rifle with a 22-inch barrel balances and handles nicely.

As I write this the majority of American factory big-game rifles are standard with 22-inch barrels. The Remington Model 600 has an 18½-inch barrel but the Model 700 in such calibers as .280, 6 mm., .30/06, and .270 has a 22-inch barrel. A rifle for one of the various magnums should never be made with a barrel of less than 24 inches. If the barrel is chopped off more than that, muzzle blast and velocity loss become serious problems.

The rifle carried by the rancher who is in the hills most of the time and demands nothing more of it than to knock off an occasional piece of meat or smoke up a coyote can well wear iron sights and be light and short of barrel. If he misses a coyote or doesn't bring in the fat little forkhorn, he will see another coyote and another fat forkhorn tomorrow or the day after. The rifle for the once-a-year dude hunter should be a better piece of ordnance, a scope-sighted rifle capable of catching good aim and capable of being held steady and shot accurately enough to knock off a trophy buck or ram at 300 yards if the need arises.

For the trophy hunter, the saddle rifle and the mountain rifle are about the same thing—a rifle with a 22-inch barrel, mounted with about a 4X scope, and chambered for an accurate flat-shooting cartridge. If nothing larger than deer, sheep, or black bear is on the menu, a cartridge like the .243 Winchester, the 6-mm. Remington, or the old .257 is perfectly all right. If, on the other hand, the hunter is apt to run into elk, caribou, moose, white goats, or grizzlies, he should have a rifle using a cartridge with more bullet weight and somewhat more energy—the .280, .270, .284, .30/06, 7 × 57, or something of the sort. Rifle and scope should weigh in the neighborhood of eight pounds.

I am a bolt-action man myself. For one thing, I cut my teeth on the old Model 1903 bolt-action Springfield. For another, I am a handloader, and the bolt action is more satisfactory for handloads than actions of other types. If the horseback hunter wants to use a lever-action rifle for a reasonably potent cartridge, there is no reason why he should not. The Model 99 Savage in .308, .300 Savage, or .284 makes a good solid saddle rifle when equipped with a 4X scope. So does the Winchester Model 88 in the same calibers. Suitable autoloaders are the Remington Model 742 or the Winchester Model 100 in .308, .30/06, or .280, or .284. The levers, pumps, and autoloaders have the advantage for saddle use of being somewhat thinner than bolt-action rifles.

All of these actions are faster than the bolt, but for open-country hunting I have never seen much need for firing a fusillade. However, many find the bolt action ugly and awkward and are bemused by fire power. If they fancy some other actions I am all for them!

When scope-sighted rifles first began to come into general use thirty years or so ago, there were simply no saddle scabbards on the market for them. My first satisfactory scope-sighted rifle was a Griffin & Howe .30/06 Springfield with a 22-inch barrel and mounted with a 2¾X Hensoldt scope on a Griffin & Howe mount so high that I could see through the Lyman 48 receiver sight underneath. I couldn't get a scabbard to fit the outfit so I used to carry the scope in a little case hung on my belt when I hunted on horseback. I never had the time to put the scope on when some frightened buck was putting geography behind him. The only times I knocked off game with the scope was when I was hunting on foot.

I eventually soured on this miserable business of mounting a scope above the receiver sight. I had a 7 × 57 with an old Noske 4X scope mounted low on the Noske side mount. This was a fine outfit. Later I acquired the flat-bolt .270 Mauser I have mentioned previously. But even with these low-mounted outfits, I still could not get a store-bought scabbard to fit.

Another horseback hunter and I, with the aid of a Mexican saddle-maker, worked out the saddle scabbard I am illustrating here and giving the dimensions for. As I show it, the scabbard will fit a bolt-action rifle

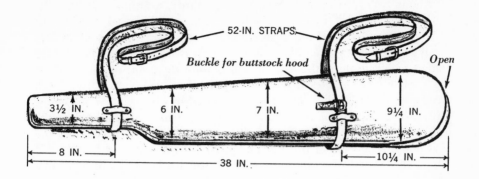

52-IN. STRAPS

Buckle for buttstock hood

Open

3½ IN. 6 IN. 7 IN. 9¼ IN.

8 IN.

38 IN.

10¼ IN.

Dimensions of rifle scabbard designed by the author and saddlemaker for a scope-sighted rifle with a 22-inch barrel. Rifle is inserted scope up so no weight is on sight.

with the scope mounted low. It can be made by any competent saddlemaker. However, since saddlemakers do not work with micrometers, it is wise to leave the rifle for which the scabbard is being made with the maker so he can make sure it fits.

There is much that can be said in favor of this scabbard. It is not very difficult to make. Nor is it frighteningly expensive. It holds the rifle securely, and yet it is easy to yank the rifle out. It is so designed that it does not bind the scope, and it does a better job than most of protecting the buttstock from scratches and gouges. If it is made of heavy saddle skirting leather and combined with a cap or hood, it can double fairly well as a rifle case. It can be made by any competent saddlemaker at a cost of from $18 to $30 depending on the leather used and whether it has a hood for the butt.

Two styles of buttstock hoods designed for the scabbard.

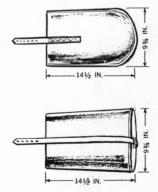

9¾ IN.

14½ IN.

9¾ IN.

14½ IN.

About twenty years ago the late Cap Hardy, a famous Los Angeles leather worker and former exhibition shooter, borrowed one of the scabbards from me and made an elaborate variation which doubles very nicely as a carrying case. The scabbard itself is made of very heavy, stiff leather which protects the rifle to well beyond the point of the comb. It has a soft leather hood which can be zipped shut, tied back to give quick access to the butt of the rifle, or even removed by unzipping. The George Lawrence Company of Portland, Oregon, used my old scabbard as the inspiration for one which I allegedly designed and which is called the "O'Connor scabbard." I did not design it, but the scabbard has most of the good features of my old one. It has a stiff leather cap which buckles on and which converts it into a carrying case.

One type of saddle scabbard on the market has a sort of a flap which snaps around the rifle at the pistol grip. This gismo is of some value in keeping the rifle from falling out of the scabbard, but it leaves the buttstock sticking out like a sore thumb. If the hunter has to ride through areas of thick brush (particularly thorny brush), he will find that a scabbard of this sort does not protect the buttstock of his rifle. Furthermore, unless the snap is on the outside, it is very clumsy to use and the scabbard must always be carried on one particular side. This limits the usefulness.

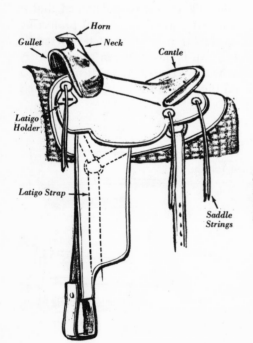

Horn
Gullet
Neck
Cantle
Latigo Holder
Latigo Strap
Saddle Strings

Scabbard is tied to saddle by fastening straps through gullet, latigo holder and to the rear saddle strings.

Position of Scabbard

The location of the scabbard on the horse depends on many things. Most important is how fast the hunter wants to get his rifle out and go into action. If he is simply using his horse to carry him and his rifle from somewhere to somewhere else where he wants to hunt, the position makes no particular difference. But if he wants to get off his horse, grab his musket, and lay down a barrage that is another story.

In some areas hunting can be done almost entirely from horseback. The hunter rides in such a way that he will move deer and see them when they move. He rides along ridges so he can see into canyons on each side. He rides along the sides of canyons and around the heads of draws. To be hunted successfully in this manner, country must be pretty open and it must be cut up and hilly. Heavy brush country and flat country generally cannot be hunted on horseback.

I have shot many mule deer in the hills and canyons of Arizona when I was hunting on horseback. I have likewise shot a great many Coues (Arizona) whitetails in Arizona and Sonora the same way. Generally such shots are at running animals and generally they are at fair ranges— from 200 to, occasionally, 300 yards. For this work I like what is generally

With rifle in Southwest position—angled down at about 45 degrees with butt to rear—rider steps off on left side, grabs gun butt, and yanks it out.

Hardy scabbard, in trail position, has muzzle end low to avoid cramping the hunter's knee during long rides.

called the Southwest position. For this I put the scabbard on the horse butt to the rear on the left side with the butt pointing up and at an angle of about 45 degrees. This slant is important for two reasons. For one thing it keeps the rifle from sliding out of the scabbard when the horse is going sharply uphill. For another, this position puts the forward portion of the scabbard low so it does not cramp the left leg. Another advantage is that since the open portion of the scabbard is at the rear, the scabbard does not fill up with leaves and twigs as it does when the open mouth of the scabbard points forward. The one disadvantage is that the hunter does not see his rifle as he rides and he can lose it and not know it.

With his scabbard in that position, the hunter steps off his horse on the left side, drops the reins (since Western horses are trained to stand when the reins are down), grabs the rifle by the small of the stock, yanks it out, sits down, and goes into action. If his horse gets nervous and takes off, the animal goes forward and the hunter keeps the rifle in his right hand and does not lose it.

Some say they like to carry their rifles on the left side with the butt forward along the horse's neck. I do not like this position. For one thing,

308

the scabbard fills up with leaves and twigs if the hunter must ride through brush. For another, the horse is often spooked if the excited hunter makes a sudden grab for the butt of his rifle. Then, if the horse takes off, the hunter will lose his hold on his rifle even if he has grabbed it. This position is all right for transporting a rifle from one place to another but I do not like it for actual horseback hunting.

Another fast position that was formerly quite popular was to sling the scabbard high on the right side, butt to the rear and projecting above the horse's rump. Then the hunter grabbed the butt with his right hand as he dismounted on the left side. This position is feasible only with a short-barreled carbine like the old Model 94 Winchester.

Most Southwestern horses and good cow horses all over the West have a high proportion of hot blood in them and as a consequence their backs are shaped to carry saddles. The position of the saddle scabbard or the rider's getting on and off doesn't tend to pull the saddle over on one side or another.

In the Canadian Rockies, from the American border to the Yukon, most of the horses are from cold-blooded work stock, and their backs are shaped like sausages. Keeping a saddle on an even keel on these goats is a chore. On such a horse, I like to carry my rifle in what I call the trail position. This is on the right side, butt to the front and at an angle of

Lawrence scabbard showing buckle used to fasten on buttstock hood.

about 45 degrees. Sometimes the rifle is carried more nearly vertical but this position puts the butt so high that if the rider bends over to dodge a branch he may knock his teeth out. In the trail position the rifle is then carried about even with the front cinch. Its weight doesn't pull the saddle over, but such tendency as it does have about balances the sudden pulls when the horseman mounts from the left side. This is no place for the man who wants to carry his rifle so he can jump off, grab it, and shoot, but it is right for a Rocky Mountain pack trip. I can see no point whatsoever in carrying a rifle on the right side butt to the rear as I have seen some do. Slung that way, the rifle and scabbard pull the rifle over to the right. The rifle is slow to get to, and if the excited hunter goes charging around Black Beauty's fanny from the left side to the right to grab his musket, he is apt to get kicked.

Now and then some innocent citizen comes around to Chez O'Connor to borrow a saddle scabbard. When he returns it, the straps are almost always on backward and it is plain to see that he has been carrying his rifle upside down with all the weight on the scope. Why anyone should want to carry his rifle so that it bounces around on the scope has always baffled me—but many do.

The rifle carried in the scabbard should have the weight resting on the muzzle and on the bottom of the rifle. Weight should never rest on either glass or iron sights. The scabbard should be roomy enough so that the scope and rifle do not wedge into the scabbard. Since I am relatively dumb, I learn these things the hard way. Once I hunted on horseback with a .30/06 fitted with a scope on a side mount with aluminum arms. The scabbard was too narrow and none of the weight rested on the muzzle. Most of the weight was on the end of the scope tube and every step the horse took wedged the scope more solidly into the scabbard. Since the wedging action bent the aluminum arms of the bracket mount and made the scope point down, this made the barrel point up in relation to the scope. I shot over a couple of nice bucks, and then when I found out what was happening I managed to kill one at 200 yards by holding a foot under the line of his chest.

Another hint is either to remove the sling from the rifle and carry it in the saddlebags if it is to be needed or to take great pains to tuck the sling inside the scabbard. If it dangles out, it may catch on a limb and yank the rifle out.

Anyone hanging a rifle scabbard on a horse should remember that his mount is only slightly less powerful than a bulldozer and that unless whatever is tied on Old Dobbin is anchored securely it is apt to get yanked off. If a sizable branch gets between horse and scabbard, the straps are apt to be torn off. Hunters are always tying binocular cases, camera cases, and whatnot to their saddles. I have seen at least three pairs of binoculars lost because they were tied to the saddle or hung over the horn. Another chap I knew lost a $600 movie camera he had tied to his saddle. Once I led a horse down a steep hill through thick brush. One of my saddlebags was ripped open and all I lost was a $300 miniature camera, a leather cartridge box, some film, and a $400 movie camera. However, I backtracked myself and found the stuff.

When the rifle is carried butt forward, the top carrying strap is put in the latigo holder or through the fork of the saddle. This is a strong place, but there is always a chance that a limb can get between horse and scabbard. When the rifle is carried butt to the rear, the top strap is tied to the saddle with the rear saddle strings and the bottom strap goes through the fork.

Another point is to sling rifle and scabbard so that the bump they cause is low enough not to twist the knee. If the scabbard causes a strained knee during a long ride, it can cause almost as bad cramps as too-short stirrups. The scabbard should never be thrust between the stirrup leathers. This makes for a bad bump and a cramped knee.

Anyone ordering a scabbard for horseback hunts out from a ranch has no need for a cap to cover the buttstock. If he wants to get into action fast it gets in his way. If he is afraid of a sudden rain, he can cover butt and scope with an old boot sock. On a long pack trip, where the rider may travel in rain and snow and where he almost never has to get to his rifle instantly, some sort of a gimmick to cover the butt with leather is a good idea. Then if the scabbard itself is of good hard, moulded leather, it can serve as a carrying case on train or plane. At that, though, it is a good idea to request permission to take rifles and scabbards into the cabin of the plane. Some baggage handlers get a bit careless with rifles at times, and a scope-sighted rifle that is tossed merrily around may come out of adjustment.

Scabbards are better off when not lined with fleece. Genuine lamb fleece attracts moisture and is apt to promote rust. The synthetic fleece I have seen goes to pieces when it gets wet. Furthermore, fleece is not needed as a rifle does not wear in a scabbard that fits properly.

Jouncing a scope-mounted rifle around on a horse is not the best way I can think of to keep it sighted in. Particularly if the mount and scope screws have some oil in the threads, the scope can get so loose it rattles. All screws should be checked with screwdrivers that fit to see if they are tight every time the rifle is cleaned.

The best type of scope mount for the saddle rifle is the popular bridge type, and the farther apart the rings are the better the scope is supported. Base screws particularly should be dipped in shellac or "Loctite" before they are tightened. Then the jolting from the horse will not loosen them.

A companion piece for the saddle scabbard is a good pair of saddle-bags to be tied on behind the cantle by the rear saddle strings. Satisfactory ones more or less on the order of the old cavalry saddlebags can be purchased at some sporting goods stores and saddle shops for around $15. In them the hunter can carry his movie camera, lunch, extra film, tape measure, and various oddments. The bags are just about a necessity. Not all outfitters furnish them.

27 | *Your Meat and Your Trophy*

The best big-game meat is as good as the choicest corn-fed beef or the tenderest lamb available at a market. The worst is so bad as to be inedible.

Whether it is good or bad, delicious or revolting, depends on many factors: the condition of the animal when it was shot, the placement of the bullet and the quickness of the kill, the care given to the meat, the way it is cooked, and the attitude of the person eating it.

As is the case with just about everything connected with big-game hunting, people with very little experience or knowledge about game meat or game cookery are quick to pass judgment on all game meat. Some are so prejudiced that if they were given a perfectly cooked filet of prime beef but were told it was moose they would be unable to eat it. In contrast, some are so romantic about game that they will declare a tough, dry steak from a half-starved and evil-smelling bull elk shot after the rut is a delicious morsel. Most of us are to some extent prejudiced about food. A Hindu regards anyone who will eat beef as being no better than a cannibal, and most Americans will not knowingly eat horse meat as the French do. When Lewis and Clark led their famous expedition from St. Louis to the Pacific they found that most of the Indian tribes along their route raised dogs for meat. The explorers ate a lot of dog meat and grew very fond of it. The very thought revolts most Americans today. The first time I was in Paris, I ordered snails in garlic butter at a fine restaurant. I felt I was taking my life in my hands. I found them delicious. When I returned and told some of my friends about my daring gastronomic escapade they turned green.

No meat from any animal is good unless the animal is killed when it is in good condition. No meat is any good if the animal has been gut-shot and chased a couple of miles before it is finished off. No meat is good unless the animal is properly cleaned, skinned, and cooled.

Anything connected with the hunting of big game is a great stimulant to the imagination, and much that is said and written about the qualities of various big-game meat defies logical analysis and explanation. Most cigarette smokers are certain that their favorite brands have unique flavors, yet when they are blindfolded most of them cannot distinguish their favorite brand from any of a half-dozen others. So it is with meat. A friend of mine once fed his cronies on roast donkey. When the roast was served he told them they were eating elk. They all declared the meat delicious with a unique and exotic flavor. When he informed them that they had just devoured a burro, all were indignant and some became ill.

During the Middle Ages, the gentry much preferred venison to beef, and today in flossy restaurants pheasant costs much more and among gourmets is considered a greater delicacy than chicken. A Scotch grouse that has been lying around bloody and uncleaned in a pile of other birds for ten days is even more expensive. Years ago in Nogales, Sonora, there was a very good restaurant that always listed venison, antelope, and mountain sheep on the menu. Venison was more expensive than beef, antelope more expensive than venison, and the meat of the mountain ram more expensive than antelope. Tourists used to order these rare morsels, devour them blissfully, and attribute to them all manner of qualities that existed only in their imaginations. All of this exotic meat was simply that of the Coues, or Arizona, whitetail, and if the market hunters who supplied the restaurant didn't come through it was domestic goat. I knew two men who sold deer to the restaurant and I also knew the head waiter.

Most foreigners who visit the United States comment on the excellence of American beef. They consider it far better than the beef available in Europe—and so it is. The reason is that the best American beef comes from mature animals that have been pen fattened, then quickly slaughtered, quickly cleaned, skinned, and cooled, and properly aged. In Europe most of the beef sold is too young to have attained the proper flavor and texture. It has not been penned up and fattened on corn, and it has not been as skillfully slaughtered, cooled, and aged. Often if European beef is not too young it is too old—some farmer's ancient and worn-out milk cow. It is for this reason that so much European beef is served with sauces or in stews.

To be at its best, game must be shot in the late summer or early fall when it is in good condition from the plentiful feed of the lush summer months—and it should also be shot before the rut. Furthermore it should have been eating plants which do not make the meat strong. I have shot several bucks up the Snake River from my Idaho home and I have never shot a bad one. I have also shot several bucks on the Salmon River upstream from the village of Riggins. I have never killed a buck there that was good eating. The reason? It simply has to be what the animals eat. In areas where deer live adjacent to farms and live on wheat and alfalfa they always provide good venison.

Animals domesticated by man do not have the regular annual rutting season like most of the herbivorous creatures of the wild, particularly those of the Temperate zone. In addition, domestic animals destined from birth to be eaten are castrated. In the Northern Hemisphere game animals go through a violent rutting period in the fall, and if they are to furnish good meat they must be shot before this time.

Elk generally start the rut about the middle of September, and so do moose and caribou. The Indians say these animals start rutting with the first full moon in September. Whether the moon has anything to do with the timing of the rut or not I cannot say. However, the timing does vary with the climate and with the gestation period of the animal. In the Rockies the mountain sheep begin to rut in late November and the rut is in full swing the first two weeks of December. Since the sheep have a five-month gestation period, this means that the lambs are generally born in May when new growth is coming on. In the desert the rams start rutting around the last part of August and the first of September so the lambs will be born right after the winter rains.

On the desert the mule deer rut over a month later than their relatives in the mountains, and their rut is in full swing a month later—well into January. The desert whitetails rut still later—or along in February.

In some states it is impossible to get first-rate elk or deer venison because the season opens too late. The flesh of rutting male animals becomes musty and since most of them eat little or not at all during the rut they soon are in poor flesh. A bull elk shot in October after it has been in the rut from two to four or five weeks is thin and the meat is dry and strong. The flesh of most bull moose in the middle of the rut is so strong that anyone trying to cook it will be driven out of the house. Venison from a rutting bull caribou tastes, to me anyway, like the strongest of domestic mutton. I have shot a couple of desert bighorns right at the beginning of the rut in early September, but at that time their meat was untainted and they were still fat. One I shot in late

November after the rut was over was not strong, but he was as lean as a greyhound and as tough as a first baseman's mitt.

Generally sheep offer no problem to the man who wants to bring home some meat, since sheep from Colorado to Alaska are hunted before the rut, from August 1 to October—well before the rut. Most deer rut in November, with the rut well under way toward the last of the month. Deer shot after the rut is in full swing never furnish as good venison as those shot before. Elk and moose are a real problem for the meat hunter. In Idaho the general elk season starts October 1. The rut is in full swing then and the meat of the bulls is past its prime. Within a week or ten days it is strong, lean, and tough. This is why residents shopping for their winter's meat prefer to knock off spike bulls and cows. Late in the rutting period I have even seen strong cow elk.

It is my experience that the best game meat comes from mature animals that are fat and in good flesh and not from young ones, just as steer beef is better than veal. The finest venison and the finest mountain mutton come from old animals that are fat.

I have always felt that the meat of the mountain sheep was the finest in the mountains. Old trophy rams are lazy. They like to lie around in some high basin, drink the pure cold water of little crystal-clear rills, eat the rich tender grass, nibble the fragrant herbs. During the long and bitter winters the rams grow thin, but they quickly fatten up when the snow goes off and the country greens up. Their flesh is new and tender.

However, any prime male animal fattened during the lush summers in the rich pastures above timberline is fine eating. Mule and whitetail deer in good condition and shot on the lowland deserts of Arizona and Sonora also furnish outstanding meat—undoubtedly because of the mild plants on which they feed. Actually, the quality of any meat depends pretty largely on what the animal has been feeding on. A berry-fed black bear or one that has got fat on piñon nuts is good eating (although I have never thought bear tasted like pork), but a bear that has been living on fish or carrion is not fit to eat. But even the finest, most prime game animal can be ruined for the table by improper handling.

Field Dress Game

No big-game hunter should ever go afield without the means of dressing his game. When I am hunting animals the size of deer, sheep, or antelope I simply take an ordinary pocketknife of good quality and a small whetstone. When I am after elk or moose I take along a hatchet and a larger knife—either a stronger and larger knife with a folding blade so it can be carried in the pocket or a "hunting" knife to be worn at the belt.

When a buck is down I turn him over on his back and make a long incision through the skin of the abdomen but taking great care not to cut into the stomach. I continue the incision through the cartilage of the brisket clear up to the neck. This requires a knife with a fairly strong blade and likewise some muscle. I then remove the sexual organs and cut around the anus to free the descending colon. If I have a piece of string I tie this off close to the vent to keep the contents away from the meat. Then I reach up into the neck and cut the windpipe to free the lungs. I cut around the diaphragm where it is attached to the body, cut away where internal organs are attached to the body, pull the descending colon into the abdominal cavity. Care should be taken not to cut or break the bladder or the intestines so the contents will not be scattered through the abdominal cavity. Deer do not have gall bladders but sheep, goats, and antelope do. This should not be damaged. If the animal has been shot through the lungs or heart the whole chest cavity is full of blood. Everything is now loose and ready to dump out. If two hunters are together the animal can be turned over, belly side down, and everything shaken out. If the hunter is alone he can still manage well with a deer-sized animal.

There is a good deal of superstition connected with the dressing of game. Many hunters run up to a dead buck and "stick" him—meaning to jab a knife into his throat. This is supposed to "bleed" him. There is no need to do this, as an animal is sufficiently bled by a properly placed modern bullet. I am convinced that the custom of cutting the tarsal and metatarsal glands out of deer is likewise a worthless ritual. I have cut them out and I have left them in and I cannot see that it makes any difference. It is important, however, to avoid getting the smell on the hands and then handling the meat. I always quickly cut the sexual organs off but I am skeptical if this is as necessary as most people think. It is probably more ritualistic than necessary.

If the head is to be mounted and the scalp, "cape," or "head skin" saved, no cuts should be made in the neck skin at the time of dressing. If the scalp is not to be saved, the hunter should open up the neck and remove the windpipe. Then the pelvis should be cut through so the air can circulate between the hams. This is done most easily with a hatchet, but it can also be done by pounding on the strong blade of a hunting knife with a stone or by the use of a sharp stone alone.

The blood in the body cavity quickly dries and does not taint the meat. Some hunters like to wipe out the cavity with dry grass or with a cloth. The hunter should wash his hands off as well as he can, with water down at the creek, with snow, or with several of the little packages of moistened tissue sold under various brand names. These can be obtained at any drugstore. If there are cuts or abrasions on the hands, game blood sometimes causes a low-grade infection which may be difficult to get rid of.

Dressing an elk or a moose is like dressing a deer except that the elk or moose is much larger. It is possible to cut through the cartilage of a deer or sheep's brisket with a strong-bladed pocketknife, but to do the same job on an elk a hatchet or a saw is needed. One man can turn over a deer or a sheep, pick the carcass up by the legs and shake the body contents out. He cannot do that with an elk, a moose, or a bull caribou.

But whatever we have down—deer, sheep, elk, or moose—we now face the problem of getting the meat to camp and seeing that it does not spoil. If the head is to be mounted, now is the time to remove the head and cape. The cut should be made behind the shoulder so the taxidermist will have plenty of skin to work with. Then a cut should be made along the top of the shoulders and the top of the neck to within a few inches of the horns or antlers. Then the skin should be removed up close to the head, and the neck severed. Care should be taken not to get blood on the scalp.

On the other hand, many hunters are after meat only and have no interest whatsoever in the horns or antlers. If this is the case, the neck can be cut off close to the head and the head thrown away. Many a superb trophy has been left in the hills by meat hunters. One of the finest Dall sheep heads ever taken in the Yukon was shot by a meat-hunting trapper. He told the late Jean Jacquot, pioneer Yukon outfitter, that he had shot a ram with bigger horns than any Jean had. Jean told him that if he would go back and get it, and if indeed it was larger than anything he had, he would give him $50 for it. The head was in the record class.

Packing Out the Carcass

If the hunter has a horse with him, getting this deer or sheep back to camp is easy, as we have seen in the chapter on the hunting horse. If he does not, he is in for some hard work. On a few occasions I have carried the whole carcasses of deer to a road or to camp. One young buck mule deer weighed 145 pounds. One mature whitetail buck weighed probably around 100 pounds. I remember these two particularly because I carried the mule deer about a mile and a half and the whitetail over three miles. At best, any deer is an awkward burden for one man. I remember another time when I carried a big ram head about seven miles on a packboard with a heavy ham in each hand. This was not nearly as awkward a load as a deer carcass, but the combined weight must have been well over 100 pounds. By the time I got to camp I was convinced that both of my arms were about six inches longer than when I had started. I also had a rifle, a pair of binoculars, and a camera.

Probably the best way for one man to pack a deer out is to tie each front leg to a hind leg and make a backpack out of it. Still better is to lash the animal to two poles and make a two-man job out of it. A deer can be dragged on snow without much damage, but if it is dragged on bare ground, hide and meat are damaged.

Many states have laws with severe penalties for leaving game meat in the woods or mountains. I am against waste, but many times game meat is not worth bringing in, and the laws should be enforced with considerable wisdom. Pressure for the passage of such laws always comes from exaggerated tales told about nonresident "head-hunters" by resident meat hunters. Since I have hunted for many years both as a resident and a nonresident, as a meat hunter and a trophy hunter, I know both sides.

Those who hunt big game should always give some thought to the problem of getting the meat out before they start. Those who thoughtlessly shoot an animal where they cannot bring out the meat should be prosecuted. It annoys me to see meat wasted. It also annoys me to see someone shoot a magnificent trophy animal and then discard the head. I have seen hunters shoot magnificent but skinny six-point bull elk out of bunches containing tender and juicy spike bulls—and then throw the heads away.

I have known stout fellas to shoot elk in deep canyons and then pack the meat out quarter by quarter on packboards, but no one who isn't young and tough and hasn't played tackle for the Green Bay Packers should consider doing it. Packing out elk, moose, or caribou is a job for a horse or a dog team—not for a flat-footed, desk-bound hunter with emphysema and varicose veins who is doing well to carry a light rifle as well as his own flabby carcass. In most sections where elk are hunted, packers set up camp and for a fee pack in the meat for those who have connected.

Skinning and Cooling

Generally the hide should be removed from game as soon as possible. The carcass should be cut into quarters and hung where circulating air can cool the meat and cause a dry rind to form. This protects the meat from blow flies and from contamination. If it is not feasible to skin an animal at once, it should either be hung up or laid over a log or a large stone with the belly cavity propped open so that the air can circulate and the meat can cool. If an animal is left on the ground, the heat is held in and putrefaction can start quickly.

This is particularly important in the case of large animals like elk and moose. The quicker the insulating hide is off and the quarters are hung up to start cooling, the better. Under no circumstances should a large animal be left overnight before it is skinned, quartered, and hung up. If it is, there's a very grave danger that the meat will sour.

The large animals have to be skinned as they lie on the ground. This is something of a chore. To skin the smaller animals, I like to hang the carcass up head down and start skinning at the first joint of the hind legs. The quicker an animal is skinned, the easier the job is. Much of the work of skinning can be done on a warm carcass by pulling the hide off with one hand and jamming a blunt instrument or the stiffened fingers of the other hand between hide and flesh. Once the hide is off, the neck is severed just behind the head and the carcass is sawed in half with a meat saw or with an ordinary carpenter's saw. Then the halves are cut in two.

Most sporting goods stores in game country sell "meat sacks" made of rough cotton cloth, and these can be put around the quarters to protect them from dust and flies when the meat is thoroughly chilled and the dry rind has formed on the outside. Keeping meat dry is almost as important as keeping it cool. The carcass of a moose or an elk tends to sour quickly if left out overnight in the rain—not only because rain is usually accompanied by warmer weather but because the meat is wet.

Once meat is thoroughly cool it can be kept for a surprisingly long time. I have kept deer and sheep carcasses in the Sonora desert when the days were quite warm until they were eaten up. In the morning I would wrap the quarters in canvas to keep them from warming up, and at night I would unwrap them so the night air would chill them.

What many people call the "gamey taste" is simply a sign of poorly cared for meat—the taint of the juices from the paunch and intestines that have covered the meat, the beginning of putrefaction because an animal has not been properly dressed and cooled. How good would the meat of the finest grain-fed beef steer be if the animal were shot three times through the stomach and intestines, terrorized, and then chased for three miles? How good would it be if the butcher then cut both stomach and intestines in dressing it out and let the juices and contents flow over the meat? Then let us suppose the butcher did not remove the hide and quarter the animal at once, but instead let it hang, part of the time in hot sun, for a couple of days while the flies crawled over it. Then to wind up, let us suppose our butcher put his steer, still wearing hide and head, over the hot hood of a truck and drove through dust and gasoline fumes for 200 miles or so before he skinned, quartered, and cooled it. The steer would then be as "gamey" as the worst deer you ever ate!

The hunter should likewise remember that just as beef is not at its best until it has been aged, neither is game meat. Too many hunters not only do not skin, quarter, and chill their game, but they deliver the carcass to a locker plant to be skinned, cut up, packaged, and frozen at once. The best beef that was killed and not allowed to age would be tough. Ideally meat should be hung in a cool place for a week or so before it is eaten or frozen.

Thoroughly chilled and dry quarters can be transported a great distance by automobile if the hunter keeps it cool. One method is to wrap a couple of quarters in a sleeping bag. At night it should be taken out, hung up, and allowed to cool again. Some meat does not keep well. The fat on sheep meat, for example, turns rancid. Bringing meat long distances by plane or train seldom works out, as the meat often gets too warm at airports between planes. If meat is once frozen it must be kept frozen or it will quickly spoil once it has thawed out.

Cooking Game

The finest and best cared for game meat can be ruined by poor cooking, just as good beef can likewise be ruined. Hell is too good for the sloppy cook who throws delicious venison or mountain sheep mutton into a pan filled with lukewarm grease and then boils it over low heat until it tastes like stale liver. Another pet gripe of mine is the cook who covers the flavor of choice cuts of venison or sheep meat with onions, garlic, and chile. I grew up in the Southwest and am as fond of chile con carne as any Mexican, but stews and mulligans can be made of the lesser cuts.

I like to pan broil chops or back strap (filet mignon) of mountain sheep or deer by cooking crisp a few pieces of bacon in a good thick frying pan that will hold the heat. The bacon grease should be so hot it smokes. Meat from 1 to 1½ inches thick, cooked in a *hot* pan until each side is brown and crisp, will come out medium to medium rare. The small amount of *hot* grease seals the flavor in the meat.

If I want to be fancy I fry the chops in butter, then set them over near the fire in a pan to keep hot. I then put a small can of mushrooms with the juice in the pan I have used, another lump of butter, a teaspoonful of meat extract, a dash of Worcestershire sauce, salt and pepper. Then I pour the sauce over the chops and serve. Country fried venison, milk gravy, and bannock or biscuits eaten by the campfire is a memorable dish. I like to cut round steak thin, flour it, and fry it in a Dutch oven or in a large, heavy frying pan with about one-half inch of hot lard in the bottom.

One of the choice dishes of the far North is roast sheep ribs. The Indians put a stick through the rib section of a Dall or Stone ram and thrust the sharpened end into the ground close enough to get the heat, far enough away to stay out of the smoke. Now and then they turn it. For the sparerib fancier this is a feast for the gods.

In general, good big-game meat should be treated like good beef, but venison in particular is drier than beef and roasts should be larded with strips of beef tallow or the finished product is apt to be pretty dry. The time to get fancy with game is when the animal was shot during or just after the rut. Then the meat is not very choice and the cook can marinate it in wine or lemon juice, cook it with onions, garlic, and chile, grind it up and mix it with pork and spices for sausage. There are many cook books to which one can refer, some devoted exclusively to game cookery.

The Trophy

One of the services performed by most outfitters is the skinning out and preparation of the scalps or head skins so they can be used for mounting the horns or antlers. In a pack outfit, the job is generally done by the horse wrangler, as once he has rounded up the horses that are to be ridden he doesn't have much to do but get wood and water—and work on the trophies.

The hunter who shoots a deer or some other game animal near his home can leave the head and scalp on the hide and have the taxidermist finish the skinning job. However, in many cases the hunter himself should skin out and preserve the scalp—or the complete hide in the case of a bear or a cougar.

To be sure that there is plenty of hide for the taxidermist to work with, it is generally best to start the cut for the scalp just in front of the forelegs, then up to the top of the shoulders, and around. Some skinners start the cut back of the forelegs to make certain there is plenty of hide for a shoulder mount. Then a cut should be made from the top of the shoulder along the top of the neck to a point about three or four inches from the antlers. Then a cut should be made to the middle of each horn or antler, leaving a flap of skin in the form of a "V."

The next step is to cut around the horns or antlers carefully. Coloman Jonas, the famous Denver taxidermist, has recommended the use of a large screwdriver to pry the skin away from the antlers without cutting. The ears should be cut off close to the skull and the hide removed slowly and carefully from the skull. Great care should be taken in skinning around the eyes and the lips. If the scalp will not go to a taxidermist for some time, one should remove the cartilage in each ear and the ear should be turned inside out and salted. However, this is a pretty delicate operation and any amateur skinner should watch the job done before he tries it himself.

Skinning out a head is a fairly delicate operation, but there is nothing very difficult about it if the skinner is willing to be slow and careful and avoid cutting through the hide. All loose flesh should be removed. The scalp should then be thoroughly salted and folded up for a half day or so.

Then it should be pulled taut and resalted so that the salt gets to every part of it and there are no creases or folds that the salt does not reach. The scalp with the salt on it should be spread out on a bush, a limb, or on a rope strung between two trees to dry in the shade. The salt draws the moisture out of the scalp and in a few days it is hard and bone dry and in good shape for the taxidermist. It is best to send scalp and horns or antlers to the taxidermist as soon as possible. American taxidermists use papier-maché forms and not the skull, so the skull can be sawn through, leaving only a portion with horns or antlers attached.

Large hides of bears, moose, and other animals should have every bit of flesh and fat removed. They should be salted at least twice, stretched, and dried in the shade. If fat is left on, it forms an acid which causes the hair to slip, just as putrefaction likewise causes it to slip. When a hide is about dry but still flexible it should be folded hair side in and tied up for transporting.

Very thick hides are thinned by scraping or by crosshatching with a knife and then thinning off the little chunks of hide. Then the thinned skin is salted. If this is not done, very thick skins will decay, even if salted, as the salt cannot reach down deep. Walrus hide is very thick and so is the skin of elephants, rhinos, and various African antelopes which fight with sharp horns.

American taxidermy is the world's best, but some reasonably good taxidermy is done in England, in Continental Europe, by a firm in Nairobi, Kenya, and on tigers by one firm in India. In Europe many trophies of horned and antlered game are not mounted with scalps. Instead the skulls are bleached white and skulls and horns are mounted on hardwood plaques. To an American this looks a bit ghastly at first but by the time I had seen such mounts in luxurious British, Continental, and Indian houses I began to feel it was quite elegant. I have some trophies so mounted.

28 | *How To Judge Big-Game Trophies*

In 1951 my son Bradford, two friends, and I went on a thirty-day big-game hunt in the Atlin section of northwestern British Columbia. At that time, if I remember correctly, the sheep and bear season opened well ahead of that on moose and caribou. One afternoon almost at the end of our hunt we took the packtrain over a high piece of country above timberline toward a new campsite on the other side of the mountains. The caribou were rutting, but the season would not open until the next day. Several times two big bull caribou, one with a magnificent set of antlers, came trotting up to our horses, apparently thinking the packhorses were cow caribou.

Bradford was then eighteen and he had never shot a caribou. He was dying to knock the big bull off and furious at me because I refused to let him do so. I told him that since we were going to camp near a road that night we might run into a mounted policeman, and that if we had an illegal caribou I'd be the guy who got in trouble.

After we had made camp, one of the guides with whom Bradford was very friendly told him he knew of a basin where he had always seen bull caribou at the beginning of the rut, but to get there they would have to walk ten miles in and ten miles out. Was Bradford game? He was!

They left long before dawn. After dark they came staggering in, dead tired but carrying a very fine caribou head. I turned the flashlight on it, took one good look, and told Bradford that it was better than any caribou head I had ever taken and probably better than any I had ever seen. I added that I thought he should win the first prize for mountain caribou in that year's Boone & Crockett contest. He did. The head was No. 5 in the 1952 edition of *Records of North American Big Game* and it is still No. 20 even in the 1964 book.

In 1955 I walked into the sporting goods store owned by George Pfeffer at Grangeville, Idaho, and George told me that he had a good elk head in the back room and he'd like to have me look at it. The instant I saw it I told him I thought it would be in the first ten in the world records. It was still No. 4 in the 1964 book.

In 1950 when Herb Klein and I were hunting Dall sheep in the Yukon he rode into camp at dusk one evening with the head and scalp of a very fine ram tied on behind his saddle. He had not measured it as he had not taken a tape measure with him. I guessed its longest horn would go 47. When we put the tape on it a few minutes later it went 47½, and today, although it has shrunk somewhat as all sheep heads do, the longest horn measures 46⅝.

All of these were pretty good guesses. How was I able to make them? By the use of trained and experienced eyes! And I think there is only one way to train the eyes in the judgment of big-game trophies—and that is by seeing many sets of horns and antlers and by intelligently evaluating them. In thinking about this chapter and talking it over with Bill Sill, the editor of the Outdoor Life book department, it was decided to depend as much on pictures as on words so we are illustrating here three types of heads of the principal species—immature, average mature, and exceptional. Anyone who wants to learn to judge heads quickly and with reasonable accuracy should study these pictures and read the accompanying text. However, of the two the pictures are more important. He should also look critically at all the game heads he encounters—in habitat groups in museums, in sporting goods stores, in homes of friends. Anyone can read about horns and antlers until he gets spots before his eyes but unless he has seen and compared many heads and knows what an exceptional head looks like evaluating trophies is a laborious business.

The first time anyone hunts a new species he simply cannot judge the heads unless he has done a good deal of homework such as I am now suggesting. Reading helps, but *seeing* is the important thing. Let us suppose that a young man grew up on a South Pacific island and had never seen a Caucasian woman or even a picture of one. Then let us further suppose that at the age of twenty-one he was to visit the United States for the first time and meet women of his own race. Let us also suppose this young man of ours wanted to learn how he could tell a beautiful girl from an ordinary one or from a downright homely one. He could read about the size of eyes among beautiful Caucasian females, the proportion of head to body, of length to width of face, the preferred shape of lips. All of these words would not mean nearly as much to him, however, as a few pictures, and in turn pictures would be less helpful than seeing some young Caucasian females in the flesh. If, let us say, he were shown some poor homely girl with small eyes, protruding teeth, greasy hair, and thick ankles, then the girl next door with adequate but not outstanding endowments, and then some gorgeous creature like Virna Lisi or Gina Lollobrigida, he would rapidly get the message.

And so it is with the judgment of trophies—a moderate amount of intelligent seeing is worth a great many words.

I'll never forget the first bull caribou I saw. I had never laid eyes on a caribou, even in a zoo. I had seen only two or three not-very-good mounted heads. Apparently the pictures I had seen had made little impression on me. My guide and I rode down into a strip of timber that fringed a little stream in a timberline basin in the Alberta Rockies. A bull caribou about three years old ran out. To my excited eyes his antlers looked tremendous and I was all for knocking him off. My guide told me not to shoot, and the bull ran off seventy-five yards or so and stopped. "Look him over," my guide told me. "He's the kind of bull not to shoot except for meat." I could hardly believe it. A few days later I killed my first bull caribou from a camp at the head of Copton Creek right at the crest of the Rockies and near the Alberta-British Columbia boundary. By the time the trip was over and I had seen seventy-five or so bulls, I realized my first trophy was only an average mature bull. Within a few years I had seen hundreds of others—in the Yukon and in northern British Columbia—and I was able to tell at once if a caribou was immature, a fair average, or outstanding.

To me one of the rules of trophy hunting is that to the man who knows something about the various animals, the really outstanding head knocks his eye out. He doesn't have to look at it hard and long to know it is good, just as a young man would not have to study a beautiful girl for some time to realize she was pretty. The heads that do not turn out well are the ones the hunter thinks about, hopes are good, tries to make grow, looks for an excuse to take.

The big ones always look big!

The Whitetail Deer

I do not think there is any doubt but that the whitetail deer is the smartest of all North American game animals, and I am likewise convinced that getting a really outstanding whitetail head is the most difficult task in trophy collecting.

There are many reasons for this. In the first place, the whitetail is generally an animal of forest and brush. When he is seen he is more often than not on the move and the hunter generally has to shoot quick or not at all. He has little time to size up a head.

Another reason is that a great many whitetails are found close to large centers of population and they are hunted hard by people who shoot at the first glimpse of an antler. Consequently, not many whitetail bucks live to become fully mature—and members of the deer family have their largest antlers when they are from five to eight years old.

Still another reason is that in many areas whitetail deer have been allowed to become too plentiful and they have overbrowsed their range. Fawns born of half-starved mothers do not become large and to grow large antlers deer have to eat food rich in protein and lime.

One pleasant thought is that good whitetail heads seem to come from just about every state where these beautiful deer are found, and the hunter wanting to collect an outstanding specimen would not have to go far from home. Actually, a high percentage of outstanding heads come from thickly populated agricultural areas where the bucks feed on nourishing crops from fertile land.

The present (1966) world-record Virginia whitetail comes from Minnesota, the No. 2 from New York, the No. 3 from Saskatchewan, the No. 4 from Montana, the No. 5 from Texas, the No. 6 from South Dakota, the No. 7 from Saskatchewan, the No. 8 from North Dakota, the No. 9 from Arkansas, and the No. 10 from Tennessee.

In the first 100 heads there are more from Saskatchewan than from any other state or province. I am surprised that there aren't more big heads recorded from the Black Hills of Wyoming. When I have driven through there I have seen many very good whitetail antlers nailed up on barns and filling stations. I have seen very good heads that have been shot in Idaho, Washington, and British Columbia. One reason for the scarcity of Northwestern whitetail heads in the record book may be that in these states they are largely shot by meat hunters.

The normal Virginia whitetail buck may be a spike or a forkhorn his first year, a forkhorn or a small three-pointer (eight-pointer by Eastern count). When the whitetail buck is mature the normal head has the brow tine or eye guard and four points. Easterners call this a ten-pointer, Westerners a four-pointer. Two characteristics that make whitetail antlers different from those of mule deer are that all of the points on whitetail antlers grow off of a main beam and the normal whitetail head has a large and prominent brow tine. On the other hand, normal mule deer antlers are dichotomous or evenly branched and the brow tine is smaller and is sometimes missing altogether. The Pacific Coast blacktail has antlers similar to those of a mule deer.

JUDGING WHITETAIL DEER

Forkhorn

IMMATURE

At least 4 points;
tines longer;
antlers heavier

Spread extends
beyond body

AVERAGE MATURE

The Arizona whitetail, a smaller relative of the Virginia whitetail, differs in that the antlers of a normal mature buck have three points and an eye guard. However, any species of North American deer may grow a great many points. My wife and I once collaborated on a whitetail buck with eighteen points in all.

Any mature whitetail buck is a very respectable trophy, and any buck with relatively massive antlers and five points to a side is a very good trophy. If Lady Luck ever sends a record-class whitetail in your direction you'll know it as he will look to be all antlers.

Sometimes whitetail antlers freak badly. They palmate, twist, turn, grow an enormous number of irregular points. Incidentally, a point is not "anything you can hang a ring on" as some believe, but instead must be an inch long. I think these freak heads are ugly and would not be caught dead getting one mounted, but some like them.

Getting a record whitetail is very difficult to manage, as even in good

328

4 or more points, massive antlers

Well-developed brow tines

EXCEPTIONAL

country one does not see many mature bucks in a season to shoot at, and he must size up those he does see in a few seconds. Most of the outstanding Virginia whitetail heads I have seen taken have been knocked off by meat hunters who would no more think of getting a head mounted than they would of lighting a cigarette with a $20 bill. You can't get a record whitetail unless you are lucky.

I have shot more of the small variety of whitetails called the Arizona whitetail, Sonora whitetail, fantail, or scientifically, *Odocoileus virginianus couesi*, than I have of any other game animal. I used to shoot a buck every fall in Arizona and for a good many years I lived close to the Sonora border when bag limits were generous and were even more generously interpreted. In spite of the fact that at least three-fourths of the bucks I shot were fully mature four-point bucks or better, I have only shot one that was well up in the record class—and I no longer have that head.

The Mule Deer

Whereas the whitetail is found from Arizona to Maine and from Florida to Washington, the mule deer's territory is much more limited. He ranges west of the Mississippi from eastern Montana to southern California and from west Texas to Washington. The Columbian blacktail deer is listed separately in *Records of North American Big Game,* but his antlers are dichotomous (evenly branched) as are those of the mule deer, and the blacktail is now considered simply a variety of mule deer. His range is low but narrow, as he is found west of the summit of the Coast Range and on the islands off the coast from southeast Alaska to the latitude of San Francisco.

In *Records of North American Big Game* there are two classifications of mule deer heads—typical and nontypical—and a world record is listed for each. Of the two kinds, the nontypical antlers with their many points and often great mass are far handsomer and more interesting.

As is the case with the whitetail, good mule deer heads are found pretty generally all over their range, wherever their browse contains the right combination of lime and protein and where the bucks are not shot before they mature. Arizona's Kaibab Forest north of the Grand Canyon used to produce some great mule deer heads, as the area is one great plateau of solid limestone, but poor management has resulted in too many deer, not enough browse, and many hunters mean that most of the bucks are killed before they get a chance to grow outstanding antlers.

Of the first ten mule deer in the list of typical heads in the 1964 record book, three (including the No. 1) were shot in Wyoming, four in Colorado, and one each in Idaho, New Mexico, and Arizona. In the nontypical list, one (the world record) is from Alberta, two are from Colorado, two from New Mexico, two from Utah, and one each from Wyoming and Nevada, and one is listed only as coming from the Rocky Mountains.

Some excellent mule deer heads used to come out of the lava-bed country around Mt. Lassen in northern California, but for many years the area has swarmed with hunters and the bucks there have been shot about as soon as they started showing antlers. The subspecies which lives farther south and is known as the California mule deer is small and does not grow large antlers.

It is rare that a good head comes from any area that is easily accessible and is pounded hard by hunters, but since most deer hunters are not found far from automobile roads there is still plenty of good mule deer country where the enterprising head hunter can go in with a backpack or a little pack outfit.

O'Connor with the best desert mule deer he ever shot. This head is quite heavy, with seven points on one side, six on the other.

JUDGING MULE DEER

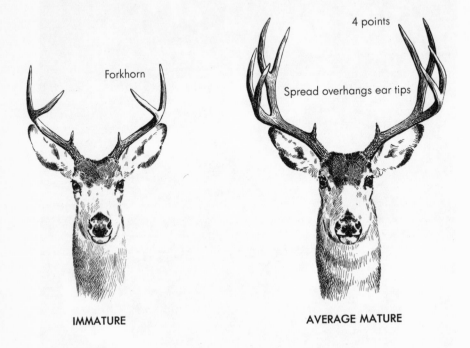

Forkhorn

4 points

Spread overhangs ear tips

IMMATURE

AVERAGE MATURE

Like the whitetail, the yearling mule deer is generally a spike but may be a forkhorn. With rich food and plenty of it he may grow four points and a brow tine his second fall. Antlers reach the maximum size between the fifth and eighth years. Warty, many-pointed heads are generally grown by deer past their prime. Antlers of very old deer become small and now and then go back to large two-point antlers. If something happens to the sex glands of deer, either through an accident or the degeneration of old age, the antlers often grow many random points and sometimes never shed the velvet.

Barbershop biologists like nothing better than to invent new species of deer and bear. In Arizona these scientists used to declare that there were two species of mule deer in the state. One was the "regular blacktail deer" (this was the name the old-timers gave the mule deer) and the other was the mule deer or "mule-tailed deer," sometimes called the "bench-legged deer." One of these species (I have forgotten which) had high antlers with little spread and it was generally conceded by these

4 or more points

Massive antlers

EXCEPTIONAL

naturalists that they were part elk. The other species was marked by antlers with wide spreads.

Of course, close-pinched and wide-spread antlers are found wherever there are mule deer. The handsomest and the most spectacular are the antlers with the wide spreads, and the average hunter ranks mule deer antlers by the spread. As far as official ranking goes, spread is of little importance, and if the spread exceeds the length of the main beam there is a penalty attached. Over thirty years ago in northern Arizona I shot a mule deer with a 37½-inch spread. I doubt if the main beam was over 26 or 27 inches. It was a far handsomer head than another one I shot in 1932 with a main beam of about 28½ inches.

For the sake of the records the important measurements are the length of the main beam, the number and length of points, and the symmetry. An Eastern hunter wanting to take home a mule deer trophy should hold out for a good average mature buck with five points, counting brow tine, on each side. If he should be fortunate enough to bump into a record-

JUDGING ELK

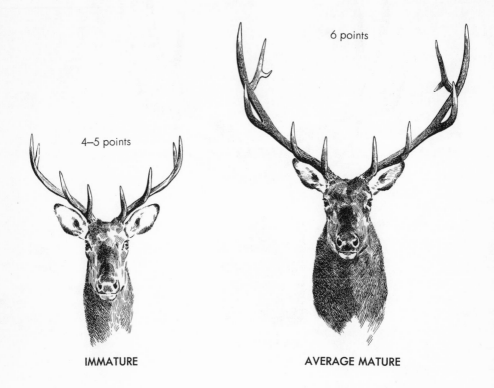

6 points

4–5 points

IMMATURE   AVERAGE MATURE

class head, particularly one of the nontypical sort with the wide spread, he will know it, as the buck will look "all horns." If there is any doubt about the head's being outstanding, it isn't. Study the illustrations.

The Elk

The American "elk" or, more properly, *wapiti* is related to the red deer of Europe, north Africa, and the Middle East, and to the Siberian and Mongolian wapitis, which look so much like the North American elk that most hunters could not tell the difference. But the red-deer–wapiti tribe reaches its greatest size and produces the best antlers in North America. Our elk is the largest round-antlered deer in the world.

The same conditions that produce large deer antlers also produce large elk antlers—rich food and the opportunity to mature. As is the case with the mule deer, elk are hunted very hard in areas that can be reached

Large royal points

6 points or more

Massive antlers

Heavy beams and points

Long brow tines,
extend almost to tip of nose

EXCEPTIONAL

by automobile road or by a short pack trip, but there are vast areas of wilderness back country difficult to get into where the big deer are seldom hunted.

Of the first ten elk heads in the 1964 record book, one (the record) is from Colorado, four from Montana, two from Alberta, and one each from Idaho, Arizona, and Wyoming. I think that if I were after a record head I would try to find some spot in the southern Alberta or British Columbia Rockies where there was little hunting.

When a bull elk is a long yearling he is a spike. As a long two-year-old he has five points to a side. The next year he grows his first pair of six-point antlers. The normal elk head is always a six-pointer. The antlers grow larger until the bull is seven or eight years old. Then they generally start to deteriorate. They grow smaller but often have more points. Probably the finest, most spectacular, and highest-scoring heads come from seven- and eight-year-old bulls. Of the first ten heads in the records

These hunters have a young six-point bull elk. He's fine meat but by no means a remarkable trophy.

only one is a six-pointer. Five have seven points on one side, eight on the other, one has nine and eight, three, seven and seven.

Bulls with more than six points are actually quite rare, and bulls with deformed and freak heads are rarer still. I have never seen such a head in the hills, and of the twenty or so bull elk I have shot only one had more than six points.

No one wanting a trophy should ever shoot a five-pointer. It is not necessary to count the points because the five-point heads are always short and have a flattened-out appearance something like the antlers of a deer. For the beginning elk hunters, the foolers are the small six-point heads grown by bulls in their fourth and fifth year. To be a real trophy the main beams of elk antlers should be at least four feet long and the nearer they approach five feet the better. If the hunter has time to look the head over (and in many areas this is possible since bulls are often found above timberline and habitually come out to feed early and late in open parks), he should note that the length of the beam approaches the height from ground to shoulder, that if the bull puts his head back the tips of the antlers come almost to the hips, that *all* the points are large and well developed. If a head looks like this it is a real trophy. If it looks long and

336

heavy and has more than six points it is very, very exceptional. For a quick check in the timber where a man must shoot instantly or not at all the most important criterion is length. If the antlers tower far over the elk's head or come back to his fanny when he lifts his head to go through the brush, crack him. He's worth shooting!

The Antelope

The American pronghorn antelope is a very odd creature, an animal with characteristics shared by many other hoofed animals but closely related to no other living animal. All of the close relatives of the pronghorn died off in North America during the Ice Age.

The horns of the antelope are branched like those of a deer, but they are true horns—the only branched *horns* in the animal world. Like the antlers of deer, the horns are shed annually but they are made of hair and it is the sheath that is shed—not the core. The fact that the core is always in evidence has led many to believe that antelope do not shed their horns. The doe antelope also have horns but they are very small and almost never noticed at a distance.

An antelope head makes a handsome and interesting trophy, particularly in states that have no antelope and no antelope hunting. However, I have seen hunters who drove from the East all the way out to Wyoming for a trophy antelope and have settled for some poor little two-year-old.

As is the case when a hunt is planned for any other trophy, the would-be antelope hunter should carefully study the pictures in this book, read the text, and in addition he should look carefully and critically at every mounted antelope head he sees.

Actually, the horns of buck antelope are very easy to classify. Those of an immature buck do not give the impression of blackness. If the hunter gets a good look at them they appear rounded, unfinished. The prong is not prominent or well developed.

The horns of a mature buck are much more massive. The prong is well developed and conspicuous. They look *black*. They project far beyond the ears. If the hunter gets a good chance to look over a buck with a high-powered binocular or a spotting scope he should notice the tips. Sometimes they are not greatly curved. At other times they are curved on the ends like fishhooks and are ivory tipped. Estimating how far the horns project above the ears doesn't do too much good because many handsome heads have much of their length in the hook. A horn that looks very black, looks heavy and massive at the base, has a well-developed prong and a pronounced hook, and with a length approaching that of the face, is a very good head. Anyone who looks for these characteristics and who does not shoot until he sees such a head will get a

JUDGING PRONGHORN ANTELOPE

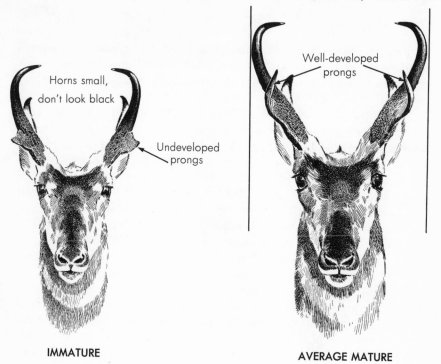

Horns larger, project far beyond ears, look black

Well-developed prongs

Horns small, don't look black

Undeveloped prongs

IMMATURE

AVERAGE MATURE

perfectly satisfactory trophy with a horn length around the curve of from fourteen to fifteen inches.

Most mature buck antelope have horns measuring about 13 to $14\frac{1}{2}$ inches. In any fairly good antelope country anyone content to wait a while and not shoot until he sees something that looks pretty good should be able to come home with a trophy in this class.

Any head with a well-developed prong and over 15 inches in length is a very good head and one to be proud of. If it is massive enough and has a good enough prong, it stands a good chance to get in the record book. Anyone who has seen some antelope heads and is lucky enough to run into a real buster will know it immediately. As is the case with almost any other trophy of top quality, the horns jump out and hit you in the eye.

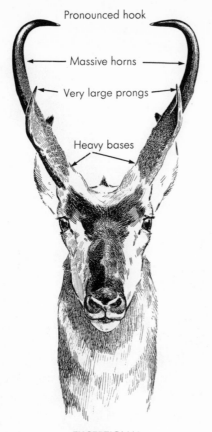

Pronounced hook

Massive horns

Very large prongs

Heavy bases

EXCEPTIONAL

Any head with a curve of 17 inches is very, very good. I have never shot such a head, but my wife's first antelope had a long prong, a heavy base, and well-hooked horns tipped with ivory and 17¼ inches long. A heavy well-developed head that is 18 inches around the curve is getting right up there. The longest I see in the current record book is an old Arizona head that was shot on the desert near Oracle, Arizona, back in 1899. It is 20⅛ and 20.

In the early 1930's on Anderson Mesa about thirty miles from Flagstaff, Arizona, there were about 5,000 antelope and many of them were ancient, mossy-horned, and arthritic old bucks. They were not wild and I used to spend a lot of time watching them. I saw several that I am sure would have measured between 19 and 21 inches and one that I thought would measure almost 24. None of these old bucks were harvested.

Eleanor O'Connor with an exceedingly fine antelope head. The top of the horn is deeply hooked, the tip ivory-colored, and the prongs are well-developed. This head measured 17½ inches.

The season remained closed and all the old antelope died off during some bad winters. When the season was finally opened some fine heads were taken, but none as good as those worn by several of my old friends that had died of cold and old age. It was during the first season on Anderson Mesa that my wife shot her 17¼-inch head. A friend of ours got a buck with an 18½-inch head but it was his first antelope and he was so innocent that he did not realize what an outstanding trophy he had. The *average* of the heads that came through a checking station when I was around was about sixteen inches.

Good antelope heads come from areas where the food grows horns and where a reasonable number of bucks have time to grow old. Some areas seem never to produce big heads. I used to take a crack at an antelope now and then in northwest Sonora and I never saw one there with a good head. On the other hand the belt of antelope that runs midway across Arizona and New Mexico produces more than its share of big heads and it is my impression that the antelope there are larger in body and heavier than the Wyoming antelope. The No. 1, No. 2, and No. 3 antelope heads in the record book are from Arizona and the No. 6 is from New Mexico. Of the top ten, four are from Wyoming, but Wyoming has the largest herd of antelope in the United States and many thousands are shot there each year. Most reasonably mature Wyoming bucks have horns that run from 13 to 14 inches.

Freak heads are fairly common among antelope. Sometimes the horns grow almost straight out from the head and sometimes one horn will grow out but the other will be normal. Occasionally one horn will twist around toward one eye. Most freak antelope heads are ugly and should be avoided by the trophy hunter.

The Mountain Sheep

The mounted head of a good trophy mountain sheep is generally conceded to be the best trophy in North America. There are two species of sheep on this continent and for the purpose of record-keeping they are divided into four subspecies. The snow-white Dall sheep (*Ovis dalli dalli*) found in Alaska and the western Yukon and the dark Stone sheep (*Ovis dalli stoeni*) found in British Columbia form one species but two subspecies. They are listed separately in the record books. In extreme northern British Columbia and south and east of the Yukon River in the Yukon the sheep are transitional between the true white Dall and the dark Stone. Very light and very dark sheep are found in the same bunch, and in which classification a particular ram would belong to would be open to argument.

Americans are great subdividers and classifiers, and several subspecies of desert sheep and bighorns (*Ovis canadensis* and its variations) have been listed. For the sake of the records, however, there are only two classifications: the desert sheep of Lower California, Chihuahua, Sonora, Southern California, Arizona, and Nevada and the bighorn sheep of Colorado, Wyoming, Idaho, British Columbia, Alberta, and Montana. A mature ram of any species is a trophy to be proud of, but a good desert ram is generally rated as the top sheep trophy because these animals are not common, permits to hunt them are difficult to obtain, and hunting desert rams is very hard work. The next most difficult ram trophy to obtain is the bighorn. The Stones and Dalls are somewhat easier to collect and are more plentiful, but getting a good ram of any species is generally an exceedingly laborious task.

Back about 1949 the late Grancel Fitz wrote a magazine article called "A Grand Slam on Sheep." In it he made the statement that only five men had ever shot all four varieties of North American sheep and that anyone who had done this had made a "grand slam." He further stated that when Ernest von Lengerke had shot a Dall in the Yukon and I had shot a couple of Stones in northern British Columbia in 1946 we became the third and fourth hunters ever to accomplish the feat. Actually he did not know about Dr. Wilson du Comb, a small-town Illinois physician, who got a grand slam by shooting a desert sheep in Sonora about 1945. Charles Sheldon and Wilson Potter, the first two men to turn the trick, have long since been dead and Ernest von Lengerke has joined them.

Fitz's article filled hundreds of hunters with the ambition to get a grand slam, and in the spring of 1966 somewhere around 100 hunters had taken the four varieties. Some of the heads that have made up these "slams," however, are a long way from being in the trophy class.

There are three types of mature sheep heads in North America—the wide spread, the close curl, and the argali type, which pinches in toward the jaw and then flares out. All three types of heads are found among the various subspecies but rams with very close curls are most common among the desert and bighorn sheep, and wide spreads and argali-type heads among the Dalls and Stones.

A very high proportion of old rams of whatever species have horns with rubbed or broken points. Rams with close-curled horns that come up past their eyes and block their side vision, rub the points on rock to shorten them so they can see. Often the horns are rubbed down so far the core shows. Among the sheep heads in my trophy room, every close-curled head has rubbed points. Rams also break points off by bumping them against rocks accidentally. In 1963 my wife shot a magnificent 44-inch Dall ram with an argali-type head in the Yukon. Apparently the ram had taken a bad tumble not long before. A piece of horn about four inches long on one side was so badly cracked it would have fallen off in a day or two and the ram's ribs and shoulder on one side were terribly bruised.

Horns that do not block the side vision are sometimes broken accidentally but are never rubbed. Both the wide-spreading and argali-type sheep horns do not block the side vision and many such heads have perfect points even on very old rams. Since the horns of the Rocky Mountain bighorn are most often of the close-curl type, they are generally rubbed. I have seen them rubbed down until they are three inches wide at the tips. The best North American ram I have ever shot was a very fine Dall of the argali type. His horns showed thirteen annual rings but the points are perfect, since his horns never blocked his side vision. Some inexperienced sheep hunters set great store by perfect points, but if a head is of the close-curl type perfect points are always a sign of a young ram and an immature head.

In the past, Dall and Stone sheep have been called the "thinhorns," and it is true that the horns average smaller in diameter than do those of the bighorns. However, the horns of both Stones and Dalls often have very respectable bases. I have shot one Dall and one Stone that had bases with diameters of over 15 inches when killed and today many years later still measure just under 15. In the old days one heard many tales of bighorn heads with 18- and even 19-inch bases but most of such heads were improperly measured. A head with a 16-inch base measured thoroughly *dry* is actually very big and was probably around 17 when killed. One Canadian bighorn and one desert bighorn in the 1964 edition of *Records of North American Big Game* have base measurements of 17 inches. The largest base on a Dall sheep I can find is $14\frac{7}{8}$ and the largest base on a Stone is $15\frac{1}{8}$. Most Dall horns have a heavy ridge around the top edge and are somewhat triangular in cross-section whereas those of the various bighorns are oval. However, oval horns are also found among the Stones. Horns are made of hair material, whereas antlers are bone, and there is a direct relationship between the hair on the head of a sheep and the horn color. The horns of the snow-white Dall are when clean a faded lemon yellow. The horns of Stones are light to medium brown, and those of bighorns are dark brown.

Every ram carries on his horns a record of his life and loves. In the lush late spring, summer, and early fall there is food aplenty and the ram's horns grow rapidly. Comes the rut in late November and December. The ram eats almost not at all. He goes into the winter lean and hungry and his horns grow very slowly. When the snow leaves and the new growth begins, the ram eats, takes it easy, and his horns again grow. A ram's age can be told by the annual rings. However, it is sometimes not too easy to tell some seasonal rings from the annual rings, particularly with desert sheep as the seasons in the south are less marked. In addition, horn growth slows down on an old ram and the growth rings of the last

JUDGING BIGHORN SHEEP

Horns thin   Flat, shallow curve

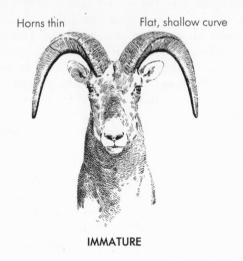

IMMATURE

Heavy bases

Deep curve

Close curl

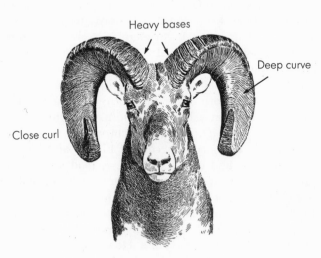

AVERAGE MATURE

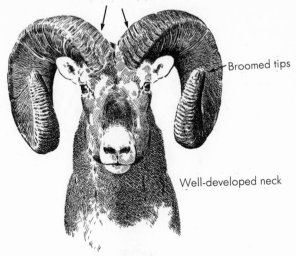

Very heavy bases

Broomed tips

Well-developed neck

EXCEPTIONAL

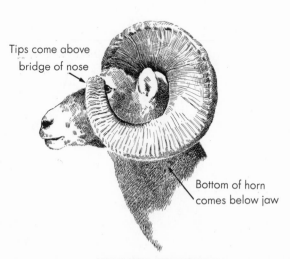

Tips come above
bridge of nose

Bottom of horn
comes below jaw

SIDE VIEW, EXCEPTIONAL

JUDGING DALL SHEEP

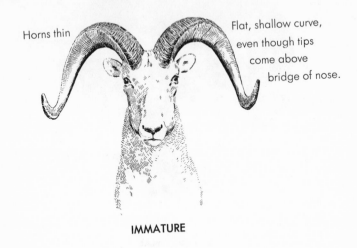

Horns thin

Flat, shallow curve,
even though tips
come above
bridge of nose.

IMMATURE

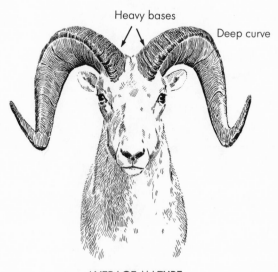

Heavy bases

Deep curve

AVERAGE MATURE

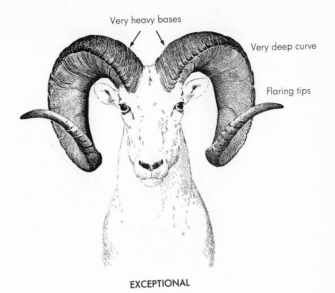

Very heavy bases

Very deep curve

Flaring tips

EXCEPTIONAL

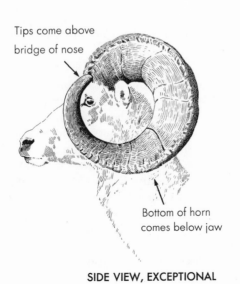

Tips come above
bridge of nose

Bottom of horn
comes below jaw

SIDE VIEW, EXCEPTIONAL

A magnificent desert bighorn ram shot in Sonora, Mexico, by Oscar Brooks. Note how massive the horns are and how the points have been rubbed down by the sheep to prevent them from obscuring his vision. This head is No. 5 in the world records.

three or four years may be difficult to count. A ram is in his prime from five to eight. At 10 he is definitely in the trophy class, a big mature ram that isn't as frisky as he used to be. When he is 11 he is old and most rams do not live beyond 12. I have shot several 13-year-old rams but I have only seen one ram shot that I was certain was 14. The big record heads come from 12-, 13-, and 14-year-old rams that had got a good healthy start when they were young and lived a long life on good feed.

Rams are generally seen at long range with binoculars and then looked over carefully with a spotting scope. The man who knows sheep heads can probably come closer to guessing just about how a ram will measure than any other trophy. At least I can.

The terms "full curl" and "three-quarters curl" mean almost nothing. In most states and provinces a ram must have a three-quarters curl to be legal. Very young rams often have "full curl" horns. Particularly among Stone and Dall sheep it is common to see rams having horns with a flat,

This is the best North American sheep the author ever shot—a Yukon Dall ram with an exceptionally heavy and symmetrical head. The horns measured 43⅝ inches; the bases are just under 15 inches in circumference. Note in the side view that the horns come down below the point of the jaw and the points come far above the bridge of the nose.

This is a very good Stone sheep head. From the annual rings on the horns, he appears to be twelve or thirteen years old. Here, too, the horns come well below the point of the jaw and the tips above the bridge of the nose.

An immature ram shot in northern British Columbia displayed by Vernon Speer (right) and guide George Edzerza. This is an example of the light-colored Stone sheep generally called Fannins.

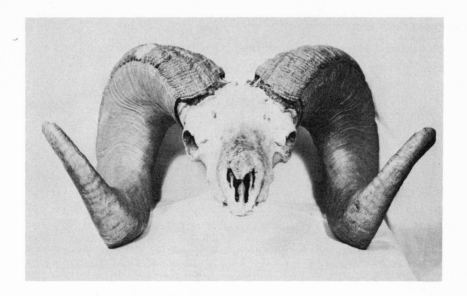

The world-record bighorn head comes from a ram shot in Lower California by an Indian poacher. The head is now owned by Carl Serivens of Los Angeles.

shallow curve with tips that go up past the bridge of the nose. But such heads are poor trophies and generally the rams wearing them are young.

Because I did my first sheep hunting on the Sonora desert, where the majority of old desert bighorn rams have close curls and broomed and rubbed horns, I have a weakness for those rugged old broomed and heavy heads even if the horns are not particularly long.

When I am looking over a bunch of rams with binoculars or a spotting scope, I look for rams with horns having deep curves with the bottom of the horn coming down even with or below the bottom of the jaw. Then if the ends of the horns come up to the bridge of the nose and have been broomed off at the tips, the ram is an old one and will be a trophy anyone can be proud of. Depending on the tightness of the spiral of the horns and the size of the ram itself, such a head will measure around the curve from 36 to 38 inches. If the horns curve down even with the jaw and then come up over the bridge of the nose and make more than a complete circle, the horns will measure 40 inches and over. As is the case with all exceptional trophies, such heads *look* big.

Any head of a North American ram nine years old or older is a good trophy. Any broomed bighorn, Stone, or Dall head 37 inches around the curve or longer is a very good head, and any such head between 37 and 39½ is a head of the highest class. Any American sheep head broomed or unbroomed that goes over 40 inches is one to celebrate in song and story, and particularly with bighorn and desert sheep a man might hunt a lifetime and never see a 40-inch head. Desert rams are quite rare and they are smaller in body than bighorns.

A desert ram with broomed horns and a close curl that goes 34 inches is an absolutely first-class trophy, and actually smaller heads are in the record book.

Caribou

The antlers of all adult bull caribou are built to the same general design, but no two are exactly alike. All antlers have a brow point just above the base. This is generally a simple point or projection on one antler and a "shovel" on the other. The shovel may be a few inches in width or as much as 20 inches. I shot a bull once with a 15-inch shovel. Rarely will a caribou have a "double shovel" on each antler. Above the brow points are the "bez formations." These curve forward and may or may not be elaborately palmated. Then above these is a single point projecting to the rear. At the top of the beam there may be considerable palmation or there may be some points not unlike those of an elk. Caribou heads are judged in contests by an elaborate formula. But the highest scoring and handsomest antlers are those with considerable length and with at least one large shovel and wide top palmation. A very long pair of antlers will appear to be almost as high as the bull caribou stands from hoofs to shoulder. However, such a head is not much good unless shovel and top formation are also good. The best heads have good shovels, good bez formations, and heavy palmation at top. Such a head is one of the most beautiful and spectacular of the world's trophies, but sad to say the bull caribou is a pretty dumb creature and I would not rate a good caribou trophy nearly as high as a really good whitetail buck.

The Moose

To me the moose trophy is the toughest of all antlered game to judge. A bull moose is such an enormous animal that to my eyes anyway even very large antlers do not look impressive. At one time moose antlers were rated entirely on spread, but now the score is a combination of spread, length and width of palm, number of points, circumference of beam, and symmetry. The bodies and antlers of moose get larger the farther north they range—and they are found beyond the farthest timber up in the willows of the arctic prairies. Enormous moose in antler and in body are found from northern British Columbia on. The best moose antlers I have ever seen on the hoof belonged to an old bull I saw in northern British

The leading caribou has an exceptional shovel which makes the head an extraordinary one. The top portion is good but not exceptional. This head would
undoubtedly have made the record book. The second caribou is a mature bull
with an adequate but not spectacular head.

JUDGING ALASKA-YUKON CARIBOU

Antlers small, undeveloped palms

Small bez formations and shovel

IMMATURE

Well-developed palms

Good bez formations

Single shovel

AVERAGE MATURE

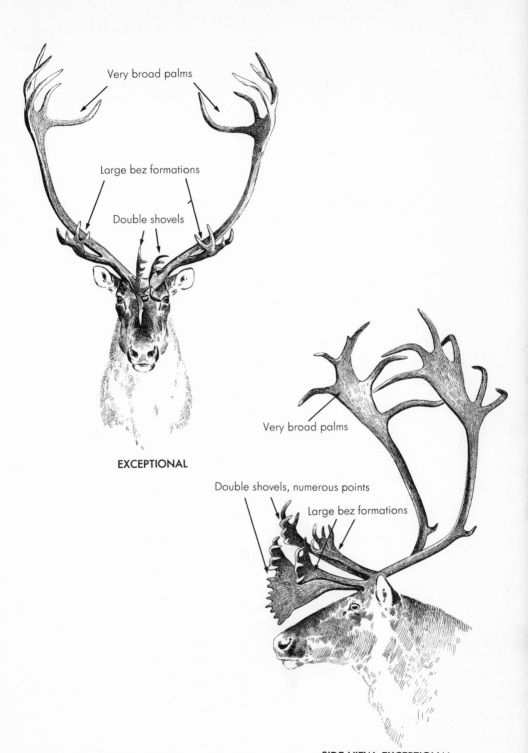

Very broad palms

Large bez formations

Double shovels

EXCEPTIONAL

Very broad palms

Double shovels, numerous points

Large bez formations

SIDE VIEW, EXCEPTIONAL

355

JUDGING MOOSE

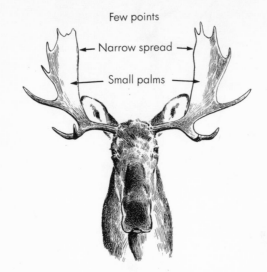

Few points

← Narrow spread →

Small palms

IMMATURE

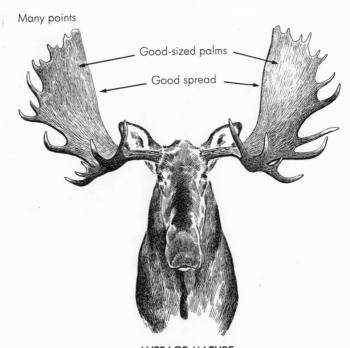

Many points

Good-sized palms

Good spread

AVERAGE MATURE

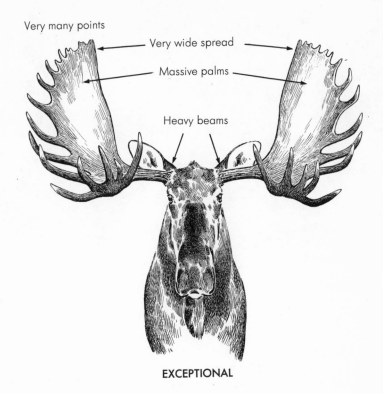

Very many points

Very wide spread

Massive palms

Heavy beams

EXCEPTIONAL

Columbia. I couldn't shoot him as I had already on that hunt taken a moose with a 62½-inch spread. This one made my trophy look like peanuts. The palms looked like table tops and I would guess the spread at around 80 inches.

The bull moose's first antlers are spikes, the second a funny little contraption called a "bootjack," the third small, palmated, but recognizable moose antlers. Like all antlered game, moose are in their prime and grow their best heads between the ages of five and eight or nine. Nevertheless a four-year-old bull is quite impressive. My first moose was such a bull. I shot him in Alberta still-hunting by myself. He had fairly narrow

Bradford O'Connor measuring his record northern British Columbia caribou. This caribou scored very high because of the massive top portion of the antlers.

palms but a 50-inch spread and he probably weighed about 1,200 pounds. My guide heard me shooting and came out from camp. He shook his head in disappointment: "That's only a little one!" he said. In Wyoming, Idaho, and Montana, where the Shiras moose are found, this would have been a large head and a fine trophy. The largest moose are those of the Alaska-Yukon variety and famous moose areas are the Alaska Kenai Peninsula, Alaska's Rainy Pass area, and the Bonet Plume country of the Yukon. The largest moose I ever saw shot was knocked off in the Yukon in 1946 by my old pal the late Myles Brown. It had a spread of 69¾ inches and stood seven feet high at the hump.

A big moose head is often a white elephant because it is so bulky and so heavy. I gave the largest head I ever shot to the owner of a sporting goods store. He got it mounted and when it came back from the taxidermist he had to tear down half the joint to get it inside. After it had been up a few years, it pulled out of the wall and came crashing down. It shattered a showcase, broke the stocks on a couple of rifles, and frightened several customers. Anyone without high, strong walls should think twice about acquiring the mounted head of a trophy moose.

Vernon Speer (left) and Bradford O'Connor with a young moose shot by Speer in northern British Columbia. The head was not exceptional; a trophy hunter should have looked for a bigger moose.

Andy Simons, the famous Alaska guide who specialized in big Kenai moose, is reputed to have carried a notched stick. He extended it at arm's length, compared it to the moose antlers, and then gave an accurate estimate of the spread. Often the hunter gets a chance to look over the head of a northern moose quite carefully as the big bulls are often feeding on willows above timberline and can be spotted a long way off.

I can only say that the best way to judge a moose head is to get a fore and aft look at it. Almost any mature head of a Yukon-Alaska moose that has wide spread rather than cupped palms will have a spread of between 58 and 62 inches. Look for points and for width and length of palm. The impressiveness of a moose head is in the mass.

Bears

Next time you go to a zoo watch the bears. Notice that the heads of old male grizzly, brown, and polar bears are wider than those of female and young bears. If the bear is alone he is pretty apt to be a male and if his head looks broad he is a male and probably a big one. A big grizzly or brown moves heavily and deliberately. He looks massive. His legs appear shorter than do those of young bears and females. Even a large, fat black bear moves deliberately.

I have never hunted polar bears, but I have hunted both Alaska browns and grizzlies. If anyone ever sees a really big bear of either species he knows it!

The Rocky Mountain Goat

I am not exactly a keen goat hunter, but I have shot a few and have been along when a few more were shot. There is not much difference between mature goat horns, and my feeling is that when you have shot one goat you have shot them all. However, the goat is a unique and interesting if not spectacular trophy and is a good addition to the trophy room.

The goat is a phlegmatic creature, not nearly as lively and wary as the wild sheep. The sheep is an animal of high upland pastures near rough country or slide rock where he can escape his enemies. The white goat likes rougher country, and he can get around in places where a sheep would come to grief.

The toughest thing about getting a goat is the climbing. It is generally exhausting, difficult, and can be dangerous. Another complication is that goats are often found on narrow ledges, and when they are shot they fall and break off their horns.

There are a few rules to follow in picking your goat trophy. If he is alone in August, September, or October, he is probably an old billy. Goats mate during November. If you see several goats together, particularly if they are of different sizes, they are undoubtedly nannies and kids. However, on occasion I have seen old billies feeding within 100 yards of nannies and kids but having nothing to do with them.

It is my impression that old billies are more often yellowish, less nearly snow white than the nannies or the young, but maybe that is just an impression. The best goat trophy I have ever seen was on the Middle Fork of the Salmon River in Idaho. He was lying in a dusty bed and was as brown as one of his Asiatic goat-antelope relatives. Farther north, where the goats usually bed on moss or grass above timberline, they are cleaner.

Bradford O'Connor with a 9½-inch billy goat shot in northern British Columbia. This is a good trophy but not in the record class.

JUDGING ROCKY MOUNTAIN GOATS

Horns less than ¾ head size

IMMATURE

Horns ¾ head size

AVERAGE MATURE

Horns more than ¾ head size

Long beard

EXCEPTIONAL

There isn't much difference between an average billy's horns and a record. The horns of a nanny are much thinner than those of a billy but they average just as long. Nannies are legal everywhere but I do not consider it sporting to shoot them. A pair of goat horns measuring 9¾ inches is just a good trophy goat, but a pair only one inch longer is up in the record class and one two inches longer is well at the top of the records. The world record goat is a 12-inch billy, but in the days when length only counted the record was held by a nanny head.

Since the hunter can usually look his goat over for as long as he wants, he should note the length of horn compared with the distance from the base of the horn to the nose. If the horn looks about as long as the face, he is looking at a hell of a goat. If the horn length appears to be about ¾–⅞ the length of the face, it is a good shootable goat. If it is less than three-fourths the length of the face it should be passed up as it is immature.

29 | *Trophy Collecting and Trophy Rooms*

Trophy hunting has increased enormously in popularity since the end of the last war. There are many reasons for this and among them are prosperity and rapid transportation. The poor man and the pioneer hunt for meat. Neither has money to spare to get heads mounted or any place to hang them. Now and then a pioneer who shot an animal with exceptionally large horns or antlers would nail the skull on the side of his cabin, but for whatever the reason the pioneer, if he ever saved horns or antlers, almost invariably cherished freaks. I once knew an old rancher in Wyoming who lived in excellent mule deer and antelope country, who was a keen hunter, but who saved only freak heads. He had a collection so grotesque as to make the blood run cold.

In Europe members of the aristocracy have been trophy hunters for hundreds of years, and the castles and manor houses of Europe contain antlers of red and fallow deer, skulls of wild boar, and horns of chamois taken before the days of sporting guns. The peasant was, of course, a poacher and a meat hunter, and he hated the aristocrat who chased stags and foxes over his crops and who protected the destructive wild boars.

The British who went out to India and Africa as army officers and administrators adopted the mores of the aristocrats. Houses, particularly in India, tended to be large and there was room to hang heads and horns. The wealth of Britain increased enormously during the 19th century.

Most of the new-rich British were descended from yeoman and peasant stock and were not to the manor born, but as they accumulated money they bought land and built large houses. Since they had some place to hang trophies and trophy hunting was fashionable among the aristocrats whom they imitated, they became trophy hunters. The indefatigable British hunted all over the world in the century between the battle of Waterloo, which made the British the top dogs in Europe and in the world, and the outbreak of World War I. No spot was too remote for them to reach if it contained worthwhile trophies. The British, riding yaks and taking with them astonishing assortments of the comforts the 19th century upper-class Englishmen considered necessary for the civilized life, hunted *Ovis poli* in the Russian and Chinese Pamirs. They went after lions and elephants in Africa, the great Siberian argali in the Altai, and shot *Ovis nivicola* on the Kamchatka Peninsula, wild reindeer in Norway, red deer in Poland, ibex in Spain.

In India high British civil servants and officers in the Indian army shot tigers, leopards, black buck, gaur in the lowlands and made expeditions into the mountains of Tibet and the Northwest frontier. They were the pioneer trophy hunters of what was then called British East Africa (now Kenya) and some of the less affluent among them became ivory hunters. It was the British who founded the profession of "white hunting."

Rich Britishers hunted in the American plains and Rockies after the Civil War. One of them, an Anglo-Irish nobleman named Gore, laid on what was probably the most expensive and bloody sports hunt in the history of the Western world. He was accompanied by an enormous entourage, took with him every luxury, and shot hundreds of buffalo, elk, antelope, deer, and sheep. Another rich Irishman, Lord Dunraven, wanted to buy a big chunk of the Colorado Rockies for a hunting preserve.

Before World War I, the British came by the dozens to hunt elk in Wyoming and Montana. They hunted bighorns in Alberta and British Columbia, Dall sheep, caribou, and grizzlies in the Yukon, moose and giant brown bear in Alaska. Back in the 1930's I knew an old Mexican who had gone along as a guide and packer for a rich Englishman and his beautiful blond wife on a sheep hunt in the Pinacates of northwestern Sonora. The lady rode side-saddle all the way from Ajo, Arizona, to the Pinacate carrying a white umbrella with a green lining to preserve her fair British beauty. She hunted in a long, modest khaki-colored skirt and shot three rams with a 6.5 Mannlicher-Schoenauer. Every night, the Englishman and his wife bathed, changed clothes, ate dinner on a clean tablecloth using china and silver, drank wine, and wound up with coffee and brandy. What impressed the old Mexican more than anything was that white umbrella with the green lining. Every time he told the story he would shake his head and say, "Ah, those English. What a people!"

Because of the interest of the rich British in trophies, an enterprising London taxidermist named Rowland Ward collected measurements of outstanding specimens of the world's game and issued a record book from time to time. I have a copy of what appears to be the first edition. It came out in 1892 and is called *Horn Measurements of Great Game.* Later it became Rowland Ward's *Records of Big Game.* The last edition appeared in 1962 and is limited to the game of Africa. As this is written in 1966, an edition for Asian records is in preparation.

The British big-game hunters set the style over most of Europe. French big-game hunters buy British rifles, generally British shotguns, wear British clothes, and manage to look British. If these French practitioners of *la grande chasse* speak English (and most of them do), it is with a decided British accent.

The Germans have their own hunting traditions, were avid trophy hunters, and they also had and have a lively arms manufacturing industry. Prior to World War I, their colony of German East Africa was one of the world's great hunting grounds.

For many years Americans did little trophy hunting. My Kentucky-born grandfather moved from Colorado to Arizona in the 1880's when the desert bighorn, the most prized of North American trophies, were still fairly common. I can remember several sets of fine trophy horns with skulls lying around the barn. I also remember cutting thin slices of mountain mutton off of the hind quarter of a ram, broiling them on top of a wood-burning stove, putting on a little salt and eating them when I was home one time with a sore throat. This must have been about 1910 or 1912. This particular ram was shot off a cliff about 150 yards away by one of my maternal uncles from his bedroll with a .30/30 carbine. If anyone had suggested that my grandfather get a head mounted by a taxidermist he would have thought him mad.

The first American trophy hunters were the very rich who lived along the Eastern seaboard. Theodore Roosevelt was an example of the class. Many of these rich men went to school in England and many others visited in English homes. Most were Anglophiles. They saw mounted heads and skulls with horns and antlers put on plaques in British homes and manor houses. All this made them decide that the collecting of heads was a very classy thing to do. They bought and used British rifles and shotguns, and some of them leased grouse moors and deer forests in Scotland. Many of them rode to hounds wearing "pink" (meaning red) coats. Owning a double-ejector rifle engraved with the name of a famous British gunmaker was almost as prestigious a caper as playing footsie with a duchess.

They were adventurous hunters. They made the laborious journey by transcontinental train, steamship, narrow-gauge railway, gas boats, and packtrain into remote reaches of the Yukon, British Columbia, and Alaska. Some made three- and six-month foot safaris in what was then called British East Africa but is now Kenya. In those days everyone walked including the dudes, and hordes of porters carried loads on their heads.

Prior to World War II, few Americans could afford the eight to twelve months necessary for the long sea voyage and an African safari or the six weeks to two months for a long pack trip in northern British Columbia or the Yukon. The first time I hunted in the Yukon there were only about three or four outfitters in the whole vast territory and perhaps four or five in northern British Columbia. Myles Brown, an old hunting companion of mine, was one of the first if not the first trophy hunters to hunt Stone sheep on the east side of the Rockies in northern British Columbia. He went by train from New York to Dawson Creek, British Columbia (and this must have taken a week), from Dawson Creek to Ft. St. John in a Model T Ford, and from there clear to the place where the old Yukon Trail crosses the Prophet River by saddle horse and packtrain. He was out of Ft. St. John for sixty-five days.

After World War II the speedy and relatively cheap transportation of the airplane and the extension of roads like the Alaska Highway made remote hunts less demanding of time, money, and endurance. The first time I went to the Yukon I traveled in two and a half days by railway from Tucson, Arizona, to Vancouver, B.C. There I took a steamship up the Inside Passage to Skagway, Alaska. This required four days. Traveling from Skagway to Whitehorse, Y.T., by narrow-gauge railway took yet another day. After a day in Whitehorse getting squared away, I drove with my outfitter to Kluane Lake, where the Jacquot brothers had a trading post. The next night we were in camp beside the Alaska Highway with our pack outfit ready to take off the next morning. The last time I hunted in the Yukon, I left Seattle in mid-morning by jet plane and was in Whitehorse not much later by Yukon time. We got our licenses, picked up our bedrolls and duffel at the customs office, and the next night we were with our pack outfit.

Many more Americans are hunting outside of their own states and in foreign countries now than ever before. Nonresident hunters are so plentiful in western states that harbor out-of-the-ordinary game that their fees contribute more to the upkeep of the game departments than do the fees of residents. People who live in Ohio, Pennsylvania, and New York hunt antelope in Wyoming and Montana, sheep, elk, mule deer, and goats in Idaho and Montana. They take pack trips into all sorts of improbable places. Because big-game hunting has now become a big business, Alaskan guides and East African white hunters comb the United States every winter for prospective clients. They show movies, exude charm, tell tall tales, but they get their men! Before the war Americans who had hunted in Africa were about as common as ex-presidents. Today a safari is within the means of anyone who has from three weeks to a month to spare and can reach down into his jeans for about $2,500. The trip can even be made on the cuff and paid off by the month. Such a trip doesn't produce the finest trophies but at least it is a safari.

World War II made many profound changes in American life. Many thousands of Americans became rich or at least well-to-do. Because the work week was shorter and paid vacations longer, Americans have had more leisure. Great prosperity combined with American international commitments have made the Americans the greatest international travelers the world has ever seen. In any de luxe hotel from the Oberoi Grand in Calcutta to the New Stanley in Nairobi the great majority of foreign visitors are Americans. Just as the globe-trotting British were the international travelers of the 19th century, the Americans are the international travelers of the 20th.

All of this has meant that Americans are today the world's greatest trophy hunters. From what I have seen I'd guess that about eighty percent of the safari clients in Kenya, Tanganyika, and Bechuanaland are American and at least that high a percentage of shikar clients in India. Several times as many Americans than Canadians patronize outfitters in Alberta, British Columbia, and the Yukon. However, big-game hunting and trophy collecting have become fashionable in all affluent societies. French, Spanish, German, Belgian, and Italian big-game hunters shoot in Africa regularly and a few have come to North America.

Most people who like to hunt big game have an interest in the size of horns and antlers and like to know how their own trophies compare with those of others. In the unsophisticated days of my youth, the relative worth of deer, elk, and moose antlers was judged by the spread or by the number of "points"—and a point was considered to be "anything you can hang a ring on." Rowland Ward's *Records of Big Game* ranks trophies by the length of the horns or the main beam antlers.

This was the practice followed by the first American record book. It was published in 1932 under the auspices of the Boone & Crockett Club. It was edited by one of the club members, the late Prentice N. Gray. Only 500 copies were printed. This first edition of *Records* is now a rare and valuable item. Remington Arms Company printed a summary of the records but listing, if I remember correctly, only the first ten heads of each species. This was given away as a promotion and some sly words about Remington products were included.

The second record book came out in 1939. It was likewise compiled by the Boone & Crockett Club and edited by Alfred Ely, who was chairman of the committee, Harold E. Anthony of the Museum of Natural History in New York, and by R. R. M. Carpenter. It was published by Scribners. Besides the records it contained articles of interest to big-game hunters—on the animals and their habits, rifles and ammunition, photography, taxidermy, and similar subjects. I wrote an article on the Arizona (Coues) whitetail for it. Like its predecessor, this edition now has considerable value to collectors.

It takes no very astute observer to realize that rating horned and antlered trophies exclusively either by length of horn or antler or by spread is not precisely satisfactory. In the 1939 edition of *Records,* my friend of many years standing, the late Grancel Fitz, had an article on the rating of trophies by taking other factors into consideration. To some extent his system for ranking the various animals was based on the Continental system used on European game by the Conseil International de la Chasse. James L. Clark, the famous big-game hunter and taxidermist at the American Museum of Natural History had also evolved a somewhat similar system.

In 1950 the Boone & Crockett Club adopted the present system for the ranking of trophies by various factors including length, symmetry, massiveness, and number of points in case of antlers. The bears and cats are ranked by length and width of skull alone, as they should be. Some wonderful things can be done in the way of stretching hides. The first record book to be published using this system came out in 1952. Another appeared in 1958 and the most recent, as this is written, in 1964. It lists 5,072 North American trophies, pictures the world-record head of each species and sometimes two or three others.

Since the war big-game trophy competitions have been held every two years until the 1963 contest at the American Museum of Natural History in New York and since then at the Carnegie Museum in Pittsburgh. The trophies are submitted well ahead of time and are judged by members of a committee. The awards (medals) are given at a dinner, a very plush affair. I have acted as judge once, and my wife, my son Bradford, and I have each picked up medals.

The Boone & Crockett Club deserves great credit for promoting an interest in trophies, as the trophy animals are in the majority of cases old-timers who have lived out their lives and do not have long to be around. The club has likewise promoted sportsmanship and has come out in its rules for fair chance against the use of such mechanical helps as airplanes, helicopters, and walkie-talkies in the pursuit of game. As this is written the club no longer includes the polar bear as a trophy animal in its competitions because of the almost universal use of the airplane in the hunting of these great white bears.

The club must also be given credit for the increasing knowledge of what a really good trophy is and for the many state and regional contests in which prizes are given for good heads measured by Boone & Crockett standards. A discriminating interest in trophies is a sign of a mature and sophisticated hunter. Every year the number of entrants in the contest increases and new world records turn up for almost every competition.

As is the case with any good thing, some have gone overboard on trophy hunting. It is not unknown for various citizens of a highly competitive nature to resort to a bit of chicanery in order to get a head in the record book or to win a medal. Heads actually shot by simple meat hunters have been known to adorn some pretty high-class trophy rooms, and one chap is reputed to have kept a very fine set of sheep horns and the skull immersed in water so it would not shrink until three months had elapsed and he could send the head in to be officially measured.

To my way of thinking a record-class head is a very nice thing to have in a trophy room, but no hunter should ever be depressed if he never gets a head worthy of inclusion in the record book. I think it is silly for anyone who wants a trophy to shoot immature animals with small heads, but it is equally silly for anyone to be thrown into a fit of depression if he does not collect a record-class head. Any good, larger-than-usual head of any species is a fine trophy and one for the hunter to be proud of. When the hunter gets a head mounted he is more than anything else preserving a memory. One Dall sheep head in my trophy room is certainly not in the record class. The ram that wore it was a little old ram with close-curled and broomed horns that came well up past the bridge of his nose. He was alone when I shot him and until I walked up to it, I thought the head was much better than it was. But the ram was almost a dwarf. He had thirteen annual rings but his horns only went about thirty-six inches around the curl. Yet I'll always cherish the trophy as a reminder of a cold, blustery day of bitter wind and driving snow above the glaciers at the head of the St. Clair River in the Yukon, of a time when I had enough iron in my legs to climb to the crests of the ridges on both sides of the river in one day.

Taxidermy has made great strides in the past half century or so. In the 1880's and 1890's trophies were literally stuffed, and even today people who know no better always ask to see my "stuffed" animals. The scalp or headskin was soaked in a pickling solution. Then two pieces of two-by-four or similar board were nailed together, one to represent the head and one to represent the neck. The horns or antlers were screwed to the piece that represented the head. Then the pickled scalp was put around the boards and excelsior was stuffed into the scalp to fill it out. The result was pretty ghastly, and no matter what species the animal belonged to, he always came out looking like a mouse. Then as the wet pickled scalp dried, it shrank. The ears twisted. The lips pulled away from the stitches in a ghastly leer. Ancient heads so mounted are still seen covered with soot and grime in ancient clubs and in old bars and restaurants. Heads are still mounted this way in such countries as Mexico and India, but one of the world's best taxidermists is in Mexico City and there is one good taxidermist in India. The pickling method of preserving scalps is still used by some taxidermists, but it is not satisfactory. The best desert mule deer head I have ever taken was mounted with a pickled scalp, and the ears have twisted.

Modern methods of taxidermy were largely pioneered by Carl Akeley, who was in charge of mounting the animals in the habitat groups in the American Museum of Natural History. Akeley brought great skill, taste, and ingenuity to his work. He was an accomplished sculptor and a clever mechanic, who among other things developed a motion-picture camera and a cement gun.

Akeley first modeled the animal in clay. He then made a plaster mould of the clay model. He then coated the inside of the clay model with glue, laid a sheet of muslin on the glue and worked it into every curve and contour of the mould. Then on this he put thin layers of papier-maché covered with shellac. From two to four layers of papier-maché were used, depending on the size of the animal. Then the mould with the muslin and papier-maché is immersed in water. The water dissolves the glue and the papier-maché form comes free. The plaster mould can be used to make more forms. The result is a light, strong, lifelike form on which to put antlers and scalp. Today taxidermists do not use the skulls. A small portion of the skull of horned and antlered animals is sawed off to be attached to the papier-maché form. For lions, tigers, and bears, papier-maché head forms with artificial teeth are used. Properly cleaned, the natural skulls make interesting mementos.

James L. Clark, who succeeded Akeley at the museum, did commercial taxidermy in addition to his museum work and used this method for mounting heads and complete animals for trophy collectors. The remarkable Jonas brothers, who started out in Denver and who at one time had shops in Mt. Vernon, New York, and in Seattle, also used the method and supplied excellent papier-maché forms to other taxidermists. Today Coloman Jonas of the Denver shop has retired and the Mt. Vernon and Seattle shops have been sold, although they still bear the Jonas Brothers name. Jonas Brothers of Denver also supplies glass eyes and other necessities to taxidermists.

The pickling method of preserving scalps is seldom used in the United States. Instead the scalps are tanned, just as glove leather is tanned. Before the scalp is put on, the form is covered with a special glue and lumps of wet papier-maché are put on for final shaping. The veins that show through the hide on the complete animal are simply heavy binding twine attached to the form. Then the tanned scalp is put on, and the final contours are modeled into the mount by manipulating the damp papier-maché—the bump on a mountain sheep's nose, the wrinkles around the lips, the contours of the binding twine that becomes "veins," and so on. Cardboard has been put in the ears to replace the cartilage that has been removed.

Small taxidermists generally buy their forms from taxidermist supply houses such as Jonas Brothers of Denver and they send their scalps to a concern which specializes in the job. The difference between one taxidermist and another consists today pretty largely in the skill with which the final moulding is done, the artistic eye of the taxidermist, his judgment in selecting a papier-maché form of the right size, his taste, the care with which he sews up rips and holes in the scalp, and the care with which the scalps and hides are tanned. No one taxidermist can do all his own work, but a good one should approve of all the jobs turned out by his hired hands. I believe Coloman Jonas, who is now retired, did the most realistic sheep mounts. I have several which he mounted himself and they are very fine indeed. Jack Atcheson, the Butte, Montana, taxidermist, also does a very fine job on sheep.

Some taxidermists are careless. Some have no taste. Some simply have no artistic eye and cannot model. The first lion I shot in Africa had a very decent mane, but when I got it back from the taxidermist it was almost maneless. The taxidermist said I had shot the lion when it was shedding and that the hair would not stay in when it was tanned. I found out later that the trouble had been careless and violent tanning. When I shot a very fine maned lion in Angola in 1962 I turned the job over to Steve Horn of Jonas Brothers of New York (Jonas Brothers Studio, Inc., 135 North High Street, Mount Vernon, New York). He did the tanning job carefully and turned out a fine lion mount which is one of my most prized trophies. Some taxidermists simply have no idea what certain animals look like, and others create corny and tasteless poses. I think the snarls of bears and lions are greatly overdone myself, but what gives me the vapors is what I call the "punch-drunk bear." One taxidermist has produced dozens of life-size mounts of brown and polar bears standing erect with their front paws down and with dazed looks on their faces. They remind me of prize fighters who have been clipped a good one right on the button and are about to fall on their faces for the count. If the trophy hunter must have a life mount I think it looks less corny to have it on all four feet as one generally sees the animals instead of standing up. A good rule when ordering taxidermy is when in doubt to have the job done as a shoulder mount with the animal looking straight forward. Dramatic, corny, and bizarre poses should be avoided. Some of the damndest taxidermy I have ever seen was in Mexico City. A customer had ordered three mountain lions mounted strung up by the hind feet with bullet wounds showing, just as he had brought them into his ranch. They were so realistic I could just about smell them, but they seemed to me to be a ghastly exhibit.

Until comparatively recently, little trophy collecting was done in the United States. A few very rich men on the Eastern seaboard and along the West Coast had trophy rooms. The average hunter, if he ever had a head mounted, put it in his "den," generally a dismal little cubicle where the harassed paterfamilias occasionally retired with a jug and a crony or where once a month he cleared a spot on what was laughingly called "daddy's desk" so he could write out checks to pay the bills. In his den daddy had a couple of whitetail heads and a .30/.30, an N.R.A. Springfield .30/06, a .22 pump, an old double inherited from his father, and a 12-gauge pump. These were in a glass case of golden oak in one corner. On top of the case, beside a pile of old copies of *Outdoor Life* and the *American Rifleman,* was a stuffed pheasant somewhat worse for wear from a battle with moths.

But affluence, more leisure, speedy transportation, and widespread publicity for trophy collecting has made having a trophy room the "in" thing to do. The Weatherby annual big-game award has been widely publicized and so have the competitions held by the Boone & Crockett Club. Some local and state trophy contests are also held. Outfitters and guides have become highly conscious of trophies, since they know that if their clients collect good ones they will get more business.

Rich Europeans who began hanging antlers up for display hundreds of years ago in their high-ceilinged and drafty manor houses had plenty of space but the modern middle-class American who wants to preserve the memories of good hunts by displaying some trophies faces plenty of hazards. Probably the number one hurdle is the Storm & Strife. She welcomes the hanging of a deer head or the spreading of a bear rug in her living room about as enthusiastically as a tigress would welcome the invasion of her den by a pack of wolves.

Many houses today have recreation rooms, where the inmates of a house resort to hoist a jug, fondle a gun, or play ping-pong. These lend themselves to the display of some of the smaller heads—deer, antelope, sheep, and goats. Ceilings in most modern houses are too low for any of the long-antlered animals such as elk and caribou.

Back in the 1930's when I was living in Tucson I had a mule deer, a whitetail, an antelope, and a desert sheep in our dining room, but my wife felt that they did nothing for the decor. I finally wound up building a rather handsome trophy room with 14-foot beamed ceilings, a good fireplace, the works. Not very long after my expensive trophy room was completed I realized that Arizona's population explosion made it advisable for me to leave my native state and find some other spot with fewer people and more game.

I took a considerable loss when I sold the Tucson house with its trophy room. We moved to a colonial house overlooking the Snake River in Lewiston, Idaho. Today my upstairs office-gunroom-trophy room is paneled in walnut, has all walnut furniture, a red wall-to-wall carpet, and an open walnut gun rack which holds twenty-one shotguns and rifles. There are two walnut beams across the white plaster ceiling. Because the ceilings are only eight feet high it is impossible to hang large heads with long horns here. The room is fifteen by thirty feet. On the walls are shoulder mounts of a lion and a tiger and several small heads ranging in size from that of a dik-dik to that of a spotted axis deer from India. If I do say so, the effect is rather pleasing.

In the upstairs hallway I have some heads and the stairway well gives me enough room to put up the head of greater kudu and a sable and hang the hide of a very large tiger I shot in northern India in 1955.

When I bought our present pad the former owner had built just behind the house a workshop where he played with power tools and indulged various hobbies. I had a window cut out at one end to give access to another room which I had built. The building is now eleven by thirty-six feet, has a fireplace at one end. Since it is electrically heated the fireplace is more ornamental than useful and I stoke it up only for atmosphere when I have guests in for drinks. The two connecting rooms are paneled in knotty fir, and bookcases on either side of the fireplace contain volumes on hunting, guns, and whatnot. At each end is a greater kudu head, and one wall is devoted to sheep. Below the sheep heads are the hides of a lion and a tiger. In one of the rooms I have my reloading bench. There is a desk, a sofa, some comfortable chairs, a low table, a few guns, some hides and Navajo rugs on the floor. It is neither a pretentious trophy room nor an expensive one, but it is not bad looking.

Just how much money the man interested in a trophy collection can afford to put into a trophy room is for him to decide. Anyone interested in something of the sort and building a new house can incorporate a special room for trophies. The lovely Dallas home of my old pal Herb Klein is built around a large and beautiful trophy room, which also serves as a living room, bar, and gun room. The late Myles Brown of Gates Mills, Ohio, built a special wing for a trophy room on a big colonial house he bought. Elgin Gates built a large house around a trophy room at Newport Beach, California, and in it was one of the world's most extensive collection of trophies. Gates has now moved to his old home town of Needles, California. As I write this I have not seen the new place.

The late Grancel Fitz lived in a large studio apartment in a New York skyscraper. High walls enabled him to display large antlered animals like elk and caribou. What is, I am convinced, the world's most extensive collection of trophies taken by one man is that belonging to Prince Abdorreza Pahlavi, brother of the Shah of Iran. When I first met his highness, most of his trophies were from Iran and India and they were housed in a large and beautifully decorated room in the basement of his palace in Tehran. Since then he had been on several safaris in various parts of Africa, has taken the rare great sheep of central Asia, has hunted in North America, and has collected more Indian trophies. Now the trophies have spread out into other rooms in the enormous basement, into a big basement hall, and they are creeping up the walls of the big stairway to the main floor of the palace. So far Princess Pari Sima has managed to keep them out of the exquisitely decorated reception rooms and living rooms but I am afraid she is fighting a battle that is lost.

But not all of us can be world hunters. Few of us can go after such exotics as bongo and *Ovis poli*. Likewise few of us can afford to build our houses around trophy rooms. However, any hard-working family man who likes animals and hunting deserves a place all his own, a place where he can display his guns, put up a few well-chosen big-game trophies, maybe do his handloading or repair with a few cronies for a friendly game of draw poker. If he has no Stone sheep heads or tiger hides, what of it? That crafty old whitetail buck above the fireplace is a lot smarter and harder to come by than any Stone sheep or any tiger that ever lived.

Ideally, I think a trophy room should look like the uncluttered room of someone interested in shooting and hunting and not like a taxidermy shop or a minor museum. If mounted heads are crowded close together and stuffed into every nook and cranny, they lose their effect and the whole place looks cluttered. The best effect to create is that of a handsome and livable room in which big-game heads are part of the decor.

Taxidermists dote on selling novelties made from spare parts of various animals. Some are in good taste and some are ghastly. Cigarette boxes and even photo albums made of zebra hide are nice looking and I believe in good taste. Cigarette trays made of mountain sheep feet do not look bad, are novel, and are in keeping with the decor of a trophy room. Various other oddments give me a seizure. Among them are humidors for cigars made of rhino feet, wastebaskets made of elephant feet, floor lamps with pedestals made out of moose feet, screens made from zebra hide, pictures framed in zebra or leopard hide, chairs made out of steer or moose horns.

Rugs made of game hides should not be laid on the floor in an area where they are walked on, for it they are they do not last long. A tiger hide or a polar bear hide is an elegant decoration for even the most baronial of rooms, but if either is walked on they quickly wear out, and anyone who has stumbled over a few heads on bear rugs in the dark soon believes their place is on the wall. Any white hide quickly gets dirty and is difficult to clean. Of these the worst is a Rocky Mountain goat. Polar bears are also bad, but the coarser hair of the white Dall sheep does not soil very easily if it is dusted regularly. Mounted heads should be regularly and gently dusted with a whisk broom, cleaned now and then with a vacuum, protected against moths and beetles. Taken care of, they'll last for generations!

Gallery of
Big Game
Trophies

Oscar Brooks of Mexico City and London with his son and his wife June in his trophy room in Mexico City where his North American heads are elegantly displayed.

Trophy room of Dr. Brandon Macomber of Albany, New York. This shows
game from the Arctic (walrus) to the tropics (jaguar).

Another part of the trophy room of Dr. Brandon Macomber.

George Parker of Amado, Arizona, in his elegant and tasteful trophy room. Parker, who at one time guided and outfitted in Sonora, has hunted all over the world.

Trophy room of Elgin Gates of Needles, California. Gates has hunted all over the world.

Part of the trophy room of Julio Estrada of Cuernavaca, Mexico. Senor Estrada has hunted all over the world. These are North American trophies.

Frank Hibben, University of New Mexico archaeology professor, with North American trophies. Shown here are all varieties of North American sheep.

African and Asiatic trophies in the home of Julio Estrada of Cuernavaca.

The author in his trophy room at his home in Lewiston, Idaho.

Two other sections of the author's trophy room, including (above) his grand slam of North American rams.

Index